Next-Generation Technologies in Cloud Computing

Next-Generation Technologies in Cloud Computing

From AI and Security to Sustainability

Edited by

Bishwajeet Pandey
GL Bajaj Institute of Technology and Management, Uttar Pradesh

Advait Patel
Broadcom Inc., United States

IEEE Press
WILEY

Published by John Wiley & Sons, Inc., Hoboken, New Jersey.

Library of Congress Cataloging-in-Publication Data Applied for:

Hardback ISBN: 9781394382453
ePUB ISBN: 9781394382460
ePDF ISBN: 9781394382477
oBOOK ISBN: 9781394382484

Cover Design: Wiley
Cover Image: © LHG/stock.adobe.com

Set in 9.5/12.5pt STIXTwoText by Straive, Chennai, India

To my wife and son—for your love, patience, and the light you bring into my life.

Contents

About the Editors *xxv*
List of Contributors *xxvii*
Preface *xxix*
Acknowledgments *xxxi*

1 Introduction: Reimagining Cloud Computing in the Age of AI and Sustainability *1*
Karan Alang and Anant Kumar
1.1 Introduction *1*
1.2 The Evolution of Cloud Computing: From Mainframes to AI-Powered Everything *1*
1.2.1 From Mainframes to Virtualization *1*
1.2.2 When Theory Met Commerce *2*
1.2.3 Modern Cloud Architecture and Service Models *3*
1.2.4 The Shifting Cloud Paradigm *4*
1.2.5 AI: Cloud's New Growth Engine *4*
1.2.6 Challenges of Supporting AI Workloads in the Cloud *5*
1.2.7 AI and Cloud Use Cases *6*
1.3 The Sustainability Imperative *7*
1.4 Challenges and Opportunities *9*
1.5 Conclusion *11*
1.6 Future Scope *11*
References *12*

2 The Evolution of Cloud Computing: From Virtual Machines to Serverless *15*
Anuj Ashok Potdar and Pronnoy Goswami
2.1 Introduction *15*

2.2 The Definition of Cloud Computing *16*
2.3 Historical Context and Significance *17*
2.4 Evolution Timeline Overview *18*
2.5 The Foundations: Virtual Machines and Early Virtualization *20*
2.5.1 The Concept of Virtualization *20*
2.5.2 Hypervisor—Virtual Machine Technology Explained *21*
2.5.3 The Transition from Physical to Virtual Infrastructure *22*
2.6 The Birth of Modern Cloud Computing *23*
2.6.1 Limitations of Traditional Virtual Machines *23*
2.6.2 The Rise of Containerization *24*
2.6.3 Container Orchestration *25*
2.7 The Serverless Paradigm *26*
2.7.1 The Concept of Serverless Computing *26*
2.7.2 Key Serverless Platforms *26*
2.7.3 Benefits and Limitations of Serverless Computing *27*
2.8 Conclusion *27*
References *27*

3 Exploring Cloud-Native Microservices Architectures and Design Patterns *31*
Prashanthi Matam and Venkata Naga Kartik Pidatala
3.1 Introduction *31*
3.1.1 Overall Objective of the Chapter *32*
3.2 Fundamentals of Cloud-Native Computing *33*
3.3 Microservices Architecture (MSA) Overview *36*
3.4 Cloud-Native Migration Strategies to Microservices *38*
3.5 Core Design Patterns in Microservices *39*
3.5.1 SDP-s Service Decomposition Patterns *39*
3.5.2 Integration Patterns *39*
3.6 Data Management Patterns *40*
3.6.1 Observability Patterns *40*
3.7 Event-Driven Architectures and Microservices *42*
3.8 Practical Considerations and Best Practices *43*
3.8.1 Testing and Quality Assurance in Microservices *44*
3.8.1.1 Compliance, Cost Optimization, and Governance *45*
3.9 Emerging Trends and Future Directions *45*
3.10 Case Studies and Real-World Applications *49*
3.11 Conclusion *51*
References *51*

4 **Multicloud and Hybrid Cloud Strategies for Resilient Infrastructure: An Observability-Driven Framework for Modern Distributed Systems** *55*
Aditya Gupta and Pronnoy Goswami
4.1 Introduction *55*
4.2 Related Work and Theoretical Foundations *56*
4.2.1 Multicloud Observability Foundations *56*
4.2.2 Distributed Tracing Technologies *57*
4.2.3 Service Mesh Observability Patterns *58*
4.3 Multicloud Observability Architecture Framework *58*
4.3.1 Key Architectural Principles *58*
4.3.2 Data Collection and Instrumentation Strategy *59*
4.3.3 Service Mesh Integration Architecture *60*
4.4 Distributed Tracing Implementation Strategy *61*
4.4.1 OpenTelemetry Integration Framework *61*
4.4.2 Cloud-Native Platform Integration *61*
4.4.3 Real-Time Processing and Analytics *62*
4.5 Multimodal Data Fusion and Analytics *63*
4.5.1 Unified Data Model Architecture *63*
4.5.2 AI-Enhanced Anomaly Detection *63*
4.5.3 Intelligent Alerting Systems *65*
4.6 Cross-Cloud Security and Compliance Observability *65*
4.6.1 Zero-Trust Observability Implementation *65*
4.6.2 Encrypted Telemetry Management *66*
4.6.3 Compliance Automation Framework *66*
4.7 Implementation Guidelines and Best Practices *67*
4.7.1 Phased Deployment Strategy *67*
4.7.2 Tool Selection Framework *68*
4.7.3 Developing Performance Optimization Techniques *68*
4.8 Performance Evaluation and Verification *68*
4.8.1 Benchmark Results Analyses *68*
4.8.2 Scalability and Resilience Testing *69*
4.8.3 Cost–Benefit Analysis *70*
4.9 Future Directions and Emerging Technological Developments *70*
4.9.1 Edge Computing Integration *70*
4.9.2 Advanced AI Integration *71*
4.9.3 Sustainability and Green Computing *71*
4.10 Conclusion *72*
References *72*

5 **Machine Learning as a Service (MLaaS): Enabling Scalable AI** *75*
Raghuram Katakam and Ashwin Prakash Nalwade
5.1 Introduction *75*
5.2 The Evolution of Machine Learning *76*
5.2.1 Background *76*
5.2.2 The Rise of Cloud Computing *76*
5.2.3 Key Drivers of MLaaS Adoption *76*
5.3 Frameworks and Tools in MLaaS *77*
5.3.1 Important Elements *77*
5.3.1.1 Data Management *77*
5.3.1.2 Model Development and Training *78*
5.3.1.3 Model Deployment and Inference *79*
5.3.1.4 Integration and APIs *80*
5.3.1.5 Security and Governance *81*
5.3.2 Use Cases *82*
5.3.3 Technical Depth: Enabling Scalability *82*
5.3.3.1 Scalable Infrastructure *82*
5.3.3.2 Scalable Model Training *82*
5.3.3.3 Scalable Inference *85*
5.3.3.4 Scalable Data Pipelines *85*
5.3.3.5 Cost Optimization *85*
5.4 Challenges and Future Outlook *86*
5.4.1 Challenges in MLaaS Adoption *86*
5.4.1.1 Data Privacy and Security *86*
5.4.1.2 Vendor Lock-In *86*
5.4.1.3 Cost Management *86*
5.4.1.4 Skill Gaps *86*
5.4.1.5 Model Interpretability *86*
5.4.2 Future Outlook *86*
5.4.2.1 Federated Learning *86*
5.4.2.2 AI Democratization *87*
5.4.2.3 Edge AI *87*
5.4.2.4 Sustainable AI *87*
5.4.2.5 Integration with Generative AI *87*
5.4.2.6 Open-Source MLaaS *87*
5.5 Conclusion *87*
References *88*

6 **Cloud Cost Optimization and the Rise of FinOps** *91*
Dhivya Nagasubramanian
6.1 Introduction: Cloud Cost Complexity and the Capital Expenditures (CapEx)-to-Operating Expenditures (OpEx) Shift *91*

6.2 From CapEx Comfort to OpEx Chaos *91*
6.3 The Rise of FinOps: Making Cloud Spending Make Sense *92*
6.4 You're Not Alone—The Data Tells the Story *92*
6.5 A New Mindset for a New Era *92*
6.6 The Emergence and Evolution of FinOps *94*
6.7 Core FinOps Principles and Lifecycle *95*
6.7.1 FinOps Principle *96*
6.7.2 FinOps Lifecycle: Inform, Optimize, Operate *97*
6.8 Holistic Cost Management Framework *98*
6.9 Beyond Single-Workload Optimization *98*
6.10 Cost-Aware Architecture and Operations *99*
6.11 AI/ML for Predictive Cloud Cost Management *100*
6.12 FinOps in Action: Real-World Case Studies *101*
6.13 The Future of FinOps: Sustainability, Cross-Cloud Arbitrage, and Decentralized Models *104*
6.13.1 FinOps Meets Sustainability (GreenOps) *104*
6.13.1.1 Why Is This Trend Significant? *104*
6.13.2 Cross-Cloud Arbitrage and Multicloud FinOps *105*
6.13.3 Decentralized Cloud and New Financial Models (FinOps 2.0?) *107*
6.14 Agentic AI Orchestration: The Next Frontier in FinOps *108*
6.15 Conclusion *109*
References *110*

7 FinOps for AI Workloads *113*
Anaranya Bagchi
7.1 Introduction *113*
7.2 Types of AI Workloads and Cost Drivers *114*
7.2.1 Types of AI Workloads *114*
7.2.2 Cost Drivers for AI Workloads *116*
7.3 FinOps Principles Applied to AI *117*
7.4 Challenges in FinOps for AI Workloads *125*
7.5 Conclusion *126*
References *127*

8 AI-Driven Cloud Services and Intelligence Automation *129*
Prashanthi Matam and Venkata Naga Kartik Pidatala
8.1 Introduction *129*
8.1.1 The Journey to AI-Driven Cloud Services *130*
8.1.2 Challenges Driving AI Adoption in Cloud Environments *131*
8.1.3 The Broader Impact of AI-Driven Cloud Services *132*
8.2 Evolution of Cloud Computing: From Virtualization to Cloud-Native Architectures *132*
8.2.1 Core AI Technologies Empowering Cloud Services *133*

8.2.2 Intelligent Automation Principles in Cloud Ecosystems *134*
8.2.3 Automated Provisioning and Dynamic Scaling *135*
8.2.4 AI-Enabled Security and Threat Detection *136*
8.2.5 Predictive Analytics for Performance Optimization and Cost Management *136*
8.2.6 AI-Powered Multicloud and Hybrid Cloud Management *137*
8.3 Intelligent Automation in Cloud Operations *137*
8.3.1 AI in Deployment Pipelines *138*
8.3.2 Self-Healing Cloud Infrastructure *138*
8.3.3 AI for Compliance and Governance Automation *139*
8.3.4 Trustworthy and Responsible AI in the Cloud *139*
8.3.5 AI-Powered Cloud Cost Optimization *141*
8.4 Emerging Paradigms: Generative and Agentic AI in Cloud Services *143*
8.4.1 Generative AI for Cloud Service Development and Automation *143*
8.4.2 Agentic AI for Autonomous Cloud Operations *144*
8.4.3 Ethical and Trust Considerations *144*
8.4.4 Future Directions *145*
8.5 Foundations of Multimodal AI *145*
8.5.1 Applications of Multimodal AI in Cloud Services *145*
8.5.2 Challenges in Multimodal Cloud AI *146*
8.5.3 Research and Future Directions *146*
8.5.4 Summary *146*
8.6 Future Trends and Opportunities *147*
8.6.1 Quantum Computing Integration *147*
8.6.2 Edge AI and the Cloud-Edge Continuum *147*
8.6.3 AI Governance and Regulatory Frameworks *147*
8.6.4 Advances in Autonomous AI Systems *147*
8.7 Conclusion *148*
References *148*

9 AIOps: Intelligent Cloud Observability and Incident Management *151*
Milankumar Rana and Jyoti Kunal Shah
9.1 Introduction *151*
9.1.1 Motivation and Scope *151*
9.1.2 Chapter Overview *151*
9.2 Background and Evolution of AIOps *152*
9.2.1 From Manual Operations to Automated Monitoring *152*
9.2.2 The Big Data Imperative *153*
9.2.3 Defining AIOps: Conceptual Foundations *153*

9.3 Cloud Observability Fundamentals *154*
9.3.1 Observability vs. Monitoring *154*
9.3.2 Pillars of Observability: Metrics, Logs, Traces *154*
9.3.3 Telemetry Collection in Cloud Environments *155*
9.3.4 Distributed Tracing and Context Propagation *156*
9.4 Architecture of AIOps Platforms *156*
9.4.1 High-Level Architectural Components *156*
9.4.1.1 Data Ingestion and Normalization Layer *157*
9.4.1.2 Feature Engineering and Data Enrichment *158*
9.4.1.3 AI/ML Engine for Anomaly Detection *158*
9.4.1.4 Event Correlation and Causality Mapping *159*
9.4.1.5 Knowledge Base and Runbook Integration *159*
9.4.1.6 Automation and Orchestration Layer *160*
9.4.1.7 Visualization and Alerting Interfaces *161*
9.5 Data Pipelines and Telemetry Management *161*
9.5.1 Sources of Observability Data *161*
9.5.2 Agent-Based vs. Agentless Data Collection *162*
9.5.3 Data Transport and Storage Considerations *163*
9.5.4 Schema Standardization and Tagging Strategies *163*
9.5.5 Handling High Cardinality and High Velocity *164*
9.6 AI/ML Techniques for Intelligent Observability *165*
9.6.1 Unsupervised Learning for Baseline Modeling *165*
9.6.2 Supervised Learning for Known Anomalies *166*
9.6.3 Time-Series Forecasting and Trend Analysis *166*
9.6.4 Clustering and Dimensionality Reduction *167*
9.6.5 Graph-Based Models for Dependency Mapping *167*
9.6.6 Reinforcement Learning for Adaptive Thresholds *168*
9.7 Anomaly Detection and Root Cause Analysis *169*
9.7.1 Types of Anomalies *169*
9.7.2 Multi-Modal Anomaly Detection (Metrics + Logs + Traces) *169*
9.7.3 Alert Fatigue Mitigation Through Noise Reduction *169*
9.7.4 Probabilistic Correlation and Causality Inference *170*
9.7.5 Topology-Aware Root Cause Localization *171*
9.7.6 Confidence Scores and Explainability *171*
9.8 Incident Management Workflow *172*
9.8.1 Incident Lifecycle: Detection → Triage → Diagnosis → Remediation *172*
9.8.2 Automated Triage: Ticket Generation and Prioritization *172*
9.8.3 ChatOps and Collaborative Incident Response *173*
9.8.3.1 Runbook Automation and Playbook Execution *173*

9.8.4 Automated Remediation: Safe Rollbacks and Remediation Scripts *174*
9.8.5 Human-in-the-Loop vs. Fully Autonomous Remediation *174*
9.9 Case Studies and Industry Implementations *175*
9.9.1 E-Commerce Platform at Scale: Reducing Flash Sale Downtime *175*
9.9.2 Financial Services: Compliance-Driven Observability *176*
9.9.3 SaaS Provider: Predictive Autoscaling and Cost Optimization *177*
9.9.4 Telecom Network: Edge Computing and Distributed AIOps *178*
9.9.5 Lessons Learned and Comparative Analysis *179*
9.10 Best Practices for AIOps Adoption *179*
9.10.1 Organizational Readiness and Cultural Shift *179*
9.10.2 Data Governance, Privacy, and Security Considerations *179*
9.10.3 Incremental Implementation and Proof-of-Value *180*
9.10.4 Key Performance Indicators (KPIs) and Metrics *180*
9.10.5 Integration with DevOps Toolchains and CI/CD Pipelines *181*
9.10.6 Vendor Selection: Open-Source vs. Commercial AIOps Platforms *181*
9.11 Challenges and Limitations *182*
9.11.1 Data Silos and Heterogeneous Tooling *182*
9.11.2 Model Drift and Concept Drift in Dynamic Environments *182*
9.11.3 Explainability and Trust in AI-Driven Decisions *182*
9.11.4 Scalability and Cost Overhead *183*
9.11.5 Regulatory Compliance and Auditing Needs *183*
9.12 Future Directions in AIOps *183*
9.12.1 Intent-Driven Operations and Policy-as-Code *183*
9.12.2 Self-Healing Systems and Closed-Loop Automation *184*
9.12.3 Integration of AIOps with APM and DevSecOps *184*
9.12.4 Emerging AI Techniques: Generative Models, Causal AI *184*
9.12.5 Toward Autonomous Cloud-Native Environments *185*
9.13 Conclusion *185*
References *186*

10 Cloud-Native DevSecOps and Shift-Left Security Practices *187*
Jay Shah and Garima Bajpai
10.1 Introduction *187*
10.2 State of DevSecOps and Shift-Left Security *188*
10.2.1 Planning and Design Phase *189*
10.2.2 Coding *190*
10.2.3 Build *190*
10.2.4 Test *190*
10.2.5 Deploy *190*

10.2.6 Monitor *190*
10.3 Adoption of DevSecOps *192*
10.4 Implementing DevSecOps with Frameworks *192*
10.5 What Is a Maturity Model? *193*
10.6 Best Practices *194*
10.6.1 Use Cases *194*
10.7 Challenges and Future Outlook *196*
10.7.1 Success Criteria for DevSecOps Implementation *196*
10.8 Conclusion *197*
References *197*

11 Autonomous Cloud Infrastructure and Self-Healing Systems *199*
Vinod Goje and Manoj Ravi
11.1 Introduction *199*
11.1.1 Motivation and Scope of Autonomous Cloud Infrastructure *199*
11.1.1.1 Defining Autonomous Cloud Infrastructure *199*
11.1.1.2 The Role of Self-Healing in Cloud Resilience *200*
11.1.2 Architectural Principles for Autonomous Systems *201*
11.2 Background and Context *203*
11.2.1 Cloud-Native and Microservice Paradigms *203*
11.2.1.1 Evolution from Monolith to Microservices *203*
11.2.1.2 Containerization and Orchestration Tools *204*
11.2.2 Kubernetes *205*
11.2.2.1 Common Orchestration Patterns *205*
11.2.3 Serverless and Function-as-a-Service Architectures *206*
11.2.3.1 Serverless Computing Model *206*
11.2.3.2 Serverless Use Cases and Patterns *206*
11.2.4 Infrastructure-as-Code and GitOps *207*
11.2.4.1 Declarative Infrastructure Management *207*
11.2.4.2 GitOps and Continuous Delivery *208*
11.2.5 Monitoring, Logging, and Observability *208*
11.2.5.1 Traditional vs. Cloud-Native Monitoring *208*
11.2.5.2 Observability Platforms and Tools *209*
11.2.6 Cloud Storage and Networking Fundamentals *209*
11.2.6.1 Cloud-Native Storage and Cloud Networks *209*
11.2.6.2 Software-Defined Networking and Cloud Networks *210*
11.2.7 Autonomic Computing and AI for IT Operations (AIOps) *210*
11.3 Self-Healing Mechanisms and Implementation Strategies *210*
11.3.1 Container Orchestration and Self-Healing *210*
11.3.1.1 Kubernetes Self-Healing Capabilities *210*

11.3.1.2 Advanced Patterns and Service Mesh Integration *212*
11.3.2 Serverless Self-Healing Patterns *212*
11.3.2.1 Retry Logic *213*
11.3.2.2 Dead Letter Queues (DLQs) *213*
11.3.2.3 Comparison of Serverless vs. Container-Based Approaches *214*
11.4 Case Study: Netflix's Implementation *214*
11.4.1 AWS Case Study: Netflix's Chaos Engineering and Auto-Scaling *214*
11.5 Conclusion *215*
11.5.1 Summary of Key Insights *215*
11.5.2 Implementation Considerations and Best Practices *215*
References *216*

12 Serverless Computing and Event-Driven Cloud Architectures *219*
Jyoti Shah and Milankumar Rana
12.1 Introduction *219*
12.2 Background and Related Work *220*
12.3 Challenges *224*
12.4 Proposed Framework *226*
12.5 Architecture Overview *229*
12.6 Implementation Considerations *232*
12.7 Case Study *235*
12.8 Challenges and Limitations *239*
12.9 Future Work *241*
12.10 Conclusions *243*
References *245*

13 Zero Trust Architecture in Cloud Environments *247*
Aparna Achanta and Vinod Goje
13.1 Introduction *247*
13.1.1 Zero Trust—Core Concepts *247*
13.1.1.1 Verify Explicitly *248*
13.1.1.2 Least Privilege *248*
13.1.1.3 Breach Is Assumed *248*
13.2 Zero Trust in the Cloud *249*
13.2.1.1 The Perimeter Is Blurred *249*
13.2.1.2 Cloud APIs Are Publicly Accessible *249*
13.2.1.3 Cloud Identity and Access Management Is Complex *250*
13.3 Threat Actors in the Cloud *250*
13.4 How the Cloud Embraces Zero Trust *250*
13.4.1 Strong Authentication *251*

13.4.2 Least Privilege Access *251*
13.4.3 Federation and Single Sign On *251*
13.4.4 Continuous Access Evaluation *252*
13.5 Zero Trust Governance for IAM *252*
13.6 Micro-Segmentation for Network Control *253*
13.6.1 The Problem of Traditional Network Segmentation *253*
13.6.2 Understanding Micro-Segmentation *254*
13.7 Zero Trust Network Access (ZTNA) *254*
13.7.1 Network Policy as Code *255*
13.8 How Micro-Segmentation Prevents Lateral Movement *255*
13.9 The Role of Unified Endpoint Management (UEM) *255*
13.9.1 How UEM Enables Zero Trust *256*
13.9.2 Key Contributions to Zero Trust *256*
13.10 Continuous Authentication and Session Monitoring *256*
13.11 SaaS-Specific Zero Trust Strategies *257*
13.12 PaaS Security Controls *257*
13.13 Visibility, Logging, and Threat Detection *258*
13.14 Centralized Log Aggregation Architecture *258*
13.15 SIEM/SOAR Integration for Zero Trust *259*
13.16 Cloud-Native Threat Detection Services *260*
13.17 Data-Centric Security *260*
13.17.1 Data Classification and Tagging *260*
13.17.2 Data Encryption at Rest and in Transit *261*
13.18 Conclusions *261*
13.19 Future Work *262*
References *262*

14 Predictive Risk Intelligence and Governance Framework in Multicloud Environments *265*
Priya Ranjani Mohan and Yugandhar Suthari
14.1 Introduction: From Reactive to Predictive *265*
14.1.1 Defining Predictive Risk Intelligence *265*
14.1.2 The Multicloud Complexity Challenge *265*
14.2 Core Challenges in Multicloud Governance *266*
14.2.1 The Fragmentation Problem *266*
14.2.2 Data Sovereignty Complexity *266*
14.2.3 Identity and Integration Gaps *267*
14.3 PRIG Framework Architecture and Components *268*
14.3.1 Conceptual Architecture *268*
14.3.2 Database Layer (Foundation) *268*
14.3.3 Intelligence Engine Layer *269*

14.3.4 Governance Rig Layer *269*
14.4 Building Your Organization's PRIG Infrastructure *270*
14.4.1 The Reality Check *270*
14.4.2 Getting the Data House in Order *270*
14.4.2.1 Splunk Enterprise Security *270*
14.4.2.2 GRC Intelligence Use Cases *270*
14.4.3 Elastic Stack (ELK) *271*
14.5 Out-of-the-Box Tools for Predictive Decisions *271*
14.5.1 IBM QRadar SOAR *271*
14.5.2 GRC Intelligence Use Cases *271*
14.5.3 Microsoft Sentinel *272*
14.5.4 GRC Intelligence Use Cases *272*
14.5.5 Palantir Foundry *272*
14.6 Building Custom ML Models and Risk Prediction *273*
14.6.1 Data Sources and Quality Challenges *273*
14.6.2 Model Selection and Performance *273*
14.6.2.1 Risk Assessment Compatibility *273*
14.6.3 Performance Metrics Alignment with GRC Objectives *274*
14.6.4 Confidence Scoring and False Positive Management *274*
14.7 Making Predictive Decisions and Taking Action *274*
14.7.1 ServiceNow GRC *274*
14.7.2 GRC Intelligence Use Cases *275*
14.7.3 RSA Archer *275*
14.7.3.1 GRC Intelligence Use Cases *275*
14.8 The Glue That Holds It Together *276*
14.8.1 MuleSoft Anypoint Platform *276*
14.8.2 Apache Kafka *276*
14.8.3 How It All Works Together *276*
14.9 Considerations for Potential Issues When Implementing PRIG Framework *277*
14.9.1 Data Consistency Problems *277*
14.9.2 Performance Issues *277*
14.9.3 Security Complexity *277*
14.10 Real-World Case Studies *277*
14.10.1 RSA Security: How One Platform Eliminated Tool Fragmentation and Reduced 10,000 Vulnerabilities to 560 Actionable Priorities *277*
14.10.2 The Hidden Cost of Fast Multicloud Deployments and How to Tackle It: A Real-Life Story by Bilfinger and Tenable *278*
14.11 Outlook and Recommendations *279*
14.11.1 Strategic Implementation Recommendations *279*
14.11.2 The Evolution Toward Autonomous Governance *280*

14.12 Conclusion *281*
References *281*

15 Security and Compliance for Cloud-Native Applications *283*
Vaishnavi Gudur and Ashish Kattamuri
15.1 Introduction *283*
15.2 Background/Context *284*
15.2.1 Why Is Compliance and Security Challenging in Cloud-Native Systems? *286*
15.3 Core Content *287*
15.3.1 Current Security Frameworks and Processes *287*
15.3.2 AI-Enhanced Security and Compliance Mechanisms *290*
15.4 Challenges *292*
15.5 Future Outlook *294*
15.5.1 Emerging Technologies in Cloud-Native Security *294*
15.5.2 Research Directions and Opportunities *295*
15.6 Conclusion *296*
References *297*

16 Data Privacy, Sovereignty, and Cloud Localization Laws *299*
Dhivya Nagasubramanian and Kiran Kumar Reddy Puram
16.1 Introduction: When the Cloud Hits the Ground *299*
16.2 Global Trends in Data Privacy and Localization *300*
16.3 Regional Regulatory Landscape *301*
16.3.1 European Union: GDPR, Schrems II, and the Quest for Digital Sovereignty *301*
16.3.2 United States: The CLOUD Act, State Privacy Laws, and Government Data Rules *302*
16.3.3 China: PIPL and Cyber Sovereignty *303*
16.3.4 India: The Digital Personal Data Protection Act and Sectoral Rules *304*
16.3.5 Other Notable Jurisdictions and Frameworks *305*
16.4 Industry Case Studies: Impact of Sovereignty Requirements *306*
16.4.1 Finance and Banking: Balancing Global Platforms with Local Control *306*
16.4.2 Healthcare: Protecting Patient Data Across Borders *307*
16.4.3 Public Sector and Government: Sovereign Clouds for National Data *308*
16.5 Architecting for Compliance: Technical Approaches to Sovereignty *309*
16.5.1 Sovereignty-Aware Cloud Architecture *310*

16.5.2 Sovereign Cloud Services and Regionalization *310*
16.5.3 Multicloud and Federated Trust Strategies *311*
16.5.4 Compliance-as-Code (CaC): Embedding Legal Rules in DevSecOps *312*
16.6 Evolution and Future Outlook *313*
16.6.1 Lessons Learned from Failed Implementations and Takeaways *314*
16.7 Conclusion *315*
References *316*

17 Sustainable Cloud Computing and Carbon-Aware Architectures *319*
Vamsi Alla and Ashish Kattamuri
17.1 Introduction *319*
17.2 Evolution of Cloud Computing: The Foundation for Sustainability *321*
17.3 Principles of Sustainable Cloud Computing *322*
17.3.1 Energy Efficiency *322*
17.3.2 Renewable Energy Integration *323*
17.3.3 Carbon-Aware Scheduling *323*
17.3.4 Edge Computing *324*
17.3.5 Serverless Architecture *325*
17.4 Core Frameworks for Sustainable Cloud Computing *325*
17.4.1 Cooling Systems and Energy-Efficient Hardware *325*
17.4.1.1 ARM-Based Approach *325*
17.4.1.2 SSDs, or Solid-State Drives *327*
17.4.1.3 Advanced Cooling Solutions *327*
17.4.2 Integrated Renewable Energy *328*
17.4.2.1 PPAs *328*
17.4.2.2 On-Site Renewable Installations *328*
17.4.2.3 Methods of Energy Storage *328*
17.4.2.4 Dynamic Load Balancing and Smart Grids *328*
17.4.3 Carbon-Aware Workload Scheduling *329*
17.4.4 Edge Computing for Sustainability *330*
17.4.4.1 Use Case Example *330*
17.4.5 Serverless Architectures *330*
17.4.5.1 Key Features *331*
17.5 Use Cases and Industry Relevance *332*
17.5.1 Google's Data Centers Carbon-Neutral *333*
17.5.1.1 Integration of Renewable Energy *333*
17.5.1.2 AI-Driven Enhancement *333*
17.5.1.3 Using Real-Time Carbon Intensity Data *333*

17.5.1.4 Scalability 333
17.5.2 Project Natick from Microsoft: Underwater Data Centers 333
17.5.2.1 Modular Scalability 334
17.5.3 IoT Edge Deployment Smart City Singapore 334
17.5.3.1 Edge Computing Adoption 334
17.5.3.2 Energy Savings 334
17.5.3.3 Latency and Efficiency Gains 334
17.5.3.4 Scalability 334
17.6 Difficulties and Future Vision 334
17.6.1 Technical Difficulties 335
17.6.2 Financial Difficulties 336
17.6.3 Policy and Legal Difficulties 336
17.6.4 Social and Adoption Difficulties 336
17.7 Sustainable Cloud Computing's Prospect 337
17.8 Conclusion 338
References 339

18 Quantum Computing in the Cloud: Opportunities and Challenges *341*
Ashwin Prakash Nalwade and Khan Shariya Hasan Upoma
18.1 Introduction 341
18.2 Background 342
18.2.1 Fundamental Quantum Gates 342
18.2.2 Quantum Operations and Execution 342
18.2.3 Important Concepts of Quantum Theory 343
18.2.3.1 Superposition 343
18.2.3.2 Entanglement 344
18.2.3.3 Decoherence 344
18.2.3.4 Quantum Volume 344
18.2.4 Encoding Data, Making Physical Models, and Loss Prevention 344
18.3 Quantum Computing in the Cloud 345
18.3.1 Quantum Computing Frameworks and Cloud Platforms 345
18.3.2 Why Quantum Computing in the Cloud? 346
18.3.2.1 Cloud-Based Quantum Computing Solves Three Core Bottlenecks 346
18.3.3 The Leaders in the Space 347
18.3.3.1 IBM Qiskit and IBM Quantum 347
18.3.3.2 Amazon Braket 348
18.3.3.3 Microsoft Azure Quantum 350
18.4 Quantum Computing—Key Strengths 350
18.5 Challenges and the Future 351

18.6 Conclusion *353*
References *353*

19 Cloud Platforms for Scientific Research and HPC Workloads *355*
Anant Kumar
19.1 Introduction *355*
19.2 Background and Context *356*
19.2.1 The Evolution of Scientific Computing *356*
19.2.2 Traditional HPC vs. Cloud HPC *357*
19.2.3 The Data Challenge *357*
19.3 Core Content: Frameworks, Use Cases, and Technical Depth *358*
19.3.1 Major Cloud Platforms for Scientific Computing *358*
19.3.1.1 Amazon Web Services (AWS) *358*
19.3.1.2 Microsoft Azure *358*
19.3.1.3 Google Cloud Platform (GCP) *359*
19.3.1.4 Specialized HPC Cloud Providers *359*
19.3.1.5 Rescale *360*
19.3.1.6 Sabalcore *360*
19.4 Container Orchestration for Scientific Workloads *360*
19.4.1 Kubernetes for HPC *361*
19.5 Workflow Management Systems *361*
19.5.1 Nextflow *361*
19.5.2 Snakemake *362*
19.5.3 Apache Airflow *362*
19.5.4 Performance Optimization Strategies *362*
19.5.4.1 Network Performance *362*
19.5.4.2 Storage Optimization *363*
19.5.4.3 Cost Optimization *363*
19.5.5 Case Studies *363*
19.5.5.1 Climate Modeling *363*
19.5.5.2 Genomics and Bioinformatics *364*
19.5.5.3 Particle Physics *364*
19.6 Challenges and Future Outlook *365*
19.6.1 Current Challenges *365*
19.6.1.1 Data Transfer and Network Latency *365*
19.6.1.2 Cost Predictability *365*
19.6.1.3 Skills Gap *365*
19.6.1.4 Compliance and Security *365*
19.7 Emerging Trends *366*
19.7.1 Serverless Computing for Scientific Workloads *366*

19.7.2 Edge Computing for Scientific Applications *366*
19.7.3 Quantum Computing Integration *367*
19.7.4 AI and ML Integration *367*
19.7.5 The Road Ahead: Where Scientific Computing Is Really Heading *367*
19.7.5.1 Federated Everything (Because Nobody Wants to Put All Their Eggs in One Basket) *367*
19.7.5.2 Sustainability and Green Computing *368*
19.7.5.3 Democratization of Scientific Computing *368*
19.8 Conclusion *369*
19.8.1 The Economics Have Changed Everything *369*
19.8.2 The Long View *370*
References *370*

20 Ethics, Bias, and Responsible AI in Cloud Environments *373*
Sreekanth B. Narayan and Karan Alang
20.1 Introduction *373*
20.1.1 Cloud AI Introduces a Security Perspective *373*
20.1.2 Ethical Considerations in AI *375*
20.2 Key Ethical Principles *375*
20.2.1 Fairness and Non-Discrimination *375*
20.2.2 Transparency *376*
20.2.3 Accountability *376*
20.2.4 Privacy and Data Protection *377*
20.2.5 Beneficence and Non-Maleficence *377*
20.3 Bias in AI *377*
20.3.1 Types of AI Bias *378*
20.3.1.1 Data Bias *378*
20.3.1.2 Algorithmic Bias *378*
20.3.2 Sources of Bias *378*
20.3.3 Importance of Addressing AI Bias *379*
20.4 Responsible AI Practices *379*
20.4.1 Core Principles of Responsible AI *380*
20.4.1.1 Ethical Risk Assessments *380*
20.4.1.2 Stakeholder Engagement *381*
20.4.1.3 Human Oversight *381*
20.4.1.4 Continuous Improvement and Adaptation *381*
20.4.1.5 Data Management and Privacy *382*
20.4.1.6 Transparency and Accountability *382*
20.5 Implementation Considerations and Good Practices *382*
20.6 Cloud Environments and AI *383*
20.6.1 Opportunities and Innovations *383*

20.6.2 Emerging Risks *384*
20.6.3 Ethical Considerations and Governance *384*
20.7 Case Studies *385*
20.7.1 Introduction to Ethical AI Case Studies *385*
20.7.2 IBM's AI Ethics Board *385*
20.7.3 Google's AI Principles *386*
20.7.4 The COMPAS System and Racial Bias *386*
20.7.5 Amazon's Recruitment Algorithm *387*
20.7.6 Healthcare AI and Racial Bias *387*
20.8 Future Directions *388*
20.8.1 Enhancing Ethical Frameworks *388*
20.8.2 Advancements in Bias Mitigation *388*
20.8.3 Collaborative Approaches to AI Safety *389*
20.8.4 Commitment to Continuous Learning *389*
20.8.5 Promoting Privacy and Security *389*
References *390*

21 Conclusion—The Future Cloud: Ethical, Autonomous, and Planet-Aware *393*
Pronnoy Goswami and Aditya Gupta
21.1 Introduction *393*
21.2 The Enduring Arc of Abstraction and Its Unseen Costs *394*
21.3 From Monitoring Silos to Multicloud Operational Resilience *395*
21.4 The Challenge of Governance-Aware Autonomy *397*
21.5 From Optimization to Obligation: The Rise of Ethical and Planet-Aware Architectures *398*
21.5.1 Engineering Ethics into the Infrastructure Layer *398*
21.5.2 Planet-Aware Computing: A First-Order Principle *399*
21.6 Redefining the Economics: Financial Operations, Sovereignty, and Zero Trust *400*
21.6.1 The Evolution of FinOps: From Cost Control to Value Optimization *400*
21.6.2 Securing the Fabric: Sovereignty and Zero Trust *401*
21.7 Synthesis and a Forward-Looking Research Agenda *402*
21.8 Conclusion and Future Scope *403*
References *403*
Glossary *405*

Index *407*

About the Editors

Dr. Bishwajeet Pandey is a professor at GL Bajaj Institute of Technology and Management, Greater Noida, India. He has been a senior member of IEEE since 2019. He holds an MTech in Computer Science from the IIIT, Gwalior, India, and a PhD in Computer Science from the Gran Sasso Science Institute, Italy. He has taught at esteemed institutions such as Chitkara University, Chandigarh; Jain University, Bangalore; Astana IT University, Kazakhstan; Eurasian National University, Kazakhstan (QS World Rank 321); Walsh College, USA; and UCSI University, Malaysia (QS World Rank 265). He is a prolific researcher with over 30 published books and more than 220 research papers indexed in Scopus. He has garnered over 4400+ citations. His leadership roles include serving as the research head of the School of CSE at Jain University, Bangalore, from 2021 to 2023 and as the head of the International Global Academic Partnership Committee at Birla Institute of Applied Science, Bhimtal, from 2020 to 2021. In 2023, Dr. Pandey was honored with the prestigious Professor of the Year Award at Lord's Cricket Ground by the London Organisation of Skills Development. Beyond his outstanding research output, his greatest strength lies in his global academic network. He has visited 49 countries, participated in 105 international conferences, and co-authored papers with 218 professors from 93 universities across 42 nations.

Advait Patel is a senior site reliability engineer at Broadcom, where he leads the design and implementation of secure, scalable cloud infrastructure across global SaaS platforms. With experience in cloud security, DevSecOps, and AI-driven monitoring systems, he specializes in Kubernetes, Terraform, GCP, and container security. He is an active member of IEEE and ISACA, a conference speaker, and the creator of DockSec—an AI-powered Docker security analyzer. He also serves as a technical reviewer for IEEE and ACM publications and is the author of multiple cloud security research papers and technical articles.

List of Contributors

Aparna Achanta
Security Architect
Austin, TX
USA

Karan Alang
Independent Researcher
Cupertino, CA
USA

Vamsi Alla
Independent Researcher
New York, NY
USA

Anaranya Bagchi
IEEE Senior Member
Seattle, WA
USA

Garima Bajpai
Founder, Canada DevOps Community of Practice
Ottawa, ON
Canada

Vinod Goje
Computer Science and Engineering
University College of Engineering
Osmania University
Hyderabad
India

Pronnoy Goswami
IEEE Senior Member
Santa Clara, CA
USA

Vaishnavi Gudur
Independent Researcher
Seattle, WA
USA

Aditya Gupta
IEEE Senior Member
Seattle, WA
USA

Raghuram Katakam
Independent Researcher
Atlanta, GA
USA

Ashish Kattamuri
Independent Researcher
Denver, CO
USA

Anant Kumar
Einstein AI Division. Member of IEEE and Sigma Xi
The Scientific Research Honor Society
San Jose, CA
USA

Prashanthi Matam
Independent Researcher
Mountlake Terrace, WA
USA

Priya Ranjani Mohan
Independent Researcher
Raleigh, NC
USA

Dhivya Nagasubramanian
Independent Researcher
Minniapolis, MN
USA

Ashwin Prakash Nalwade
AI Research Pythia
Seattle, WA
USA

Sreekanth B. Narayan
Sr. IEEE Member
Okemos, MI
USA

Venkata Naga Kartik Pidatala
Independent Researcher
Mountlake Terrace, WA
USA

Anuj Ashok Potdar
IEEE Senior Member
Boston, MA
USA

Kiran Kumar Reddy Puram
Independent Researcher
Charlotte, NC
USA

Milankumar Rana
University of the Cumberlands
Williamsburg, KY
USA

Manoj Ravi
Sr. Software Architect & IEEE Member
Eastern North Carolina Section
Raleigh, NC
USA

Jay Shah
Independent Researcher
Canada DevOps Community of Practice
Toronto, ON
Canada

Jyoti Shah
Independent Researcher
Edison, NJ
USA

Yugandhar Suthari
Independent Researcher
Raleigh, NC
USA

Khan Shariya Hasan Upoma
Independent Researcher
Dhaka
Bangladesh

Preface

Cloud computing has transformed the way organizations build, deploy, and secure applications. As enterprises increasingly rely on platforms like Google Cloud, understanding how to design secure, compliant, and resilient cloud environments is critical. This book was born out of real-world experience—from securing large-scale cloud workloads to automating compliance and implementing Zero Trust architectures.

This book is written for engineers, architects, and security professionals who want actionable guidance, not just theory. Each chapter blends hands-on practices, design principles, and real-world examples to help readers confidently secure their Google Cloud environments.

We hope this book not only serves as a guide but also inspires you to push the boundaries of what's possible in cloud security.

Bishwajeet Pandey
GL Bajaj Institute of Technology and Management
Uttar Pradesh

Advait Patel
Broadcom Inc., United States

Acknowledgments

This book wouldn't have been possible without the support of many people. I want to thank:

My amazing wife, whose support and patience helped me focus during countless late-night writing sessions. My parents, for instilling in me a deep love for learning and perseverance. My colleagues at Broadcom for the daily inspiration and collaboration that shaped many of the ideas in this book. The Wiley's editorial and production team for their guidance, professionalism, and encouragement throughout this process. The vibrant cloud security and DevOps communities, whose blogs, tools, and feedback keep this field moving forward.

Wiley's editorial, production, and publishing team—especially my editors and coordinators—for their incredible professionalism, feedback, and encouragement from proposal to publication.

Finally, my son, Avyakt, whose arrival reminded me of the future we are building—and protecting—with every secure cloud we deploy.

1

Introduction: Reimagining Cloud Computing in the Age of AI and Sustainability

Karan Alang[1] *and Anant Kumar*[2]

[1] *Independent Researcher, Cupertino, CA, USA*
[2] *Einstein AI Division. Member of IEEE and Sigma Xi, The Scientific Research Honor Society, San Jose, CA, USA*

1.1 Introduction

Cloud computing has undergone a radical transformation since its inception. It started as a flexible infrastructure for storage and computation but has subsequently transformed to being central to digital transformation initiatives across nearly every industry.

The convergence of two dominant forces—artificial intelligence (AI) and sustainability—requires a reassessment of how cloud infrastructure is built, operated, and governed. It requires a reassessment of how cloud computing can play an even more important role in providing the benefits of AI to various industries.

This chapter introduces understanding this transformation and sets the stage for the themes that will be explored throughout this book.

Before we dive into AI and sustainability, we will first examine the historical evolution of cloud computing.

1.2 The Evolution of Cloud Computing: From Mainframes to AI-Powered Everything

1.2.1 From Mainframes to Virtualization

Contrary to popular belief, cloud computing didn't start with Amazon or Google. Its roots go way back to 1960, when DARPA threw $2 million at MIT's Project MAC—which sounds like loose change today but was serious money back then. The goal is "developing a computer to be used by two or more people, simultaneously" [1].

Think about it—we're talking about massive mainframes with magnetic tape memory that took up entire rooms. The idea of sharing these computational beasts was basically the Stone Age version of what we now call virtualization.

But here's where it gets interesting. J.C.R. Licklider came along in 1969 with his wild vision for ARPANET. He called it an "Intergalactic Computer Network"! He envisioned the future of the internet before anyone really knew where it was headed. His idea was simple yet profound: everyone interconnected through computers, accessing information from anywhere [2].

The 1970s saw virtualization really hit its stride; by the 1990s, virtual machines were becoming the norm rather than the exception. Then in 1997, Professor Ramnath Chellapa dropped what I consider one of the most prescient definitions of cloud computing ever: "a new computing paradigm, where the boundaries of computing will be determined by economic rationale, rather than technical limits alone" [3].

Economic rationale over technical limits. That's basically the cloud in a nutshell!

1.2.2 When Theory Met Commerce

The late 1990s and early 2000s—now that's when things got really interesting. Salesforce kicked things off in 1999 with their SaaS offering [4]. But the real game-changer was Amazon Web Services (AWS) launching EC2 in 2006 [5]. Amazon basically said, "Hey, why don't we rent out some of our massive computing power?" and this started the democratization of enterprise computing.

Of course, once Amazon proved the model worked, everyone wanted in. Microsoft rolled out Azure in 2010, bringing their signature hybrid approach and deep enterprise integration [6]. Google came to the party with Google Cloud Platform (GCP), throwing their weight behind containerization and Kubernetes [7].

Then you had IBM and Oracle doing their thing with industry-specific solutions [8, 9], plus Alibaba Cloud basically conquering Asia [10]. Each player brought something unique to the table, and suddenly we weren't just talking about renting servers anymore. We were talking about AI, multicloud orchestration, sustainability … the works.

Before cloud computing became popular, organizations had to plan the purchase of physical servers based on projected peak usage. This involved effort to set them up in data centers as well, and then hoping the projections were accurate so the servers could handle the peak traffic. Over-provisioning was the name of the game because nobody wanted their website to crash during high-traffic events like Black Friday. This led to underutilization of resources during nonpeak periods.

1.2.3 Modern Cloud Architecture and Service Models

By 2011, National Institute of Science and Technology (NIST) had gotten their act together and defined the five essential characteristics of cloud computing [11]. You know the drill: on-demand self-service, broad network access, resource pooling, rapid elasticity, and measured service. Sounds bureaucratic, but these definitions actually mattered—they gave everyone a common language.

The ISO folks expanded on this later, describing cloud computing as "a paradigm for enabling network access to a scalable and elastic pool of shareable physical or virtual resources with self-service provisioning and administration on-demand" [12].

As shown in Figure 1.1, Infrastructure-as-a-Service (IaaS), Platform-as-a-Service (PaaS), and Software-as-a-Service (SaaS) are the holy trinity of cloud services. Each one abstracts away different layers of complexity. This abstraction is what made cloud computing accessible to everyone, not just the big players with dedicated IT teams.

The growth has been tremendous, driven by data-intensive apps, cheaper internet, and everyone's desperate need for digital transformation [13]. Small businesses suddenly had access to enterprise-grade infrastructure; startups could scale without massive upfront investments. Game-changing stuff.

Of course, it hasn't all been smooth sailing. Security concerns, vendor lock-in, and compliance headaches—these issues keep Chief Information Officers (CIOs) up at night [5]. And now with AI workloads demanding ever more performance, cloud providers are constantly under pressure to innovate while keeping costs reasonable.

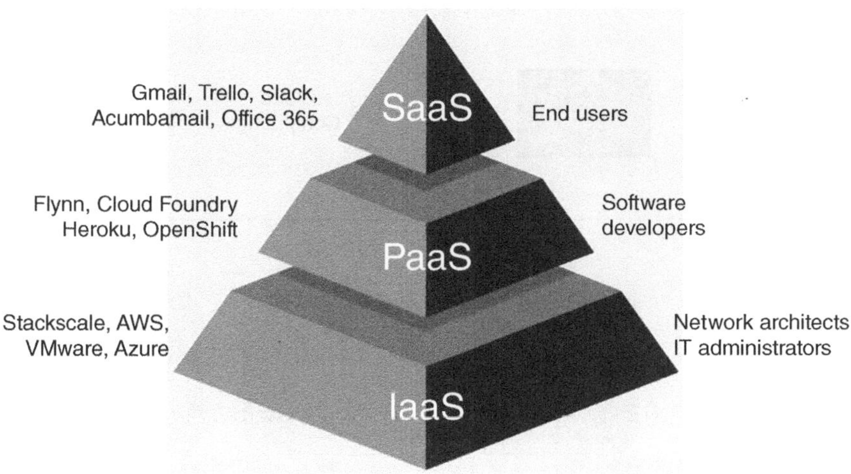

Figure 1.1 Cloud service models [1].

1.2.4 The Shifting Cloud Paradigm

The original cloud promise was pretty straightforward: scalability, cost-efficiency, and flexibility [14]. But modern enterprises wanted it all—performance, cost-effectiveness, intelligence, automation, and accountability [15]. And it needs to be sustainable too, because everyone's suddenly worried about carbon footprints [16, 17].

This is where AI comes in, both as cloud computing's biggest beneficiary and its primary driver. Think about it: AI needs massive computational power for training those complex models, and the cloud provides exactly that. Meanwhile, AI is making cloud services smarter—predictive analytics, autonomous operations, you name it.

It's a symbiotic relationship that's spawned some impressive innovations.

1.2.5 AI: Cloud's New Growth Engine

AI has become both a driver and a beneficiary of cloud computing. The cloud offers the computational horsepower and scalability needed for training and deploying complex models, while AI infuses intelligence into cloud services, enabling predictive analytics, autonomous operations, and smarter decision-making.

As shown in Figure 1.2, the symbiotic relationship between AI and cloud has catalyzed innovations in:

- **AutoML and AI as a Service:** Have basically democratized machine learning. Google Cloud AutoML, AWS SageMaker Autopilot, and Azure AutoML—these

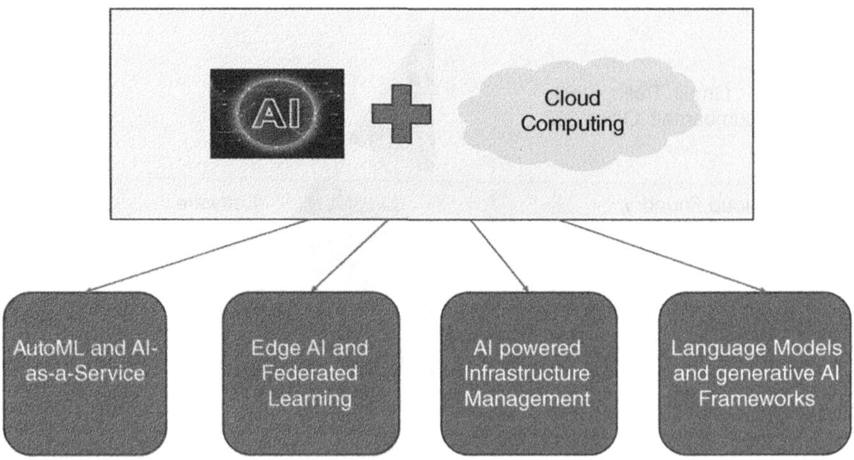

Figure 1.2 AI enhancement is driving growth in cloud computing.

platforms let nonexperts build decent models without writing much code. Time-to-value has plummeted, which is great for business but maybe not so great for traditional data scientists' job security.
- **Edge AI and Federated Learning:** Are solving the latency problem. Why send all your data to the cloud when you can process it locally? Google's federated learning approach is particularly clever—train models on decentralized data without ever moving that data. Privacy preserved, performance maintained.
- **AIOps Platforms:** Are the unsung heroes here. Azure Monitor, Google Cloud Operations Suite, and third-party tools like Dynatrace and Datadog—they're using ML to predict infrastructure failures, detect anomalies, and allocate resources dynamically. It's like having a crystal ball for your data center.
- **Large Language Models:** OpenAI's GPT, Google's PaLM, Meta's LLaMA, and others—have democratized the usage of machine learning/AI and have been instrumental in powering applications like customer service bots and code generation tools. The fact that you can access these capabilities through simple API calls That's the cloud doing what it does best.

1.2.6 Challenges of Supporting AI Workloads in the Cloud

Supporting large-scale AI workloads presents substantial challenges. The energy requirements alone are staggering. Training frontier models can require tens of thousands of graphics processing units (GPUs) and cost millions per run [18]. These computational requirements can have a significant environmental impact.

Then there's the performance pressure. AI assistants, live transcription, and fraud detection—these use cases demand sub-second response times at a global scale. AWS Inferentia, Google's TPUv5, and NVIDIA's Triton Inference Server—everyone's racing to build faster inference accelerators [19].

Complexity of supporting AI workloads remains a significant challenge. Model versioning, reproducibility, and access control in multi-tenant environments—these are key aspects that need to be managed effectively and planned for. Tools like MLflow, SageMaker Model Registry, and Vertex AI Model Monitoring [20–22] can be leveraged to manage the complexity. However, the field and tools are still evolving, and the best practices need to be fully established.

Moreover, regulations are changing faster than we can keep up. The EU AI Act and data localization laws in China and India—cloud providers are constantly adapting their infrastructure to comply with regional requirements [23]. The dynamic environment and regulatory changes require constant vigilance and the operational/design flexibility that would allow adapting to the changing regulations.

1.2.7 AI and Cloud Use Cases

As shown in Figure 1.3, the AI and cloud use cases are extensive and varied, despite the challenges.

In **healthcare**, large language models (LLMs) are handling triage support and patient interactions while staying HIPAA-compliant through edge processing [24]. Imagine having an AI that can pre-screen patients and annotate medical images—all without sending sensitive data to the cloud.

Retail has gone all-in on generative AI for dynamic content, personalized marketing, and demand forecasting [25]. These systems adapt promotions in real time based on inventory levels and customer behavior. The conversion rate improvements are pretty remarkable.

Industrial IoT is where predictive maintenance really shines [26]. Sensors on manufacturing equipment feed data to edge AI models that can predict failures before they happen. Just-in-time maintenance isn't just a buzzword anymore—it's saving companies millions in downtime costs.

Autonomous Systems are the crown jewel of edge AI [27]. Real-time object detection, navigation, and decision-making—all happening locally while syncing with cloud services for updates and coordination. The safety implications are huge.

Finance might be traditionally conservative, but they've embraced AI for fraud detection and credit scoring [28]. Multicloud pipelines process millions of transactions in real-time, using both supervised and unsupervised learning. The accuracy improvements are impressive, even if banks are still cautious about adopting cutting-edge techniques.

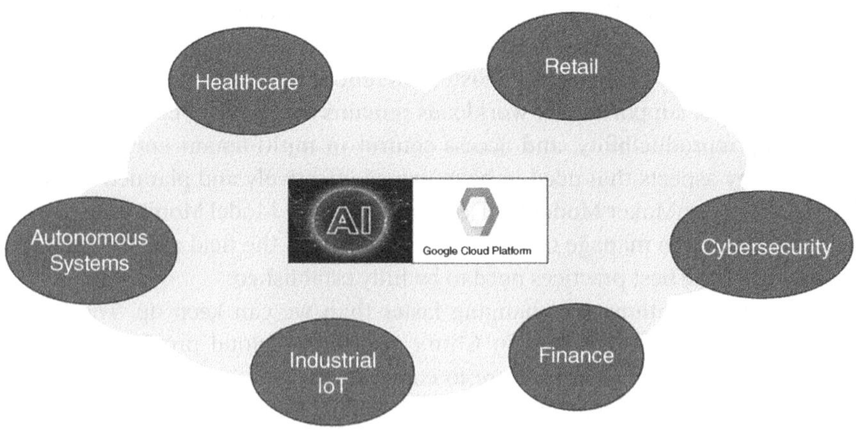

Figure 1.3 AI and cloud use cases.

Cybersecurity platforms are using cloud-based Security Information and Event Management (SIEMs) and Extended Detection and Response (XDR) systems with AI-enhanced threat detection [29, 30]. These systems ingest logs from everywhere—endpoints, APIs, and network traffic—and flag anomalies faster than any human analyst could.

As cloud platforms race to deliver AI infrastructure and services, they're juggling three critical requirements: performance, cost-efficiency, and compliance. It's not easy maintaining agility while embedding sustainability and ethics into everything you do [31, 32].

1.3 The Sustainability Imperative

Let's talk about something that's been keeping a lot of us in the industry up at night lately. Data centers—those massive, humming temples to our digital age—can be a bit problematic from an environmental standpoint. It is true that cloud infrastructure still offers unparalleled scalability and flexibility. But it is also a fact that it consumes a staggering amount of energy.

And then AI came along and basically threw gasoline on the fire.

Training large LLM models like GPT-4, LLaMa 3, Claude 4, and PaLM does take a lot of resources. We're talking about "compute" requirements that would make a supercomputer from the 1990s look very small. These models demand specialized hardware, extensive data pipelines, and round-the-clock inferencing for real-time applications. The energy consumption across the entire AI lifecycle is extensive.

The use cases of ML/AI (specifically LLMs) are varied—real-time content generation, AI chatbots, smart search, and autonomous decision systems, to name a few. Finance, healthcare, and cybersecurity—all domains need and benefit from the AI advancement, which means cloud workloads are higher than they've ever been.

So here we are caught between the promise of AI-powered everything and the reality that our planet has limits.

In response, the sustainability imperative pushes the cloud industry toward operational practices and architectural innovations that minimize ecological impact while maintaining service performance and economic viability.

As highlighted in Figure 1.4, the key AI, cloud, and sustainability strategies shaping this evolution are discussed below.

1) **Renewable Energy Commitments**
   The big players—Google, Microsoft, and Amazon—have made some pretty bold commitments. Operating entirely on renewable energy by 2030 or earlier. Solar, wind, hydroelectric, you name it. Microsoft's pledge to go carbon negative by 2030 and remove all their historical emissions by 2050? That's not just

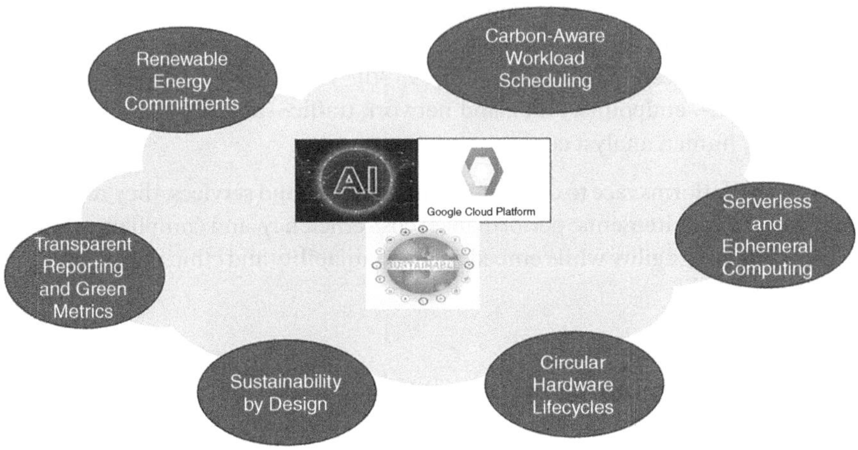

Figure 1.4 AI, cloud, and sustainability.

PR speak; they're actually tracking this stuff with sustainability dashboards and third-party audits.

Power purchase agreements (PPAs) are becoming the norm rather than the exception. It's fascinating to watch these tech giants essentially become major players in the green energy development game.

2) **Carbon-Aware Workload Scheduling**

Here's something that's cleverer than it sounds: carbon-aware workload scheduling. The idea is beautifully simple—dynamically shift compute jobs across geographic locations based on real-time carbon intensity data.

Got a machine learning training job that isn't super urgent? Route it to the data center where renewable energy is abundant right now. Google Cloud's carbon-aware computing platform and Microsoft's emissions impact dashboard are making this kind of optimization accessible to customers. It's like traffic routing, but for carbon footprints.

3) **Serverless and Ephemeral Computing**

Serverless computing—AWS Lambda, Azure Functions, and Google Cloud Functions—turns out to be an environmental win, not just a developer convenience. When you think about it, it makes perfect sense. These ephemeral compute environments eliminate idle resource consumption. No more servers sitting around burning electricity waiting for something to happen.

Event-driven architectures allow for micro-optimizations at runtime, which is great for both sustainability and your AWS bill. Win-win.

4) **Circular Hardware Lifecycles**

This one's particularly interesting. Instead of the traditional "buy new, throw away old" approach, cloud providers are embracing circular economy principles. Refurbishing servers, recycling rare earth metals, and designing equipment for modularity and extended life.

Google's 2022 Sustainability Report showed that over 25% of their deployed servers were refurbished machines. That's thousands of metric tons of avoided carbon emissions. Not bad for what basically amounts to smart recycling.

5) **Sustainability by Design**
Rather than bolting sustainability onto existing infrastructure (which, let's face it, never works well), modern cloud infrastructure is being designed with eco-efficiency as a first-class objective. We're seeing innovations in liquid cooling to reduce HVAC loads, AI-driven power and thermal management systems, and data centers co-located with renewable energy sources.

Custom chips like Google's TPU and AWS's Graviton processors are optimized for performance per watt. It's amazing what happens when you design for efficiency from the ground up rather than trying to retrofit it later.

6) **Transparent Reporting and Green Metrics**
Cloud customers are getting increasingly demanding about visibility into their environmental impact—and honestly, it's about time. Providers are publishing sustainability reports, real-time dashboards, and APIs that offer transparency on carbon intensity, water usage effectiveness (WUE), and power usage effectiveness (PUE).

Tools like the AWS Customer Carbon Footprint Tool and the Azure Sustainability Calculator let enterprises actually track and reduce their environmental impact rather than just hoping for the best. The thing is, this isn't just about doing the right thing anymore (though that matters). It's becoming a competitive differentiator, a driver of innovation, and surprisingly often, a source of long-term cost savings.

Sustainability, when treated as a design principle rather than a constraint, can yield not only environmental benefits but also operational efficiency and cost savings.

1.4 Challenges and Opportunities

Integrating AI and sustainability into cloud ecosystems introduces a complex landscape of challenges and opportunities that must be navigated thoughtfully to ensure future-proof architectures.

1) **Managing the Energy-Intensive Nature of Large-Scale AI**
Training large foundation models like GPT and PaLM requires computational resources that translate directly to high energy consumption and carbon emissions [33, 34]. We're talking about training runs that consume as much electricity as dozens of US households use in a year. For a single model.

The response has been interesting, though. Hyperscalers and AI firms are turning to renewable energy sources, hardware optimization (ASICs like Google TPUs), and energy-aware scheduling algorithms. It's not solving the fundamental problem, but it's making progress.

2) **Balancing Performance and Eco-Efficiency**
   Here's the rub: achieving high performance for AI workloads often means provisioning extensive computational infrastructure, which directly conflicts with sustainability goals. Finding the sweet spot between latency, throughput, and energy usage demands some pretty novel optimization strategies.

   Serverless AI architectures are helping. Edge deployment for inference workloads reduces long-distance data transfer and energy consumption. But we're still figuring out the optimal approaches.

3) **Ensuring Ethical AI Development and Deployment**
   AI models hosted on cloud platforms can exhibit bias, opacity, and unfairness unless they're governed by strict ethical standards. Integrating responsible AI practices—explainability, fairness-aware learning, or transparent documentation—into cloud-based development pipelines is becoming essential.

   And there's the environmental justice angle too. The impact of siting data centers in resource-strained communities is something we need to talk about more openly.

4) **Standardizing Green Cloud Metrics and Benchmarks**
   A lack of universal standards for assessing the environmental impact of cloud-based AI limits progress. There's a growing call for standardized sustainability metrics, such as PUE, carbon usage effectiveness (CUE), and ML-specific emissions per training run. Benchmarking frameworks like MLPerf must evolve to include eco-efficiency metrics alongside performance measures.

5) **Opportunities at the Intersection of Technology, Policy, and Ethics**
   While the challenges are significant, they also create space for groundbreaking innovation.

   Opportunities include:

   - Green AI research that optimizes models not just for accuracy but also for carbon footprint
   - AI-powered sustainability applications, such as optimizing power grids, reducing waste, and improving climate models
   - Policy innovations, such as carbon credits for eco-friendly compute jobs
   - Cross-sector collaborations to set global standards for sustainable AI deployment

These intersecting trends highlight the importance of a multidisciplinary approach to building the future of cloud computing.

1.5 Conclusion

In this chapter, we explored the changing face of cloud computing, and how AI and sustainability have refined how cloud computing architectures are being reimagined. We delved into the evolution of cloud computing from the early roots in mainframe time-sharing to its current role as a backbone of AI and sustainability efforts.

We also examined the modern cloud architecture and service models, highlighting how they are evolving to support the demands of AI advancements. We explored how AI has become the growth engine for cloud computing, with the symbiotic relationship between the two. We delved into the AI and cloud use cases, which have seen extensive growth.

While AI has fueled the growth of cloud computing, there are multiple challenges to supporting AI workloads in the cloud. The chapter delved into some of these challenges. Further, the chapter provided an introduction on the sustainability imperatives and requirements on the cloud computing industry with the increasing datacenter (i.e., energy) demands for ML model training and inference. The chapter highlights the key "AI, Cloud, and Sustainability" strategies that companies are adopting to balance performance, cost, and sustainability considerations. Finally, we look at the challenges and opportunities in integrating AI and sustainability with cloud computing.

In summary, the chapter explores the advancements and synergies of cloud computing, AI, and sustainability and highlights the importance of balancing performance, cost, and ethical considerations in building next-generation cloud systems. As organizations continue to adopt AI at scale, these themes will become even more central to how cloud architectures evolve and sustainability becomes a "key" requirement of how infrastructure is designed and governed.

1.6 Future Scope

In the chapters ahead, we're going to dive deep into how cloud computing is being reshaped by AI and sustainability working together. You'll see how platforms are evolving to meet demands for intelligent, efficient, and ethical digital infrastructure.

We'll explore the transition from basic virtual machines to highly abstracted, serverless, event-driven architectures. Cloud-native design patterns, microservices, and multicloud strategies—all the stuff that's making modern infrastructure both more resilient and more complex.

AI plays the central role throughout this journey, naturally. AI as a service, intelligent automation, AIOps, and the increasingly critical challenge of managing cost and complexity through FinOps—especially for generative AI workloads that can burn through budgets faster than you can say "transformer architecture."

Security, privacy, and regulatory compliance receive focused attention as well. Zero Trust architectures, embedded DevSecOps practices, and data localization laws ensure that as cloud-native threats grow, organizations use proactive security strategies that strengthen threat detection and cyber resilience.

Then we'll look toward the future: sustainable architectures that reduce the environmental impact of AI workloads, the promise and limitations of quantum computing in the cloud, and using cloud infrastructure for scientific research and high-performance computing.

Throughout all of this, we'll maintain a strong ethical lens. Questions of bias, fairness, and responsible AI deployment—these aren't nice-to-haves anymore; they're fundamental to building systems that work for everyone.

By the end, you'll have a holistic understanding of how cloud computing is evolving in the AI age and, more importantly, the practices that will define its sustainable and secure future.

Because ultimately, reimagining cloud computing through these lenses opens the door to a future where digital progress actually aligns with ecological and ethical imperatives. And frankly, it's about time!

References

1 M. M. Waldrop, *The Dream Machine: J.C.R. Licklider and the Revolution that Made Computing Personal*. New York: Viking Penguin, 2011.

2 A. L. Norberg and J. E. O'Neill, *Transforming Computer Technology: Information Processing for the Pentagon, 1962–1986*. Baltimore: Johns Hopkins University Press, 1996.

3 R. Chellapa, "Intermediaries in cloud-computing: A new computing paradigm," in *INFORMS Conf. Inf. Syst. Technol. (CIST)* Dallas, 1997. p. 26-27.

4 M. Benioff and C. Adler, *Behind the Cloud: The Untold Story of How Salesforce.com Went from Idea to Billion-Dollar Company*. San Francisco, CA: Jossey-Bass, 2009.

5 Q. Zhang, L. Cheng, and R. Boutaba, "Cloud computing: State-of-the-art and research challenges," *J. Internet Serv. Appl.*, vol. 1, no. 1, pp. 7–18, 2010, doi: 10.1007/s13174-010-0007-6.

6 S. Guthrie, "Introducing windows Azure," *Microsoft Azure Blog*, 2010. [Online]. Available: https://azure.microsoft.com/en-us/blog/introducing-windows-azure.

7 B. Burns, B. Grant, D. Oppenheimer, E. Brewer, and J. Wilkes, "Borg, omega, and kubernetes: Lessons learned from three container-management systems over a decade," *ACM Queue*, vol. 14, no. 1, pp. 70–93, 2016.

8 "IBM: IBM cloud strategy overview," 2017. [Online]. Available: https://www.ibm.com/cloud/strategy.

9 "Oracle: Oracle cloud infrastructure overview," 2019. [Online]. Available: https://www.oracle.com/cloud.

10 J. Liu, *Alibaba Cloud: A Leader in China and Growing Globally*. Boston, MA: Harvard Business Review Digital Articles, 2018.

11 P. Mell and T. Grance, *The NIST Definition of Cloud Computing*. National Institute of Standards and Technology, 2011. [Online]. Available: https://nvlpubs.nist.gov/nistpubs/Legacy/SP/nistspecialpublication800-145.pdf.

12 ISO/IEC: ISO/IEC 17788, *Information Technology – Cloud Computing – Overview and Vocabulary*. International Organization for Standardization, 2014. [Online]. Available: https://www.iso.org/standard/60544.html.

13 D. C. Marinescu, *Cloud Computing: Theory and Practice*. Boston, MA: Morgan Kaufmann, 2013.

14 M. Armbrust *et al.*, "A view of cloud computing," *Commun. ACM*, vol. 53, no. 4, pp. 50–58, 2010, doi: 10.1145/1721654.1721672.

15 R. Buyya *et al.*, "A manifesto for future generation cloud computing: Research directions for the next decade," *ACM Compu. Surv. (CSUR)*, vol. 51, no. 5, pp. 1–38, 2018, doi: 10.1145/3241737.

16 A. Shehabi *et al.*, *United States Data Center Energy Usage Report*. Lawrence Berkeley National Laboratory, 2016. [Online]. Available: https://eta.lbl.gov/publications/united-states-data-center-energy.

17 E. Masanet, A. Shehabi, N. Lei, S. Smith, and J. Koomey, "Recalibrating global data center energy-use estimates," *Science*, vol. 367, no. 6481, pp. 984–986, 2020, doi: 10.1126/science.aba3758.

18 D. A. Patterson *et al.*, "Carbon emissions and large neural network training," *arXiv preprint arXiv:2104.10350*, 2021.

19 Google, "Carbon-aware computing: The next frontier of Green Cloud," 2023. [Online]. Available: https://sustainability.google.

20 Google Cloud, "Vertex AI model monitoring overview," [Online]. Available: https://cloud.google.com/vertex-ai/docs/model-monitoring/overview.

21 MLflow, "Open source platform for the machine learning lifecycle," [Online]. Available: https://mlflow.org.

22 Amazon Web Services, "Amazon SageMaker model registry developer guide," [Online]. Available: https://docs.aws.amazon.com/sagemaker/latest/dg/model-registry.html.

23 M. Veale and F. Z. Zuiderveen Borgesius, "Demystifying the draft EU Artificial Intelligence Act," *Comput. Law Rev. Int.*, vol. 22, no. 4, pp. 97–112, 2021. [Online]. Available: https://papers.ssrn.com/sol3/papers.cfm?abstract_id=3896852.

24 A. I., Prem, "Enterprise AI trends for 2025: What's next for businesses?," *Prem AI Blog*, 2025. [Online]. Available: https://blog.premai.io/enterprise-ai-trends-for-2025-whats-next-for-businesses.

25 PwC, "AI is no longer an option – It's the future of retail," *PwC Global*, 2024. [online]. Available: https://www.pwc.com/gx/en/services/alliances/microsoft/ai-retail-transformation-future.html.

26 C. Grant, F. Wallace, L. MacKay, and J. B. Adelusi, *Edge AI for Predictive Maintenance in Industrial IoT Environments*. ResearchGate, 2024. [Online]. Available: https://www.researchgate.net/publication/391384065_Edge_AI_for_Predictive_Maintenance_in_Industrial_IoT_Environments.

27 J. Kaur, "Edge AI for autonomous vehicles," *XenonStack Blog*, 2024. [Online]. Available: https://www.xenonstack.com/blog/edge-ai-for-autonomous-vehicles.

28 PwC, "Leveraging GenAI in banking," *PwC Middle East*, 2024. [Online]. Available: https://www.pwc.com/m1/en/publications/leveraging-generative-ai-in-banking.html.

29 "Google cloud: Chronicle SIEM – Cloud-native security information and event management," *Google Cloud*, 2024. [Online]. Available: https://cloud.google.com/chronicle?hl=en.

30 Microsoft, "Microsoft defender XDR – Unified threat protection across endpoints and cloud," *Microsoft Security*, 2024. [Online]. Available: https://www.microsoft.com/en-us/security/business/siem-and-xdr/microsoft-defender-xdr.

31 R. Schwartz, J. Dodge, N. A. Smith, and O. Etzioni, "Green AI," *Commun. ACM*, vol. 63, no. 12, pp. 54–63, 2019, doi: 10.1145/3381831.

32 P. Henderson, J. Hu, J. Romoff, E. Brunskill, D. Jurafsky, and J. Pineau, "Towards the systematic reporting of the energy and carbon footprints of machine learning," *J. Mach. Learn. Res.*, vol. 21, no. 248, pp. 1–43, 2020. https://www.jmlr.org/papers/volume21/20-312/20-312.pdf.

33 A. de Vries, "The growing energy footprint of artificial intelligence," *Joule*, vol. 7, no. 10, pp. 2191–2194, 2023, doi: 10.1016/j.joule.2023.09.004.

34 D. Patterson *et al.*, "Carbon emissions and large neural network training," *arXiv preprint arXiv:2104.10350*, 2021. https://arxiv.org/abs/2104.10350.

2

The Evolution of Cloud Computing: From Virtual Machines to Serverless

Anuj Ashok Potdar[1] *and Pronnoy Goswami*[2]

[1] *IEEE Senior Member, Boston, MA, USA*
[2] *IEEE Senior Member, Santa Clara, CA, USA*

2.1 Introduction

This section explores how the term "cloud computing" came into existence and traces its roots from the traditional time-sharing systems and ARPANET in the 1960s [1], followed by the advent of Software-as-a-Service (SaaS) in the 1990s [2], and finally to the mainstream adoption of the term in the 2000s [3]. It also dives deep into terms like virtualization, hypervisors, the birth of the modern container architecture and orchestration, and the serverless paradigms [4, 5].

The chapter also breaks down the NIST definition of cloud computing in detail and explains each term of the definition with examples [6]. Going through the historical context and significance, this section covers each development throughout the last 50 years that has laid the foundation of the current cloud computing architecture, highlighting the contributions of various tech companies like IBM, Salesforce, Google, and Amazon in creating technologies and solutions that are used in some form or another throughout the world for the deployment and hosting of their applications [2, 3, 7] and briefly touching on different types of service models in cloud computing, the SaaS, Platform-as-a-Service (PaaS), and Infrastructure-as-a-Service (IaaS), and the level of flexibility and customization offered by each of them [8].

Listing various types of virtualizations and the different technologies used in virtualization and cloud computing, we discuss types of hypervisors, their advantages, and shortcomings in detail [9]. Finally, we discuss the limitations of traditional computationally intensive virtualization techniques and how the modern containerization and serverless architectures provide a much lighter and extensible solution, crucial for modern-day high-speed and high-scale applications that need to scale up and down on demand as the load increases and decreases [4, 5, 10].

Going through containerization, we discuss the role of Docker and how it has led to the ease of development for software engineers to concentrate solely on the functionality and business needs while developing an application without having to worry about how the application would behave differently in production compared to the development environment [11].

2.2 The Definition of Cloud Computing

As per the National Institute of Standards and Technology (NIST), the definition of cloud computing is as follows [6]:

> *Cloud computing is a model for enabling ubiquitous, convenient, on-demand network access to a shared pool of configurable computing resources… that can be rapidly provisioned and released with minimal management effort or service provider interaction.*

Let us break down the definition to understand it better. Cloud computing stands for the use of the internet or a network (depending on the type of cloud) to access computer resources from a shared pool of resources, which can include resources like servers, databases, and even Graphic Processing Units (GPUs) in a modern context, without the need to own these resources and their physical hardware components yourself [6].

The term "ubiquitous" in the definition points to the accessibility aspect of cloud computing, where a pool of resources can be at any one location and accessed from a completely different location seamlessly without needing to move it from one place to another, given that you are connected to the network (often the internet) that it is hosted on [6].

Additionally, the mention of "rapidly provisioned and released with minimal management effort" means that the time required to start and stop using these resources should be less, and there should not be a need for someone to manually set up these resources for you every time as there is a change in the computational needs or configuration requirement [6].

This paradigm emphasizes renting. In cloud computing, instead of keeping a particular piece of hardware permanently, you rent a specific configuration temporarily as needed [4, 6].

2.3 Historical Context and Significance

Today, we rely heavily on cloud computing, which we often don't fully understand. From our Google Photos and Apple iCloud to ChatGPT, everything works on cloud computing [12]. We use it effortlessly and with a high level of abstraction, which has made it a crucial part of our lives. It is ubiquitous; we do not spend efforts on managing whether we need to scale it up or down. Let us go back in time and trace where the term was originally coined.

The term "cloud computing" first gained widespread popularity in 2006 when Eric Schmidt, the then CEO of Google, used this term publicly at the Search Engine Strategies (SES) Conference in San Jose, California, in August 2006 [13]. During a Q&A session at the conference, he explained Google's approach to web-based applications and stated:

> *What's interesting is that there is an emergent new model. I don't think people have really understood how big it's going to be. It starts with the premise that the data services and architecture should be on servers. We call it cloud computing; they should be in a 'cloud' somewhere* [13].

Eric Schmidt's mention of "cloud computing" at a 2006 tech conference was one of the first times the term appeared in a high-profile public setting, describing a move away from local software to internet-based services, a concept that had existed internally for years but only gained mainstream traction after that moment. However, the modern cloud era truly began later that year when Amazon Web Services (AWS) launched Elastic Compute Cloud (EC2), offering businesses on-demand access to virtual servers [3]. Although Schmidt popularized the term, it gained more widespread use in the modern context after the launch of AWS EC2, where Amazon introduced its infrastructure as a service (IaaS), providing raw computing power for applications to be built with higher control and flexibility [3].

In 1997, during a lecture at Emory University, Professor Ramnath Chellappa, a well-known researcher in digital business and technology, introduced the concept of cloud computing and provided the following definition:

> *A computing paradigm where the boundaries of computing will be determined by economic rationale rather than technical limits* [5].

This definition has been pivotal for a few reasons, mainly because it emphasized the on-demand access of computing resources and also highlighted the economic scalability, which is very relevant and important even today.

However, the term had been used internally much earlier, but it had not gained widespread popularity; for example, Compaq had used it internally since 1996. In a 1996 document entitled "Internet Solutions Division Strategy," Compaq executives drafted an internal document that referenced "cloud-computing-enabled applications" [5].

The foundation of this term can be traced back to the 1960s, during the mainframe era, when the foundation of virtualization was established. In this period, resources to carry out heavy computation operations were in short supply because they were very expensive and novel for the time. As necessity is the mother of invention, this led to the development of systems and strategies used for time-based sharing systems, facilitating multiple users to access the same mainframe system simultaneously [7, 14].

2.4 Evolution Timeline Overview

The cloud computing paradigm has evolved over the past few decades, and it has been evolving ever since. From the early 1960s to the present day, there have been constant developments in the areas of virtualization, resource sharing, networked utilities, and distributed systems that have shaped it into what it is today [1, 14].

During the first mentions of cloud computing in 1960s and 1970s in the form of virtualization, it primarily focused on abstracting physical hardware. In the 1960s" Mainframe Era, the computers were huge, and they were primarily owned by larger entities like government offices, universities, or giant corporations. Because of these factors, access to computers and their giant computational resources was limited to a single user, which resulted in a waste of computational power. A solution to this was proposed and designed by projects like MIT's CTSS (Compatible Time-Sharing System) in 1961 and followed by Multics in 1965. Both of these worked on the concept of time-sharing that allowed multiple users to access the same mainframe computer simultaneously, which in turn reduced the idle time for the machines and facilitated resource pooling, which is a core cloud computing principle [14].

The ARPANET, which is the precursor to the modern-day internet, was developed in 1969 as a project of the U.S. Defense Department that connected computers across different locations. This has been pivotal in demonstrating the power and potential of networked resources, where the resources can be in various places and still be provided with "ubiquitous access" [1]. This also led to the foundation of remote job entry (RJE), which allows users to submit their tasks to the mainframe over a network, similar to how APIs work in today's cloud services [1].

With the advent of the UNIX operating system during the 1970s, developed at Bell Labs, along with it came the multi-user, multi-tasking architecture and the ability to run on various hardware, which influenced future cloud-friendly operating systems like Linux [10]. Decentralized computing was getting explored by projects like Xerox PARC's Alto (1973) and Ethernet (1973) that primarily worked on decentralized computing, which allows resources to be shared across networked machines [10]. Concepts like virtual memory came into existence, allowing and enabling programs to use more memory than what was physically available, all of which has been a precursor to the modern-day distributed cloud architecture [10].

In the 1990s, the World Wide Web (1991) was launched, and it transformed the internet from a niche academic tool into a full-fledged commercial platform. This introduced HTTP for transferring data and HTML for structuring the content on the web. Alongside came some other inventions that aided the growth of information transfer like Common Gateway Interface scripts (CGI, 1993) for dynamic web content, JavaScript (1995) for client-side interactivity to browsers, and Java (1995) for platform-independent applets that could run in browsers [5].

Server-side innovations occurred during this era. Open-source technologies like Apache became a key contributor to empowering over 50% of the websites by 1996 [5]. Hypertext Preprocessor (PHP) (1994–1995) allowed the software to have embedded logic directly into HTML, and it simplified the creation and enhanced the usage of dynamic web applications [5].

The Dot-Com Boom happened, and businesses raced to be a part of it, which created a demand for scalable software solutions. Companies like Salesforce emerged that primarily focused on changing the way people used to consume software, changing the mode of software delivery from on-premise software like Microsoft Office and Oracle databases, which required expensive licenses, installation, and IT maintenance, into a more portable solution delivered directly through the web browser. This helped reduce the cost and time to get up and running, and this was the birth of the modern-day SaaS model, most commonly referred to as SaaS [2]. Small businesses could pay a monthly subscription fee rather than an expensive license, which made this model even more popular.

Even though SaaS became popular for using software, for building their software, many companies still relied on physical servers, managed hosting, and colocation, which required a lot of physical space, hiring people, and building infrastructure, and scaling up would require a huge amount of investment for increasing the server space and capacities. This used to be a huge bottleneck, especially when a smaller web application gained overnight popularity and the servers were not enough to handle the increased load and requests [3].

This problem was addressed during the Modern Cloud Era (2006–2010), during which PaaS and IaaS started gaining increasing popularity. The key invention of virtualization decoupled software from hardware, which in turn allowed platforms to be turned into a self-service, Application Programming Interface

(API)-driven utility [4, 8]. One such key platform is AWS, launched in March 2006. AWS unveiled S3 (Simple Storage Service), which worked on RESTful APIs to provide standard GET/PUT commands to access storage over HTTP [3]. Companies building software could now store their data on AWS just by interacting with a GET and PUT request. They also introduced EC2 (Elastic Cloud Compute), which enabled on-demand virtual machine (VM) instances with root access and was the first true IaaS, allowing developers to rent compute power by the hour [3]. Microsoft launched Windows Azure in 2008 (later rebranded as Microsoft Azure in 2014), focusing on PaaS for .NET developers, then later pivoted to IaaS in 2010 by introducing Windows Server VMs [3]. Similarly, Google offered its cloud solution through Google Cloud Platform (GCP) with the App Engine in 2008, offering a sandboxed PaaS where developers could deploy Python and Java applications. GCP expanded to IaaS with Google Compute Engine (GCE) in 2012 with an open-source hypervisor for Linux/Windows VMs [3].

In 2013, with the advent of Docker, the containerization revolution began, which provided a more lightweight and portable alternative to traditional VMs [11]. These platforms transformed the software architecture paradigms by enabling microservices, DevOps, and the cloud-native movement [4, 15]. Each one of these innovations has increased the levels of abstraction and automation, slowly and gradually freeing software developers from their focus on infrastructure and concentrating more on building the functionality. Finally, serverless computing emerged in 2014 with AWS Lambda, further abstracting infrastructure management and enabling a pure focus on code [4, 15].

2.5 The Foundations: Virtual Machines and Early Virtualization

2.5.1 The Concept of Virtualization

Virtualization is the backbone of cloud computing, the process of abstracting and creating software-based demarcations of physical computing resources [6]. NIST defines virtualization as follows:

> *Virtualization is the simulation of the software and/or hardware upon which other software runs. It allows multiple operating systems and applications to run on the same physical hardware* [6].

Let us break down the definition to understand it better. Simulation of the software refers to creating a virtual version of an entire operating system or application environment that mimics the behavior of a real one. Hardware simulation refers to emulating physical computer components like CPUs, memory, and storage. In a very oversimplified language, we can think of it as one or more logical computers inside a real computer. This hardware or software virtualization system behaves just like a real machine, and the software running on top of it can run as if it is running on an independent machine. In a non-virtualized or traditional computing environment, one operating system controls one physical machine, but virtualization breaks this limitation by allowing multiple VMs to run on one physical machine, and each VM thinks it has its dedicated hardware [8].

The core idea of virtualization revolves around the abstraction of physical resources, enabling multiple environments on the same hardware. The concept of virtualization started in the 1960s–1970s with the early mainframe era. IBM invested heavily in developing IBM CP-40 (1967) and CP/CMS (later renamed as VM/CMS), which introduced hypervisors that allowed a single mainframe to host multiple independent VMs [7]. Time sharing and resource pooling allowed CPU time, memory, and storage to be dynamically allocated to users, creating a facade of dedicated machines while sharing the dedicated underlying hardware [7].

Virtualization in a cloud context is offered in four prominent verticals [8, 9]:

- Server Virtualization
- Storage Virtualization
- Network Virtualization
- GPU Virtualization

The invention of full virtualization enabled each VM to have the ability to run its operating system and applications. Most importantly, they were isolated from each other, which allowed running applications of different natures on the same hardware. This resulted in significant improvements in resource utilization and cost-effectiveness, positioning cloud computing as an attractive option for software deployment [4, 8]. Another key advantage of virtualization is how it offers disaster recovery and portability. In the event of a site failure, VM snapshots and live migration enable seamless recovery [4, 8].

2.5.2 Hypervisor—Virtual Machine Technology Explained

Let us take a minute to understand a little bit about hypervisors. Hypervisors are the monitors of VMs. They are software layers that are used for creating and managing VMs by performing operations like allocation of physical hardware resources to each VM while keeping the isolation, security, and fairness between the VMs [9].

There are two main types of hypervisors, and this section will go through both of them in detail:

- *Type-1 Hypervisor, also known as Bare-Metal Hypervisor:*
  This hypervisor runs directly on the physical hardware, without the need for a host OS. It offers higher performance and security and is used in enterprise data centers and cloud computing [9].

Since there is no underlying operating system layer, they offer near-native performance, making the overhead minimal while also focusing on strong isolation and providing direct hardware access, which is crucial for high-performance workloads [9]. Examples are VMware ESXi, Microsoft Hyper-V, Xen, and kernel-based VM (KVM) [9].

- *Type-2 Hypervisor, also known as the Hosted Hypervisor:*
  This hypervisor runs on top of a conventional operating system such as Windows, macOS, or Linux. It is commonly used for development and testing on various platforms without having to invest in purchasing different hardware [9]. The presence of a host OS makes it easy to install and use this type of hypervisor, which is a great solution for running multiple OSes on a single machine [9].

  However, due to the presence of a host OS, the performance suffers as there is a higher overhead, and it is less secure, as a compromise in the host OS will affect all the VMs hosted on it [9]. Examples are Oracle VirtualBox, VMware Workstation/Fusion, and Parallels Desktop [9].

2.5.3 The Transition from Physical to Virtual Infrastructure

Before virtualization, in an enterprise setting, each application was bound to one server. The servers were powerful and expensive machines, often dedicated to a single critical application. Needless to say, this approach was proven to be very cost-intensive with a lack of resource utilization; each machine would run at 15–20% of the server's CPU, memory, and I/O capacity, causing huge amounts of expensive computing power to be idle. This represented significant amounts of wasted capital expenditure, and beyond the hardware cost, this inefficiency resulted in several other problems as well, namely:

- **Data Center Footprints:** Underutilized servers demanded enormous space and would require a higher number of servers to fulfill the enterprise server demands.
- **High Power and Cooling Costs:** Each physical server, irrespective of the workload or idle time, would consume significant electricity and generate a high amount of heat that requires expensive cooling.
- **Lack of Operational Flexibility:** Adding a new physical server was a slow and labor-intensive task, involving procurement, physical racking, cabling, installation of the operating system, and configuration, which could take weeks or months, making resource scaling equally painful.
- **Difficult Disaster Recovery:** In case of loss of physical servers, recovery/restoration would rely on complex, slow, and often unreliable backup/restore processes.

Virtualization greatly counters these constraints using hypervisors, where each VM operates like a self-contained physical computer running its own operating system and applications. Also, multiple VMs can be hosted on a single physical host server, which further helps in reducing the amount of physical hardware required. Some of the key enablers of the virtualization concepts are hardware-assisted virtualization (Intel VT-x, AMD-V), which uses CPU extensions to significantly reduce the performance overhead of the hypervisor by handling complex privilege-level translations, and mature hypervisor software (ESX/ESXi) developed by companies like VMware, Xen, Microsoft Hyper-V, and KVM that provide robust, enterprise-level management and features.

All of these techniques provide a lot of cost efficiency by consolidating *n* number of physical servers into a single powerful host, which helps reduce the idle time and dramatically improves the hardware resource utilization. This reduced the CapEx by having fewer physical servers that needed to be purchased, and reduced operational expenses were significantly reduced by optimizing power consumption, cooling requirements, and data center real estate space.

Despite the benefits and various features, enterprise adoption was not easy; there were significant challenges to be addressed. With the early hypervisors (especially without hardware assist), performance overhead concerns were very prevalent, as they had measurable overheads. Enterprise software architects would often be concerned about the impact of virtualization on large databases and transaction systems and whether consolidating multiple VMs on a single physical hardware would hurt system performance. Compatibility issues among applications and hardware peripherals would cause some of these not to interact well with each other.

2.6 The Birth of Modern Cloud Computing

2.6.1 Limitations of Traditional Virtual Machines

The traditional VMs were great for the time, but as computing started becoming heavier and demand increased, certain challenges and limitations were observed. This section will go through each limitation and challenge in detail:

- *Resource Overhead*

  Traditional VMs require a full operating system instance, which consumes substantial memory and storage even when idle and not in use. In high-density environments where resource utilization is maximum, this becomes even more problematic [4].

  Let us take an example to understand this better. Consider a host that is running 20 VMs on it, with each VM instance consuming 1 GB of RAM, which could waste up to 20 GB of RAM just on OS kernels. In such a configuration, high-density microservices that have hundreds of instances would become infeasible [4].

- *Slow Startup Times*
  Traditional VMs also suffered from slow startup and boot times, which would take up minutes of boot time, something that is unacceptable in today's computing scenario, where we sometimes need to scale up for handling sudden traffic spikes due to unexpected increased usage [4].
  The complete process of traditional VM boot involves steps like BIOS/UEFI initialization, hypervisor hardware checks, and full OS kernel initialization. This makes serverless functions that require less than 100 ms initialization impossible to achieve [4].
- *Operational Complexity*
  With multiple operating systems across all the VMs on the host, their management becomes an administrative burden. Here, a system administrator would be required to manage each VM OS individually [4].
  It was impossible to have 2 applications that require 2 different versions of a dependency to be deployed on the same VM; this would lead to dependency conflicts, security overhead, and admin burden [4].
- *Deployment and Portability Challenges*
  The most important and biggest challenge faced by traditional VMs was deployment and portability. Applications that were developed in one environment would often behave differently when deployed to production systems due to configuration differences between their environments [4, 8].
  Applications would fail if the host hypervisor were not similar to the development environment's kernel versions. Library dependency, network/firewall rules, and storage configuration mismatches were among other problems that would cause "mystery failures" in the production environment [4, 8].
  All these limitations and challenges collectively paved the way for the container revolution, which introduced a lighter approach to virtualization [4, 11].

2.6.2 The Rise of Containerization

To overcome the limitations of traditional VMs, containerization came into existence. The approach of containerization is a revolutionary one, where application deployment was transformed from the traditional isolation concept into a cloud-native superpower. In 1979, Unix introduced "chroot," which allowed a form of filesystem isolation [10]. During the early 2000s, technologies like FreeBSD Jails and Solaris Containers added further isolation capabilities, which helped in orchestrating this technology [10]. Building on all these technologies, in 2013, with the introduction of Docker, the term "containerization" achieved mainstream acceptance and adoption [11]. Docker's approach was very developer-friendly; it transformed containers from a complex and specialized technology into an accessible tool for machines. The core differentiator of Docker containers from VMs is that, unlike a VM, which virtualizes the entire hardware stack along with the operating systems, containers virtualize at the operating system level, allowing them to share the host's kernel and use namespaces and control groups (cgroups) technologies to maintain isolation among containers [11].

This architectural paradigm difference allows a container to be extremely light compared to VMs, in the order of megabytes rather than gigabytes, and allows a quick start-up time in the order of seconds, or if of a lower complexity, then even milliseconds [11]. This has revolutionized application deployment by ensuring consistency across development, testing, and production environments, also dramatically improving resource utilization and making applications truly portable [11].

2.6.3 Container Orchestration

With the increasing adoption of containers, managing large numbers of them has become a challenge. Since manually managing containers became impractical, container orchestration platforms rose to address the complex challenges of deploying, scaling, networking, and maintaining containerized applications at scale [16].

In 2014, Google introduced Kubernetes, leveraging its experience running containerized workloads via its Borg system [16]. Through the use of a strong mechanism for automated deployment and for scaling and load balancing, the platform's architecture consists of a control plane that manages the cluster state in addition to worker nodes that run the containerized applications; this architecture creates a powerful but complex system for managing containerized environments [16]. Notably, Docker Swarm gave a simpler alternative, smoothly integrating with Docker, while Apache Mesos gave wider, general-purpose cluster management capabilities to run containers besides workloads [16]. Other cloud providers have developed managed Kubernetes services such as Amazon EKS, Google Kubernetes Engine, and Azure Kubernetes Services that work for reducing the complexity of maintaining orchestration platforms [16].

The container orchestration model has fundamentally transformed the applications deployed and managed within cloud environments. It has also enabled organizations to operate on a scale that was previously impossible [16].

2.7 The Serverless Paradigm

2.7.1 The Concept of Serverless Computing

Serverless computing represents a transformative advancement in cloud architecture, significantly reshaping traditional approaches to application deployment and management. Despite its nomenclature, "serverless" does not imply the absence of servers; instead, it encapsulates the abstraction of server management away from developers. In this paradigm, developers exclusively focus on crafting application logic, while cloud service providers manage infrastructure provisioning, scaling, security, and maintenance responsibilities [17, 18].

The foundational principles of serverless computing include infrastructure abstraction, ephemeral compute instances triggered only when necessary, an event-driven execution model, and a consumption-based pricing structure [19]. Function-as-a-service (FaaS) is the predominant implementation of the serverless model, decomposing applications into discrete, event-driven functions. These functions activate in response to events such as HTTP requests, database updates, or file uploads, enabling granular scalability and optimizing resource efficiency significantly compared to traditional architectures [18–21].

2.7.2 Key Serverless Platforms

Serverless computing gained significant momentum with Amazon Web Services' introduction of AWS Lambda in 2014, establishing the foundational architecture for mainstream FaaS implementations. Lambda offered developers automatic scaling and infrastructure-free execution triggered by specific events, rapidly becoming a blueprint for subsequent serverless platforms [17, 20].

Following AWS Lambda's success, major cloud providers developed their respective platforms. In 2016, Microsoft introduced Azure Functions, emphasizing comprehensive integration across the Azure ecosystem and multilingual support. Simultaneously, Google launched Cloud Functions, targeting lightweight, event-driven workloads seamlessly integrated within Google Cloud's extensive infrastructure [18, 21].

Additional noteworthy platforms include IBM Cloud Functions, developed around the open-source Apache OpenWhisk project; Cloudflare Workers, designed to execute functions at the network edge; and platform-neutral tools like the Serverless Framework, simplifying cross-provider deployments. These platforms collectively form a versatile ecosystem, enabling developers to select environments best aligned with specific application requirements and technical constraints [17–19].

2.7.3 Benefits and Limitations of Serverless Computing

Serverless architectures provide significant advantages, driving widespread adoption across various industry domains. The most immediate benefit is cost efficiency, driven by a consumption-based pricing model eliminating payments for idle capacity, notably advantageous for workloads with fluctuating demand. Furthermore, automatic, rapid scalability from zero to high concurrency simplifies operational overhead, facilitating agile application development and quicker deployment cycles [17, 19].

Nonetheless, serverless architectures possess inherent limitations. "*Cold start*" latency, representing delays in initializing function instances, remains problematic, particularly impacting latency-sensitive or infrequently executed functions. Additionally, vendor lock-in emerges as a significant concern due to proprietary APIs and deep integration within provider-specific ecosystems, complicating migrations across cloud platforms. Moreover, the highly distributed nature of serverless architectures amplifies complexity in monitoring, debugging, and maintaining observability, necessitating specialized tools and methodologies [24–26].

2.8 Conclusion

The evolutionary transition from VMs to containerization and ultimately to serverless computing underscores a clear progression toward heightened abstraction and simplified operational management within cloud computing paradigms. Each evolutionary step addressed specific limitations inherent in prior approaches, reflecting iterative refinement and innovation.

Serverless computing, with its radical abstraction of infrastructure management, epitomizes the latest advancement in this sequence, substantially influencing how applications are designed, implemented, and operated. Future developments in serverless computing are anticipated to incorporate automation-driven infrastructure management, further addressing existing challenges like observability and vendor lock-in and enhancing interoperability across diverse cloud ecosystems.

For researchers and industry practitioners alike, understanding these evolutionary dynamics is critical. It informs strategic technology adoption decisions, ensuring that organizations can optimally leverage evolving cloud paradigms for enhanced operational efficiency, scalability, and innovation.

References

1 DARPA, "ARPANET timeline," 1969. [Online]. Available: https://www.darpa.mil/about-us/timeline/arpanet.

2 http://Salesforce.com, "Company history," 1999. [Online]. Available: https://www.salesforce.com/company/news-press.

3 Amazon Web Services, "AWS launches elastic compute cloud (EC2)," 2006. [Online]. Available: https://aws.amazon.com/about-aws/whats-new/2006/08.

4 M. Armbrust *et al.*, "A view of cloud computing," *Commun. ACM.*, vol. 53, no. 4, pp. 50–58, 2010.

5 A. Rashid and M. Chaturvedi, "Understanding the evolution and emerging trends in cloud computing," *J. Cloud Comput.*, vol. 8, no. 1, pp. 101–121, 2019.

6 P. Mell and T. Grance, "The NIST definition of cloud computing," NIST Special Publication 800-145, Sep. 2011. [Online]. Available: https://nvlpubs.nist.gov/nistpubs/Legacy/SP/nistspecialpublication800-145.pdf.

7 IBM Archives, "IBM CP-40 and CP/CMS virtual machines," 1967. [Online]. Available: https://www.ibm.com/ibm/history.

8 R. Buyya, C. Vecchiola, and S. T. Selvi, *Mastering Cloud Computing: Foundations and Applications Programming*. Waltham, MA: Morgan Kaufmann, 2013.

9 VMware, "Understanding full virtualization, paravirtualization, and hardware assist," *VMware White Paper*, 2006. [Online]. Available: https://www.vmware.com/pdf/Virtualization.pdf.

10 Free Software Foundation, "History of UNIX, GNU, and FreeBSD jails," 2005. [Online]. Available: https://www.gnu.org/gnu/history.html.

11 Docker Inc., "What is a container?," 2013. [Online]. Available: https://www.docker.com/resources/what-container.

12 OpenAI, "Cloud infrastructure and LLMs," *OpenAI Blog*, 2023. [Online]. Available: https://openai.com/blog.

13 Google Cloud Blog, "Eric schmidt coins 'Cloud Computing'," 2006. [Online]. Available: https://cloud.google.com/blog.

14 Multics Project, "CTSS and multics time-sharing system," 1965. [Online]. Available: https://multicians.org.

15 D. Rountree and I. Castrillo, *The Basics of Cloud Computing: Understanding the Fundamentals of Cloud Computing in Theory and Practice*. Waltham, MA: Syngress, 2013.

16 Kubernetes Authors, "Kubernetes concepts," 2021. [Online]. Available: https://kubernetes.io/docs/concepts.

17 Amazon Web Services, "What is serverless computing?," [Online]. Available: https://aws.amazon.com/what-is/serverless-computing.

18 Google Cloud, "What is serverless computing?," [Online]. Available: https://cloud.google.com/discover/what-is-serverless-computing.

19 Revstar Consulting, "Understanding serverless computing: A beginner's guide," [Online]. Available: https://revstarconsulting.com/blog/understanding-serverless-computing-a-beginners-guide.

20 Techahead, "History of AWS," [Online]. Available: https://www.techaheadcorp.com/knowledge-center/history-of-aws.

21 Cognixia, "How has Microsoft Azure evolved over the years?," [Online]. Available: https://www.cognixia.com/blog/how-has-microsoft-azure-evolved-over-the-years.

22 Unix Manual Pages, "chroot(2) — Linux manual page," 1979. [Online]. Available: https://man7.org/linux/man-pages/man2/chroot.2.html.

23 Antstack, "The history of serverless: Everything you need to know," [Online]. Available: https://www.antstack.com/blog/the-history-of-serverless-everything-you-need-to-know.

24 CloudZero, "Serverless vs containers: Which should you use?," [Online]. Available: https://www.cloudzero.com/blog/serverless-vs-containers.

25 Datadog, "Serverless architecture: Serverless vs containers," [Online]. Available: https://www.datadoghq.com/knowledge-center/serverless-architecture/serverless-vs-containers.

26 IBM, "Serverless computing explained," [Online]. Available: https://www.ibm.com/think/topics/serverless.

3

Exploring Cloud-Native Microservices Architectures and Design Patterns

Prashanthi Matam and Venkata Naga Kartik Pidatala

Independent Researcher, Mountlake Terrace, WA, USA

3.1 Introduction

Cloud-native computing and microservices architectures (MSAs) have become a new focal point in current software engineering. These ideas appeared as a result of a reaction to restrictions of old-fashioned monolithic applications, which are prone to issues of scalability, maintainability, and deployment. With more businesses moving toward cloud structures, there is also an increased demand for software constructions that leverage the elasticity, resilience, and automation features of the cloud. Microservices architectures, cloud-native, respond to this challenge and break large applications into loosely coupled and separately deployable services that can be developed, scaled, and maintained in an agile and efficient way [1].

Cloud-native is not only closely related to the process of deploying applications to cloud-based systems but also a series of principles and best practices that take advantage of the distinctive opportunities of the cloud. These are containerization, orchestration, continuous integration and deployment (CI/CD), and infrastructure as code (IaC), and, collectively, they achieve fast delivery of software and operation robustness. Microservices architecture goes hand-in-hand with cloud-native, thus optimizing modularity, scalability, and fault isolation. This architecture pattern breaks an application into a collection of mini-services, each operating in its own process and cooperating through lightweight mechanisms, usually HTTP Application Programming Interface (APIs).

Microservices are also important in the cloud-native space due to factors other than scalability and agility. It promotes organizational alignment because services can be owned and managed by small, cross-functional teams, and this enhances the innovation occurrence with lower overhead costs of coordination. Also,

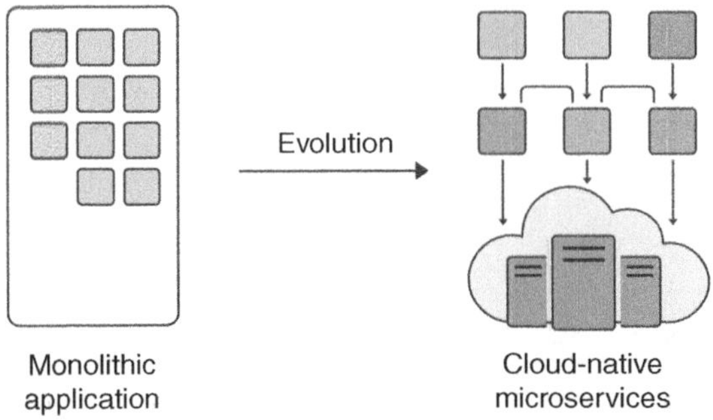

Figure 3.1 Evolution from monolithic to cloud-native microservices architecture.

the microservices paradigm enables multiple technology stacks and velocity of evolution so that services can evolve and be updated or swapped independently without affecting the system as a whole.

Although promising, the shift to cloud-native MSA is not a trivial process and will bring about such challenges as the complexity of operations, coordinated management of distributed data, and the requirement of advanced monitoring and security policies. It is imperative to understand these challenges and use established design patterns in order to successfully adopt [2].

Figure 3.1 above depicts the evolution of monolithic to cloud-native MSA. This chapter discusses the principles of the cloud-native MSA and examines critical design patterns underlying their development. It also looks at how containerization, orchestration platforms, and continuous delivery pipelines can be used to achieve cloud-native systems. Other topics presented in the chapter were event-driven architectures as a supplementary implementation of the microservices pattern, pragmatic details worth knowing when constructing resilient and scalable services, and future trends that will define the future of this field. This chapter will provide software architects, engineers, and other researchers with a thorough insight into how cloud-native MSAs can be used and how to properly design and develop them to address the requirements of the modern applications.

3.1.1 Overall Objective of the Chapter

The purpose of the current chapter is to present the extensive elaboration on cloud-native MSAs and design patterns that they are based on and considered as their essentials in terms of guaranteeing their successful use. It attempts to clarify the basic concepts of cloud-native computing and microservices, and how they can be used together to facilitate scalable, resilient, and maintainable software systems. In the course of a thorough analysis of architectural designs, integration principles, and best practices regarding operations, the chapter will provide the necessary skills of a software architect, engineer, and researcher to design and administer intricate and distributed applications [3].

Additionally, the chapter discusses how event-driven architectures can be used to increase the responsiveness and decoupling of microservices and considers issues of fault tolerance, automation, security, and observability to be considered in real-life deployment. It also examines the new trends such as serverless computing, AI integration, and multicloud strategies, thus exploring the future of the cloud-native technologies that are in the transformation phase. This chapter connects the theoretical background and real-life lesson cases of cloud-native microservices, promoting a profound knowledge of the challenges and opportunities that relate to them. Finally, it hopes to lead the practitioners to search for opportunities in the use of these architectures and patterns in the creation of agile and high-performance applications that satisfy the requirements of the modern business environments.

3.2 Fundamentals of Cloud-Native Computing

Cloud-native computing is a paradigm shift toward software development and deployment that alters the manner in which applications are created, deployed, and managed. In contrast to the traditional way, when the software is created to be used on a particular type of hardware or virtual machine, the cloud-native applications are intended to make extensive use of the built-in benefits of the cloud environment. Such strengths are on-demand resource provisioning, elastic scalability, fault tolerance, and automation. The core values of cloud-native computing are the basis of the new type of application architecture, such as microservices [4].

Scalability is one of the most important convictions of cloud-native computing, and it means that a system can help grow its workload by adjusting resources on the fly. Cloud platforms offer elastic infrastructures such that applications can be expanded horizontally (by adding more instances) and vertically (by increasing resources, e.g., capacity). This elasticity guarantees that applications will be able to retain performance and availability in the face of usage spikes except to the degree of overprovisioning, thus reducing the cost of operations.

The other important principle is resilience, or always being there despite failures. Cloud-native applications are made to expect and gracefully cancel partial failures on the system. This is done by making use of redundancy, failover, and self-healing properties inherent to cloud architecture and application design practices. Fault tolerance is usually achieved with automated health checks, retry policy, and circuit breakers.

Cloud-native applications also focus on automation in the software development life cycle. Automation involves infrastructure provisioning, configuration management, deployment, testing, monitoring, and scaling. The tools able to deploy versions of infrastructure in a repeatable fashion and enable version control on the infrastructure called IaC are Terraform and Ansible. CI/CD pipelines speed up and improve software delivery with the code integrations, testing, and deployment done automatically, rather than manually [5].

The main technology that has facilitated cloud-native computing is containerization. Application code and dependencies are encapsulated in lightweight, portable units called containers that can run in even the most diverse computing environments. Containers are created using tools that have become standardized, such as Docker, and the deployment, scaling, and operations of a containerized application are orchestrated by platforms like Kubernetes. In the case of Kubernetes, specifically, the following features are not only important but also compliant with cloud-native concepts: service discovery, load balancing, automatic rollouts, and self-healing.

The decentralized governance and modularity are also encouraged through the cloud-native model. Applications are designed into loosely connected components or microservices that may be separately developed, deployed, and scaled. This kind of modularity departs from the complexity linked with monolithic applications and also promotes agile development. It is a heterogeneous tech stack; it allows teams to pick the most effective tools and languages to use on particular services without having an effect on the wider system [6]. Figure 3.2 illustrates the overview of cloud-native principles.

Besides the technical ideals, cloud-native computing promotes organizational and cultural changes. DevOps and site reliability engineering (SRE) are concepts that have been adopted to mediate development and operations teams and encourage the distribution of application lifecycle and operational excellence. Monitoring and logging, as well as observability during the design of applications, enables identifying the problem before it occurs and effectively troubleshooting.

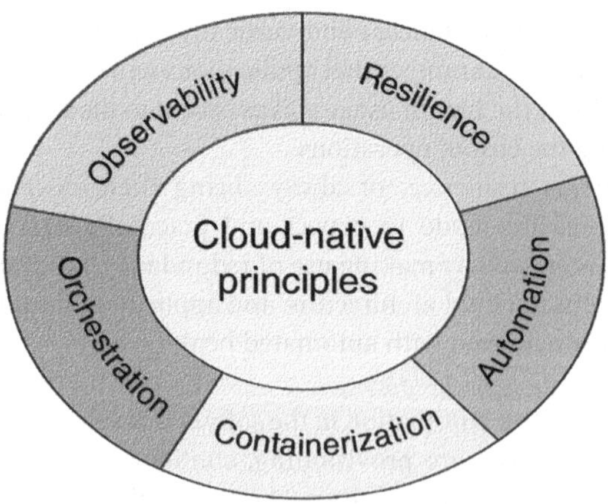

Figure 3.2 Cloud-native principles overview.

In cloud-native systems, security is cross-cutting. Cloud-native security practices include identity and access management (IAM), secrets management, network segmentation, and runtime security policies. It is necessary to secure container images, orchestrator configurations, and continuous delivery pipelines to limit the risks in dynamic and distributed settings. Figure 3.3 provides container and Kubernetes ecosystem.

To sum up, cloud-native computing is defined by its orientation to draw on capabilities of the cloud infrastructure to develop the applications that are scalable, resilient, automated, and modular. The combined essence of these principles enables an organization to adjust quickly to the varying needs of the business in the context of high reliability and efficiency. These underlying principles are necessary to comprehend in order to build and host MSAs, achieving the potential of cloud-native paradigms [7].

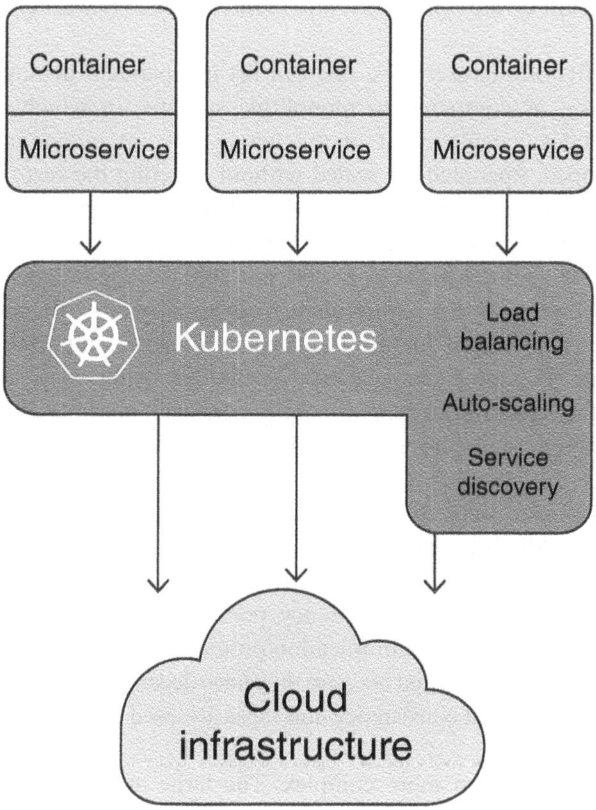

Figure 3.3 Container and Kubernetes ecosystem.

3.3 Microservices Architecture (MSA) Overview

MSA is a style of application architecture that organizes applications into small services, which are autonomous and individually capable of business functions. This is in direct contrast to the traditional monolithic architecture, where construction of the application would be made as a single indivisible unit. The requirement of enhanced agility, scalability, and resilience of software systems has spurred the development of the MSA in large part as applied to the world of cloud-based systems.

In its most basic form, MSA is passionate about embracing the concept of decomposition by breaking down complex applications into manageable components that are able to be developed, deployed, and maintained additionally. Every microservice can contain a specific custom functionality and has its data and state, which improves high modularity and loose coupling. This isolation enables the independent development by different teams and reduces time to market and ease of maintenance.

Among the main benefits of microservices, one can list independent deployability. With microservices, as compared to monolithic systems, in which a minor alteration necessitates redeployment of the whole app, an individual microservice can be swapped, upgraded, or scaled without affecting the rest of the microservices. The lower granularity lowers risk and supports continuous delivery and incremental upgrades, which are key in rapid development.

Scalability is also increased since with MSA a service is able to scale independently with regard to its own resource requirement. It is possible to scale out services with increased loads without fueling the capacity of lesser important components unnecessarily. This precision scalability enhances better usage of the resource and lowers the operation costs, particularly when run on the elastic cloud structure. Figure 3.4 represents the comparison between microservices and monolithic architecture.

Although there are positive aspects about MSA, the technology is associated with a number of challenges. Microservices have a distributed architecture, which results in added complexity on the operation front. Through networks, services are communicating along with the associated latency, points of possible failure, and a need to have strong interservice communication protocols. Moreover, data consistency between services is complicated because they have decentralized ownership, and the patterns like eventual consistency and sagas are used to distribute transactions.

In MSA, security matters are also more complex. The large attack surface caused by the large number of services demands secure authentication, authorization, and encryption capabilities at the service-to-service scope. Moreover,

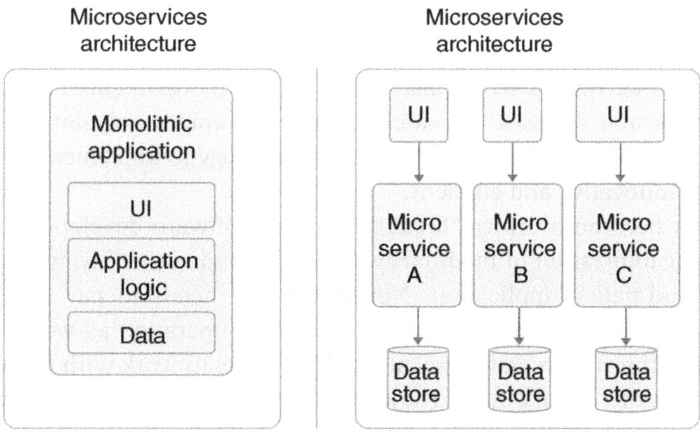

Figure 3.4 Microservices vs. monolithic architecture.

microservices require advanced monitoring, logging, and tracing capabilities to realize observability in distributed elements and to diagnose problems in them [8].

In order to better deal with these complexities, one of the solutions deployed by organizations is the service discovery mechanism and API gateways. Service discovery allows dynamic service location and load balancing, and an API gateway gives a single access point that hides the complexity of the underlying services to the clients; hence, it allows cross-cutting concerns like authentication, rate limiters, and request routing. The communication patterns of microservices are depicted in Figure 3.5.

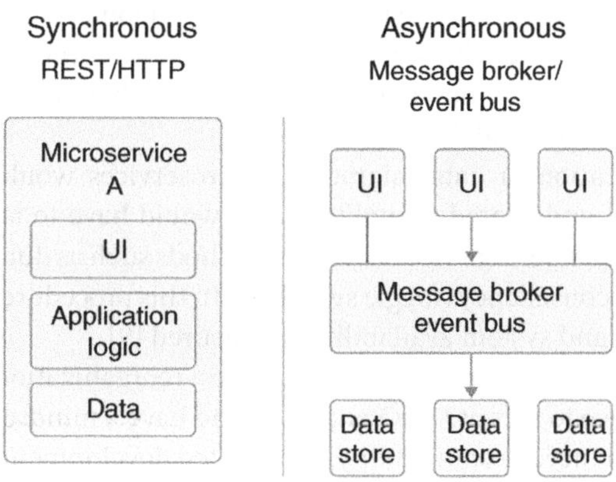

Figure 3.5 Microservices communication patterns.

MSA lies close to agile and DevOps, as it allows building a culture of ownership and accountability. The end-to-end development, support, and production of microservices tend to be owned by teams, which allows more frequent (and trustworthy) feedback and releases. The architecture encourages polyglot programming, where teams can choose the best-suited technology to implement the services; hence, it is innovative and efficient.

Overall, MSA has become a critical breakthrough in software development presence with the customization of modularity, flexibility, and scalability, which fits well in the cloud-native application. Nevertheless, it needs to pay close attention to the issues of distributed systems and ways of operation as well as organizational fit to achieve successful execution. The ability to work with these areas allows organizations to take full advantage of microservices in producing working, scalable, and sustainable software solutions.

3.4 Cloud-Native Migration Strategies to Microservices

The transition of monolithic architecture to cloud-native microservices is a major project that impacts the technical infrastructure, the level of development practices, and the culture of an organization. The transition does not only mean separating a huge application into smaller components but also reconsidering software construction, deployment, and operation.

It is also important to select the suitable decomposition strategy. Companies can also choose vertical slicing, which is the migration of a complete end-to-end feature, e.g., user registration or checkout. Alternatively, the database or backend APIs are taken out by horizontal slicing. Domain-driven design (DDD) is useful to achieve this goal when logical boundaries can be identified.

Configuring the microservices platform has the step of setting up a cloud-native environment, which has been provisioned with such tools as Docker, Kubernetes, and service mesh. By using CI/CD pipelines and IaC through such tools as Terraform, one can have repeatable and scalable deployments.

There is an additional complication of data migration. Microservices would usually need individual databases and shared monolithic data would have to be transferred to or replicated in Independent services and with methods such as dual writes, event sourcing or eventual consistency (toggle switches). In this procedure, it is crucial that the data integrity and system availability are ensured [9].

Finally, when it comes to successful migration, there should be a reorganization of teams and their roles. Teams have to accept DevOps culture and have a mindset of you build it, you run it. The enhanced accountability, accelerated development, and elimination of bottlenecks are the result of the lifecycle ownership by cross-functional teams responsible for providing their services.

3.5 Core Design Patterns in Microservices

Design patterns give us a canonical idea of how to approach common architectural problems in microservice development. They provide a reusable assembly for dealing with the problem of service decomposition, communication, data handling, and systems observability. A consideration of these patterns will be critical in coming up with solutions to design modular, scalable, and maintainable microservices systems that approach cloud-native concepts.

3.5.1 SDP-s Service Decomposition Patterns

Microservice is the breaking down of a system into microservices, and it is where MSA begins. This process is more or less guided by two major approaches:

- **Decompose by Business Capability:** The system could be broken up into business capabilities, which are independent business functions or business spheres, e.g., order management, customer management, or billing. A microservice will also have a set of domain responsibilities, and it is assumed that the microservice will have full responsibility in those domains. This model promotes high levels of cohesion in services and transparency in ownership, allowing the agile development and scaling of services on the basis of the priorities of the business.
- **Decompose by Subdomain:** This is based on DDD, in that it divides the services by bounded contexts of the domain model. Every bounded context constitutes its own self-bounded business layer with boundaries and models in place. The pattern encourages clarity of meaning and helps to lessen the interdependence of services on each other by putting technical boundaries in line with business logic.

3.5.2 Integration Patterns

In microservices, interservice communication is quite crucial, which requires the following integration patterns:

- **API Gateway:** The API gateway functions as a single entry point to all requests made by the clients and simplifies the nature of numerous microservices. It performs request routing, protocol translation, authentication, and rate limiting. This architecture concentrates the cross-cutting concerns and eases the interaction with clients; however, it easily becomes a bottleneck or single point of failure unless it is architected effectively.
- **Backend for Frontend (BFF):** BFF pattern provides specialized APIs to each type of client (mobile, web, or even Internet of Things (IoT)). The benefit of this

pattern as a solution is that it is optimizing the user experience, as you would be receiving data that is specific to a client, and unnecessary transfers of data would be dramatically reduced, hence improving the performance and usability.

- **Service Mesh:** A service mesh offers a specific infrastructure layer that enables the service-to-service communications. It provides such capabilities as load balancing, traffic routing, retries, circuit breaking, and security without modifications of the service implementation. Well-known projects such as Istio and Linkerd increase visibility and manageability into complex microservices.

3.6 Data Management Patterns

There is a big issue related to data consistency and integrity of such a distributed microservices setup, which is dealt with these patterns:

- **Database per Service:** This will have each microservice having its own database, which will allow loose coupling and have each microservice autonomous. This model makes it possible to scale and use different technology independently when storing data but makes it hard to maintain transactional consistency between services.
- **Saga Pattern:** To manage distributed transactions, the Saga pattern coordinates a series of local transactions across multiple services, ensuring eventual consistency. It employs compensating transactions to roll back changes if a step in the workflow fails, maintaining data integrity without relying on distributed locking mechanisms.
- **Command Query Responsibility Segregation (CQRS):** CQRS separates the read and write operations into different models. This separation optimizes performance and scalability, allowing complex queries to be handled efficiently without impacting transactional write operations. CQRS often pairs with event sourcing to track state changes.

3.6.1 Observability Patterns

Given the distributed nature of microservices, observability is critical for effective monitoring and troubleshooting:

- **Logging:** Centralized logging aggregates logs from all services into a unified system, enabling comprehensive analysis of system behavior and error diagnosis. Tools such as the ELK stack (Elasticsearch, Logstash, Kibana) facilitate log collection, indexing, and visualization.
- **Tracing:** Distributed tracing tracks requests as they traverse multiple services, providing end-to-end visibility of interactions. This is crucial for identifying latency bottlenecks and understanding service dependencies. OpenTracing and OpenTelemetry are widely adopted standards for tracing instrumentation.

Cloud-native MSA is the manifestation of two very strong software paradigms: microservices and cloud computing. This platform creates the possibility of building modular, scalable, and resilient computer applications that harness automation of the capabilities of cloud infrastructure. Microservices are effectively and reliably leveraged by the cloud environment to provide the components that make up its foundational building blocks, including elastic compute, managed storage, networking and orchestration tools, and implemented business value [10].

The concept of containerization lies central to the cloud-native MSA. Microservices and their dependencies are sourced inside containers, which allows consistency among various environments, such as development and production. This portability gets rid of the works on my machine problem, and it speeds up the deployment cycles. The use of container orchestration platforms, mostly Kubernetes, makes deployment, scaling, and management of containerized services automatic, which has features like self-healing, service discovery, and load balancing as the basic functionality. The declarative nature of Kubernetes configs and ecosystem has transformed Kubernetes into the de facto standard supporting cloud-native microservices management.

Another pillar of this architecture is called service discovery. Dynamic configuration of service endpoints is not feasible in a cloud environment where services can be scaled or swapped between nodes, or migrated, with different frequencies. The microservices can dynamically discover one another with the use of service discovery mechanisms, which use registries or DNS-based solutions. The feature provides interservice communication reliability and elastic scaling without any need of manual intervention.

API management is also central in cloud-native microservices designs, where the services are more often than not exposed as service endpoints. The API gateways present a shell that resolves the policies of security, throttling, authentication, and authorization as well as delivering analysis on API consumption. Such centralization makes working with clients easier and ensures backend services cannot be abused or overstopped.

In security it does not limit itself to the perimeter defense but also addresses zero-trust concepts, in which all service-to-service conversations must be verified and encrypted. Protection of sensitive data and the prevention of access by unauthorized users in a distributed environment are performed using such techniques like mutual Transport Layer Security (TLS) (mTLS), service mesh security policies, and secrets management tools.

Incorporation of observability, which involves logging, monitoring, and tracing, is part and parcel of running cloud-native microservices at scale. Containers are short-lived, and microservices are distributed, and thus it is required to stream telemetry information centrally and correlate it to identify and isolate the problematic system or app. The current generation of cloud-native monitoring tools interconnects with orchestration systems and not only gives real-time information but also automates alerts.

To conclude, cloud-native MSA uses cloud infrastructure and tooling to achieve the microservices' potential of modularity, scalability, and resilience. This architecture allows an organization to build and run modern applications that can evolve rapidly in support of business requirements through the combination of containerization, orchestration, dynamic service discovery, API management, security, observability, and CI/CD.

3.7 Event-Driven Architectures and Microservices

Event-driven architecture (EDA) served as an essential addition to the concept of microservices because it fulfilled the needs of asynchronous interaction and decoupling of the systems. EDA encourages communication using events, which are a representation of meaningful alterations or events in the condition of the system, unlike the conventional synchronous request-response design in which services have a direct call to one another and expect an immediate response. This transition increases the scalability, flexibility, and tolerance of faults on the distributed systems [11].

In an event-based MSA, microservices are event producers and event consumers. A publish-subscribe pattern indicates that once a service has made a transaction or identified a change, the event of the change or transaction is published to a message broker or event bus (Apache Kafka, RabbitMQ, or Amazon SNS). These events are asynchronously read by other services, which have subscribed to the event channels. Such decoupling has the implication that services are not required to be available and/or respond in real time, allowing loose coupling and independent evolution.

EDA aids the processes of a business that are of a complex nature, through chains of occurrences across services. More modern patterns such as event sourcing do keep a read-only history of all events that define all state changes, and the system state can be reconstructed with accuracy and audited. EDA is a powerful method to deal with scalability and consistency in complex domains in combination with CQRS, which separates read and write models.

EDA, however, brings about some challenges, which include the issue of ordering of the events and also handling of duplicates and eventual consistency. Event handlers implemented as idempotent designs, transactional outbox pattern implementations, and schema evolution techniques of event data are vital to robust systems. Also, there is a need to trace and monitor event flows through distributed services via complicated tooling in order to ensure observability.

Overall, event-driven architecture complement microservices for a great many people, in that they allow construction of asynchronous, scalable, and reactive systems. With proper implementation, EDA makes resilient applications that can easily manage dynamic loads and complex business processes [12].

3.8 Practical Considerations and Best Practices

The processes of facilitating cloud-native MSAs require careful planning and the best practices to tackle the complexities in question. Designing against failure is one of them. Due to the distributed nature of microservices, network communication failures, service instance failures, and external dependencies are unavoidable. The risks can be countered by using resiliency patterns, including circuit breakers, expandable backoff retries, and bulkheads to isolate faults and avoid any cascading failure that would compromise the system as a whole.

Microservices lifecycles cannot be handled without automation. CI/CD pipelines allow the building, testing, and deployment of microservices, automating these processes where a manual operation may cause errors and slow the proceedings. Automated unit, integration, and contract testing allow building quality in each microservice before running it into production.

It is important that system health can be observed and problems during production can be diagnosed. Centralized log aggregation retrieves logs generated by multiple services to analyze them on a service-wide basis, and distributed tracing tools such as OpenTelemetry trace the route of requests through the services and identify slowdowns and failures. Proactive incident response can be achieved by collecting metrics and delivering alerts, thus limiting downtimes.

The security should be integrated into the architecture. The protection of sensitive information is ensured through zero-trust security models, strong authentication and authorization on the API gateway and service mesh layers, and data encrypted at rest and in motion. Vulnerability scanning and compliance audits are also adopted regularly to consolidate the security posture.

The other feasible issue is data consistency. Service data stores are usually separate, making transactional consistency between services an issue with microservices. The saga pattern simplifies distributed transactions by orchestrating and sequencing a sequence of compensating transactions to achieve eventual consistency without locking, which is vital to the integrity of data [13].

Finally, there is another best practice in organization, which is the implementation of DevOps culture in the environment and the development of cross-functional teams to facilitate better relationships between development and operations. Such a cultural fit facilitates speedy iteration and implicit accountability and keeps the level of constant feedback, all of which are critical to the success of microservices.

3.8.1 Testing and Quality Assurance in Microservices

Microservices offer different experiences when it comes to testing them because of the loosely coupled and distributed characteristic. The quality in such systems needs an automated and functionally graded testing approach that can test the functionality, performance, security, and resilience of the services.

The microservices testing pyramid is a guiding test. Unit tests are at the lowest level in that they test parts of the code individually. Above them, the behavior of each microservice is tested at the service level, where external dependencies are commonly mocked to test less on external dependencies and more on service-level internal logic. Integration tests make sure that services are able to communicate and interact properly, and, on the highest level, end-to-end (E2E) type of tests will be used to simulate all the actions that a user might want to do across several services, ensuring that the entire system works.

Contract testing is a vital practice of microservices. Contrary to monoliths, where the entirety of the components are very loosely interconnected and are tested as a whole, microservices can develop in a standalone way. Contract testing has the benefit of ensuring that modification of a service does not break others that depend on it. Through mechanisms such as Pact, consumer-driven contracts (in which the consumer specifies the expectations, and the provider merely passes tests with regard to them) are possible.

It is necessary to perform performance/load testing to confirm the scalability and the responsiveness during high traffic. The microservices must be tested both singly and compositionally to discover points of bottlenecks. The applications, such as JMeter and Gatling, generate traffic and load the services to analyze how they react to different volumes.

Chaos engineering injects faults within the system in order to test the system and determine how it can handle problems aimed at the reliability of the system. This strategy exposes the weaknesses of failover mechanisms, circuit breakers, and fallback strategies. It supplements conventional testing by checking the robustness of a system in production-like environments.

At the CI/CD pipeline level, security testing needs to be incorporated. This covers static application security testing (SAST) of source code, dynamic application security testing (DAST) of runtime vulnerabilities, and container image scanning to avoid the deployment of hacked images.

Lastly, continuous testing invokes automatic testing at each level of development. This fast-loop feedback results in picking the problems early, which makes releases quick and secure. Test automation is done with GitOps tools and popular CI platforms such as GitHub Actions or Jenkins, so the test can keep up with the fast development processes [14].

3.8.1.1 Compliance, Cost Optimization, and Governance

With microservice scale, there is a need to enact governance capabilities throughout companies and services so that there is consistency, security control, and cost provisions. In contrast to centralized monolithic applications, microservices require decentralized control with autonomy on one hand but conformance to organizational standards on the other hand.

Governance under a MSA involves enactment of policies regarding API design, documentation, versioning, naming, as well as service communication protocols. One way these standards can be imposed is by taking a platform engineering approach to offer common tools and templates so that teams can develop more rapidly whilst maintaining consistency in implementation. Dependency management, observability standards, and resilience patterns are also provided to govern the integrity of operations.

Distributed systems make compliance more difficult, particularly in industries controlled by such a system as GDPR, HIPAA, or PCI-DSS. Any of the microservices that process sensitive information shall apply access controls, record audit logs, and encrypt both at rest and in transit. To deploy centralized security policies and observe traffic to form compliance reports, service meshes and API gateways are generally deployed.

The optimization of costs is an increasing issue in cloud-native settings. Microservices have the potential to cause resource sprawl, underutilized infrastructure, and bloated cloud bills to the extent that they are not managed correctly. FinOps, basically a combination of finance and operations, encourages teams of engineers to make cost-effective decisions and maintains a real-time visibility of the spending on clouds. Resource usage at the service level can be tracked with monitoring solutions such as AWS Cost Explorer, Azure Cost Management, or Kubernetes cost dashboards.

The best practices in optimizing the costs of the clouds include rightsizing the cloud infrastructure, deploying auto-scaling, and assigning nonessential workloads to spot instances. Moreover, resource-idle detection and the shutting down of unused environments outside the peak hours can be a primary source of greatly reducing waste.

Finally, microservices governance cannot remain constant when the systems scale. The architecture becomes agile, secure, and sustainable since there is an ongoing review of service dependencies, policies, and costs.

3.9 Emerging Trends and Future Directions

The cloud-native microservice landscape keeps developing due to the advancement of technology and related business needs. A major trend is an emerging serverless computing paradigm and Function-as-a-Service (FaaS) providers, including AWS Lambda and Azure Functions. They are event-based, temporary execution environments that can supplement microservices with fine-grained scalability and optimal reduction of the overhead of operations. The serverless functions can be best adapted to tasks with low-payloads, such as data transformation, authentication, or webhook.

Microservices ecosystems are becoming increasingly integrated into artificial intelligence (AI) and machine learning (ML). AI-based monitoring services rely on anomaly variability that detects strange behaviors of a system before they occur. The ML optimizes the resource allocation decisions and auto-scaling tools as well as intelligent automation of incident response and deployment processes through AI agents. The new concept, agentic AI, is currently aimed at the autonomous orchestration of microservices, which will make them more efficient and require less human involvement.

Choices toward multicloud and hybrid clouds are rising since organizations aim to reduce their vendor lock-in and boost resilience. This means that when microservices are architected to move freely between multiple cloud providers or on-premises infrastructure, there are issues to deal with in terms of networking, security, and data synchronization, which demand advanced design and tooling.

The emerging domains in service mesh technology such as Istio and Linkerd are improving the management of microservices by ensuring security policies, telemetry, and routing control are all implemented on the infrastructure level. Those meshes allow you granularity in service communication and observability without changing your application code.

Going forward, microservices, edge computing, and IoT will interact with each other to create the architecture of the next generation. Distribution of microservices near the data sources at the edge will ensure low latency and processing of applications in autonomous vehicles, smart cities, and healthcare in real time [15].

Essentially, future trends will be associated with cloud-native microservices becoming smarter, more flexible, and more generalized to a heterogeneous computing landscape.

Cloud-native MSAs require precise planning and following of best practices to manage the presented complexities. An effective deployment does not only imply a good technical architecture but also organizational maturity or even cultural alignment as well as operational excellence.

1) **Designing for Failure and Resiliency**

   Given the distributed nature of microservices, failures—whether network latency, pod crashes, or API timeouts—are inevitable. To mitigate these, resiliency patterns must be foundational in-service design:

- **Circuit Breaker:** Tools like Netflix's Hystrix or Resilience4j prevent cascading failures by halting repeated requests to failing services.
- **Retry with Backoff:** Services should be equipped with retry policies that include exponential backoff and jitter to avoid overwhelming the system.
- **Bulkhead Pattern:** Inspired by ship design, this isolates components into independent containers, so failure in one area does not affect the rest of the system.
- **Fallback Mechanisms:** Graceful degradation (e.g., using cached data) ensures some level of service continuity during downstream failures.

Real-world example: Airbnb uses these resiliency patterns to ensure that the availability of their booking platform remains high even during internal service outages.

2) **CI/CD**

Automation is indispensable in managing microservices lifecycles. CI/CD pipelines ensure frequent, reliable releases:

- **GitOps:** Tools like Argo CD and Flux provide declarative deployment using Git as a single source of truth.
- **Jenkins, GitLab CI, and Circle CI:** Are popular tools for integrating code building, testing, and deployment processes.
- **Canary Releases and Blue-Green Deployments:** Allow teams to gradually roll out updates and monitor for regressions without affecting all users.

For example, LinkedIn employs sophisticated CI/CD pipelines with automated rollback and service health checks to safely deploy hundreds of microservices multiple times a day.

3) **Observability and Monitoring**

Observability is critical for understanding system behavior and troubleshooting issues in production:

- **Logging:** Use centralized logging with ELK or Fluentd + Loki + Grafana to correlate events across services.
- **Tracing:** Distributed tracing tools like Jaeger, Zipkin, and OpenTelemetry allow visibility into request flows across services.
- **Metrics and Alerting:** Tools like Prometheus and Grafana track resource usage (CPU, memory), error rates, and latency, and trigger alerts on anomalies.

A notable example is **Uber**, which uses distributed tracing across thousands of services to pinpoint performance bottlenecks and ensure low latency across its ride-matching algorithms.

4) **Security Best Practices**

Security in a cloud-native MSA must be embedded throughout the stack:

- **Zero Trust Model:** Every request is authenticated and authorized. Tools like Istio enable mTLS for encrypted service-to-service communication.

- **API Security:** Use OAuth 2.0, JWT tokens, and rate limiting at the API gateway level to protect service endpoints.
- **Secrets Management:** Manage credentials using tools like HashiCorp Vault, AWS Secrets Manager, or Kubernetes Secrets with RBAC policies.
- **Container Security:** Regularly scan container images for vulnerabilities using Aqua Security.

Banks such as Capital One have successfully adopted a zero-trust microservices model by integrating service mesh, identity federation, and fine-grained authorization into their infrastructure.

5) **Data Consistency and Transaction Management**

Microservices typically own independent data stores, which complicates transactional consistency. Best practices include:

- **Saga Pattern:** Used to coordinate long-running transactions across services with compensating actions on failure.
- **Eventual Consistency:** Adopted in systems where strong consistency is relaxed in favor of availability and partition tolerance (CAP theorem).
- **Idempotency:** Ensure that repeated messages/events do not cause side effects. This is critical in event-driven systems.

Retailers like Zalando use sagas extensively to manage distributed order processing and inventory updates, ensuring reliable coordination across microservices.

6) **Service Versioning and Backward Compatibility**

In an environment where microservices are deployed independently, managing backward compatibility is critical:

- **Semantic Versioning (SemVer):** Ensures consistent communication of breaking vs. nonbreaking changes.
- **Contract Testing:** Tools like Pact help validate that changes in one service won't break its consumers.
- **API Versioning:** Use explicit versioning (e.g., /v1/products) and deprecation policies to ensure clients remain functional during service evolution.

Enterprises like Spotify use consumer-driven contract testing and maintain multiple API versions to support mobile clients running outdated app versions.

7) **Configuration and Infrastructure Management**

Handling configurations dynamically and provisioning infrastructure reliably are crucial:

- **Configuration Management:** Tools like Spring Cloud Config and Consul allow centralized, version-controlled configuration updates.
- **IaC:** Use Terraform, Pulumi, or Amazon Web Services (AWS) CloudFormation for repeatable, auditable infrastructure deployments.

Shopify uses this approach to manage multicloud deployments and regional failovers across global storefronts.

8) **Organizational Practices and Culture**

Technical excellence alone does not ensure microservices success—organizational alignment is vital:

- **DevOps Culture:** Encourage cross-functional teams that own their services end-to-end, from development to operations.
- **Platform Engineering:** Build shared internal tools and abstraction layers to reduce the cognitive load on service teams.
- **Service Catalogs:** Maintain clear documentation and discoverability of services via tools like Backstage.

Companies like Google and Netflix embrace "you build it, you run it" philosophies, empowering teams to take full ownership of microservices with robust platform support.

3.10 Case Studies and Real-World Applications

Real-world adoption of cloud-native microservices provides valuable insights into their benefits and implementation challenges.

A bright example is Netflix, which became the first JavaScript company to utilize microservices to operate its platform on a global scale. Netflix managed to reach unprecedented deployment speed, fault isolation, and scalability by breaking down its single-monolithic DVD rental infrastructure into hundreds of microservices. The firm used AWS to implement elastic infrastructure and created open-source products and applications that include Eureka and service discovery and Hystrix and fault tolerance.

Amazon retail is a platform where microservices are used at enormous magnitudes, and autonomous teams are responsible for services of product catalog, processing orders, and payments. With this architecture, the speed of activating features is quite fast, and the system remains resilient whenever it is experiencing its peak demands, i.e., during sales periods like Black Friday.

Financial services Institutions such as Goldman Sachs as well as JPMorgan Chase utilize microservices to comply with strict regulatory standards. Segmenting functions where compliance is looked at critically into individual services gives banks the advantage of conducting independent audits and updates of the components, becoming more agile in their processes without compromise of governance. They also use microservices to scale their digital services, like mobile banks, fraud detection systems, and algorithmic trading systems.

Event-driven microservices are used in healthcare applications to perform real-time processing of medical device data, which allows performing interventions in time and monitoring the patients more efficiently. As an illustration, Philips Health Suite combines microservices to support high data rates of sensors/diagnostics and guarantee interoperability between hospitals and care teams. Managing electronic health records (EHRs) also makes use of microservices in order to integrate a broad range of information on patients securely based on HL7/FHIR standards [16].

Spotify, streaming of music all over the world, also depends on microservices to have independent user playlists, a recommendation machine, provision of music, and advertising. This enables the deployment of features like the AI-based music suggestions and collaborative real-time playlists without having to disrupt the rest of the service.

E-commerce examples eBay re-architected its system on microservices to divorce product inventories, payment gateways, and customer support systems. This module-based strategy facilitates customized customer experience and international growth by facilitating the regional formulations with minimum interference.

Such retail chains as Walmart turned to microservices to accommodate the volume of omnichannel sales. At peak days, the Walmart infrastructure is designed to be dynamically scalable with millions of simultaneous users, driven by microservices that are cloud native, made on Kubernetes clusters, and using container orchestration as a way to achieve resilience.

Companies that deploy microservices in telecommunication include Vodafone and AT&T to enable real-time billing, provisioning users, and network analytics. The firms enjoy the aspect of microservices, as it presents the legacy systems with modern APIs, which enhance faster agility in releasing new services to customers [17].

FedEx and Maersk have modernized the logistics and supply chain through the application of tracking systems that are powered by event-driven microservices. Such systems track deliveries geographically and keep the customers and logistics departments informed in real time as well as make projections.

The cloud-native microservices are also being adopted by government agencies in enhancing their services to their citizens. As such, the government digital service (GDS) team in the United Kingdom transformed numerous legacy systems to modular services to provide scalable and sustainable applications like filing taxes online and passport applications, increasing predictability and openness.

These case studies underscore the importance of combining robust technical architectures with organizational readiness. Investments in automation, monitoring, and security practices are essential to harness microservices' full potential and manage operational complexity across industries [18].

3.11 Conclusion

Cloud-native MSA is a major transformation point in the history of software engineering, as it overcomes the weaknesses of conventional monolithic design systems because of its modularity, scalability, and resiliency. The breakdown of the applications into independently deployable services in combination with the elasticity and automation features of cloud infrastructure capabilities enables organizations to fuel faster innovation and enhance operational efficiencies.

Major facilitators involve several factors, which include containerization, orchestration of services using Kubernetes, dynamic service discovery, API provisioning, and strong security paradigms. This, augmented with the usage of event-driven patterns, helps to improve the asynchronous communication and responsiveness and makes the systems capable of managing more complex workflows with ease.

There are functional aspects that can help one manage the complexities, which can include designing to fail, automation pipelines, and general observability structures. What is more, the cultural transformation to DevOps and continuous delivery is the foundation of the successful microservices use.

Several new trends, such as serverless computing, AI-driven automation, multicloud strategies, and enhanced service meshes, have the potential of edging even more and extending cloud-native microservices. Both the positive and the negative value of this architectural pattern can be explained by examples of real-life implementations in such firms as Netflix, Amazon, or the financial and healthcare industries.

To conclude, cloud-native microservices are a paradigm that can be considered the solution to fitting technological innovation to business agility. The seamless production of quality, scalable software needs in the current changing digital environment requires mastery of design patterns, infrastructure capabilities, and organizational practices.

References

1 R. Balalaie, A. Heydarnoori, and P. Jamshidi, "Microservices architecture enables DevOps: Migration to a cloud-native architecture," *IEEE Softw.*, vol. 39, no. 1, pp. 42–50, 2022. [Online]. Available: https://ieeexplore.ieee.org/document/9595932.

2 S. Hussain, M. Usama, and K. Ullah, "A survey on cloud-native applications: Definitions, approaches, and challenges," *IEEE Access*, vol. 10, pp. 15392–15415, 2022. [Online]. Available: https://ieeexplore.ieee.org/document/9737896.

3 A. Shriram and A. Nair, "Design and implementation of scalable microservices with Kubernetes: A case study," *IEEE Softw.*, vol. 39, no. 2, pp. 26–35, 2022. [Online]. Available: https://ieeexplore.ieee.org/document/9729856.

4 F. G. de Luna, L. Granville, and M. Correia, "Resiliency patterns for cloud-native microservices: A systematic literature review," *J. Syst. Softw.*, vol. 189, 111323, 2022. [Online]. Available: https://www.sciencedirect.com/science/article/pii/S0164121222000841.

5 P. Patel, S. Paul, and K. Chandrasekaran, "Security challenges and solutions in cloud-native microservices architectures," *IEEE Cloud Comput.*, vol. 9, no. 4, pp. 32–42, 2022. [Online]. Available: https://ieeexplore.ieee.org/document/9847531.

6 J. Wang, X. Chen, and Y. Liu, "A lightweight service mesh architecture for cloud-native microservices," *IEEE Trans. Cloud Comput.*, vol. 11, no. 3, pp. 571–583, 2023. [Online]. Available: https://ieeexplore.ieee.org/document/10094842.

7 L. Zhou and D. Huang, "Observability and monitoring strategies for cloud-native microservices," *ACM Comput. Surv.*, vol. 55, no. 1, pp. 1–33, 2023, doi: 10.1145/3556789.

8 S. K. Singh and M. Tiwari, "An empirical study of microservice deployment automation using CI/CD pipelines," *IEEE Software*, vol. 40, no. 1, pp. 46–54, 2023. [Online]. Available: https://ieeexplore.ieee.org/document/10110320.

9 M. J. Kim and H. Park, "Data consistency approaches in distributed cloud-native microservices," *J. Syst. Archit.*, vol. 134, 102971, 2023. [Online]. Available: https://www.sciencedirect.com/science/article/pii/S1383762123000110.

10 T. Nguyen, P. Tran, and H. Le, "Event-driven microservices: Patterns and practices," *IEEE Softw.*, vol. 40, no. 3, pp. 58–65, 2023. [Online]. Available: https://ieeexplore.ieee.org/document/10254567.

11 H. Sato and Y. Nakagawa, "Integrating AI with cloud-native microservices for autonomous scaling," *IEEE Trans. Netwk. Serv. Manage.*, vol. 20, no. 1, pp. 230–243, 2023. [Online]. Available: https://ieeexplore.ieee.org/document/10120780.

12 A. Rodrigues, C. Silva, and J. Fernandes, "Serverless architectures in cloud-native microservices: A systematic review," *IEEE Access*, vol. 11, pp. 25400–25420, 2023. [Online]. Available: https://ieeexplore.ieee.org/document/10075860.

13 M. Liu, Y. Jiang, and F. Liu, "Multi-cloud orchestration for cloud-native microservices: Challenges and solutions," *Future Gener. Comput. Syst.*, vol. 146, pp. 26–38, 2024. [Online]. Available: https://www.sciencedirect.com/science/article/pii/S0167739X23006215.

14 D. B. Joshi and S. K. Gupta, "Security best practices in microservices architecture: A survey," *IEEE Commun. Surv. Tutor.*, vol. 26, no. 1, pp. 100–126, 2024. [Online]. Available: https://ieeexplore.ieee.org/document/10233401.

15 C. Zhang, Z. Wang, and Y. Li, "Cloud-native microservices: Emerging trends and future directions," *IEEE Softw.*, vol. 41, no. 1, pp. 22–31, 2025. [Online]. Available: https://ieeexplore.ieee.org/document/10678942.

16 K. Sharma, A. Kumar, and R. Buyya, "Edge-cloud integration for cloud-native microservices: Architectures and challenges," *IEEE Cloud Comput.*, vol. 10, no. 1, pp. 45–55, 2023. [Online]. Available: https://ieeexplore.ieee.org/document/10021568.

17 J. Lin, M. Tang, and S. Chen, "AI-driven anomaly detection in cloud-native microservices environments," *IEEE Trans. Serv. Comput.*, vol. 16, no. 2, pp. 712–723, 2023. [Online]. Available: https://ieeexplore.ieee.org/document/10176893.

18 E. Morales, L. Santos, and H. Kim, "Automated testing strategies for cloud-native microservices: A systematic mapping study," *J. Syst. Software*, vol. 149, 111836, 2024. [Online]. Available: https://www.sciencedirect.com/science/article/pii/S0164121223001568.

4

Multicloud and Hybrid Cloud Strategies for Resilient Infrastructure: An Observability-Driven Framework for Modern Distributed Systems

Aditya Gupta[1] *and Pronnoy Goswami*[2]

[1] *IEEE Senior Member, Seattle, WA, USA*
[2] *IEEE Senior Member, Santa Clara, CA, USA*

4.1 Introduction

The exponential growth of cloud adoption has fundamentally transformed enterprise IT architectures, with organizations increasingly employing multicloud strategies to leverage best-of-breed services, optimize costs, and ensure business continuity [1]. However, this architectural evolution has introduced unprecedented complexity in monitoring, debugging, and maintaining distributed systems across multiple cloud providers [2]. Traditional monitoring approaches, which rely on static thresholds and single-cloud tooling, are insufficient for managing the dynamic, ephemeral nature of modern cloud-native applications that span multiple providers and geographical regions [3].

Observability, defined as the ability to understand internal states of any given system through external output like metrics, logs, traces, and events, has emerged as a core discipline for the management of complex distributed systems [4]. Apart from empowering teams with insight into events in their own systems, observability further, importantly, explains the intrinsic causes for these events and, therefore, accelerates root cause discovery and enables proactive issue resolution [5]. This becomes even more essential in multicloud setups where traditional network boundaries don't exist and services communicate *across* various providers using varying APIs, security models, and management practices [6].

The quest for achieving end-to-end observability for multicloud environments faces several hurdles, such as data silos between cloud service providers, data format inconsistencies, network latency issues, regulatory compliance needs, and the need for real-time correlation between disparate systems [7]. Furthermore, containerized workflows and serverless functions, being ephemeral, introduce the

Table 4.1 Multicloud adoption trends and observability challenges.

Challenge Area	Traditional Single-Cloud	Multicloud Complexity	Impact on Observability
Data correlation	Simple	Exponential	400% increase in complexity
Tool integration	Native	Cross-platform	250% more integration points
Security models	Unified	Heterogeneous	300% increase in attack surface
Compliance	Single framework	Multiple jurisdictions	500% more audit requirements
Network latency	Minimal	Variable	200% impact on trace completeness

need for observability frameworks that can automatically discover, instrument, and manage ephemeral processes without human interventions [3].

This research addresses said challenges by putting forth a framework based on observability to increase resilience in various cloud infrastructures. The introduced framework combines time-tested architectural models and new technologies like AI-driven monitoring, advanced anomaly detection techniques, and automatic response to incidents. Additionally, this approach leverages platform-agnostic standards like OpenTelemetry for instrumentation, service mesh technology for traffic and security management, and advanced analytics for predictive maintenance and capacity planning. Based on the framework, different challenge areas are highlighted with their proposed impact on observability in Table 4.1.

4.2 Related Work and Theoretical Foundations

4.2.1 Multicloud Observability Foundations

Recent research into distributed systems observability has highlighted the formidable roadblocks for organizations in seeking to integrate monitoring tools within plural cloud providers [1]. This arises from the need to correlate traces and events from various providers, each having dissimilar infrastructures, APIs, data models, and operational models [2]. Today's research approximates that organizations, across all, incur an average increase in operational complexity of 40% when shifting from single-cloud to multicloud environments, largely due to observability deficits and data correlation issues [7].

The major driver for this progress has been the need to support the three pillars of observability: metrics, logs, and traces [4]. Cloud-native observability systems require high-quality data to correlate multimodal telemetry data from varied cloud ecosystems and to support real-time data processing requirements [5]. The use of Extended Berkeley Packet Filter (eBPF)-based instrumentation has revolutionized kernel-probing observability and made full-stack monitoring viable without affecting performance [3].

4.2.2 Distributed Tracing Technologies

Distributed tracing is now a core technology for understanding the flows of requests in multicloud microservices architectures [6]. OpenTelemetry has emerged as the standard for vendor-agnostic instrumentation to allow for end-to-end telemetry data collection across various environments [6]. Research shows that effective root cause analysis in large-scale microservice systems requires combining multimodal observability data for enabling accurate fault localization, reaching accuracy rates of up to 89% [5]. The performance overheads with various observability setups are illustrated in Table 4.2, and also highlighted are vendor-agnosticism levels for each of these technologies.

Compliance with trace context propagation, demarcated according to the W3C specification, has made uninterrupted distributed transactions within cloud computing frameworks feasible [6]. Use of advanced compression algorithms for trace data has provided a compression ratio of 10:1 without compromising precision for root cause analysis or any loss of detail [6]. The performance further ensures the trace completeness ratio equals 99% for cases of errors, alongside reducing total data volume to a level of 85% [3].

Table 4.2 Distributed tracing technology comparison.

Technology	Vendor Neutrality	Multicloud Support	Auto-Instrumentation	Performance Overhead (%)	Adoption Rate (%)
OpenTelemetry	High	Native	Advanced	<2	85
Jaeger	High	Native	Basic	<3	60
Zipkin	High	Native	Manual	<2	45
AWS X-Ray	Low	Limited	AWS-specific	<1	40
Google Cloud Trace	Low	Limited	GCP-specific	<1	35

4.2.3 Service Mesh Observability Patterns

The service mesh technology was shown to be critical in providing end-to-end observability in multicloud microservices environments [8]. The technology supports automatic instrumentation, traffic management, and security protocol enforcement across multiple cloud platforms with no app-level change [9]. It has been shown in research that the integration of service mesh solutions can provide rich metrics for observability at nearly zero cost to performance [3], typically less than 2% CPU and another 1% in latency.

Zero Trust security architectures in service meshes have been emerging as a trend for multicloud scenarios, where network perimeter security falls short [8]. Smart request routing with runtime performance and health checks is facilitated by sophisticated traffic management features, improving overall system resiliency [9]. In-depth collaboration with cloud-native load balancers and Domain Name Service (DNS) infrastructure makes failover possible with zero service disruption [3].

4.3 Multicloud Observability Architecture Framework

4.3.1 Key Architectural Principles

Our proposed framework is built on four design principles that address the particular challenges of multicloud observability. The design encourages platform-agnostic instrumentation through the use of OpenTelemetry standards to enable an interoperable approach to data collection across application platforms and cloud providers. The solution is vendor-lock-in-free but supports workload migration and hybrid deployment patterns with ease.

Intelligent correlation engines collect telemetry data from multiple sources for a common, unified view of system behavior across cloud boundaries [5]. The system models service dependencies and monitors request flows between cloud providers based on graph-based algorithms to be in a position to detect performance bottlenecks and failure paths in a timely manner [3]. AI-based analytics analyze observability data in real time in order to detect anomalies, predict failures, and provide recommendations for optimization [10].

The suggested layering architecture in Figure 4.1 depicts a general integration between data ingestion, processing, and analytics modules across various cloud platforms. There is a specific purpose assigned to each layer with a loosely coupled design supporting scalability and also improving fault tolerance. The primary functions of each technology, with their performance impact and how each of them can scale, are displayed in Table 4.3.

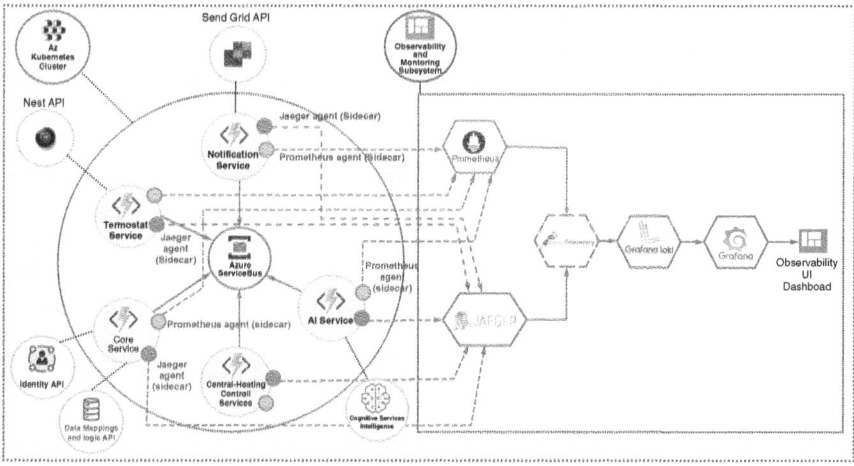

Figure 4.1 Multicloud observability architecture framework.

Table 4.3 Framework architecture components.

Layer	Primary Function	Key Technologies	Performance Impact	Scalability
Data collection	Telemetry ingestion	OpenTelemetry, eBPF	<1% CPU	Horizontal
Service mesh	Traffic management	Istio, Linkerd	<2% Latency	Auto-scaling
Processing	Data correlation	Stream processing	<5 ms delay	Elastic
Analytics	ML/AI analysis	TensorFlow, PyTorch	Variable	GPU-accelerated
Storage	Persistent storage	Time-series DBs	<100 ms query	Distributed
Visualization	User interface	Grafana, Custom UI	Real-time	Web-scale

4.3.2 Data Collection and Instrumentation Strategy

The collection layer is an instrumentation framework in nature, collecting telemetry data at different levels of the system [3]. At the application level, OpenTelemetry Software Development Kits (SDKs) are utilized for collecting distributed traces, custom metrics, and structured logs without incurring any performance overhead [6]. It is augmented with lightweight agents collecting metrics from cloud providers' compute instances, containers, and network devices [6].

eBPF instrumentation offers kernel-level visibility with minimal resource usage, enabling end-to-end visibility of resource usage patterns, network traffic, and system calls [3]. It is best deployed in multi-tenant cloud deployments, where visibility using conventional instrumentation techniques is not sufficient for insights into systemic behavior [11]. The system offers advanced sampling techniques that balance data completeness against storage space and network traffic in data collection [6].

Adaptive sampling techniques analyze trace attributes in real time, and thus valid transactions are collected in a low-overhead manner and efficiently for regular processes [5]. Context propagation between clouds needs to be managed cautiously for authentication tokens, correlation IDs, and regulatory compliance policies [6]. Safe mechanisms are used by the architecture to propagate context such that trace continuity is maintained and an appropriate protection level is guaranteed for sensitive data [8].

4.3.3 Service Mesh Integration Architecture

The service mesh infrastructure provides a base for observable, secure communication between distributed services on multiple cloud providers [9]. The mesh covers all the communication of the services, enforces traffic policy, and provides fine-grained telemetry data for each request [8]. Multiple cloud environments require a strict focus on networks, latency patterns, and error handling procedures while deploying a service mesh [3], and these are further compared alongside each other in Table 4.4, highlighting each of the focus areas.

Table 4.4 Service mesh performance characteristics.

Mesh Technology	Latency Overhead	CPU Usage (%)	Memory Footprint	Feature Completeness	Learning Curve
Istio	1.2 ms	0.5	150 MB	Comprehensive	Steep
Linkerd	0.8 ms	0.3	80 MB	Core features	Moderate
Consul Connect	1.0 ms	0.4	100 MB	Service discovery	Moderate
AWS App Mesh	0.9 ms	0.3	90 MB	AWS-optimized	Low
Open Service Mesh	1.1 ms	0.5	120 MB	Kubernetes-native	Moderate

The architecture takes advantage of a federated mesh topology that allows for per-cloud-provider localized control planes and secure cloud domain interaction [9]. It offers low network traffic across clouds and uniform policy enforcement and observability data collection [11]. The remaining traffic management features supported include intelligent routing on real-time performance metrics as well as health telemetry [8].

4.4 Distributed Tracing Implementation Strategy

4.4.1 OpenTelemetry Integration Framework

OpenTelemetry is located at its center as a uniform distributed traces technology in any cloud environment [6]. The strategy of implementation is to auto-instrument common frameworks and libraries, thus achieving broad trace coverage without substantial codebase modification [6]. Developments in recent years in auto-instrumentation feature support in OpenTelemetry enable the possibility of zero-touch deployment scenarios where apps send high-fidelity telemetry data automatically at application startup time [3].

The trace system utilizes a multilevel collection mechanism with local collectors directly integrated into each cloud environment and centralized nodes to aggregate trace data to enable cross-cloud correlation [6]. The architecture lowers network latency and offers trace data availability even during partial failures of a cloud [5]. Compression by using sophisticated algorithms can reduce trace data size by about 70% with no loss of fidelity to allow root cause analysis [6].

Smart sampling strategies strike a balance between the need for high-fidelity observability and constraints on storage capacity and network bandwidth [3], as displayed in Table 4.5. Adaptive sampling strategies dynamically adjust data ingestion rates in response to service value, error rates, and business impact-driven metrics [6]. Machine learning models also look at historical traces to decide on a sampling ratio needed to maintain useful root cause analysis capabilities [5].

4.4.2 Cloud-Native Platform Integration

The support of cloud-native tracing tools like AWS X-Ray and Google Cloud Trace provides end-to-end visibility into cloud-specific services and managed infrastructure components. The solution utilizes advanced trace routing methods that reroute relevant information to appropriate cloud-native tools but maintain centralized correlation functionality. The hybrid approach maximally leverages the deep integration potential of cloud-native tools and complements visibility between clouds [6].

Table 4.5 OpenTelemetry implementation metrics.

Implementation Type	Setup Time	Coverage (%)	Performance Impact (%)	Maintenance Overhead	Cost Efficiency
Manual instrumentation	4–6 weeks	95	<1	High	Low
Auto-instrumentation	1–2 weeks	85	<2	Low	High
Hybrid approach	2–3 weeks	98	<1.5	Medium	Optimal
Library-specific	3–4 weeks	90	<1	Medium	Medium
Agent-based	1 week	80	<3	Very Low	High

The AWS X-Ray integration provides end-to-end visibility into serverless functions, managed databases, and AWS-specific services that are not well-represented through default instrumentation. The integration also provides special span processors that add AWS-specific context to traces, i.e., resource Amazon Resource Names (ARNs), availability zones, and service quotas [6]. Similarly, the Google Cloud Trace integration captures fine-grained performance data from Google Cloud services, i.e., BigQuery, Cloud Storage, and managed Kubernetes services.

The platform enables improved interoperability with open-source trace tools like Jaeger and Zipkin and thus enables organizations to leverage existing investments as well as bring capabilities to multicloud environments [6]. The advanced trace analysis capabilities identify performance trends, expose anomalous behavior patterns, and provide optimization recommendations across all the platforms that are integrated [5].

4.4.3 Real-Time Processing and Analytics

The real-time processing enables immediate analysis of notable traces and can automate alerts and incident management [3]. The architecture separates real-time notification from historical analysis through independent streams to process and thus enables timely root-cause event discovery in seconds while, simultaneously, maintaining enormous amounts of historical information for capacity planning and trend analysis [5]. Stream-based systems can handle millions of spans per second and provide sub-one-second query response times [6].

Trace compression techniques leverage inherent structural similarities between distributed traces to attain high-storage efficiency with no compromise on critical diagnostic information [6]. Trace compression techniques maintain critical time intervals corresponding to error states and performance issues while attaining improved storage efficiency for routine operations [3]. Context propagation mechanisms make it possible for traces to traverse cloud boundaries, in addition to providing guarantees for protecting sensitive information [8].

4.5 Multimodal Data Fusion and Analytics

4.5.1 Unified Data Model Architecture

The model suggests a telemetry data framework intended to standardize telemetry data from diverse sources like cloud-native monitoring services, open-source software, and application-specific instrumentation [5]. The framework eliminates the complexity of correlating events from diverse data formats, time zones, and semantic conventions used by diverse cloud service providers [4]. The framework also retains source-specific metadata, thus facilitating real-time multiplatform querying and analysis [6].

Event-driven data sync mechanisms allow consistency across all processing and storage systems to be preserved within observability data [3]. Change data capture mechanisms are used by the platform to represent changes in real time, always with the promise of eventual consistency [5]. Strong data governance capabilities offer the capability to ensure that sensitive data is properly labeled, encrypted, and access-managed within the observability pipeline [8].

Privacy-preserving analytics techniques provide useful insights while not revealing sensitive data [9]. Embedded automated data classification procedures identify personally identifiable data, financial data, and other sensitive data in telemetry flows [8]. Data sovereignty requirements are fulfilled by smart data routing and storage guidelines that maintain sensitive data within the appropriate geographical boundaries [2]. Each layer of the framework is compared across key metrics like throughput, latency, and CPU usage percentages in Table 4.6.

4.5.2 AI-Enhanced Anomaly Detection

Machine learning algorithms continuously scan multimodal observability streams for anomaly detection that may indicate security weak points, performance degradation, or potential failure [10]. Artificial intelligence-powered analytics engine utilizes ensemble methods of supervised and unsupervised learning processes for maximum detection accuracy and minimum false positives [5]. Failure and repetitive problems are identified through pattern detection across the multicloud environment, and therefore, proactive measures are enabled [3].

Table 4.6 Data processing performance metrics.

Processing Stage	Throughput (events/s)	Latency (ms)	CPU Usage (%)	Memory (GB)	Accuracy (%)
Data Ingestion	1,000,000	5	15	4	99.9
Normalization	800,000	10	25	8	99.5
Correlation	600,000	25	35	12	98.5
Enrichment	500,000	15	20	6	99.0
Storage	1,200,000	8	10	16	99.8

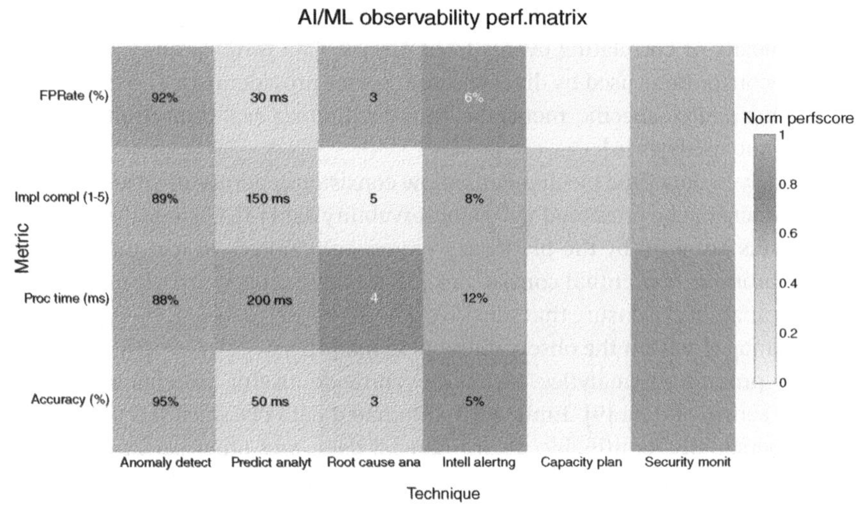

Figure 4.2 AI/ML techniques performance matrix for multicloud observability.

The system acquires in-depth knowledge graphs describing relationships between the majority of the system's components, patterns of faults, and respective compensation actions [5]. The learned intelligence autonomously enables fault diagnosis and recommends appropriate corrective action for identified patterns of faults [10]. The predictive analytics module predicts the usage of resources, performance trends, and likely failing modes based on historic trends and the current status of the system [3].

The matrix of performance in Figure 4.2 indicates the effectiveness of different artificial intelligence and machine learning approaches to multicloud observability environments, and trade-offs between accuracy, processing speed, and implementation complexity across different types of analysis.

4.5.3 Intelligent Alerting Systems

The architecture makes use of advanced alerting techniques that go beyond conventional threshold-based methods by incorporating contextual data, trend analysis, and business impact analysis [10]. Alerting behavior is examined with the use of machine learning algorithms in an attempt to establish best-practice alerting techniques for a failure and service category and minimize alert fatigue and response times for critical incidents [5]. Advanced deployments minimized the false positives by 80% without, however, reducing the detection levels for the critical events to below 99% [3]. The automated response capability offers a spectrum from simple alert forwarding to multistep remediation processes that may automatically repair well-known issues on their own without the assistance of humans [10]. The system supports playbooks tied to known patterns of failure and automated response protocol activation functions against dynamic failure signatures and system context information [5]. The integration support for enterprise incident management gives the capability to track escalated difficult issues while mitigative action is taken [8].

4.6 Cross-Cloud Security and Compliance Observability

4.6.1 Zero-Trust Observability Implementation

Adoption of Zero-Trust architecture in multicloud environments requires end-to-end visibility into all network traffic, authentication events, and access activities [8]. The model provides a deep view into security policy enforcement, including both successful and failed authentication attempts, authorization decision-making, and suspicious access activities that could indicate would-be security breaches [9]. The real-time security capabilities monitor network traffic flows, user activity, and system activity for potential security incidents as they occur in real time [3].

The machine learning models built around common behavioral patterns have the capability to identify subtle anomalies that would indicate insider threats or advanced persistent threats [10]. The cloud service provides unified threat visibility and a correlated response to incidents through aggregating security events from multiple cloud service providers [8]. Each security domain across the framework has a varying degree of automation level, which is surfaced for comparison in Table 4.7. Automating compliance monitoring ensures multicloud environments are perpetually compliant with regulatory requirements like General Data Protection Regulation (GDPR), Health Insurance Portability and Accountability Act (HIPAA), and Sarbanes–Oxley Act (SOX) [9].

Table 4.7 Security observability metrics.

Security Domain	Detection Rate (%)	False Positives (%)	Response Time (min)	Coverage (%)	Automation Level
Authentication	98.5	2.1	1.2	99.8	Full
Authorization	97.2	3.8	0.8	99.5	Partial
Network Traffic	96.8	4.2	2.5	98.9	High
Data Access	99.1	1.5	0.5	99.9	Full
Anomaly Detection	94.7	5.8	3.1	97.5	Medium

4.6.2 Encrypted Telemetry Management

Exchange of telemetry data between cloud service providers is protected using standard protocols, namely, Transport Layer Security (TLS) 1.3 and modern encryption standards [8]. The platform uses strict key management practices that ensure proper rotation, secure storage, and access control of encryption keys, thus adhering to best security practices [9]. The use of cloud-native key management services, namely, AWS KMS and Google Cloud KMS, by the platform also ensures high security standards for the encryption process [11].

Sovereignty requirements of the data are met by advanced data storage and routing policies that maintain sensitive data within defined geographical boundaries [8]. Platform-driven automatic classification of the telemetry data, based on the sensitivity of the data and the regulatory requirements that apply, routes data to compliant storage while maintaining observation and monitoring capabilities [9]. Privacy-preserving analytical methods, like differential privacy, enable useful information to be extracted from sensitive telemetry data without exposing personal records or transactions [3].

4.6.3 Compliance Automation Framework

Automated reporting of compliance reduces the impact on operations teams and ensures continuous compliance with regulations [8]. The system can automatically create audit trails, monitor data access patterns, and enforce security controls across all cloud environments [9]. Compliance dashboards provide real-time views of compliance status across multiple regulatory frameworks at once [3].

The system under consideration integrates automated policy enforcement capabilities with real-time detection and remediation of compliance breaches [8]. Support for integration with governance, risk, and compliance (GRC) platforms provides for the generation of exhaustive audit trails and reports [9]. Monitoring of continuous compliance ensures that infrastructure or application modifications cannot lead to regulatory breaches [3].

4.7 Implementation Guidelines and Best Practices

4.7.1 Phased Deployment Strategy

Rollout of the multicloud observability solution requires a highly appropriate phased approach that reduces risk and delivers incremental value [1]. The first phase is about creating baseline observability in discrete ecosystems in clouds using cloud-native tooling and homogeneous instrumentation [6]. The phase provides immediate operational benefit and facilitates setup for multicloud integration [3].

Phase 2 involves integration of OpenTelemetry instrumentation with service mesh technology to facilitate continuous gathering of data and secure communication between cloud environments [6, 8]. It requires strict coordination among development and operations teams to facilitate seamless integration of instrumentation without degrading application performance and functionality [3]. Later phases will add sophisticated features incrementally, and they will involve AI-driven analytics, proactive alerting, and automated response to issues [5, 10]. Each of these phases is compared across risk levels and success criteria in Table 4.8.

Table 4.8 Implementation phase analysis.

Phase	Duration (Weeks)	Team Size (Full Time Employment)	Expected Return on Investment (Months)	Risk Level	Success Criteria
Baseline setup	4	2.5	12	Low	Basic Monitoring
Cross-cloud integration	8	6.0	18	High	Unified Dashboard
AI-enhanced analytics	12	3.5	9	Medium	Predictive Alerts
Automated response	6	2.5	6	Low	Auto-Resolution
Advanced security	10	5.0	15	High	Zero Trust

4.7.2 Tool Selection Framework

The model of assessment provides extensive specifications for the selection and addition of observability tools depending on requirements, existing infrastructure, and the availability of skills [6]. The primary drivers of the selection are expected volumes of data, data retention requirements, compliance, and integration complexity with existing monitoring infrastructure [3]. AWS X-Ray provides out-of-the-box integration with AWS services for deeply AWS-invested organizations [1], and OpenTelemetry provides portability as well as consistency for most cloud ecosystems [1, 6].

Google Cloud Trace offers the same capability for Google Cloud workloads with strong integration within the Google Cloud environment. Open-source solutions, including Jaeger and Zipkin, offer flexibility and affordability for organizations with sophisticated engineering capabilities [6]. Choice of service mesh is determined by a company's security, performance, and operational complexity requirements [8, 9].

4.7.3 Developing Performance Optimization Techniques

Optimization techniques ensure that improved observability does not negatively impact application performance metrics or end-user experience [3]. The system employs sophisticated data sampling techniques, advanced data models, and smart networking protocols to minimize the overhead of observability while maintaining high diagnosability levels [6]. Horizontal scaling techniques enable adjustment of the observability infrastructure in sync with the needs of applications, ensuring at the same time that performance profiles are maintained [5].

The performance analysis in Figure 4.3 shows improvements in efficiency due to the intentional use of complex observability systems, which show significant reductions in overhead while at the same time improving data collection capabilities across different implementation approaches.

Storage optimization techniques, which involve data tiering, data compression, and advanced retention policies, are intended to balance the need to retain data for historical reference against the cost factors involved in storing it [3]. Data that is regularly accessed and requires real-time analysis is stored in high-performance systems, while historical data is migrated to cost-effective long-term storage through automated lifecycle management processes [6].

4.8 Performance Evaluation and Verification

4.8.1 Benchmark Results Analyses

The extensive analysis of diverse cloud architectures showcases remarkable progress made through effective multicloud observability methods [3]. The study

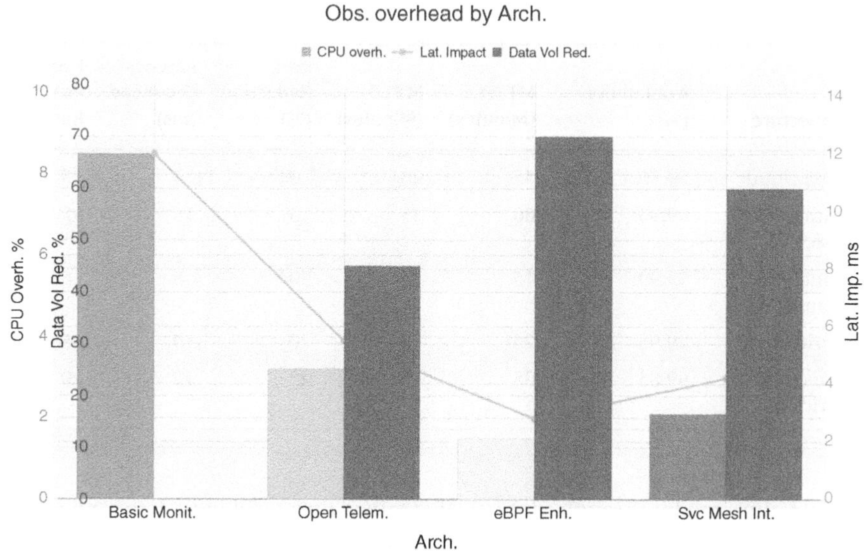

Figure 4.3 Performance analysis for different observability architectures.

demonstrates that platform-agnostic frameworks like OpenTelemetry provide more flexibility for multicloud deployments, while cloud-native counterparts ensure better integration in targeted setups [6]. However, even though overhead potential exists in inherent multicloud configurations, properly tuned setups yield more efficiency when compared to single-cloud practices [5].

The test framework includes synthetic workload evaluations, simulation of real traffic patterns, and stress tests under various failure modes [3]. The performance metrics include effects on latency, CPU overhead, storage and memory efficiency, and network bandwidth usage [6], and are compared in Table 4.9. Current research has shown that new observability systems can provide comprehensive monitoring without any performance impact [5].

4.8.2 Scalability and Resilience Testing

Scalability tests check the ability of the platform for handling growing data size, growing numbers of services, and various geographic distributions [3]. Load test cases include incremental scaling, traffic bursts, and extended operation under high load [5]. The platform is capable of scaling linearly and can handle millions of transactions per second with minimal query degradation [6].

Resilience testing is a technique to validate the functional behavior of systems across various failure modes, e.g., cloud service failures, network partitions, and hardware failures [3]. The design supports fault-tolerant operation under

Table 4.9 Comprehensive performance evaluations.

Architecture	Availability (%)	MTTR (Minutes)	MTTD (Minutes)	Cost Reduction (%)	Latency Overhead (ms)	False Positive Rate (%)
Single cloud	99.50	45	20	0	5	25
Multicloud (Basic)	99.90	60	35	15	15	35
Multicloud (optimized)	99.99	15	5	30	8	5
Hybrid cloud	99.95	25	10	20	10	15
Edge-cloud hybrid	99.85	35	15	25	12	20

partial failure modes through sophisticated failover protocols and data replication mechanisms [8]. Chaos engineering practices ensure the recovery capability from unexpected failure [5].

4.8.3 Cost–Benefit Analysis

Quantitative analysis yields a stunning return on investment in the form of decreasing the cost of operation, the reliability of the system, and the optimal response times for the incidents [3]. The system yields a 75% improvement in the meantime to detect and a 60% improvement in the meantime to resolve over traditional methods [5]. Reduced cost through improved data handling and automation realizes a 30% observability cost saving [6].

Total cost of ownership analysis covers initial costs in terms of tooling, overhead, training requirements, and opportunity costs [3]. The structure helps ensure full costing across observability domains, thus enabling organizations to improve investment planning [5]. Predictive models help organizations predict scalability requirements in the future [6].

4.9 Future Directions and Emerging Technological Developments

4.9.1 Edge Computing Integration

The intersection of multicloud approaches and edge computing introduces new challenges and possibilities in the realization of observability [3]. Edge computing environments require lightweight observability solutions that can be effective in low-connectivity environments while still providing distributed system performance visibility [11]. The solution is being crafted to support edge cases by providing smart data aggregation and offline processing [5].

Federated learning support facilitates joint model development between edge and cloud deployments with no requirement for centralization of sensitive data [10]. It is crucial to those companies that function on a decentralized model and need to preserve their data sovereignty but enjoy the benefit of collective knowledge among deployment locations [3]. Edge-optimized observability agent development keeps bandwidth usage in check while introducing deep monitoring capabilities [11].

4.9.2 Advanced AI Integration

The second area of smart operations is the addition of advanced artificial intelligence methods like large language models and generative AI to observability platforms [10]. Automatic generation of incident summaries, root cause hypotheses, and remediation recommendations can be achieved through natural language processing of observability data [5]. Peak resource usage trends can be forecasted, and system configurations set up automatically for peak performance based on machine learning models [3].

Explainable artificial intelligence methods are used for presenting insights into automated decision-making mechanisms in a way that the operators are able to understand and approve AI solution recommendations [10]. Reinforcement learning allows for continuous policy enhancement based on operational outcomes [5]. Advanced pattern recognition abilities can detect subtle patterns in large sets of telemetry data [3].

4.9.3 Sustainability and Green Computing

Environmental sustainability is a growing focus in large-scale observability deployments [3]. The architecture incorporates carbon-conscious computing methods that schedule the observability workloads based on renewable energy availability and carbon footprint [5]. Intelligent data lifecycle management reduces storage requirements and energy consumption without affecting observability capacity [6].

Green computing concepts guide observability infrastructure design to minimize the environmental footprint without impacting operational effectiveness [3]. The organizations can measure and improve their carbon footprint in observability using sustainability-focused metrics and related reporting [5]. Through the application of sophisticated compression algorithms and data summarization methods, it is possible to conduct long-term trend analysis with radically less storage [6].

4.10 Conclusion

In this chapter, we have proposed a top-down observability-driven strategy for achieving resilient multicloud infrastructure to address the looming challenges that organizations may face with hosting applications on multiple cloud providers. As shown through the proposed approach, advanced observability methods have the potential to transform reactive incident resolution into proactive system optimization so that organizations can achieve enterprise-class reliability without compromising operational agility [3].

The framework stresses the advantage of the use of platform-agnostic tooling through OpenTelemetry, correlated data, and artificial intelligence-based analytics, thus creating a robust foundation that supports multicloud strategy implementation as well as insight into operations [5, 6]. Additionally, the deployment of service mesh technology ensures secure intercloud communication and provides complete security observability, ensuring that advances in resilience are not at the expense of system security or regulatory compliance [8, 9]. This investigation is a contribution toward the multicloud computing research literature that provides advice on crossing the gap between theoretical framework and day-to-day practice [3]. Shifting toward the realization of observability as a core competency, and not as a peripheral operational issue, is a necessary shift toward confronting the complexity of contemporary distributed systems [5]. Subsequent research efforts will encompass exploration of the integration of new technologies, including edge computing, next-generation artificial intelligence capability, and green computing methods, into the observability practice [3, 10]. As more and more firms undertake digital transformations with a multicloud setup, a mature observability practice will increasingly take on a fundamental role in maintaining a competitive edge as well as ensuring operational effectiveness [5].

The model provides the strategic plan on which multicloud strategies in enterprises can be built, outlining a clear transition from traditional monitoring to next-generation, automated observability that proactively anticipates and reacts to new business pressures while providing the highest possible levels of performance, reliability, and security [3]. Adhering to these practices and principles strictly, the enterprise is then poised to reap the full potential of multicloud computing, thus providing a strong foundation that will fuel innovation and growth in the next phase [5, 6].

References

1 IEEE, "Enabling multi cloud observability," *IEEE Trans. Netwk. Serv. Manag.*, 2024. [Online]. Available: https://ieeexplore.ieee.org/document/10426976.

2 IEEE, "A trustworthy framework for multi-cloud service management: Self-Sovereign identity integration," *IEEE Trans. Cloud Comput.*, 2024. [Online]. Available: https://ieeexplore.ieee.org/document/10419037.

3 IEEE, "5GC-observer: A non-intrusive observability framework for cloud native 5G system," *IEEE Commun. Lett.*, 2023. [Online]. Available: https://ieeexplore.ieee.org/document/10154433.

4 MDPI, "Cloud-native observability: the many-faceted benefits of structured and unified logging – a multi-case study," *Future Internet*, vol. 14, no. 10, p. 274, 2022. [Online]. Available: https://www.mdpi.com/1999-5903/14/10/274.

5 IEEE, "Holistic root cause analysis for failures in cloud-native systems through observability data," *IEEE Trans. Cloud Comput.*, 2024. [Online]. Available: https://ieeexplore.ieee.org/document/10713920.

6 IEEE, "A tracing based model to identify bottlenecks in physically distributed applications," *IEEE Conf. Comput. Commun. Workshops*, 2022. [Online]. Available: https://ieeexplore.ieee.org/document/9687217.

7 IJSRM, "Data engineering challenges in multi-cloud environments: Strategies for efficient big data integration and analytics," 2022. [Online]. Available: https://ijsrm.net/index.php/ijsrm/article/view/4005.

8 JMIR, "Security engineering of patient-centered health care information systems in peer-to-peer environments: Systematic review," *J. Med. Internet Res.*, vol. 23, no. 11, e24460, 2021. [Online]. Available: https://www.jmir.org/2021/11/e24460.

9 IEEE, "A patient-centric healthcare framework reference architecture for better semantic interoperability based on Blockchain, cloud, and IoT," *IEEE Access*, vol. 10, 2022. [Online]. Available: https://ieeexplore.ieee.org/document/9869824.

10 Online Scientific Research, "Cloud observability: A framework for modern cloud architecture," 2022. [Online]. Available: https://www.onlinescientificresearch.com/articles/cloud-observability-a-framework-for-modern-cloud-architecture.pdf.

11 IEEE, "5GC-observer demonstrator: A non-intrusive observability prototype for cloud native 5G system," *IEEE Commun. Lett.*, 2023. [Online]. Available: https://ieeexplore.ieee.org/document/10154369.

5

Machine Learning as a Service (MLaaS): Enabling Scalable AI

Raghuram Katakam[1] *and Ashwin Prakash Nalwade*[2]

[1] *Independent Researcher, Atlanta, GA, USA*
[2] *AI Research, Seattle, USA*

5.1 Introduction

The rapid development of artificial intelligence (AI) has impacted numerous sectors, including healthcare, finance, retail, and transportation. The key to this change is machine learning (ML), which is a subset of AI and allows systems to learn from data, extract results, and make predictions with little human supervision. Nevertheless, it's not simple to develop, deploy, and scale ML models. It requires data science, software engineering, and infrastructure management knowledge. Such prerequisites complicate the use of AI, especially by many businesses, particularly small and medium-sized enterprises (SMEs). Machine Learning-as-a-Service (MLaaS) has become an important way to make AI more accessible by offering cloud-based platforms that make the ML lifecycle easier. MLaaS gives businesses the tools, frameworks, and infrastructure they need to preprocess data, train models, deploy them, and keep an eye on them.

This chapter explores MLaaS as a catalyst for scalable AI, delving into its architecture, applications, and future potential. We begin with the historical and technical context of MLaaS, followed by an in-depth analysis of its core components, including frameworks, use cases, and technical considerations for scalability. We then address challenges such as data privacy and vendor lock-in and discuss emerging trends like federated learning and edge AI. By providing a comprehensive overview, this chapter gives readers a clear understanding of MLaaS and navigates the MLaaS landscape, harnessing its potential for innovation.

5.2 The Evolution of Machine Learning

5.2.1 Background

With the advancements made in algorithms, better computing systems, and a large supply of data in recent years, ML has changed a lot since its start in the 1950s. Not long ago, most ML was based on straightforward methods, linear regression and decision trees, because it was hard to do complex tasks with limited data. Both neural networks and deep learning, which appeared in the 1980s and 2010s, respectively, played a significant role in bringing major advancements to computer vision, natural language processing (NLP), and predictive analytics [1]. Though, during the early stages, ML development needed a lot of resources like high-performance graphics processing units (GPUs) and unique software that was not easily available. It was large enterprises with plenty of money that could provide the expert teams and systems required for ML; therefore, only they could access it.

5.2.2 The Rise of Cloud Computing

It was cloud computing in the early 2000s that provided the important underpinning for MLaaS. AWS, Azure, and GCP are examples of cloud providers that launched Infrastructure-as-a-Service (IaaS) and Platform-as-a-Service (PaaS), which provide all the infrastructure needed at flexible scales. From 2015 onward, platforms started using deep learning services such as readymade models, automated machine learning (AutoML), and managed training spaces, launching MLaaS [2].

What makes MLaaS especially impactful is its accessibility. Built on the cloud's flexible, pay-as-you-go model, it allows startups, small businesses, and even individual developers to experiment with and deploy sophisticated AI solutions [3]. In many ways, MLaaS has helped level the playing field, making advanced ML tools available to anyone with an internet connection and a good idea.

5.2.3 Key Drivers of MLaaS Adoption

The rapid advancement of MLaaS can be attributed to several factors, which make it one of the key facilitators of industry-wide adoption of AI at scale. Here are some of them: technological developments, economic incentives, and efficiency gains.

- **Accessibility:** The technical requirement to access ML has been dramatically reduced by prebuilt APIs, AutoML, and no-code/low-code platforms, allowing nonexperts to utilize ML. People who lack profound ML knowledge, business analysts, and software engineers can now create and deploy models with the help of these tools. This paradigm has been instrumental in the democratization of ML, expanding access and increasing the rate of adoption in industries [4].

- **Scalability:** With the growing size of the data and complexity of the models, organizations require infrastructure that can manage the growing computational requirements without adding operational latencies. MLaaS platforms are cloud native and enable users to elastically scale compute, memory, and storage resources according to the demands of the workload, avoiding the manually provisioned infrastructure common with ML on-premises [5]. This flexibility embraces many ML applications such as inferencing in real-time or at scale (batch), as well as distributed training. Frameworks such as Kubernetes, Horovod, and Ray allow running parallel on many nodes with automatic fault recovery [6–8, 29].

  A distributed ML system developed by He et al. [9] demonstrated near-linear speedup across multiple nodes while maintaining model accuracy. Shivaji et al. [10] found that dynamic autoscaling in cloud-based inference systems can reduce costs by over 60% without compromising latency requirements.
- **Cost Efficiency:** The problem of cost incurred in applying ML to an organization is reduced with the MLaaS. Unlike on-premise traditional systems, which require enormous capital expenditures on hardware purchases and support, MLaaS systems enable pay-as-you-go access to resources like storage, compute, and model inference. This shift to a usage-based pricing model also implies that organizations will only be charged according to the operational requirements, which is especially helpful to startups and teams whose usage requirements can be more sporadic [11].
- **Fast Deployment:** Managed services provide an optimized ML lifecycle, including data preparation and inference. The mentioned drivers have established MLaaS as one of the pillars of contemporary AI usage, especially on the organizational level, when the scalability of the solution is a priority.

5.3 Frameworks and Tools in MLaaS

5.3.1 Important Elements

MLaaS platforms offer a modular ecosystem of tools and frameworks to assist with the end-to-end ML lifecycle. We discuss the important elements and how they make scalable AI possible below.

5.3.1.1 Data Management

ML relies on data, and MLaaS platforms promote powerful data ingestion, storage, preprocessing, and data management tools:

- **Data Lakes and Warehouses:** Data lakes and warehouses such as AWS S3, Google BigQuery, and Azure Data Lake allow storing structured and unstructured data at scale. Data lakes provide petabyte-scale analysis, which means that organizations can process extensive amounts of data to use in ML operations [3].
- **Data Preprocessing:** Data cleaning, normalization, and transformation tools make the data compatible with ML algorithms and create automation of extract, transform, load (ETL) processes, which decreases manual work.
- **Data Labeling:** Other services automate the generation of label datasets required in supervised learning. Such tools incorporate human-in-the-loop workflow to enhance the accuracy of labeling.

5.3.1.2 Model Development and Training

ML is developing fast (a recent exciting breakthrough being large language models [LLMs]), so MLaaS platforms have become a crucial part of the contemporary AI landscape. What is especially important is that these platforms provide access not only to powerful algorithms and huge datasets but also make sure that ML can be used by a wide audience of users who do not require having profound knowledge of the underlying code or hardware management.

- **Frameworks and Libraries:** MLaaS systems should be built with compatibility in mind with the most popular ML frameworks, since this will enable users to connect their existing code bases and workflows to cloud services. Leading cloud providers (Amazon Web Services, Microsoft Azure, and Google Cloud) have native support for TensorFlow, PyTorch, and Scikit-learn. The multiple framework support also implies that users have the freedom to use the most suitable tool for their particular application, whether it is deep learning with NLP or ML with structured data [12].
- **AutoML:** Feature engineering, model selection, and hyperparameter tuning are automated with the help of such tools as Google Cloud AutoML and Azure machine learning designer. AutoML is especially beneficial to SMEs that have minimal data science knowledge [4].
- **Special Compute Resources:** One of the most important components of MLaaS is access to specialized computing resources. GPUs and tensor processing units (TPUs) are types of hardware accelerators offered by modern cloud platforms and are central to the efficient training of complex models. As an example, Google Cloud provides TPUs, which are custom-designed to run high-throughput ML workloads [13]. TPUs were demonstrated to significantly speed up the training of deep neural networks, allowing researchers and businesses to experiment with bigger models and datasets. Besides TPUs, cloud providers also grant access to scalable GPU instances that can be used to meet a variety of computational needs, including low-latency inference workloads, as well as massive parallel processing. These infrastructures are

elastic in nature, i.e., they can scale up or down automatically according to need, i.e., compute resources are allocated on demand and deallocated when not in use. This flexibility is important to cost-sensitive applications because it eliminates overprovisioning and helps to minimize wastage of idle resources. A 2025 study by Wang *et al.* [14] introduced an intelligent resource allocation framework that utilizes reinforcement learning to predict workload demands and adjust compute allocation accordingly. This approach achieved up to a 26% reduction in operating costs while maintaining robust performance.

5.3.1.3 Model Deployment and Inference

The release of trained models marks not only the start of the ML workflow but also the start of a flexible, production-ready life. MLaaS platforms have progressed to include not just powerful model hosting and scale inference but also advanced monitoring and adapting systems like drift detection and active learning. The following components are essential toward sustaining the model performance in real nonstationary settings.

- **Model Hosting:** MLaaS vendors provide managed endpoints, which conceal the complexities of server setup, scaling rules, and health checking. Services such as AWS SageMaker, Azure ML, and Google Vertex AI enable models to be deployed with little configuration and enable versioned rollouts, A/B testing, shadow deployments, and autoscaling. SageMaker multimodel endpoints can load models on demand, using minimal memory and computational overhead, without affecting latency.
- **Scalable Inference:** Inference workloads may involve real-time transaction scoring or large-batch document processing. To tackle such varied requirements, MLaaS platforms offer elastic compute supporting GPUs, TPUs, and inference accelerators such as AWS Elastic Inference or Google Cloud TPU v5e. These infrastructures may autoscale with the number of incoming requests and latency goals and frequently combine with service mesh layers in load balancing.
- **Monitoring and Logging:** Production-grade reliability requires post-deployment monitoring. MLaaS platforms offer real-time dashboards that track latency, accuracy, error rates, and resource utilization. With AWS CloudWatch, Azure Monitor, and Google Vertex AI Monitoring systems, it is possible to initiate alerts and autoscaling events. They also support telemetry pipelines to detect data drift—such as covariate drift (changes in input feature distributions) and concept drift (changes in target distributions).
- **Covariate Drift and Concept Drift:** Covariate Drift is when the distribution of input features varies across time, but the association amongst inputs and outputs is consistent. This may occur as a result of changing real-world scenarios like changing consumer behavior, seasonal changes, or any other

external factors to the economy, which may render a model that has already been trained useless. To use an analogy, a fraud detection model that has been taught on past transaction data might not perform well when customer spending patterns change radically. Continuous monitoring, feature engineering changes, and adaptive retraining are some of the strategies adopted by MLaaS platforms to alleviate the covariate drift and keep the models up-to-date with the current data patterns.

Conversely, *concept drift* is defined as a shift in the underlying association between inputs (X) and outputs (Y), i.e., the model predictions will gradually become less precise with time. This happens when there is a change in the external rules, business policies, or behaviors so that the underlying data correlations that the model is based on are changed. To provide an example, a model of loan approval, which was trained on historical data of credit scores, may be rendered useless in case of a change in the lending policy, such that the predictions of the model and the true risk evaluation no longer correlate. Concept drift requires solving by updating the model frequently, retraining on newly labeled data, and using drift detection methods to change with the current trend. MLaaS vendors usually deploy reinforcement learning techniques and real-time anomaly detection to automatically manage those changes and ensure model reliability.

- **Active Learning and Continuous Improvement:** Active learning is a process in which models or people dynamically choose the most informative data points or knowledge to gain performance in a smart way. In ML, this is performed by algorithms that sample on uncertain or high-consequence examples to train efficiently, needing not as large quantities of labeled data. Within the organizational or educational context, active learning promotes first-hand experience, critical reasoning, and flexibility, which guarantee the effective changes of both people and systems. Whereas continuous improvement is an iterative refinement in which feedback loops, performance measurement, and progressive refinement of methodologies lead to constant improvement.

5.3.1.4 Integration and APIs

MLaaS platforms provide APIs and SDKs for seamless integration:

- **Prebuilt APIs:** These are pretrained APIs that offer out-of-the-box ML capabilities, enabling developers to add AI features to applications without needing to train models. These APIs include NLP capabilities to detect sentiment, identify entities, and perform translation, computer vision to recognize images and objects, speech and audio processing to convert speech to text and vice versa, Predictive Analytics to make forecasts and detect anomalies, and Fraud Detection to identify suspicious activities in financial transactions.

With such pretrained models, organizations gain faster deployment time, reduced development costs, and guaranteed scalability in the AI-powered applications.

- **Custom APIs:** Custom APIs provide enterprises with the flexibility of model deployment, improved security, and scalability that exceeds the functionality of the prebuilt APIs. Compared to generic MLaaS services, custom APIs allow organizations to optimize models, specify custom endpoints, and use specialized algorithms that address unique operational requirements. These APIs enable real-time data processing, adaptive learning, and integrations, which are easier with enterprise systems, making the AI workflow more controlled and optimized.
- **DevOps Integration:** MLOps (ML operations) is a set of practices, tools, and principles that combines ML with DevOps to streamline and automate the ML lifecycle. MLOps can be used to simplify deploying, scaling, and monitoring of ML models using continuous integration (CI), continuous deployment (CD), and automated orchestration [15]. Automated pipelines allow businesses to seamlessly turn on data ingestion, model retraining, and validation so that AI systems remain up-to-date with changing datasets. Also, the practices of MLOps increase scalability, security, and governance, allowing organizations to put ML models into cloud and edge computing settings without losing compliance and performance enhancement. Enterprises would achieve speed, operational efficiency, and AI-driven innovations by adopting MLOps in MLaaS.

5.3.1.5 Security and Governance

Security is paramount, especially for sensitive data:

- **Data Encryption:** Data encryption helps companies ensure that sensitive information is protected from unauthorized access and cyberattacks. As MLaaS platforms deal with a lot of confidential data, such as financial data, personal healthcare data, and confidential business data, they should have end-to-end protection. Encryption should be applied to store information safely and according to all the requirements. General Data Protection Regulation (GDPR), Health Insurance Portability and Accountability Act (HIPAA), and California Consumer Privacy Act (CCPA) are the most significant laws that safeguard personal information. Providers in MLaaS secure their services by using trusted encryption techniques. AI is considered secure and reliable, as it observes regulations and can withstand evolving threats to ensure the solutions provided are more secure and reliable.
- **Access Control:** Access Control ensures that data, models, and rules are secure and consistent with rules. MLaaS implements role-based access control (RBAC), discretionary access control (DAC), and mandatory access control (MAC) to

ensure that people cannot access ML models or data that they are not entitled to use. They decide who gets access to ML models and make the process secure and compatible with industry regulations. In order to assist in securing essential AI operations, privileged access management (PAM) is utilized, which grants access only to the individuals in control. Providers of MLaaS can use granular access controls to assure the safety of AI-based applications, as well as their scalability and adherence to the rules established in the enterprise domain.

- **Compliance:** Adherence to all requirements is an essential aspect of ensuring data security, applying AI correctly, and not violating the law. Since they handle a lot of confidential information, these platforms must legally conform to GDPR, HIPAA, and CCPA to ensure the privacy of users and prevent possible misuse [16]. When applied with the aid of compliance, robust access controls, encryption regulations, and open records, AI models are clear and behave justly. Additionally, users of MLaaS must be concerned with bias, variations, and security concerns at all times, as it will maintain trust and reliability in AI systems. By ensuring powerful compliance measures, MLaaS vendors can help scale AI software in businesses without affecting their legal and ethical practices.

5.3.2 Use Cases

Table 5.1 describes how MLaaS empowers scalable AI deployments across various industries.

5.3.3 Technical Depth: Enabling Scalability

Scalability is the cornerstone of MLaaS, enabling organizations to handle growing workloads. Below, we explore the technical mechanisms that drive scalability.

5.3.3.1 Scalable Infrastructure

MLaaS platforms offer elastic resources by leveraging cloud infrastructure.

- **Distributed Computing:** These frameworks can parallelize large-scale data and perform model training.
- **Auto-Scaling:** Resources are dynamically allocated according to the workload, which lowers the costs during times of low demand.
- **Serverless Architectures:** Serverless ML services remove the administration of servers, leading to smooth scaling.

5.3.3.2 Scalable Model Training

Deep neural networks are large models that require significant computational power to train.

Table 5.1 Key applications where MLaaS enables scalable AI.

Industry	Use Case	Description
Finance	Fraud detection	MLaaS enables real-time anomaly detection on transaction streams using trained classification models, allowing banks to identify fraudulent activities at scale [17].
	Algorithmic trading	Time-series forecasting models trained on historical market data are deployed using MLaaS to automate stock price prediction and trading decisions [3].
	Credit scoring	Financial institutions use MLaaS to build scalable risk assessment models that integrate with customer data APIs for real-time credit decisions.
Healthcare	Medical imaging	Deep learning models for X-ray and MRI analysis are hosted via MLaaS to assist radiologists with fast, AI-driven diagnostics [2].
	Predictive analytics	Ensemble models deployed via MLaaS help predict readmission risks, patient deterioration, and length of stay using structured EMR data.
	Drug discovery	MLaaS platforms accelerate molecular structure prediction and simulation, significantly reducing computation time in early-stage drug development [3].
Retail and e-commerce	Recommendation systems	Personalized recommendation engines are deployed using MLaaS to provide real-time product suggestions based on user behavior and preferences.
	Inventory management	Demand forecasting models powered by MLaaS help optimize inventory and supply chains using historical sales and seasonal trends.
	Sentiment analysis	NLP models analyze customer reviews and social media text to generate real-time insights on consumer satisfaction and brand perception.

(Continued)

Table 5.1 (Continued)

Industry	Use Case	Description
Manufacturing	Predictive maintenance	MLaaS platforms use sensor data from machinery to forecast equipment failures, reducing unexpected downtimes through proactive interventions [2].
	Quality control	Computer vision models detect defects on assembly lines in real time, with scalable inference pipelines for high-throughput inspection.
	Supply chain optimization	MLaaS tools predict logistical disruptions and optimize inventory flow, improving delivery accuracy and vendor coordination.
Transportation	Route optimization	Delivery and logistics companies use MLaaS to dynamically optimize vehicle routes, reducing fuel costs and delivery times.
	Autonomous vehicles	MLaaS facilitates the distributed training and deployment of perception models for self-driving systems (e.g., object detection, lane tracking).
	Demand forecasting	Ride-sharing platforms use time-series models to forecast peak usage patterns and align driver supply with rider demand [3].

- **Distributed Training:** Data parallelism (distributing data across nodes) and model parallelism (distributing model layers) are used to accelerate the training of LLMs [17].
- **Hardware Acceleration:** Using GPUs, TPUs, and custom accelerators can dramatically speed up training time, allowing ML models to process data more efficiently. For instance, TPUs are optimized for matrix operations in deep learning [13].
- **Checkpointing and Resumption:** Tools save a state of training, which can then be resumed if the training is interrupted, which is important when training takes a long time to complete.

5.3.3.3 Scalable Inference

Inference must scale to meet real-time demands:

- **Load Balancing:** Distributing inference requests across multiple model instances minimizes latency. GCP's Vertex AI uses load balancing for high-throughput applications [3].
- **Caching:** Storing frequently requested predictions reduces compute overhead [18].
- **Edge Deployment:** Deploying models on edge devices (e.g., Internet of Things [IoT] devices) using AWS IoT Greengrass or Google Edge TPU reduces latency for time-sensitive applications [19].

5.3.3.4 Scalable Data Pipelines

Data pipelines need to be able to deal with increasing datasets:

- **Stream Processing:** Processing streams of real-time data used in applications such as fraud detection.
- **Batch Processing:** Managing batch processing of data at scale, guaranteeing optimization of data processing. For example, Apache Airflow and Google Cloud Dataflow [20].
- **Data Versioning:** Version Control Systems (e.g., data version control [DVC]) monitor changes to datasets, making ML processes reproducible [21, 27].

5.3.3.5 Cost Optimization

The scalability should be economical:

- **Pay-as-You-Go Pricing:** Pricing that is based on utilization of resources helps to reduce initial outlay.
- **Resource Optimization Tools:** Functionality such as AWS SageMaker Neo can tune models to run on particular hardware, decreasing inference expenses.

5.4 Challenges and Future Outlook

5.4.1 Challenges in MLaaS Adoption

Although MLaaS is advantageous, it is encountered with a set of challenges:

5.4.1.1 Data Privacy and Security

- **Data Breaches:** Saving sensitive information on the cloud brings up the issue of breaches [16].
- **Regulatory Compliance:** Adhering to regulations like GDPR and HIPAA is complex in multi-tenant environments.
- **Mitigation:** MLaaS providers offer encryption, private clouds, and compliance certifications.

5.4.1.2 Vendor Lock-In

Vendor lock-in happens when organizations become too dependent on a single provider's AI tools, making it expensive or difficult to switch platforms. This will result in limited flexibility, increasing long-term costs and a slowdown in innovation if the vendor changes pricing or service terms.

5.4.1.3 Cost Management

- **Unpredictable Costs:** Pay-as-you-go pricing can lead to unexpected expenses.
- **Mitigation:** Tools like AWS Cost Explorer and Azure Cost Management optimize spending.

5.4.1.4 Skill Gaps

- **Complexity:** Advanced use cases require expertise, despite AutoML simplifications.
- **Mitigation:** MLaaS providers offer training programs and documentation.

5.4.1.5 Model Interpretability

- **Black-Box Models:** Deep learning models are often hard to interpret, posing challenges in regulated industries [22, 28].
- **Mitigation:** Techniques like SHAP and LIME improve explainability.

5.4.2 Future Outlook

The MLaaS landscape is evolving rapidly. Key trends include:

5.4.2.1 Federated Learning

Federated learning allows the training of models on decentralized data, where privacy is conserved [23]. Federated learning is being incorporated into MLaaS platforms to apply to applications such as healthcare and finance, where the centralization of data is not possible.

5.4.2.2 AI Democratization

Advancements in AutoML and low-code platforms will further lower barriers, enabling nontechnical users to build AI solutions [4].

5.4.2.3 Edge AI

MLaaS is expanding to edge devices, enabling low-latency inference for IoT and autonomous systems.

5.4.2.4 Sustainable AI

To minimize the carbon footprint of AI, MLaaS providers are energy-optimizing by operating in green data centers and using low-power hardware [24].

5.4.2.5 Integration with Generative AI

MLaaS platforms are also integrating generative AI models, such as text-to-image generation models, and making use of them in applications such as content generation and design automation [25].

5.4.2.6 Open-Source MLaaS

Open-source frameworks, such as H2O.ai and MLflow, are becoming popular, providing flexibility and cost-effectiveness to organizations that do not require vendor-specific solutions [26].

5.5 Conclusion

MLaaS has changed the AI game, allowing organizations to utilize ML without the intricacies of customary development. MLaaS enables business innovation in all industries by offering scalable infrastructure, prebuilt tools, and easy integration. It is a foundation of scalable AI because of its capacity to deal with increasing amounts of data and user requests, as well as its capability to manage complexity in computation. Although issues such as data privacy, vendor lock-in, and cost control remain, current developments in federated learning, edge AI, and sustainable AI are alleviating them. Vendors of MLaaS, such as AWS, Azure, and GCP, are still innovating and providing a general-purpose platform that supports a wide variety of applications, including fraud detection or medical imaging. In the future, MLaaS will be very important in the democratization of AI, where scalable AI can be available to large and small organizations. However, by approaching the idea of best practices, which include setting clear goals, selecting the suitable provider, and investing in training, businesses will open up new opportunities, efficiency, and the ability to compete in the AI-driven world. The future of MLaaS is promising as it will bring a new age of innovations and accessibility in AI.

References

1 I. Goodfellow, Y. Bengio, and A. Courville, *Deep Learning*. Cambridge, MA, USA: MIT Press, 2016.

2 Microsoft Azure, "Azure machine learning documentation", 2024. [Online]. Available: https://docs.microsoft.com/en-us/azure/machine-learning.

3 Google Cloud Platform, "Vertex AI documentation", 2024. [Online]. Available: http://cloud.google.com/vertex-ai/docs.

4 H. Wang, L. Zhang, and Q. Yang, "AutoML in cloud-based machine learning services," *ACM Comput. Surv.*, vol. 53, no. 4, pp. 1–36, 2020.

5 Amazon Web Services, (2026) "Train ML models at scale using distributed training," [On line]. Available: https://docs.aws.amazon.com/sagemaker/latest/dgdistributed-training.html.

6 Kubernetes, "Production-grade container orchestration," 2024. [Online]. Available: https://kubernetes.io/docs/home.

7 A. Sergeev and M. D. Balso, "Horovod: Fast and easy distributed deep learning in TensorFlow," arXiv preprint arXiv:1802.05799, 2018. [Online]. Available: https://arxiv.org/abs/1802.05799.

8 P. Moritz, et al., "Ray: A distributed framework for emerging AI applications," in *13th USENIX Symp. Oper. Syst. Design Implement. (OSDI)*, 2018, pp. 561–577. [Online]. Available: https://www.usenix.org/conference/osdi18/presentation/moritz.

9 L. He, J. Sun, J. Yang, Y. Chen, C. Li, and L. Zhou, "A scalable distributed training system for deep learning," *Proc. VLDB Endow.*, vol. 10, no. 11, pp. 1349–1360, 2017.

10 A. Shivaji, D. Reddy, and V. K. Adhikari, "Cost-effective autoscaling for machine learning inference services in the cloud," in *Proc. IEEE Int. Conf. Cloud Comput. (CLOUD)*, 2020, pp. 150–159.

11 H. Wang, J. Yang, G. Liang, Y. Lee, and Z. Cao, "Analyzing the usability, performance, and cost-efficiency of deploying ML models on BigQuery ML and vertex AI in google cloud," *in Proc. 2024 Int. Conf. Cloud Big Data Comput. (ICCBDC)*, Oxford, UK, Aug. 2024, pp. 1–11.

12 TensorFlow, "TensorFlow documentation," 2024. [Online]. Available: https://www.http://tensorflow.org.

13 Google Cloud Platform, "Cloud TPU documentation," 2024. [Online]. Available: https://cloud.google.com/tpu/docs.

14 Y. Wang and X. Yang, "Intelligent resource allocation optimization for cloud computing via machine learning," 2025, arXiv preprint arXiv:2504.03682.

15 Amazon Web Services, "AWS CodePipeline documentation," 2024. [Online]. Available: https://docs.aws.amazon.com/codepipeline.

16 Amazon Web Services, "AWS compliance programs," 2024. [Online]. Available: https://aws.amazon.com/compliance.
17 Amazon Web Services, "AWS SageMaker: Developer guide," 2024. [Online]. Available: https://docs.aws.amazon.com/sagemaker.
18 Amazon Web Services, "AWS ElastiCache documentation," 2024. [Online]. Available: https://docs.aws.amazon.com/elasticache.
19 Amazon Web Services, "AWS IoT Greengrass documentation," 2024. [Online]. Available: https://docs.aws.amazon.com/greengrass.
20 Apache Airflow, "Airflow documentation," 2024. [Online]. Available: http://airflow.apache.org/docs.
21 DVC, "Data version control documentation," 2024. [Online]. Available: http://dvc.org/doc.
22 S. M. Lundberg and S.-I. Lee, "A unified approach to interpreting model predictions," in *Adv. Neural Inf. Process. Syst.*, 2017, pp. 4765–4774.
23 A. Smith, R. Jones, and T. Lee, "Federated learning for privacy-preserving MLaaS," *in Proc. IEEE Int. Conf. Artif. Intell. Data Sci.*, 2022, pp. 123–130.
24 T. Brown and S. Kim, "Sustainable AI: Reducing the carbon footprint of MLaaS," *J. Sustain. Comput.*, vol. 12, no. 2, pp. 89–102, 2024.
25 E. Roberts, J. Lee, and P. Gupta, "Generative AI in MLaaS: Opportunities and challenges," in *Proc. Int. Conf. Mach. Learn.*, 2023, pp. 456–463.
26 H2O.ai, *H2O: Open-source machine learning platform*, 2024. [Online]. Available: https://www.h2o.ai.
27 Databricks, "Unified data analytics platform," 2024. [Online]. Available: http://databricks.com.
28 J. Chen and X. Zhang, "A survey of machine learning as a service (MLaaS) platforms," *IEEE Trans. Cloud Comput.*, vol. 7, no. 3, pp. 654–667, 2019.
29 Y. Li, Z. Wang, and H. Liu, "Scalable machine learning in the cloud: Challenges and opportunities," *J. Cloud Comput.*, vol. 10, no. 1, pp. 45–60, 2021.

6

Cloud Cost Optimization and the Rise of FinOps

Dhivya Nagasubramanian

Independent Researcher, Minniapolis, MN, USA

6.1 Introduction: Cloud Cost Complexity and the Capital Expenditures (CapEx)-to-Operating Expenditures (OpEx) Shift

The first cloud bill often comes as a shock. For many organizations, it arrives not with celebration, but confusion. After months of planning, migrating, and anticipating savings, the numbers on that invoice can feel like a betrayal. Instead of reduced costs, there's a sudden spike—unexpected charges, unexplained overages, and a growing sense that something isn't adding up.

What was pitched as a more agile, cost-effective infrastructure suddenly looks like a runaway expense. And in that moment, many teams realize the cloud isn't just a technical shift—it's a financial reckoning.

The cloud, for all its promises—scalability, flexibility, innovation—has a dark side when it comes to costs. Unlike the old days of IT, where expenses were mostly upfront and predictable (think servers in a data center, long-term contracts, perpetual licenses), today's cloud costs behave more like a utility bill. One that fluctuates wildly based on usage—and sometimes, no one's even quite sure what caused the spike.

6.2 From CapEx Comfort to OpEx Chaos

In the traditional world of enterprise IT, we had control. We budgeted in neat annual cycles. We knew when we were going to buy hardware, renew licenses, or expand our data centers. Costs were stable and could be depreciated over time.

Then came the cloud—and with it, the shift from CapEx to OpEx [1]. Suddenly, infrastructure became something we rented, not owned. Every compute cycle, every API call, and every gigabyte transferred had a price tag, and with that flexibility came financial uncertainty.

On paper, this OpEx model looked great. You could scale up during peak demand, scale down when things were quiet, and only pay for what you used. But the reality is more complex. Most organizations don't scale down. Or they forget to turn things off. Or they overprovision "just in case." And without the right visibility, the costs pile up silently—until the bill hits.

6.3 The Rise of FinOps: Making Cloud Spending Make Sense

This is exactly why FinOps (Finance + DevOps)—short for financial operations—has emerged as one of the fastest-growing disciplines in tech today. It's not just another buzzword. It's a practical, necessary response to the chaos of cloud economics.

FinOps is where engineering, finance, and product teams meet to ask one simple question: Are we getting the most value for every dollar we spend in the cloud? It's not just about slashing budgets or nickel-and-diming development teams. It's about spending smarter, not necessarily spending less. It's about visibility, accountability, and aligning technical decisions with financial outcomes.

6.4 You're Not Alone—The Data Tells the Story

If this sounds familiar, you're not imagining it. One study found that nearly 80% of enterprises overspend on their cloud budgets, often due to a lack of governance or just plain inefficiency. Another reported that 69% of Chief Financial Officer (CFOs) who prioritize cost optimization still struggle to rein in cloud expenses, especially without compromising performance or speed.

Why is this so hard? Because cloud cost optimization isn't a one-time project. It's a continuous, cross-functional effort. It requires real-time insights, shared responsibility, and—perhaps most of all—a cultural shift.

6.5 A New Mindset for a New Era

Moving to the cloud is more than just a technology decision. It's a business model transformation. And with that comes a new financial mindset. One where teams ask not just "Can we do this?" but "Should we do this?" from both a technical and a financial perspective.

And this is where FinOps shines—by making cost part of the conversation, not just at the end of the month when the invoice arrives, but at the moment a service is designed, deployed, or scaled.

We're still learning. We're still evolving. But one thing is clear: if we want to harness the full potential of the cloud without breaking the bank, we need to treat cloud costs not as a technical problem but as a team sport. I still remember the look on our CFO's face when she saw our first full-quarter cloud bill after we'd migrated half of our infrastructure. It wasn't just surprise—it was disbelief. After months of promises about cost savings and increased agility, we were staring at a number that was almost 30% higher than our legacy infrastructure costs. And that was just the beginning.

This wasn't an isolated case. It's happening all over.

The cloud, for all its promises—scalability, flexibility, innovation—has a dark side when it comes to costs. Unlike the old days of IT, where expenses were mostly upfront and predictable (think servers in a data center, long-term contracts, perpetual licenses), today's cloud costs behave more like a utility bill. One that fluctuates wildly based on usage—and sometimes, no one's even quite sure what caused the spike.

To illustrate the paradigm change, consider some key differences between traditional IT spending and cloud spending in Table 6.1.

"So, why is my cloud bill out of control?"

When I first heard that the cloud was "pay-as-you-go," I figured that meant we'd only pay for what we use—like a phone bill. Simple, right?

Well, turns out it's not that simple.

In the cloud, you can spin up a hundred servers with just a few clicks. It feels almost magical. But here's the catch: if nobody's keeping an eye on things, that magic trick turns into a giant, confusing bill at the end of the month.

This is what some people are calling a cloud cost complexity crisis. Teams are trying to keep up with unpredictable expenses, figure out who's spending what, and avoid waste—all while still moving fast. It's kind of like trying to drive a sports car and balance your checkbook at the same time. For engineers and cloud financial operations (CTOs), figuring this out has become a big deal. It's not just about saving money—it's about regaining control and making sure cloud spending actually supports the business.

That's where something called FinOps comes in. I hadn't heard of it before either—it stands for "CTOs." Basically, it's a way to bring a bit of budgeting sense to the free-for-all world of cloud computing. It's about helping finance people and tech people speak the same language when it comes to spending.

In the next section, I'll dive into what FinOps actually is, where it came from, and how it helps companies stop their cloud bills from running wild.

Table 6.1 Key differences between CapEx (on-premises) and OpEx (cloud) cost models.

Aspect	Traditional CapEx (On-Premises IT)	Cloud OpEx (Cloud Computing)
Cost commitment	Large upfront investments in hardware and data centers, with costs amortized over years. Budgeting is periodic and predictable.	Pay-as-you-go for services with continuous, variable billing. Budgets must adapt dynamically to usage spikes.
Capacity limits	Fixed capacity (bound by purchased infrastructure). Scaling requires new CapEx outlays, creating a natural cap on spending.	Elastic capacity (virtually infinite resources on demand). Easy to scale up instantly, removing the natural brake on spending.
Governance	Centralized procurement and IT controls. Finance has clear oversight of purchases before they occur, enabling "water-tight" budgeting.	Decentralized, distributed spending by engineering teams. Developers can spin up resources at will, making cost control looser and harder to enforce.
Cost visibility	Relatively straightforward cost tracking—bills for equipment and software are well-defined line items.	Highly granular, complex billing with millions of line items is possible. Real-time monitoring and tagging are needed to attribute costs and avoid surprises.

6.6 The Emergence and Evolution of FinOps

As cloud adoption accelerated, forward-thinking organizations began searching for ways to bring financial accountability to this new IT model. The term "FinOps" started appearing in the early 2010s as companies experimented with practices to better control cloud spend [2]. Early pioneers recognized that the traditional siloed approach—where engineering builds and finance pays—was untenable in a pay-as-you-go cloud world. By the late 2010s, as cloud usage skyrocketed, these ideas coalesced into a formal practice.

A major milestone was the founding of the FinOps Foundation in 2019, which signaled broad industry uptake [2]. The FinOps Foundation began as a community of practitioners (originating from discussions led by cloud cost management startup cloudability) who needed a forum to share best practices beyond any single vendor tool [3]. In 2020, this foundation joined the Linux Foundation, underscoring the importance of FinOps as an open, collaborative discipline [3]. Since then, thousands of FinOps practitioners from companies across industries (from tech startups to large banks and manufacturers) have come together to develop standard frameworks and education around cloud financial management [4].

FinOps is defined as "an evolving cloud financial management discipline and cultural practice that enables organizations to get maximum business value by helping engineering, finance, technology and business teams to collaborate on data-driven spending decisions" [2]. In simpler terms, FinOps is about making sure every dollar spent in the cloud translates to value for the business. It borrows from the DevOps ethos of breaking down silos and emphasizes cross-functional teamwork: engineering, finance, and product teams work together in near real-time on cloud cost decisions [4]. This interdisciplinary approach is crucial because controlling cloud costs is not purely a technical problem or purely a finance problem—it lives at the intersection of the two.

Crucially, FinOps shifts the culture of cloud usage. In the old model, a central procurement or IT asset management team approved every purchase; now, with on-demand cloud, individual teams have autonomy to consume resources, so they must also take ownership of their cloud spending [5]. FinOps creates a shared language and set of processes that align everyone—from engineers to CFO—on how to balance cost, speed, and quality [2]. It is *not* simply about cutting costs; it's about maximizing the value of the cloud by spending wisely. A common saying in FinOps circles is *it's not about saving money; it's about getting more value per dollar*. This means sometimes spending more on the cloud is fine if it yields proportional business value, but waste (spending that doesn't translate to value) should be eliminated.

The evolution of FinOps as a discipline has also been propelled by economic pressures. In times of rising cloud bills or tighter IT budgets, organizations have been forced to mature their cost management. The market around FinOps tools and services is growing rapidly—for example, analysts project the cloud financial management market will grow from about $832 million in 2023 to $2.75 billion by 2028 (18.8% compound annual growth rate [CAGR]) [5]. This growth reflects how vital FinOps has become for enterprises worldwide.

In summary, FinOps emerged to fill a critical gap: bringing financial accountability and business-driven decision-making to the dynamic world of cloud. Next, we'll delve into the principles and frameworks that FinOps provides to achieve this goal.

6.7 Core FinOps Principles and Lifecycle

To implement FinOps, organizations rely on a set of core principles and a continuous improvement lifecycle. The FinOps Principles, established by the FinOps Foundation, serve as guiding tenets for any FinOps practice. Meanwhile, the

FinOps lifecycle (inform, optimize, operate) provides a framework for iterative cloud cost management. Let's explore each in turn.

6.7.1 FinOps Principle

FinOps practitioners adhere to key principles that shape how teams think about cloud spend [4]. In essence, these principles promote collaboration, accountability, and a value-driven mindset. The six commonly cited FinOps principles are as follows:

- **Teams Need to Collaborate:** Cloud cost is a team sport. Finance, tech, and business teams must work together closely (ideally in real-time) because cloud usage is decentralized and continuously changing [4]. Breaking down silos is non-negotiable—effective FinOps creates a culture of cooperation between historically separated functions.
- **Business Value Drives Decisions:** Cost is not looked at in isolation—it's weighed against the value or revenue it brings. FinOps encourages measuring unit economics (e.g., cost per customer transaction) to link cloud spend to business value, rather than just tracking aggregate spending [4]. This principle reminds us that the cheapest solution is not always the best; the goal is optimal ROI.
- **Everyone Takes Ownership of Usage:** Engineering and product teams are empowered and accountable for the resources they use [4]. Instead of a central IT controlling all spending, FinOps pushes responsibility to the "edges"—meaning developers and managers owning services need to monitor and optimize their cloud usage. This fosters a culture where architects consider cost as a dimension of software design (just like performance or security).
- **Financial Data Should Be Accessible and Timely:** To make informed decisions, teams need real-time visibility into their cloud costs and usage [4]. FinOps emphasizes building reliable cost reporting, tagging, and metrics. When engineers can see the cost impact of their applications immediately, they can adjust behavior quickly (fast feedback loops). Accurate, shared data is the single source of truth that drives FinOps decisions.
- **FinOps Is Centrally Enabled:** Most organizations establish a central FinOps team or function that acts as a center of excellence [4]. This team provides tooling, best practices, and governance, much like a security or cloud center of excellence. Importantly, they don't "own" all cost optimizations themselves; they enable other teams to do so in a coordinated way. Executive buy-in for this FinOps function is critical to enforce accountability across the org [4].
- **Take Advantage of the Cloud's Variable Cost Model:** Rather than fear the variability of cloud costs, FinOps advocates embracing it as an opportunity [4]. Teams are encouraged to use the cloud's flexibility to their advantage—for

example, scaling down environments when not needed or using on-demand resources strategically. The principle here is to favor agile, just-in-time use of resources (and purchasing of capacity) over static over-provisioning. Continuous experimentation and adjustment are preferred over infrequent, reactive cost-cutting [4].

These principles create a mindset where *cost optimization is a continuous, shared responsibility*. An engineer building a new microservice, for instance, will think about the cost impact (and perhaps choose a more efficient architecture) because FinOps has made cost an important metric of success. At the same time, finance people become more agile, learning to work with real-time data and engineering cycles. Together, they focus on maximizing business value for every dollar spent.

6.7.2 FinOps Lifecycle: Inform, Optimize, Operate

FinOps isn't something you "complete." It's a continuous practice that evolves with your cloud usage. The FinOps Foundation breaks it down into three key phases: Inform, Optimize, and Operate [6]. These aren't isolated steps—they loop into each other, helping teams improve over time.

Inform: See What You're Spending: Everything starts with visibility. Teams need to know what they're spending, which services are driving the cost, and who's responsible. This requires tagging, account structure, and a way to allocate costs clearly across projects and teams [6]. Budgets and forecasts help translate usage into business terms. Dashboards often come into play—showing teams how their spending tracks against budget or metrics like cost per user. Without this foundation, it's hard to hold anyone accountable or even understand what "expensive" means.

Optimize: Use Data to Make Things Better: Once the picture is clear, the next step is improvement. That might mean shutting down idle instances, resizing machines that are underused, or moving to cheaper service tiers. Discounts like reserved instances or long-term agreements can help [6]. Some changes are quick, like deleting resources no one's using. Others, like redesigning an application to reduce compute time, take more work but can offer big gains. Teams need to weigh effort, cost, and impact. Not every optimization is worth it if it hurts performance or slows delivery.

Operate: Make It Part of the Routine: The last phase is about habits. FinOps becomes part of how teams work. Companies might set policies that require tagging or alerts for any spend over a certain amount. Some automate these rules. Others use playbooks or training to teach engineers how to build with cost in mind.

Culture plays a big role. Internal newsletters, success stories, and even things like team leaderboards can help build momentum. What matters most is keeping the loop going. As teams operate, they discover better ways to track (inform) and new chances to improve (optimize) [6].

Not every team will be in the same place. One might still be figuring out visibility, and another might already be running optimizations. A central FinOps group can help guide the organization forward. There's no final stage—just a cycle that keeps making the business smarter about how it uses the cloud.

6.8 Holistic Cost Management Framework

One major shift in cloud financial management has been the rise of structured, organization-wide frameworks. FinOps is at the heart of this movement—not just as a set of tools, but as a shift in how people, processes, and technology align to manage cloud spend.

Many large enterprises pair FinOps with broader financial governance models like technology business management (TBM). One financial services firm, for instance, had long used TBM to manage on-prem IT. When cloud adoption surged, they introduced a FinOps operating model, creating a core team and embedding FinOps leads within each business unit. This federated structure helped manage cloud spend across thousands of accounts while keeping financial accountability aligned to central governance.

Another key development is the push for open cost data standards. The FinOps Foundation's FOCUS specification (FinOps open cost and usage specification) offers a vendor-neutral way to describe billing and usage data. As major cloud providers begin adopting it, analyzing costs across multicloud environments becomes easier and more consistent. For cloud engineers, this means smoother integration into dashboards and tooling—and a growing ecosystem of third-party platforms offering unified visibility across providers.

6.9 Beyond Single-Workload Optimization

Cloud cost control often starts with small, targeted fixes—adjusting one database, trimming an unused cluster. But for many teams, that approach only goes so far. To make a bigger impact, organizations are starting to zoom out.

Multicloud strategies are gaining attention. Instead of relying on a single provider, teams are spreading workloads across clouds to take advantage of pricing differences. One vendor might offer lower storage rates, while another is better for Graphics Processing Unit (GPU)-heavy tasks [7]. Years ago, this was too complex for most. Now, with containers and orchestration platforms, it's becoming far more manageable. Even the ability to move between providers gives companies an edge during pricing discussions.

There's also value in looking beyond engineering. Enterprise agreements can deliver real savings—often in the range of 10–30%—just by committing to longer terms or higher usage. This isn't about technical tuning, but it lowers costs all the same. FinOps teams usually work with procurement and vendor managers to handle these negotiations.

For newer companies or those just starting out, cloud credits can go a long way. Providers frequently offer these to startups, research projects, or early users of new services. They don't last forever, but they can cover a meaningful portion of spending in the early months—giving teams time to build better cost habits before the bills grow.

6.10 Cost-Aware Architecture and Operations

A truly novel approach to cost optimization is baking cost awareness into architecture and operational decisions from the start. This goes beyond cleaning up waste—it means *designing systems for cost-efficiency as a core requirement*. Some techniques and concepts in this realm include:

- **Cost as an Architectural Pillar:** Just as architects consider reliability, scalability, and security, leading cloud architects now consider cost-efficiency when evaluating solutions. For instance, choosing serverless or event-driven architectures can eliminate idle resource costs (you pay only per execution)—this might be more cost-effective for sporadic workloads than a server-based design. In FinOps terms, these shifts cost optimization "left" (earlier in the development lifecycle) so that the cheapest solution that meets requirements is chosen upfront.
- **Chaos Engineering for Cost:** An emerging practice is running experiments to test cost-related behaviors. For example, deliberately doubling the load on a system to see how costs scale or turning off a portion of servers to see if auto-scaling replaces them (and how quickly). This is akin to chaos engineering (which tests resilience) but focused on cost dynamics. It can reveal opportunities to tune auto-scaling or catch services that aren't scaling down as expected.
- **Showback and Chargeback Models:** A crucial part of advanced cost management is not just optimizing the costs but ensuring the right accountability and incentives are in place. FinOps often implements showback (reporting costs back to the teams who incurred them) or chargeback (directly charging those costs to team budgets). These models create a financial feedback loop. For instance, at a large bank, as soon as they started breaking

down the monthly \$1.6 million cloud bills into line items per team and service, it became clear who the top spenders were. With that visibility, teams were given the mandate to justify or reduce their portion of spending. In practice, showback/chargeback encourages teams to self-optimize. It essentially decentralizes cost responsibility, which is exactly aligned with FinOps principles.

- **Automated Governance (Guardrails):** Automation is key to managing cloud costs at scale. Advanced strategies use policies and scripts to automatically enforce cost-saving measures. For example, implementing automated scheduling that shuts down non-production environments at 8 PM or using policies to prevent provisioning of certain high-cost instance types without approval. Some organizations set up automated alerts or even automated actions (like downsizing an overprovisioned resource) when cost anomalies are detected. These guardrails act as a safety net that catches overspending before it spirals. They allow engineers to move fast while still adhering to cost policies set by FinOps governance.

In summary, beyond rightsizing lies a whole world of strategic cost management. It encompasses financial negotiations (rates and credits), architectural choices, cultural shifts (like chargeback accountability), and advanced automation. The most successful cloud cost optimization initiatives treat it not as a one-time project but as a continuous, multidimensional effort—exactly what FinOps is designed to facilitate. Every organization will have a different mix of strategies depending on its size and complexity, but the common theme is thinking bigger about cloud economics: it's about *architecting* for cost efficiency and building a *culture* that values efficient cloud usage at all levels.

6.11 AI/ML for Predictive Cloud Cost Management

As cloud environments grow, the volume of usage and billing data quickly surpasses what teams can analyze manually. This is where artificial intelligence (AI) and machine learning (ML) come in—shifting FinOps from a backward-looking process into a real-time, predictive discipline.

Real-Time Analytics and Anomaly Detection: Traditional cost reviews often happen after the fact—teams wait for a bill, then investigate spikes; AI changes that by monitoring spending patterns continuously. ML models learn what "normal" looks like for a given service or team and flag outliers in real time. For example, if a test environment suddenly incurs 10x its usual cost due to a runaway job, the system can catch it quickly and notify engineers—or even shut it down automatically [8]. These tools are built to minimize false alarms while focusing attention on real issues.

Forecasting and Early Warnings: Cloud forecasting is notoriously difficult, with variables like app scaling, project launches, and seasonal usage. ML can analyze past trends alongside contextual inputs—like release schedules or expected traffic—and predict future spending with surprising accuracy [8]. Some teams use these forecasts daily, spotting overages before they happen. With each cycle, the model improves, learning from past variances to become more reliable over time.

Intelligent Resource Optimization: The most advanced use of AI in FinOps is dynamic resource adjustment. AI systems can recognize workload patterns and automate infrastructure scaling—shutting down idle servers during off-hours or shifting workloads to more efficient configurations [9]. In multicloud environments, this gets even smarter: AI can route workloads to whichever provider or region offers the best value in the moment, a form of automated cross-cloud arbitrage [9, 10]. For example, a batch job might run in Cloud B over the weekend because of temporary capacity discounts.

In summary, AI and ML are infusing FinOps with predictive power and automation. They enable a scale of analysis and responsiveness that would be impossible manually. As cloud complexity grows (especially with trends like microservices, Kubernetes, and serverless, which produce even more granular cost data), AI will be an indispensable ally in cloud cost optimization. We're heading toward a future where your "cloud cost manager" might partly be an AI system watching over your environment 24/7, ever ready to tune and tweak for optimal efficiency.

6.12 FinOps in Action: Real-World Case Studies

FinOps isn't just theory—many organizations have successfully implemented its practices and seen dramatic results. In this section, we'll look at several real-world case studies across different industries, showing how FinOps has led to optimized costs, cultural change, and better business outcomes. Each case illustrates a different aspect of FinOps in practice.

- **Banking (US Regional Bank):** A regional bank running substantial workloads in Azure found its annual cloud costs swelling to \$18 million [11]. By partnering with a FinOps consultancy, they established a FinOps program that prioritized quick wins in cost reduction and instilled a culture of cloud cost awareness. Within the first year, the bank secured \$3 million in annual savings and identified opportunities to reach \$6 million (50% additional savings) [11]. These savings were not merely pocketed—they were reinvested into strategic IT projects that the bank previously lacked budget for. A key to success was training the IT staff in FinOps practices and shifting teams from a reactive stance ("shock at the bill") to a proactive stance where costs were monitored and optimized continuously. This case highlights how even highly regulated industries like banking can adopt FinOps to simultaneously cut costs and fund innovation.

- **Insurance (Nationwide Insurance):** Large enterprises often have sprawling cloud footprints. In one published case, Nationwide Insurance adopted FinOps and saved over \$4.3 million in annualized cloud costs [12]. The FinOps Foundation's 2019 case study on nationwide revealed that by breaking down costs to business units and implementing cross-functional cost optimization initiatives, significant waste was eliminated. This underscores how visibility and accountability (FinOps Inform phase) combined with collaborative optimization efforts can yield millions in savings even for companies that were already savvy in the cloud.
- **Software/SaaS (Atlassian):** Atlassian, a leading software company, was an early FinOps adopter. By 2020, Atlassian reported it had managed to cut about 66% of its cloud costs through FinOps practices [12]. This staggering reduction was achieved by aggressively rightsizing resources, increasing the usage of spot instances where possible, and instilling cost accountability among engineering teams. Atlassian's story is often cited to show the potential of FinOps in a "cloud-native" tech company—even highly cloud-forward companies can sometimes operate inefficiently until a focused FinOps effort unlocks huge savings.
- **Digital Entertainment/Tech (Spotify):** Spotify, the global audio streaming service, faced a situation where cloud infrastructure costs were rising faster than user growth—an unsustainable trajectory. In response, Spotify developed internal FinOps tooling and practices. They built "Cost Insights"—a custom plugin to their developer portal—giving every engineering team visibility into their cloud spend and guidance on optimization. By making cost data self-service and tying it to engineering decisions, Spotify managed to bend the cost curve, cutting annual cloud spending by millions of dollars. Engineers became more conscious of resource usage when they could clearly see the cost implications of their designs. Spotify even open-sourced this tool, demonstrating the cultural mindset of FinOps: they treated cost optimization as an engineering problem and solved it with software and transparency. This case illustrates the power of shifting cost responsibility "left" to engineers—when given the right information and incentives, teams can significantly optimize their own costs.
- **Manufacturing/Consumer Electronics (Samsung):** FinOps is not just for software companies; even hardware and electronics giants benefit from it. Samsung, for example, operates massive cloud-based services (from mobile

backends to Internet of Things [IoT] platforms). By leveraging FinOps principles and cloud cost management tools, Samsung achieved roughly 30% savings on its cloud spending. This was done through a combination of eliminating over-provisioned resources and optimizing workloads across different cloud providers and regions. For a company of Samsung's scale, 30% equates to substantial dollar amounts. It shows that FinOps methodologies can be scaled to very large, globally distributed cloud environments.
- **Energy/Industrial (Schneider Electric):** Schneider Electric, a global energy management firm, used a cloud management platform (VMware's Cloud-Health) in tandem with FinOps best practices to optimize their multicloud usage. The result was a 30% reduction in cloud costs while maintaining performance. Schneider's approach included detailed cost allocation (to find internal inefficiencies), turning off non-critical systems out of hours, and enforcing tagging policies to prevent "shadow IT" cloud spend. A notable outcome was that cost optimization efforts also aligned with the company's sustainability goals (less wasteful usage equals lower energy consumption in data centers). This case is a good example of FinOps delivering both financial and environmental benefits.

Each of these case studies reinforces a few important points:

- **FinOps Delivers Tangible Savings:** From 30% up to 66% cost reductions and millions of dollars saved. The financial impact is real and significant.
- **It's Applicable Across Industries:** Finance, insurance, tech, manufacturing, and more—any organization using the cloud at scale can apply FinOps.
- **Success Involves Culture and Tools:** The common recipe is *visibility* (the teams got clearer insight into costs) plus *accountability* (teams were empowered or mandated to act on those insights). Tools (like dashboards or Cloud Health) play an enabling role, but equally important are executive support and process changes to ensure the insights turn into action.
- **Reinvesting Savings:** Many organizations choose to reallocate the money saved to higher-value activities. This is a smart approach that frames FinOps not as "cloud cost cutting" but as "investing cloud dollars where they matter most." It turns cost optimization into a business enabler, not just a bean-counting exercise.

For cloud engineers and CTOs reading this, the takeaway is that FinOps is not just a theory; it's a proven approach that peers in your industry are using to great effect. Whether you're a startup trying to extend your runway or an enterprise striving for efficiency, these real-world examples show that a systematic focus on cloud financial management pays off.

6.13 The Future of FinOps: Sustainability, Cross-Cloud Arbitrage, and Decentralized Models

Cloud technology continues to evolve, and FinOps is evolving with it. Looking ahead, several emerging trends are poised to shape the next generation of FinOps practices. In this final section, we explore some of these trends—from integrating sustainability goals to leveraging multiple clouds and even decentralized infrastructure to new financial models inspired by decentralized finance (DeFi). Each of these trends extends the FinOps conversation beyond cost and into broader strategic arenas.

6.13.1 FinOps Meets Sustainability (GreenOps)

An important trend is the convergence of cloud cost optimization with sustainability initiatives. As companies commit to reducing their carbon footprint, the cloud's energy usage and carbon emissions are under scrutiny. Enter green operations (GreenOps), a concept parallel to FinOps that focuses on minimizing the environmental impact (carbon footprint) of cloud operations. In essence, GreenOps applies similar principles—measuring, optimizing, and governing—but the metric of concern is carbon emissions rather than dollars. According to Forrester Research, "*GreenOps is the practice of minimizing a cloud environment's carbon footprint through the efficient use of cloud resources.*" This aligns closely with FinOps: efficient use of resources not only saves money but also reduces energy consumption.

Cloud providers have begun offering tools for customers to gauge their carbon emissions from cloud usage. For example, all major clouds now have carbon footprint calculators or dashboards that estimate the Greenhouse Gas (GHG) emissions associated with a customer's usage, often breaking it down by service. FinOps teams are increasingly pulling this data into their reports alongside cost. The Inform phase of FinOps can easily extend to include sustainability metrics—indeed, FinOps practitioners are now talking about "cost per unit of value *and* carbon per unit of value." In the FinOps Foundation's framework, cloud sustainability is recognized as a key consideration, and they note that many activities (like rightsizing and eliminating waste) are dual-beneficial: they save money and reduce emissions [13, 14].

6.13.1.1 Why Is This Trend Significant?

Beyond corporate social responsibility, regulations are emerging that may require carbon reporting. Tech and cloud usage are estimated to contribute a substantial share of global emissions, roughly 3% of global greenhouse gas emissions (on par with the aviation industry), with data centers alone making up about 1%

and projected to grow rapidly [15]. Businesses know that unchecked cloud growth could become not just a cost issue but a compliance and reputation issue if it leads to a large carbon footprint. FinOps teams are well-positioned to tackle this because they already monitor and optimize resource usage. By adding a "carbon lens," FinOps becomes the bridge between IT, finance, and sustainability offices.

Soon, we might see FinOps reports that justify recommendations based not only on cost savings but also on carbon reductions. For instance, moving infrequently accessed data from high-cost storage to a cheaper, less energy-intensive tier could save around $50,000 annually and significantly lower energy consumption by X kWh, thereby reducing Y tons of CO_2 emissions. These types of dual-benefit recommendations will be especially appealing.

Additionally, cloud cost optimization inherently supports more sustainable IT practices because efficiency improvements naturally cut down unnecessary resource use—the greenest computing is the computing you avoid altogether. Some companies are already incentivizing teams based on achieving sustainability goals. Just like FinOps teams set budget objectives, GreenOps teams might establish carbon-reduction targets. The combined approach of FinOps and GreenOps, often referred to as "Sustainable FinOps," promotes close collaboration between financial and sustainability teams. They share data and jointly advocate strategies such as scheduling workloads during off-peak periods, when renewable energy availability might be higher, or selecting data center regions known for lower carbon footprints.

In short, sustainability is quickly becoming a key factor in cloud optimization efforts. FinOps professionals are broadening their roles to incorporate sustainability, ensuring that financial optimization aligns closely with the overarching objective of sustainable IT.

6.13.2 Cross-Cloud Arbitrage and Multicloud FinOps

Another future trend is the rise of multicloud strategies, not just for resilience or vendor neutrality, but explicitly for cost optimization. We touched on multicloud cost optimization earlier (using different clouds for their cost advantages), but the future may amplify this with more real-time and automated decision-making across clouds. Think of it as cloud computing akin to the stock market—with organizations dynamically "trading" where their workloads run to get the best price-performance at any given time.

While few organizations today are dynamically shifting workloads across clouds day-to-day (it's complex and often not worth the effort manually), advances in containerization, Kubernetes, and cloud-agnostic workload platforms are laying the groundwork for this flexibility. For example, a company might deploy a Kubernetes cluster that spans multiple cloud providers or can redeploy on another cloud in hours. If one cloud provider has a significant price drop or a spot instance availability, an intelligent scheduler could move some workloads there.

AI will be a big enabler of cross-cloud arbitrage. As discussed, AI systems can analyze pricing and performance data across providers continuously. We can imagine an AI recommendation engine that says, "Given your last 30 days of usage, you could save 20% by shifting these specific workloads from Cloud X to Cloud Y." Or even more dynamically, "This week, provider A in region East has excess capacity deals on GPUs—move your training jobs there for the week." Some early signs of this are already visible in products and open-source projects aiming to make workloads portable. FinOps teams of the future might operate like commodity traders or portfolio managers, except the assets are compute, storage, and network capacity. They'll need to understand the market prices and trends of each major cloud and perhaps use broker platforms to purchase capacity in the most cost-effective way.

In addition, multicloud FinOps entails managing cost data and optimization across multiple platforms in a unified way. This is a challenge because each cloud has its own billing, its own discount options, etc. FinOps practices and tools are evolving to provide a single pane of glass for multicloud spend. For instance, companies are adopting tags and account structures that work across clouds and using third-party cost management platforms that aggregate data from Amazon Web Services (AWS), Azure, Google Cloud Platform (GCP), and others into one report. Policies and guardrails are being defined in a cloud-agnostic manner ("no VM over 4xlarge unless approved" regardless of cloud). The FinOps Foundation has even started work on cross-cloud comparison benchmarks, so companies can answer if their cost of running a workload on Cloud A is truly better or worse than Cloud B.

The motivation for cross-cloud arbitrage is straightforward: competitive pressure. If your competitor figures out how to consistently get 10–20% lower cloud unit costs by being smart about multicloud usage, they have an advantage—they can spend less for the same customer demand or invest those savings elsewhere. As tools and automation make multicloud easier, more companies will pursue this path. It's likely that cloud providers will respond with more innovative pricing models to retain workloads (we already see things like committed spend discounts and multi-year agreements as "loyalty" incentives). So FinOps teams will have to be increasingly savvy, almost playing clouds off each other to secure the best deals for their business.

In summary, multicloud cost optimization is moving from a niche strategy to a mainstream consideration. FinOps of the future may involve dynamic decisions about *where* to run a workload, not just *how* to run it, to optimize costs. The complexity is high, but so are the potential savings, especially for large-scale cloud users.

6.13.3 Decentralized Cloud and New Financial Models (FinOps 2.0?)

Among the more forward-leaning developments in FinOps is its growing overlap with decentralized technologies and evolving financial models. Several emerging trends are shaping how organizations might manage cloud costs in the coming years.

Decentralized Cloud Marketplaces: Beyond the major cloud providers, new platforms like Akash Network, Filecoin, and Golem are opening up marketplaces where anyone can offer compute or storage. Users pay with blockchain-based tokens, and providers compete on price. Akash, for instance, claims compute pricing that's 60–90% lower than traditional options. These systems are still emerging but could appeal to workloads suited for distributed environments—like batch processing or dev/test scenarios. It's easy to imagine FinOps teams eventually treating these decentralized networks as part of a broader, multicloud strategy—even if the model is quite different from what they're used to.

Cloud as a Commodity: There's speculation that compute resources might one day trade like electricity or oil. That would open the door to futures contracts and hedging strategies, allowing teams to lock in pricing across providers. While this isn't yet mainstream, the idea is already visible in smaller ways—AWS has a secondary market for reserved instances, and some third parties broker cloud capacity. Meanwhile, in the DeFi space, tokens representing compute or storage capacity have already been created. A FinOps lead might, in the not-so-distant future, purchase GPU capacity months in advance via financial instruments, just like commodities traders do today.

DeFi Mechanisms for Cloud Payments: Smart contracts and decentralized governance could offer new models for managing spending. A Decentralized Autonomous Organization (DAO) might control budget distribution, or a contract could halt cloud use once a limit is reached. While enterprise adoption of crypto-native systems is still rare, the principles—automation, built-in guardrails, and transparency—align closely with what FinOps seeks to achieve.

Tokenization of Internal Cloud Budgets: Some organizations are exploring ways to bring more tangible cost awareness into engineering teams. One idea involves issuing internal "cloud tokens" or credits that developers spend when using cloud services. These budgets reset quarterly and make cloud consumption more visible. While not technically decentralized finance, this approach borrows from token-based economics to build cost-conscious behaviors internally.

It's unclear which of these models will gain traction, but the broader message is clear: FinOps is expanding. Technical teams will need to understand not only usage and architecture but also economics and financial mechanics. In some ways, cloud spend is becoming a portfolio—one that includes on-demand, reserved, spot, and now potentially decentralized capacity. Spot instance bidding, for example, already mirrors market dynamics: flexible workloads snap up spare capacity at low cost, with the trade-off being preemption risk. That's cost arbitrage in practice.

Looking forward, the FinOps toolkit will continue to evolve. Sustainability efforts are weaving carbon awareness into optimization goals. AI-driven automation is reshaping how teams forecast and react. And decentralized infrastructure may challenge the very definition of what a "cloud provider" is.

Yet the mission stays the same: align cloud costs with business value, reduce waste, and foster accountability across teams. Tomorrow's FinOps won't just be about saving money; it will be about navigating a much more dynamic, interconnected ecosystem—effectively, creatively, and with a broader view of what optimization truly means.

6.14 Agentic AI Orchestration: The Next Frontier in FinOps

As cloud environments grow in complexity and FinOps practices mature, a new chapter is beginning—**Agentic AI for FinOps**. This emerging approach moves beyond scripted automation toward coordinated, intelligent systems that manage cloud costs dynamically and autonomously.

At the heart of this model are specialized AI agents, each tasked with a focused responsibility: forecasting, anomaly detection, rightsizing, sustainability alignment, or policy enforcement. These agents operate independently but within shared goals and policies, working together through a central orchestration layer to keep cloud usage efficient, compliant, and aligned with business value.

Consider a near-future scenario:

- A forecasting agent detects a potential budget overrun weeks in advance.
- It alerts a scheduling agent, which reshuffles non-critical workloads to run in lower-cost regions.
- A compliance agent validates the new plan against data residency and security policies.
- An execution agent applies the changes, and the FinOps dashboard reflects the action automatically.

This vision is already taking shape. Early examples include GenAI copilots that summarize spending or suggest optimization steps and multi-agent frameworks that coordinate decisions across cloud operations. The combination of real-time telemetry, programmable infrastructure, and self-improving agents is turning FinOps from a manual discipline into an intelligent, adaptive system.

For cloud teams and CTOs, the shift to agentic orchestration promises more than efficiency. It offers real-time agility, reduced operational burden, and a more direct link between cloud investment and business outcomes. As infrastructure becomes increasingly modular and API-driven, AI agents will evolve from advisors to trusted co-operators, managing cost, performance, and compliance at scale.

6.15 Conclusion

Cloud cost management is no longer just a technical problem—it's a leadership issue. What was once buried in the back office now sits squarely in the boardroom. The assumption that "cloud is always cheaper" has faded. Organizations have learned that without discipline, the cloud can just as easily become a source of runaway costs. FinOps has emerged as a response to that reality, tying together engineering, finance, and operations into one unified effort.

This chapter has explored how the shift to the cloud's consumption-based model introduced new complexity and how FinOps developed to address it. The discipline isn't just about saving money. It's about aligning how cloud is used with how value is created, building shared visibility, and encouraging collaboration between teams that don't always speak the same language. For engineering leaders and technology executives, FinOps is a reminder that cloud spend is something to be managed, not tolerated. It requires strategy, process, and, above all, participation. A few takeaways worth remembering:

FinOps Is a Team Sport: The organizations that see the most impact bring finance, engineering, and product together. When these groups understand and influence cloud spend, they make smarter choices. When cost decisions map directly to business goals, the cloud becomes a better investment.

The Lifecycle—Inform, Optimize, Operate: This isn't a checklist; it's a continuous process. Get your data right, use it to uncover inefficiencies, and then build cost awareness into daily operations. Repeat. There is no "done" in FinOps.

Go Deeper Than Surface-Level Savings: The easy wins—deleting unused resources, shutting down idle VMs—are just the start. Real value comes from redesigning systems, securing enterprise discounts, and knowing when a more efficient architecture makes more sense. These are engineering decisions with financial outcomes.

Let Intelligent Tools Do the Heavy Lifting: As infrastructure scales, AI and automation help detect issues before they become expensive problems. They're not here to replace humans—they help teams respond faster, see trends earlier, and work more proactively.

Case Studies Tell the Story Best: Across industries, organizations are saving 30–50% on the cloud by combining strong tools with stronger teamwork. The lesson? You need both. Technology helps, but the results come when teams shift their mindset.

Keep an Eye on What's Coming: Cloud cost optimization is evolving. It's starting to intersect with sustainability. It's expanding to multicloud environments, decentralized compute, and new types of financial instruments [15].

Learning Is Part of the Work: FinOps community exists to help you stay informed. At its core, FinOps is about turning cloud spend into business value. That means treating it with the same level of discipline and planning as any major investment. Maturity in the cloud isn't just about the applications you build—it's about how you run them, scale them, and pay for them wisely.

Building a FinOps Practice Takes Time: Start by making cloud spend visible. From there, build cost ownership into teams. Set goals that reflect real accountability. Celebrate the small wins—shutting down what's unused—but don't stop there.

Aim for Structural Changes: Cost-aware design decisions, OKRs tied to efficiency, and a culture that treats optimization as part of good engineering. When cloud costs are no longer someone else's problem, and everyone understands their role in managing them, the benefits compound.

That's the shift FinOps enables. In the end, cloud cost isn't just a line item; it's a story about how your organization builds, scales, and delivers value. FinOps helps you tell that story well—and turn it into a long-term advantage.

References

1 "The real source of cloud overspend? The shift from CapEx to OpEx," [Online]. Available: https://www.networkcomputing.com/cloud-networking/the-real-source-of-cloud-overspend-the-shift-from-capex-to-opex.

2 "FinOps 101: An intro to the basics of FinOps | cloudZero," [Online]. Available: https://www.cloudzero.com/guide/finops-101.

3 "About the FinOps foundation," [Online]. Available: http://www.finops.org/about/.

4 "FinOps principles," [Online]. Available: https://www.finops.org/framework/principles/.

5 "Using FinOps and cloud managed services to combat growing cloud costs," [Online]. Available: https://www.torryharris.com/insights/articles/finops-a-new-perspective-on-cloud-cost-management.

6 "FinOps phases," [Online]. Available: https://www.finops.org/framework/phases/.

7 "Think beyond rightsizing when it comes to cloud cost optimization," [Online]. Available: https://www.itprotoday.com/edge-computing/beyond-rightsizing-when-it-comes-to-cloud-cost-optimization-think-big.

8 "Optimizing cloud costs helps bank fund strategic IT initiatives | cognizant," [Online]. Available: https://www.cognizant.com/us/en/case-studies/optimizing-banking-cloud-costs.

9 "AI-Powered FinOps: 8 best practices for cloud cost optimization," [Online]. Available: https://www.nusummit.com/ai-powered-finops-best-practices-cloud-cost-optimization/.

10 "Juggling multiple clouds? How AI makes it manageable," [Online]. Available: https://www.linkedin.com/pulse/juggling-multiple-clouds-how-ai-makes-manageable-narayanan-cvcnc.

11 "Shifting cost optimisation left: Spotify backstage cost insights – James governor's Monkchips," [Online]. Available: https://redmonk.com/jgovernor/2021/04/28/shifting-cost-optimisation-left-spotify-backstage-cost-insights/.

12 "GreenOps, FinOps, and the sustainable cloud – Forrester," [Online]. Available: https://www.forrester.com/blogs/greenops-finops-and-the-sustainable-cloud/.

13 "Cloud sustainability and its intersection with FinOps," [Online]. Available: https://www.finops.org/wg/sustainability/.

14 "GreenOps vs. FinOps: What's the difference? – Hyperglance," [Online]. Available: https://www.hyperglance.com/blog/greenops-v-finops/.

15 "Akash network: Another protocol revolutionizing cloud computing," [Online]. Available: https://www.linkedin.com/pulse/akash-network-another-protocol-revolutionizing-cloud-computing-fidel-r0l2c.

7

FinOps for AI Workloads

Anaranya Bagchi

IEEE Senior Member, Seattle, WA, USA

7.1 Introduction

The rapid adoption of artificial intelligence (AI) across industries has ushered in a new era of opportunity and complexity in technology management. As organizations leverage AI to drive innovation, productivity, and customer value, the financial implications of these workloads have become increasingly significant. The discipline of financial operations (FinOps), which originated to optimize cloud spending and align technology costs with business objectives, is now evolving to meet the unique challenges presented by AI workloads [1]. This evolution presents an exciting opportunity for organizations to push the boundaries of what's possible with AI, driving innovation and productivity to new heights.

AI workloads, particularly those that involve large language models (LLMs), generative AI, and machine learning (ML), exhibit fundamental differences from traditional cloud applications regarding their resource consumption patterns and cost structures. Unlike conventional workloads, which are primarily billed based on compute hours or storage usage, AI services frequently introduce novel pricing models that depend on token consumption, model selection, and sporadic, unpredictable usage patterns [2]. This complexity complicates the ability of organizations to forecast, allocate, and optimize costs solely using legacy FinOps methodologies.

Recent industry analyses highlight the urgency of this shift. According to International Data Corporation (IDC), by 2027, 75% of organizations are expected to integrate FinOps practices with generative AI deployments to manage spending effectively [3]. The financial stakes are high: Gartner projects that global spending on generative AI will reach $644 billion in 2025, with cost management cited as a top challenge for enterprise adoption [4]. Without robust FinOps strategies, organizations risk inefficiencies, budget overruns, and missed opportunities to maximize the business value of their AI investments. This underscores the need for immediate action to implement updated FinOps practices.

Although AI and ML services have existed for years, their adoption has historically required extensive technical knowledge and considerable effort. Recent advancements from cloud providers and AI vendors have significantly simplified the deployment of generative AI, making it more accessible to a broader range of organizations. This increased user-friendliness has spurred rising demand for graphics processing unit (GPU)-based infrastructure, scalable cloud platforms, and professionals skilled in managing AI systems [4]. As a result, nontechnical teams—such as product, marketing, sales, and executive leadership—are now actively engaged in AI-related cloud spending. Meanwhile, the limited availability of GPUs has increased infrastructure instability, while the variety of AI deployment models and pricing frameworks introduces new challenges for FinOps practitioners as they work to understand usage, manage costs, and effectively evaluate business value.

The collaborative nature of FinOps represents a fundamental aspect in the contemporary context. It is imperative for the finance, engineering, product, and business teams to collaborate to ensure that investments in AI are both fiscally prudent and aligned with strategic objectives. As the adoption of AI accelerates, practitioners of FinOps are encouraged to expand their skill sets, embrace innovative tools, and cultivate a culture of transparency and accountability concerning expenditures on AI.

This chapter will examine the foundations, challenges, and best practices of FinOps for AI workloads, drawing upon the latest research, industry frameworks, and real-world case studies. By comprehending the nuances of AI cost drivers and implementing a tailored FinOps approach, organizations can unlock the full potential of AI while upholding financial discipline and driving measurable business value.

7.2 Types of AI Workloads and Cost Drivers

AI workloads can be effectively categorized by their operational characteristics and their place within the ML lifecycle. This classification is essential for both technical planning and financial management, as each workload type has distinct resource requirements, cost implications, and optimization strategies.

7.2.1 Types of AI Workloads

1) **Training Workloads:** Training workloads involve developing ML models by exposing algorithms to large datasets and iteratively adjusting their parameters

to minimize errors or maximize predictive accuracy. This process is computationally intensive, often requiring specialized hardware such as Graphical Processing Units (GPUs) or Tensor Processing Unit (TPUs), and can run for hours or days, depending on the model's complexity and the volume of data. Training is typically performed in batch mode and is a foundational step before any model can be deployed for inference.

Training AI models, intense learning, and large language models require substantial computational resources (often GPUs or TPUs) and can result in unpredictable, high costs. FinOps teams play a critical role in optimizing these expenses by leveraging reserved or spot instances, right-sizing hardware, and scheduling training jobs during off-peak hours to capitalize on lower rates.

2) **Inference Workloads:** Inference workloads refer to the deployment and use of trained models to generate predictions or classifications on new, unseen data. Inference can be further split into two main types:
   a) **Batch Inference:** Predictions are generated on large datasets at scheduled intervals (e.g., hourly, daily). This is common for use cases like generating periodic reports or scoring large customer datasets. Batch inference enables more predictable and scheduled resource allocation, facilitating cost optimization through capacity planning and automation.
   b) **Interactive Inference:** Predictions are generated in real time, responding to user or system requests with minimal latency. This is critical for applications such as fraud detection, recommendation systems, or conversational AI, where immediate feedback is necessary. Interactive inference requires always-on, scalable infrastructure, which can drive up costs if not carefully managed.
3) **Batch Workloads:** Batch workloads process data or perform computations in discrete chunks at scheduled times. In the context of AI, this often includes both batch training (periodic retraining of models with new data) and batch inference. Batch workloads are typically optimized for throughput and cost efficiency, making them suitable for nonurgent, large-scale processing tasks that require high volume and low latency.

   Batch workloads, encompassing data preprocessing and periodic retraining, may be scheduled during intervals of reduced cloud demand. This practice enables organizations to capitalize on discounted rates while optimizing resource utilization.
4) **Interactive Workloads:** Interactive workloads require immediate or low-latency responses, often driven by user or application interactions. Unpredictable traffic patterns and strict performance requirements characterize these workloads. Real-time inference and continual learning (where the model updates incrementally as new data arrives) are examples of interactive workloads.

Interactive workloads require low latency and high availability, which can lead to increased costs due to the need for over-provisioning or premium services. FinOps must balance performance requirements against financial constraints, utilizing monitoring and alerting to identify and address inefficiencies quickly.

5) **Pipeline Workloads:** Pipeline workloads, as well as machine learning workloads, encompass the orchestration, automation, and monitoring of the entire ML lifecycle. Machine learning operations (MLOps) pipelines facilitate the automation of the end-to-end AI lifecycle, which includes data ingestion, training, validation, deployment, and monitoring. FinOps plays a critical role in ensuring that each stage is optimized for cost efficiency, ranging from eliminating unused resources to automating model retirement and retraining.

7.2.2 Cost Drivers for AI Workloads

The financial profile of AI workloads is shaped by several distinct cost drivers, which vary in impact depending on whether the workload involves training, inference, batch processing, interactive tasks, or is part of an MLOps or pipeline process. Understanding these drivers is crucial for implementing effective FinOps practices and ensuring the sustainable deployment of AI.

1) **Compute Resources (GPUs, TPUs, CPUs)**
   - Training workloads are particularly compute-intensive, frequently necessitating thousands of GPU or TPU hours for large models. The costs associated with hardware, encompassing the acquisition or rental of high-performance accelerators in the cloud, represent the foremost expenses incurred during the training phase.
   - Inference workloads also necessitate specialized hardware; however, the associated costs are amortized across numerous prediction requests. In the context of large-scale, real-time inference, computational expenses may surpass those incurred during the model's training phase throughout its operational lifespan, particularly as user demand and data volumes escalate.
   - Batch and interactive workloads may exhibit distinct computational profiles. Batch jobs can be scheduled for cost efficiency, whereas interactive workloads necessitate continuously available, low-latency resources. This often results in elevated per-request costs.
2) **Data Storage and Processing**
   - Training and inference necessitate considerable storage resources for datasets, model checkpoints, and logs. Extensive datasets can substantially elevate storage expenses, particularly in the context of managing unstructured or high-frequency data streams. Model storage sprawl—from abandoned experiments or multiple model versions—can accumulate substantial hidden costs if not actively managed.

3) **Data Transfer and Networking**
   - The transfer of large datasets between storage units and computational resources and across various regions or cloud environments incurs data transfer fees. This consideration is especially pertinent in the context of distributed training, hybrid cloud configurations, or the servicing of global inference requests. For example, transfer of data between regions or between two different clouds can be costly.
   - Cross-regional or multi-cloud deployments can considerably augment networking expenses, particularly for latency-sensitive interactive workloads.
4) **Vendor and Platform Fees**
   - Proprietary models and managed AI platforms (e.g., OpenAI, Amazon Web Services [AWS] Bedrock) often charge by API call, token processed, or compute time, with significant cost variance across providers and models.
   - Vendor lock-in can result in higher long-term costs due to limited portability and reduced negotiation leverage.

The implementation of generative AI (Gen AI) has resulted in the development of a comprehensive technology stack of services offered by major cloud providers, designed to accommodate a diverse array of use cases. Similar to any technology stack, Gen AI services are constructed by integrating various components that are customized to meet the particular requirements of specific use cases as given in Table 7.1. The available options span from entirely self-managed and self-hosted hardware to fully managed AI services provided by cloud or third-party vendors.

7.3 FinOps Principles Applied to AI

FinOps principles provide a structured framework for managing the financial complexity of AI. The tenets of FinOps offer a systematic framework for navigating the financial complexities associated with AI workloads. By tailoring these principles to address the distinct requirements of AI, including fluctuating resource consumption, specific hardware necessities, and dynamic pricing models, organizations can attain cost transparency, accountability, and sustainable innovation. Consumption, specialized hardware needs, and evolving pricing models enable organizations to achieve cost transparency, accountability, and sustainable innovation.

As shown in Figure 7.1, the FinOps Framework, with AI added as a scope for the year 2025, is illustrated below.

Although managing AI costs may initially be viewed as entirely novel, filled with unfamiliar terminology and concepts, FinOps practitioners will acknowledge that numerous similarities exist with other managed services. Additionally, various

Table 7.1 Mapping of AI service names by the top cloud providers.

GenAI Category	GenAI Component	Amazon Web Services (AWS)	Google Cloud	Microsoft Azure
Foundation models	Runtime	Amazon Bedrock	Vertex AI	Azure OpenAI
	Text/Chat	Amazon Bedrock	PaLM	GPT
	Code	Amazon Q, Amazon Bedrock	Codey	GPT
	Image Generation	Amazon Bedrock	Imagen	DALL-E
	Translation	Amazon Bedrock	Chirp	None
Model catalog	Commercial	Amazon SageMaker AI, Amazon Bedrock Marketplace	Vertex AI Model Garden	Azure ML Foundation Models
	Open Source	Amazon SageMaker AI, Amazon Bedrock Marketplace	Vertex AI Model Garden	Azure ML Hugging Face
Vector database	—	Amazon Kendra, Amazon OpenSearch Service, and Amazon RDS for PostgreSQL with pgvector	Cloud SQL (pgvector)	Azure Cosmos DB, Azure Cache
Model deployment and inference	—	Amazon SageMaker AI and Amazon Bedrock	Vertex AI	Azure ML
Fine-tuning	—	Amazon SageMaker AI and Amazon Bedrock	Vertex AI	Azure OpenAI
Low-code/ No-code development	—	AWS App Studio and Amazon SageMaker AI Unified Studio	Gen App Builder	Power Apps
Code completion	—	Amazon Q Developer	Duet AI for Google Cloud	GitHub Copilot

Source: [5] / FinOps Foundation Project a Series of LF Projects / CC BY-4.0.

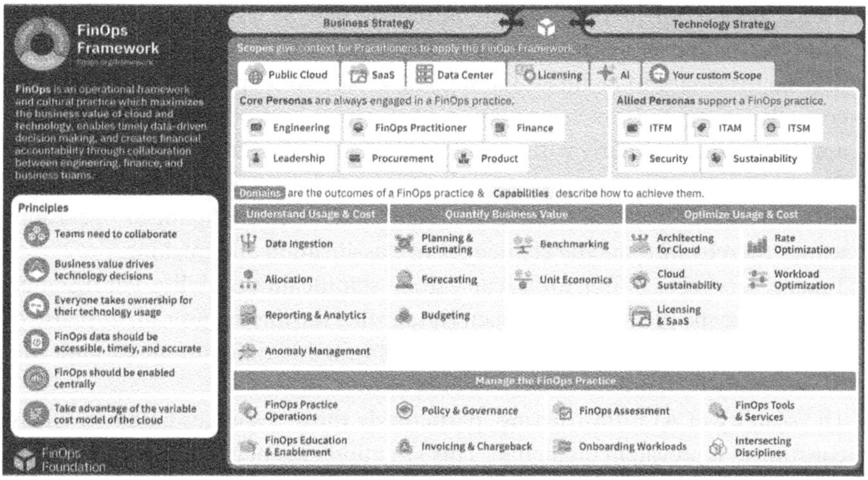

Figure 7.1 FinOps framework 2025. *Source:* [6] / FinOps Foundation Project a Series of LF Projects / CC BY-4.0.

elements of contemporary FinOps practices can already be employed to oversee the costs and usage of generative AI effectively.

Similarities:

- The fundamental equation price × quantity = cost remains applicable. Costs can be managed by either reducing the price (rate) or decreasing the quantity of resources consumed.
- Cloud-based AI service costs are reflected in cloud billing data alongside other cloud services. However, alternative data ingestion methods may need to be considered for services sourced from noncloud vendors or AI-specific observability systems.
- Tagging or labeling can be applied to many cloud services to enable cost allocation. Nevertheless, modifications may be necessary when dealing with shared environments, training workloads, or API-driven resources.
- Numerous components of AI services are eligible for commitment-based discounts (such as Reservations). The processes involved in rate management are mainly consistent with those used for traditional cloud services.

Differences:

- AI models and services often exhibit inconsistent pricing structures and are frequently offered in multiple versions or variants, leading to significant price fluctuations. An example from AWS is Amazon SageMaker, which offers multiple model deployment options—such as real-time endpoints, batch transform, and asynchronous inference—each with different pricing models.

- Cloud service providers frequently introduce new SKUs, many of which lack sufficient native support for tagging. Consequently, custom engineering tools may be necessary to facilitate the tagging of key-value pairs for cost tracking, cost allocation, and the computation of the total cost of ownership (TCO) of applications, particularly within multi-tenant environments.
- The naming conventions and service types associated with AI workloads may substantially differ from those traditionally managed by financial operations teams, thereby introducing challenges in classification and tracking.
- Tokens, serving as billing units, can exhibit significant variability. For instance, charges may be predicated on tokens quantified during the user input phase or upon a compressed and semantically transformed iteration of the prompt that is ultimately transmitted to the API endpoint.
- The scarcity of AI infrastructure, particularly those resources based on GPUs, constitutes a prevalent challenge. This situation engenders limitations in both availability and pricing, thereby necessitating the adoption of capacity management techniques. Such techniques encompass contractual commitments, orchestration strategies, and specialized purchasing methods—approaches that are less frequently requisite in conventional cloud environment services.

FinOps domains shown in Figure 7.1 are the outcomes of a FinOps practice, and the capabilities describe how to achieve them.

Below is a breakdown of how the four FinOps domains apply to AI:

Understand Usage and Cost: Effectively managing AI workloads within financial operations commences with a comprehensive approach to comprehending usage and expenditure. This process encompasses not only monitoring consumption and expenditure but also analyzing data flow through the system, attributing costs appropriately, reporting insights accurately, and identifying and rectifying anomalies. The following outlines how these key capabilities are applicable in the context of AI.

- **Ingestion:** The first step involves ingesting detailed usage and cost data from various sources, including cloud providers, AI service APIs, and internal systems. For AI workloads, this means capturing metrics such as GPU/TPU hours, token/API usage, storage consumption, and data transfer volumes. Modern FinOps for AI relies on near-real-time ingestion pipelines, enabling organizations to monitor usage spikes or cost anomalies as they occur, rather than waiting for delayed billing cycles to occur.
- **Allocation:** Implementing an effective tagging strategy is essential for the organization and tracking of resources in relation to projects, teams, or specific AI workloads. Although tagging is frequently utilized for cost

allocation, in this context, it enhances visibility regarding resource consumption. This practice ensures that each dollar expended can be traced to its origin [7].

By allocating costs to specific experiments, models, or business units, organizations foster accountability and facilitate showback or chargeback models. This is particularly vital for AI, where workloads can swiftly scale and encompass multiple teams or departments. Effective allocation supports anomaly detection by enabling the precise pinpointing of unexpected costs, down to the workload, user, or environment [8].

- **Reporting and Analytics:** Reporting mechanisms, encompassing dashboards and automated reports, present stakeholders with a comprehensive and up-to-date overview of AI resource utilization and expenditures. FinOps practitioners can employ cloud-native services or third-party FinOps tools to define, categorize, and analyze data across various teams, models, and projects, thereby facilitating the identification of cost drivers and usage patterns.
- **Anomaly Management:** Anomaly detection is of paramount importance in FinOps for AI, as it empowers organizations to swiftly identify unconventional fluctuations or declines in resource utilization and expenses. By utilizing real-time monitoring and ML methodologies, teams can automatically flag deviations from typical expenditure patterns, such as unforeseen GPU usage or token consumption, prior to the occurrence of budgetary overspend. Timely alerts facilitate prompt investigation and response, enabling teams to rectify misconfigurations, inefficiencies, or security vulnerabilities. In conclusion, effective anomaly detection not only preserves financial integrity but also enhances ongoing optimization in alignment with the increasing demands of AI workloads change.

Quantify Business Value: Quantifying business value in FinOps for AI entails establishing a connection between expenditures and outcomes. This is achieved through planning and estimation processes aimed at predicting requirements, as well as budgeting and forecasting mechanisms designed to set and monitor financial objectives. Additionally, unit economics plays a crucial role in determining the cost associated with each business result, such as the cost per prediction. Conducting benchmarking against internal or industry standards is essential to ensuring that both performance and expenditure remain competitive. Collectively, these methodologies empower organizations to substantiate their investments in AI and illustrate their influence on overarching business goals.

- **Planning and Estimation:** To achieve a detailed cost modeling framework, it is essential to decompose AI workloads into fundamental components, specifically data preparation, training, and inference. Subsequently, one

Table 7.2 Cost comparison for sentiment analysis workloads.

Platform/Model	Monthly Cost (12 h/day)
OpenAI GPT-4 8K	$2,700
Amazon Bedrock Claude 2	$1,183

Source: [1] / FinOps Foundation Project a Series of LF Projects / CC BY-4.0.

should estimate the associated costs for each phase by utilizing historical data alongside vendor pricing models. A comparative analysis of costs across various deployment models, such as software-as-a-service (SaaS) versus self-hosted solutions, can be conducted employing tools like spreadsheets or code-based estimators. An example is given in Table 7.2.

- **Budgets and Forecasting:** Establish mechanisms for continuous improvement by incorporating feedback loops into your FinOps processes. Regularly review cost trends, optimization efforts, and business outcomes to refine strategies. For instance, after conducting an analysis of cost spikes observed in prior deployments, formulate actionable policies to avert similar issues in the future. Continuous improvement guarantees that your FinOps practices evolve in tandem with your AI strategy technology.
- **Unit Economics:** In the context of FinOps for AI, unit economics pertains to the measurement of the costs and value associated with each activity, including predictions or user queries. This approach enables organizations to meticulously track their expenditures in order to accurately achieve specific business outcomes. By deconstructing costs to such a granular level, organizations can identify which AI workloads or features are genuinely profitable or delivering value, as well as discern which are contributing to unnecessary expenses. For instance, if an AI chatbot incurs a cost of $2,000 per month and processes 1 million queries, the unit cost per query is thus determined to be $0.002.
- **Benchmarking:** Benchmarking is the process of comparing essential performance and cost metrics, such as cost per prediction or GPU utilization, across internal teams or against industry standards to evaluate efficiency and value. By establishing clear benchmarks, organizations can identify areas where their AI workloads may be underperforming or incurring excessive costs, set realistic performance targets, and promote continuous improvement. Practitioners should define relevant key performance indicators (KPIs), automate data collection, and employ dashboards to transparently communicate results, thus fostering a culture of accountability and constructive engagement competition.

Optimizing Usage and Cost: Optimizing the usage and cost associated with AI workloads necessitates the design of cloud architectures that scale efficiently. This involves employing workload optimization techniques such as model pruning and batch processing, as well as securing the most advantageous rates through the utilization of spot or reserved instances. Furthermore, it entails the selection of sustainable deployment options to minimize environmental impact and the active management of SaaS and licensing to prevent unnecessary expenditures. Collectively, these practices enable organizations to extract maximum value from their AI investments while simultaneously managing costs and reducing their carbon footprints.

- **Architecting for the Cloud:** Optimize resource allocation by strategically utilizing features such as auto-scaling and spot instances when available. For instance, leverage auto-scaling to dynamically adjust the number of GPU instances in accordance with real-time demand for your generative model API.

  Data that is infrequently accessed should be stored in cost-effective cold storage solutions, such as S3 Glacier or Azure Archive, while frequently accessed data should be maintained on high-performance storage systems. It is advisable to regularly review and automate data tiering processes to prevent incurring unnecessary expenses associated with high-tier storage alternatives.

  To enhance model optimization, techniques such as pruning, quantization, and distillation should be employed to minimize model size and computational requirements, thereby facilitating faster and more cost-effective deployments without compromising accuracy.

  For workloads that are sporadic or experimental in nature, it is recommended to utilize serverless solutions, such as AWS Lambda or Azure Functions, allowing for payment solely based on usage, thus reducing costs and operational overhead.

  Appropriate hardware should be selected for your models, including AWS Inferentia, TPUs, or NVIDIA GPUs. Furthermore, edge computing should be utilized for low-latency requirements, non-real-time requests should be processed in batches, and frameworks such as ONNX or TensorRT should be leveraged to maximize inference efficiency costs. [5]
- **Rate Optimization:** Leverage reserved instances and commitment plans to achieve significant savings compared to on-demand pricing. Analyze usage patterns to utilize reserved instances and commitment plans, achieving substantial savings compared to on-demand pricing. Analyze usage patterns to enable informed decision-making regarding capacity reservations.

When training or inference workloads are predictable, it is advisable to commit to GPU capacity reservations in advance. This practice ensures availability and significantly mitigates the risk of resource scarcity while also securing enhanced performance pricing.

Purchase commitments specific to AI—such as advance discounts on API usage (e.g., OpenAI's Scale Tier)—should be thoroughly explored and evaluated. In light of the swift progression of pricing models in the AI sector, it is essential to conduct regular reviews of new offers from cloud service providers to identify potential savings opportunities. For instance, Azure has recently launched monthly pay-as-you-go token units (PTU), which enhance flexibility beyond the previously mandated annual commitment [9].

Conduct an analysis of historical and projected usage patterns to ascertain whether reserved instances (RIs), savings plans, or committed use discounts (CUDs) provide a cost advantage relative to on-demand pricing models. For example, a 1-year reservation for GPU instances may result in substantial savings for continuous model training requirements, particularly when precise workload forecasting is difficult. Furthermore, broader commitment options, including savings plans or flexible CUDs, present the advantage of applying discounts across multiple instance-type services.

- **Workload Optimization:** AI workloads require significant computing power and dynamic resource management, making cost and efficiency critical concerns. AI workloads necessitate substantial computing power and dynamic resource management, rendering cost and efficiency pivotal concerns for organizations. As the adoption of AI increases, optimizing these workloads—by aligning resources with actual needs and mitigating waste—becomes imperative for maximizing performance and controlling expenditures. Aligning resources with actual needs and preventing waste is essential for maximizing performance and controlling expenses.

Continuously ensure that AI workloads are deployed on the most appropriate instance size and type. It is advisable to utilize smaller graphics processing units for inference whenever feasible, transition to central processing units for lightweight models, and regularly analyze utilization metrics to prevent overprovisioning and underutilization [10].

Establish stringent usage restrictions and quotas regarding API calls, token consumption, and GPU utilization in order to manage expenses and avert unforeseen surges in resource consumption. Implement throttling mechanisms for noncritical workloads during peak hours and in conjunction with anomaly detection tools to swiftly identify and resolve atypical consumption patterns. These practices are substantiated by research demonstrating that dynamic resource allocation and proactive workload management—utilizing AI-driven or automated systems—can considerably enhance cost efficiency and operational stability within cloud and AI environments. [11].

The optimization of prompts represents a pivotal strategy for minimizing the operational costs associated with AI models, particularly those that employ token-based pricing mechanisms, such as LLMs. Through the development of concise, clear, and targeted prompts, organizations are able to reduce superfluous token utilization and improve the efficiency of each API call, thereby yielding a direct reduction in expenses. [12].

- **Cloud Sustainability:** Sustainability in FinOps for AI is centered on minimizing the environmental impact of AI workloads while concurrently optimizing costs and performance. This encompasses strategies such as carbon-aware resource allocation, selection of energy-efficient hardware, and the scheduling of workloads during periods of low-carbon energy availability.
- **Licensing and SaaS:** Optimizing licensing and SaaS within FinOps for AI entails meticulous monitoring of software utilization, the removal of redundant or underutilized subscriptions, and ensuring that acquisitions correspond with genuine requirements. Periodic assessments and the deployment of automated tools are instrumental in recognizing opportunities for cost savings, averting excessive expenditures, and guaranteeing that each license provides significant value to the organization.

Manage the FinOps Practice: The management of the FinOps practice necessitates the regular assessment of your organization's FinOps maturity, the implementation of transparent chargeback processes to effectively allocate costs, and the establishment of robust policies and governance to guide financial decisions. The utilization of dedicated FinOps tools automates reporting and optimizations, while ongoing education assures that all teams comprehend and apply FinOps best practices. Collectively, these endeavors foster a disciplined, transparent, and collaborative approach to financial management in the realms of cloud and AI management.

7.4 Challenges in FinOps for AI Workloads

Managing FinOps for AI workloads is significantly more complex than traditional cloud cost management due to unpredictable cost patterns, specialized infrastructure needs, and evolving pricing models. Some common challenges are described below:

- Managing FinOps for AI workloads presents unique and intricate challenges when compared to traditional cloud cost management. With the rapid acceleration of AI adoption, organizations face novel challenges in forecasting, allocating, and optimizing costs, stemming from the dynamic nature of AI workloads, specific infrastructure requirements, and evolving pricing models. The following outlines some of the primary challenges that practitioners face when implementing FinOps principles in AI environments.

- **Volatile and Unpredictable Cost Patterns:** AI workloads, particularly those involving large language models and generative AI, often exhibit unpredictable bursts, resulting in sudden spikes in GPU usage and costs that are challenging to forecast or control [12].
- **Inefficient GPU Utilization and Scarcity:** The elevated costs and restricted availability of GPUs necessitate effective resource optimization. However, the presence of idle or underutilized GPUs may swiftly result in considerable waste and excessive expenditures. [13].
- **Complex and Evolving Cost Structures:** AI services introduce new pricing models (such as token-based billing) and diverse infrastructure layers, making it challenging to understand, predict, and manage costs across the stack.
- **Lack of Granular Cost Allocation Tools:** Many AI workloads run on managed services or specialized hardware where traditional tagging and cost tracking are limited or unavailable, complicating accurate cost attribution and showback/chargeback [14].
- **Multi-Cloud and Hybrid Complexity:** Managing AI workloads across multiple cloud providers increases operational complexity and the difficulty of tracking and optimizing costs at scale.
- **Cross-Functional Impact:** AI-driven cloud expenses now affect a broader range of teams, including product, marketing, and leadership, making governance, education, and collaboration more challenging and essential for effective FinOps [14].
- **Rapid Pace of Change and Lack of Standardized Benchmarking:** The rapid evolution of AI technologies, combined with the absence of standardized benchmarks, makes it challenging to measure business value, optimize spending, and compare performance across teams or providers.
- **Need for Real-Time Monitoring and Automation:** Traditional monthly cost reports and manual processes are insufficient; organizations require real-time cost alerting, automated resource management, and dynamic forecasting to keep up with AI workload demands.

7.5 Conclusion

In conclusion, FinOps for AI workloads constitutes an evolving discipline that necessitates the implementation of novel strategies, tools, and cross-functional collaboration to effectively address the unique financial complexities associated with contemporary AI systems. As AI and generative AI adoption accelerate, organizations can no longer rely on traditional cloud cost management methods. With the average company spending 30% more on the cloud than last year—mainly due to these new workloads—businesses must embrace real-time visibility, precise allocation, and continuous optimization to keep costs aligned with business value.

The challenges—ranging from unpredictable usage patterns and intricate pricing models to resource scarcity and rapid technological advancements—demand a proactive, data-driven approach grounded in core FinOps principles. By integrating robust assessment mechanisms, governance frameworks, automation, and educational initiatives into their FinOps practices, organizations can not only manage costs effectively but also foster innovation, sustainability, and measurable business outcomes stemming from their AI investments. This comprehensive approach guarantees that as AI workloads scale and diversify, financial operations remain agile, transparent, and closely aligned with organizational objectives and goals.

References

1 B. Eubanks et al, "Cost estimation of AI workloads," [Online]. Available: https://www.finops.org/wg/cost-estimation-of-ai-workloads/.

2 R. Dilallo, "Managing Azure OpenAI costs with the FinOps toolkit and FOCUS: Turning tokens into unit economics," [Online]. Available: https://techcommunity.microsoft.com/blog/finopsblog/managing-azure-openai-costs-with-the-finops-toolkit-and-focus-turning-tokens-int/4413886.

3 IDC FutureScape, "Worldwide developer and DevOps 2025 predictions," [Online]. Available: https://my.idc.com/research/viewtoc.jsp?containerId=US52623424.

4 Gartner, "Gartner forecasts worldwide GenAI spending to reach $644 Billion in 2025," [Online]. Available: https://www.gartner.com/en/newsroom/press-releases/2025-03-31-gartner-forecasts-worldwide-genai-spending-to-reach-644-billion-in-2025.

5 B. Eubanks, *et al.*, "FinOps for AI overview," [Online]. Available: https://www.finops.org/wg/finops-for-ai-overview/.

6 FinOps Foundation, "FinOps framework," [Online]. Available: https://www.finops.org/wp-content/uploads/2025/05/English-FinOps-Framework-2025.pdf.

7 FinOps Foundation, "State of FinOps 2025 report," [Online]. Available: https://data.finops.org/.

8 FinOps Foundation, "Anomaly management," [Online]. Available: https://www.finops.org/framework/capabilities/anomaly-management/.

9 Microsoft Azure, "Azure OpenAI service pricing," [Online]. Available: https://azure.microsoft.com/en-us/pricing/details/cognitive-services/openai-service/.

10 H. Davé, "Why it's time to embrace FinOps for AI," [Online]. Available: https://www.kyndryl.com/us/en/perspectives/articles/2025/05/finops-for-ai-and-gen-ai.

11 S. Ghasemi, N. Poddar, M. H. Karim, and A. Pashazadeh, "Optimizing scalable online services: A dynamic resource allocation approach utilizing artificial intelligence," [Online] Available: at SSRN: https://ssrn.com/abstract=4825737.

12 B. Eubanks *et al.*, "Effect of optimization on AI forecasting," [Online]. Available: https://www.finops.org/wg/optimizing-genai-usage/.

13 P. Kurra, "Role of AI in cloud cost optimization and FinOps (Financial Operations)," [Online]. Available: https://journalwjaets.com/sites/default/files/fulltext_pdf/WJAETS-2025-0218.pdf.

14 P. R. Yakkanti, "AI-enabled FinOps for cloud cost optimization: Enhancing financial governance in cloud environments," *Eur. J. Comput. Sci. Inf. Technol.*, vol. 13, no. 11, pp. 17–29, 2025. [Online] Available: https://eajournals.org/ejcsit/wp-content/uploads/sites/21/2025/05/AI-Enabled-FinOps.pdf.

8

AI-Driven Cloud Services and Intelligence Automation

Prashanthi Matam and Venkata Naga Kartik Pidatala

Independent Researcher, Mountlake Terrace, WA, USA

8.1 Introduction

Cloud computing has become a key tool for digital transformation in almost every business in the last several years. Cloud services have completely transformed how organizations build, deploy, and manage applications and services by giving them IT infrastructure that is on-demand, scalable, and adaptable. Companies today use cloud platforms to be more flexible in their operations, save money, and get products to market faster. With cloud ecosystems getting complex and dispersed, hybrid and multicloud architectures increasingly gaining ground, there is an urgent necessity to have innovative mechanisms for managing and enhancing these ecosystems [1].

In this regard, artificial intelligence (AI) is emerging as an effective instrument to enhance the nature of the cloud computing capability further. A merging of AI and cloud services has produced AI-driven cloud services. These services have highly effective AI algorithms, machine learning (ML) models, and data analytics to enable automating and enhancing cloud operations. With the help of AI, cloud platforms have the potential to predict the evolution of demands, the optimal utilization of resources, detect and eliminate security risks before a crisis can occur, and automatically establish solutions to system malfunctions. This interface ensures that the cloud deployments are reliable, secure, and efficient simultaneously.

Intelligent automation, which refers to the automation of cloud management tasks that are both repetitive and rule-based and complex processes, is associated with this change. Smart cloud automation reduces the glue factor, reduces errors, hastens deployment cycles, and builds infrastructures that are capable of repairing themselves as they can diagnose and repair themselves. These characteristics are very crucial in facilitating the use of continuous delivery models and ensuring that service-level agreements (SLAs) are not breached at any time [2].

This chapter aims to offer a comprehensive glimpse of the world of AI-based cloud services and intelligent automation. Introductory, we begin by examining some of the fundamental technologies on which this convergence lies, including cloud-native architectures, microservices, containerization, and the AI approaches that are fueling automation and decision-making. We will then discuss practical, real-world AI applications that enhance the advantages of provisioning, security, monitoring, and management of cloud resources. The chapter also discusses the concepts of new chapters in AI, such as generative AI and agentic AI, which are soon going to transform cloud service design and operation itself.

In a large measure, cloud computing has transformed the world of IT, so that one can now provide computer resources of unparalleled scalability, flexibility, and affordability. The use of clouds has even skyrocketed ever since companies were introduced to their use in the mid-2000s. This is because businesses need to speed up innovation, save costs, and make their operations more flexible. Gartner says that by 2025, more than 85% of businesses will have a cloud-first strategy. This demonstrates that cloud computing is relevant in any type of business digital transformation initiative. Meanwhile, the development of intense AI has brought about an era of intelligent automation where computers have ML models, natural language processing (NLP), and autonomous agents that supplement human skills and perform challenging tasks.

8.1.1 The Journey to AI-Driven Cloud Services

At first, cloud computing only offered basic virtualization services that let numerous tenants safely share physical hardware. Over time, this turned into a large network of Infrastructure-as–a-Service (IaaS), Platform-as-a-Service (PaaS), and Software-as-a-Service (SaaS) services. But when businesses moved important workloads to the cloud and started using hybrid and multicloud methods, cloud systems became very complicated, often changing, and hard to manage manually. Because of this complexity and the need for fast deployment and high dependability, cloud management solutions need to be smarter and more automated. Enter AI: AI models can discover trends, find problems, forecast resource demands, and automate decision-making by using the huge volumes of telemetry and operational data that cloud systems create. Gartner thinks that by 2024, AI-powered technologies will be able to handle 75% of cloud infrastructure and platform operations on their own. This change is not only making cloud services more efficient and secure, but it is also letting companies come up with new ideas quicker by freeing up human specialists from boring, error-prone jobs [3].

The AI-driven cloud services architecture is shown in Figure 8.1.

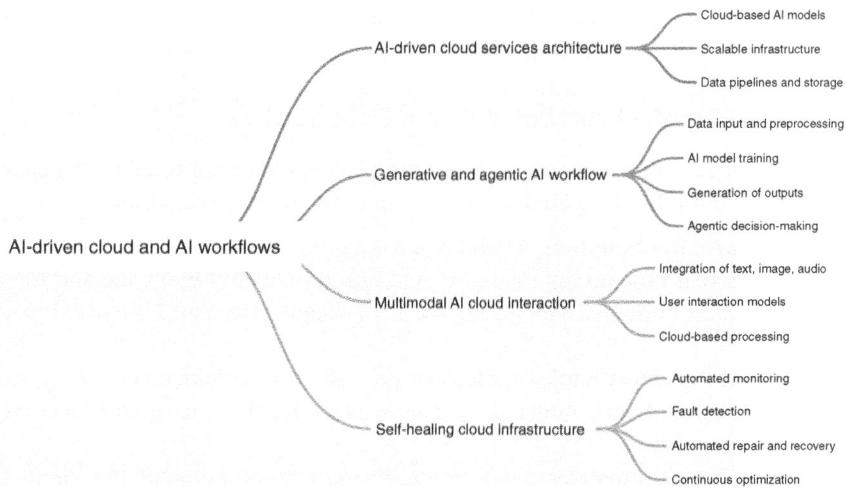

Figure 8.1 The AI-driven cloud services architecture.

8.1.2 Challenges Driving AI Adoption in Cloud Environments

Despite its promise, managing modern cloud infrastructures presents numerous challenges that fuel the adoption of AI-driven automation:

- Scale and Complexity: Cloud environments are made up of hundreds of services, containers, virtual machines (VMs), and network parts that are all linked together. Managing things by hand is prone to mistakes and can't keep up with the fast changes.
- Dynamic Workloads: Dynamic workloads in applications need to be handled with elastic scaling and real-time re-allocations of resources in order to balance costs and performance.
- Security Threats: The cyber threats charged against the cloud platform are continually developing. Detection before a threat and automated response to these incidents is the most important method to safeguard information and services.
- Compliance Requirement: Organizations will need to constantly check cloud resources in terms of whether they are compliant with complicated regulatory requirements like General Data Protection Regulation (GDPR), Health Insurance Portability and Accountability Act (HIPAA), and Payment Card Industry Data Security Standard (PCI DSS).
- Cost Control: Cloud expenses can easily grow out of control when unintelligent cost control and optimization are not put in place.

The ML capabilities of AI-driven cloud services are designed to overcome all these pain areas: resource provisioning, workload orchestration, security protection, compliance audit, and cost management, thus allowing businesses to run resilient, efficient, and secure cloud infrastructure across scale [4].

8.1.3 The Broader Impact of AI-Driven Cloud Services

This convergence of AI and cloud computing has not been confined to IT departments only, but it has triggered innovation in other areas. For example:

- **Healthcare:** By combining AI and cloud computing, companies will be able to use scaled real-time access to analyze video and images of medicine and information about patients, which will speed up diagnostics and individual treatment.
- **Financial Services:** Banks implement the use of AI-enhanced cloud services in detecting fraud, modeling risk, and algorithmic trading with greater accuracy and faster execution.
- **Retail:** The e-commerce businesses use smart automation of the cloud in demand forecasting, price flexibility, and supply chain.

Integrating AI intelligence into the cloud platform enables organizations to achieve new business models, customer experiences, and timing, adjusting to market requirements.

8.2 Evolution of Cloud Computing: From Virtualization to Cloud-Native Architectures

Virtualization was the initial milestone toward advanced cloud computing, as it allows multiple VMs to run on the same physical server and decouples software and hardware. The concept opened a possibility to utilize better hardware and more elastic allocation of resources. Some of the early cloud providers that made use of virtualization to develop their infrastructure include Amazon Web Services (AWS), Google Cloud Platform (GCP), and Microsoft Azure. That enabled them to offer IaaS, which enables you to scale your computation and storage to your needs [5].

However, when more users began putting the cloud into use, it was when the shortcomings of the VM-based systems were evident. Growing and sustaining monolithic apps on VMs in ever-evolving settings were difficult to develop. This spawned the cloud-native architectures, which are the practices that enable the applications to perform better in the cloud.

Cloud-native revolves around the microservices architecture (MSA) concept. However, microservices divide programs into small, less closely joined services, which can be used separately and communicate with each other by Application Programming Interface (APIs). This mellow approach facilitates flexibility,

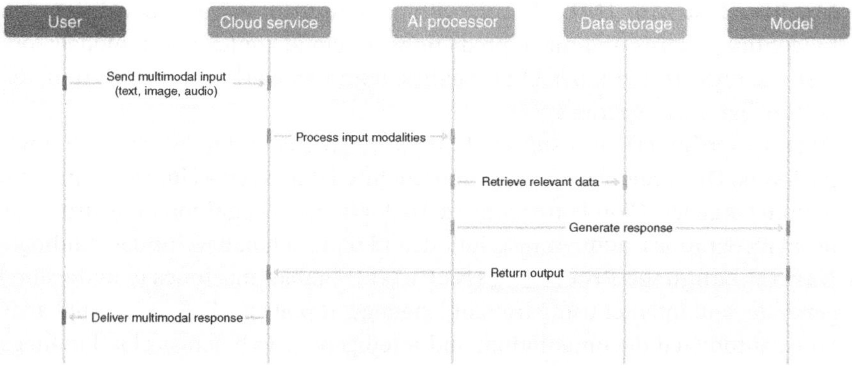

Figure 8.2 The multimodal AI cloud interaction.

expansion, and bug-free code. A case example is Netflix, which is one of the pioneers of microservices in order to deliver very scalable and reliable streaming services on AWS to millions of users worldwide.

Containerization (the grouping of software and its dependencies in lightweight, portable containers, also known as containerization) is related to microservices. One of those tools is Docker, and it transformed the way that software is delivered, ensuring that development, testing, and production environments were kept identical. Containers also make better use of resources as compared to regular VMs [6].

Container orchestration solutions like Kubernetes came along to help manage containers on a large scale. They automate the deployment, scalability, and maintenance of containerized applications. Kubernetes makes self-healing, load balancing, and rolling upgrades easier, which are all important for cloud-native operations that can withstand problems.

FaaS, often known as serverless computing, is the most recent change. It totally abstracts infrastructure issues so that developers may concentrate only on code. Cloud providers only dynamically assign resources while functions are running, which saves money and makes the service more scalable.

These improvements, such as virtualization, microservices, containerization, orchestration, and serverless, are the building blocks of current cloud infrastructures. They make it possible for AI systems to work well in settings that may grow and change.

Figure 8.2 shows how multimodal AI may interact with the cloud.

8.2.1 Core AI Technologies Empowering Cloud Services

The explosion of data generated by cloud applications, infrastructure telemetry, and user interactions forms a rich substrate for artificial intelligence. Several AI subfields are instrumental in transforming cloud services:

- **Machine Learning (ML):** ML algorithms analyze historical and real-time data to identify patterns and make predictions. In cloud contexts, ML models forecast resource demand, detect anomalies, optimize workload distribution, and personalize user experiences.
- **Deep Learning (DL):** A subset of ML leveraging neural networks with multiple layers, DL excels at processing unstructured data such as images, voice, and natural language. Cloud providers use DL for image recognition in security (e.g., facial recognition), audio transcription, and natural language understanding.
- **Natural Language Processing (NLP):** NLP enables machines to understand, generate, and interact using human language. It powers chatbots, virtual assistants, automated documentation, and intelligent search across cloud management portals.
- **Reinforcement Learning (RL):** RL trains AI agents to make sequential decisions by learning through trial-and-error interactions with the environment. RL is used in cloud operations for dynamic resource allocation, autoscaling policies, and optimizing energy consumption.
- **Generative AI:** Recent breakthroughs in generative models like transformers enable the creation of new content, from code snippets and infrastructure templates to technical documentation and even synthetic data. This accelerates software development and cloud provisioning.

Cloud vendors now offer AI-as-a-Service platforms, democratizing access to these AI capabilities. For example, Google's Vertex AI, AWS SageMaker, and Microsoft Azure ML provide tools to build, train, deploy, and manage ML models seamlessly on cloud infrastructure [7].

8.2.2 Intelligent Automation Principles in Cloud Ecosystems

Intelligent automation integrates AI capabilities with workflow and process automation frameworks to orchestrate cloud service management efficiently. It encompasses the following key principles:

- **Robotic Process Automation (RPA):** RPA employs software "robots" to perform repetitive, rule-based tasks traditionally done by humans. Within cloud operations, RPA automates provisioning, configuration management, and routine maintenance, reducing manual errors and operational overhead.
- **Event-Driven Automation:** Cloud environments generate massive event streams—from log files, performance metrics, and security alerts. Intelligent automation tools process these events in real time to trigger automated responses. For example, an event signaling a sudden Central Processing Unit (CPU) spike might trigger automatic scaling of resources.

- **Self-Healing Systems:** Self-healing systems use AI-driven anomaly detection to discover faults in real time and address them automatically. To give an example, Kubernetes identifies malfunctioning containers and automatically relaunches them or replaces the application to ensure availability.
- **AI-Enhanced DevOps:** The intelligent automation will play an enhanced role in supporting Development and Operations (DevOps) functions, such as DevOps testing, integration, and deployment. The purpose of AI in predictive analytics is to predict the failures of deployment, improve build pipelines, and integrate continuous integration/continuous deployment (CI/CD) cycles.

The combination of said principles allows developing self-managed, scalable, and ready-to-self-adjust cloud systems with the ability to proactively identify any problem and constantly optimize themselves, which are the building blocks of modern AI-enabled cloud services.

AI (AI) has emerged as one of the factors that enhance cloud services beyond the capacity of classical automation. By implementing AI-based intelligence on cloud infrastructure and platforms, there are potential provider services to enhance beyond delivering services that would be not only more efficient but also proactive, adaptive, and secure. This section discusses the main methods through which AI assists in other crucial aspects of cloud services, like resource provisioning and capacity, security and threat identification, predictive analysis, and multiple cloud management.

8.2.3 Automated Provisioning and Dynamic Scaling

Among the most evident examples of how AI has transformed the world of cloud services, there is the automation of resource provisioning and the adaptation of the infrastructures to smartly adapt to the fluctuating demand. The traditional way of autoscaling employs predetermined thresholds and rules, which may lead to the scaling that happens too late or too much, thus slowing down performance or being a waste of money.

With the help of ML models of prior usage times, trends over the seasons, and external factors such as marketing campaigns or holidays, AI-powered autoscaling can accurately predict how many resources will be required prior to requiring them. An example would be Netflix increasing ML, which has advanced algorithms that can determine the time of the year when popular shows are expected to be popular. This allows them to reserve computing and streaming resources in advance, which enables users to have a smooth experience, despite having many of them.

Examples of cloud services that leverage AI: AWS Auto Scaling looks at real-time measurements and makes guesses about the most appropriate scaling actions.

To maintain the low cost and application responsiveness, these systems can vary the number of compute instances, containers, or serverless functions that are simultaneously running [8].

AI models also learn and enhance their scaling strategies with time by examining the impact of the previous scaling measures on the system and making more sound decisions. This reduces the necessity of people becoming involved, minimizes risk in operations, and increases the availability of services.

8.2.4 AI-Enabled Security and Threat Detection

Cloud security proves to be challenging due to the immense attack surface, shared infrastructure, and workload changes. Cloud security is improved with the use of AI because it detects threats, spots unusual activity, and acts automatically.

Existing AI-based security technology uses behavioral analytics and unsupervised learning to determine what normal behavior is to or within individuals, devices, and applications. Any deviation from these baselines is highlighted as a potential risk; e.g., logging in at unusual locations, abnormal access to data, or network traffic that is abnormal [9].

As an example, Microsoft Azure Sentinel is a ML-based tool that gathers and indexes security data from multiple sources to connect events to identify advanced threats quickly. Similarly, AWS GuardDuty applies AI to continuously scan network flows and logs and issue an alarm, which can be responded to.

Not only does AI detect problems, but it can automatically resolve them by performing such actions as isolating resources that are saved, cancelling access credentials, or changing firewall rules. This reduces the response time to the danger from hours to minutes, and this significantly reduces the risk.

AI can also assist financial cloud services in identifying fraud by viewing trends in the data of transactions. This allows banks to look up and prevent suspicious transactions virtually instantly.

8.2.5 Predictive Analytics for Performance Optimization and Cost Management

Cloud operators need constant monitoring and data analysis to make sure their systems work well and don't cost too much. AI-powered predictive analytics turns raw monitoring data into useful information.

AI models can predict when a system could slow down or malfunction by looking at telemetry data like CPU and memory use, response times, and error rates. For example, AI may utilize query patterns to forecast that a database is about to become overloaded. This would lead to scaling or redistributing the load before users have problems.

Cloud providers provide predictive analytics in their monitoring suites. For example, Google Cloud Operations Suite employs ML models to find problems and anticipate when resources will run out, making it easier to manage resources before they run out [10].

AI looks at billing data and resource consumption to find resources that aren't being used enough or are sitting around doing nothing. It also suggests rightsizing and finds unusual expenditure spikes. AWS Cost Explorer and Cloudability are two platforms that use AI to provide businesses with information that helps them get the most out of their cloud spending without losing performance.

Some businesses use Financial Operations (FinOps) methods that are improved by AI. These practices combine financial responsibility with technological optimization to make sure that costs are kept under control and that everything is clear in hybrid and multicloud systems.

8.2.6 AI-Powered Multicloud and Hybrid Cloud Management

To save money, avoid being locked into a single provider, and fulfill regulatory requirements, many businesses use multicloud and hybrid cloud solutions. However, it is hard to manage these different settings since the APIs, networking, security regulations, and monitoring tools are all different.

AI gives you smart orchestration and governance tools that make it easier to manage all of your clouds. AI agents look at things like workload characteristics, compliance limitations, latency, and cost to suggest the best way to move workloads around. AI is also used to detect failures and to switch between clouds without the need of human intervention to ensure the availability of services. The AI-enhanced systems can transfer workloads automatically to the healthy regions, if a single location in a cloud has issues. This saves on idle time.

The compliance monitoring is also assisted by AI that makes continuous checks against resources in one or more clouds of policies and rules, informs the administrator about noncompliant configurations, and automates the associated process.

8.3 Intelligent Automation in Cloud Operations

Intelligent automation is becoming the reality because of the advanced AI technologies. This is transforming cloud operations by minimizing human intervention and automating repetitive tasks that are time-consuming and error-prone. Deployment, dependability, and compliance in cloud systems can no longer be managed using old manual methods, which are becoming larger and more sophisticated. With intelligent automation enabled by AI, you can deliver things any time, detect and remedy problems in a short period of time, and be more efficient in following the rules faster and more correctly. This section elaborates even more on the key impacts of intelligent automation on clouds. Those range from the incorporation of AI into the CI/CD pipelines, the realization of cloud infrastructures capable of self-healing, and the automation of compliance and governance tasks.

8.3.1 AI in Deployment Pipelines

The ability to deliver software in an agile way in the cloud involves cloud pipelines. They allow you to publish code frequently and with confidence, as they automate integration, testing, and deployment. With the incorporation of AI into such pipelines, they become enhanced since they are able to predict and make intelligent choices. AI models see prior commit data, test results, and code modifications and begin to make estimates as to which builds or deployments have the highest likelihood of failure before they are executed, which could save tons of money.

This early warning enables teams to intervene prior to the occurrence of the problem, reducing the downtimes. Such platforms as Harness.io rely on AI algorithms to identify risky deployments and immediately roll them back if anything goes wrong after deployment. This keeps things stable. Also, AI-driven test case creation makes testing more efficient. Testim.io and other tools use ML to choose and rank test cases based on changes to the code and how it is used. This makes tests more efficient while maintaining coverage. After deployment, AI keeps an eye on how well the app is working and how users are using it. If it sees any problems or regressions, it may automatically fix them or provide notifications to developers to limit the damage.

8.3.2 Self-Healing Cloud Infrastructure

Cloud services need to be very reliable and always available, especially for applications that are very important to the business. AI-enabled self-healing infrastructures can find problems and fix them on their own. This cuts down on the mean time to recovery (MTTR) and makes the system more resilient.

Kubernetes and other container orchestration solutions use AI-based monitoring techniques to find failed nodes or containers (pods). Once the system finds a problem, it automatically moves workloads to healthy nodes without needing any help. This automation makes sure that there is very little service downtime.

Netflix's Chaos Engineering method is an example of AI-driven resilience. Netflix's AI models learn about possible fault patterns by purposefully causing failures and then starting automatic recovery operations. This keeps the system stable on a large scale. Google Cloud Operations Suite also uses ML to predict when resources may degrade and automatically carry out scaling, restarts, or load redistribution, which keeps performance at its best.

8.3.3 AI for Compliance and Governance Automation

Companies that use cloud workloads always have trouble following the rules. Manual audits and enforcing policies take a lot of time, are prone to mistakes, and can't keep up with changing cloud environments. AI-driven compliance automation solves these problems by constantly checking cloud resources and settings against rules like GDPR, HIPAA, and PCI DSS.

Microsoft Azure Security Center and AWS Config are two tools that use ML to find misconfigurations, suspicious activity, and resource use that isn't legal. For instance, Capital One uses AI to find violations of internal rules and government rules. This triggers alarms and automated remedial procedures to quickly bring things back into compliance.

NLP further supports compliance by translating complex regulatory texts into machine-readable policies, enabling automatic enforcement and comprehensive compliance reporting. This integration reduces operational overhead while enhancing governance transparency. Figure 8.3 shows the self-healing cloud structure [11].

8.3.4 Trustworthy and Responsible AI in the Cloud

As AI becomes increasingly integrated into cloud infrastructure, ensuring that these systems are trustworthy, responsible, and ethical has become imperative. Trustworthy AI in the cloud involves the design and deployment of AI systems that are transparent, fair, accountable, secure, and aligned with human values.

Important elements of cloud AI-responsible AI should comprise the following:

- **Transparency and Explainability:** AI models in clouds are expected to be explainable, or their users and administrators should be able to interpret the grounds of the prediction or decision. This is particularly important in the regulated industries such as healthcare and the financial sector.
- **Ethics and Bias Hypocrisy:** Cloud AI services should be checked concerning any bias in the algorithms. To achieve equity in outcome, preprocessing (e.g., re-weighting data), in-processing (e.g., fairness constraints), and postprocessing (e.g., outcome adjustments) approaches are involved.
- **Security and Privacy:** Since the cloud AI deals with sensitive data, the use of strong encryption, federated learning, and differential privacy will be required to preserve the information that can be used by the user, as well as guarantee its adherence to legislation, including GDPR and HIPAA.
- **Human-Centric Design Backup:** AI is supposed to support human functioning, rather than to substitute it. The four core principles of responsible AI in the cloud are user control, user feedback, and ethical guardrails.

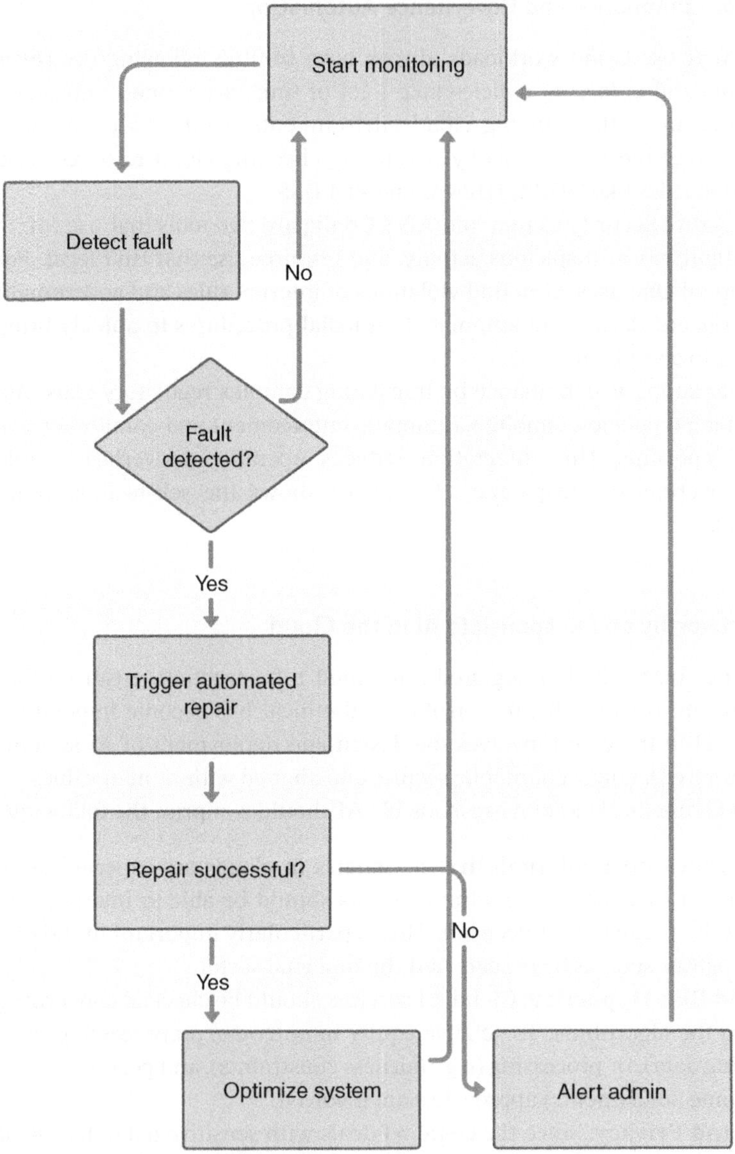

Figure 8.3 The self-healing cloud structure.

Even the largest cloud vendors, Microsoft, Google Cloud, and AWS, are integrating AI responsibility with their cloud systems. As an example, the Responsible AI Standard created by Microsoft and Model Cards generated by Google improve transparency and inform the ethical use. These frameworks provide the assurance of compatibility of AI innovations with the expectations and rules of the society and long-term confidence in the use of cloud-enabled AI services.

8.3.5 AI-Powered Cloud Cost Optimization

Another considerable benefit of AI adoption to a cloud platform is the opportunity for sophisticated cost optimization. Because organizations are pursuing complex multicloud and hybrid cloud strategies, it becomes more difficult to manage. AI offers highly efficient tools in cloud expense analysis, forecasting, and optimization without much human interference.

The strategies presented are the keys:

- **Machine Learning-Assisted Resource Rightsizing:** The usage patterns are then examined over a period during which ML models can suggest opportune instance types, storage arrangements, and schedules. This would guarantee that workloads make available only the bare essentials as opposed to over-provisioning.
- **Idle Resource Detection and Termination:** AI will recognize idle VMs, containers, and storage volumes and can automatically deallocate or reallocate the resources to avoid extra expenditure.
- **Predictive Cost Forecasting:** It is used to project future costs based on past spending patterns using time-series forecasting models, which enable operations and finance teams to allocate budgets and budget proactively as well as manage cloud spend based on budgets.
- **Dynamic Workload Scheduling:** AI can determine the best times and locations to run the workloads and so can run non-urgent workloads at times when resources are cheap or using regions of the cloud that are cheap or spot instances that are cheap.
- **Cost Anomaly Detection:** AI detects cloud bills that have unexpected peaks or have performance detriments, which could be misconfigurations, data-egress costs, or unauthorized consumption.

The cost optimization options to be used continuously have been added to the functionality of platforms, which include, among others, AWS Cost Explorer, Google Cloud Billing, and Azure Cost Management. Businesses that have adopted these tools have also said they have achieved a 30% reduction in cloud expenses, proving the utility of AI in enhancing financial management in cloud operations [12].

Case Studies and Industry Examples

Case Study 1: Netflix—AI-Driven Cloud Automation and Resilience

Netflix has an immense cloud system, which delivers services to millions of users simultaneously. AI has enabled Netflix to be able to predict its demand surge and automatically scale its streaming infrastructure and maintain its user experience even at peak traffic times. Through the Chaos Monkey tool that is now powered with the AI to monitor it, Netflix causes and deals with failures in order to test how robust the system is. The use of AI-powered CI/CD pipelines may locate troublesome deployments, in that the development automatically reverses the deployment, which in turn reduces service outages.

Case Study 2: Capital One—AI-Powered Cloud Security and Compliance

Capital One uses AI to keep cloud environments safe and compliant with strict rules. AI looks at how networks behave to quickly find dangers, and constant compliance monitoring makes sure that standards like PCI DSS and GDPR are followed. Automated remediation procedures and reporting make compliance management easier by lowering the amount of work that has to be done by hand and the risk of exposure.

Case Study 3: Google Cloud—AI in Multicloud Management

Google Cloud employs AI-powered technologies to find the best places for workloads and save money in multicloud scenarios. AI makes failover automatic by moving workloads from cloud areas that are failing to ones that are healthy. This keeps services running. The Security Command Center collects threat data and ranks vulnerabilities across clouds, which lets you plan ahead for protection.

It is important to summarize this section because it makes complicated ideas about AI-driven intelligent automation easy to understand and put into action. The explanation goes into detail about a wide range of subjects that are all related to each other, such as AI-enhanced deployment and testing, autonomous infrastructure healing, and regulatory compliance automation. This shows how AI may change the way cloud operations work.

A short description helps readers understand how AI can help make the cloud more reliable, flexible, and well-governed. It also uses case studies to put theory into practice in the actual world, connecting theory with what happens in the business. This gets readers ready for the next chapters and tells cloud architects, developers, and IT managers about the real-world advantages and strategic value of intelligent automation.

Summary of Section 4: Intelligent Automation in Cloud Operations

This part shows how intelligent automation driven by AI is changing how cloud operations function by automating deployment procedures, making infrastructure self-healing, and making compliance management easier. Integrating AI into CI/CD pipelines improves software delivery by anticipating build failures, improving test coverage, and automating rollback operations. Systems such as Kubernetes and Netflix are examples of self-healing systems, i.e., systems that identify and resolve issues automatically to ensure that things go well and reduce downtime. AI can also constantly scan cloud environments relative to a set of rules, identify misconfigurations, and initiate automatic repairs, where NLP is used to translate complex policies. Examples of such companies and organizations are Netflix, Capital One, and Google Cloud companies, where intelligent automation was established to enhance the efficiency, resilience, and compliance of their intricate cloud environments.

8.4 Emerging Paradigms: Generative and Agentic AI in Cloud Services

Due to the maturity of AI technologies, new paradigms like generative AI and agentic AI play an increasing role in affecting the development of cloud services. These methods have surpassed some of the traditional predictive analytics to the extent that the cloud systems can create content by themselves and even make complex decisions with limited human interaction. Our fourth section takes a look at these paradigms, their underlying technologies and applications, and what they have to do with cloud computing.

8.4.1 Generative AI for Cloud Service Development and Automation

- **Automate Code Generation:** Such tools as GitHub Copilot or OpenAI Codex can help developers in the code generation process as they provide code fragments or even functions based on the text description of a task. This makes the development of cloud-native applications fast and avoids manual coding mistakes.
- **Infrastructure-as-Code (IaC) Generation:** Generative AI can be used to convert system descriptions in a high-level language to executable scripts (IaC)

to conceptualize systems (e.g., using Terraform or AWS CloudFormation) as a means to easily and reliably deploy complex cloud architecture.

- **Create Documentation and Design Artifacts:** Generating technical descriptions, API specifications, and architectural drawings based on a current codebase or systems metadata improves collaboration and reduces development cycles.
- **Generate Synthetic Data:** Synthetic data generated through generative AI helps to train AI models without sharing sensitive data, and this can be used to achieve compliance and privacy because it is possible to create realistic datasets.

8.4.2 Agentic AI for Autonomous Cloud Operations

The agentic AI systems refer to fully independent agents, which perceive the environment, make decisions, and act based on the decisions to realize the goals. Such agents are able to act in a multi-agent setting, making dynamic decisions in response to versatile cloud circumstances.

Autonomous Lifecycle Management: The agents furnish resources, install software, oversee the health of a system, and make configuration changes, all without human control, to combine performance and decentralization.

RL-Based Optimization: The optimal action policies for scaling, load balancing, and fault recovery will be learned by the agents through interacting in cloud settings and being given feedback.

Multi-Agent Coordination: Distributed agents work across the hybrid clouds and multi-infrastructures to coordinate intricate workflows, provide fail-safes, and implement security policies.

An example is that Google AutoML uses agentic AI principles to automate model selection and tuning of ML and dynamically responds to workload changes. On the same note, agentic agents are used in the AI-driven orchestration infrastructure to check the health of the network, do security check-ups, and align resource utilization.

8.4.3 Ethical and Trust Considerations

The increased autonomy of generative and agentic AI raises important questions about transparency, accountability, and trust. Cloud providers must ensure:

- **Explainability:** AI decisions and generated outputs should be interpretable to gain user trust and meet regulatory requirements.
- **Bias Mitigation:** Training data and models must be audited to prevent reinforcing biases or unfair practices.
- **Security:** Autonomous agents must be secured against adversarial attacks and misuse.

8.4.4 Future Directions

The integration of generative and agentic AI with emerging technologies such as quantum computing and edge AI promises even greater capabilities:

- Quantum-enhanced AI agents may optimize cloud resource allocation with unprecedented speed.
- Edge-based agentic AI will enable localized autonomous decision-making, reducing latency and bandwidth.

These advances are expected to drive the next generation of fully autonomous, self-optimizing cloud ecosystems.

8.5 Foundations of Multimodal AI

Multimodal AI systems can use architectures that can fuse heterogeneous data into a common representation. As recent examples, Contrastive Language-Image Pre-training (CLIP) and DALL-E from OpenAI show that joint training on both image and text allows cross-modal retrieval and generation challenges. Likewise, multimodal actions that use transformers are large-scale models that are over sequences of heterogeneous inputs and learn complex correlations inaccessible to single-modality models.

Cloud computing offers the scalable infrastructure for training and rollout of such models. Distributed computing using high-performance Graphics Processing Units (GPUs) and Tensor Processing Units (TPUs) installed in cloud data centers allows processing huge multimodal data sets with parallelism. Also, cloud storage systems can process a wide range of data at the required level of throughput and latency to apply the inference in real-time.

8.5.1 Applications of Multimodal AI in Cloud Services

- **Intelligent Virtual Assistants:** Cloud-based virtual assistants that have multimodal AI that comprehends voice instructions, discerns images that users send, and answers them through speech and multimedia-rich visual data. An example may be a situation when a user can display an image of a product, pose a question orally, and get detailed information or buy alternatives without any difficulties.
- **Automation of Customer Support:** Multimodal chatbots will perform text-based support diagnostics in combination with screenshots or video feedback to diagnose problems more accurately, which results in quicker and more customized service.

- **Healthcare Diagnostics:** Using multimodal cloud-based AI systems, medical images, patient records, and sensor data can be used to help clinicians perform thorough diagnostics and plan treatment.
- **Security Monitoring:** Ensuring a hybrid coordination of video surveillance, audio sensors and text logs in cloud-based monitoring facilities enhances anomaly detection and response to incident.
- **Individualized Content Delivery:** Streaming services can rely on multimodal AI to recommend to the viewer on the basis of what he/she has watched (video), text metadata, and even sentiments he/she has included in his/her commentaries.

8.5.2 Challenges in Multimodal Cloud AI

- **Data Synchronization and Integration:** The existence of heterogeneous data streams of differing format, sampling frequency, and quality can prove to be complex to behave synchronously and in unison.
- **Computational Requirement:** Multimodal models usually need extensive amounts of computation to train and conduct inference in the real world, which is taking optimized cloud architectures.
- **Privacy and Adherence:** Processing of sensitive multimodal data can be very compliance-sensitive, in particular, in the health care or finance fields, and will demand mechanisms of data protection and anonymity.

8.5.3 Research and Future Directions

Most developing work is on cross-modal reasoning, where it is possible to extrapolate missing information on one modality using other modalities to be able to make the system more robust. Multimodal RL in clouds is expected to deliver efficient systems with the ability to learn in complicated systems.

With the maturity of both 5G and edge computing, pushing the inference of multimodal AI to users will also decrease latency, making ways to interact immersively via applications and real-time collaborative tools powered by the cloud AI a possibility.

8.5.4 Summary

Multimodal AI integrates diverse data types—such as text, images, audio, and sensor inputs—to enable cloud services that offer richer, more natural user experiences and enhanced decision-making. Foundational models like OpenAI's CLIP and DALL-E showcase how joint training on multiple modalities advances cross-modal understanding and generation. Cloud infrastructure, with its scalable

GPUs and storage, supports the demanding computation and data handling needs of these systems.

Applications include intelligent virtual assistants, multimodal customer support chatbots, healthcare diagnostics, security monitoring, and personalized content delivery. Challenges encompass data synchronization, high computational demands, and privacy concerns. Future research aims at improved cross-modal reasoning and edge AI deployment to reduce latency, fostering immersive, real-time cloud applications such as augmented reality and collaborative tools.

8.6 Future Trends and Opportunities

8.6.1 Quantum Computing Integration

Quantum computing holds the promise to accelerate AI model training and optimization through quantum algorithms and quantum ML. Though still nascent, quantum cloud services are beginning to emerge, offering hybrid quantum-classical workflows that may redefine computational limits for AI-driven cloud automation.

8.6.2 Edge AI and the Cloud-Edge Continuum

The proliferation of IoT devices and latency-sensitive applications drives the need to distribute AI inference closer to data sources. The cloud-edge continuum integrates centralized cloud intelligence with edge computing, enabling real-time AI applications such as autonomous vehicles, smart cities, and Augmented Reality (AR)/Virtual Reality (VR).

8.6.3 AI Governance and Regulatory Frameworks

As AI becomes more and more common in cloud services, governments and businesses are putting rules in place to make sure that AI is used responsibly. Standards for ethical AI, data stewardship, accountability, and auditability will help with development and deployment, which will encourage innovation and public confidence.

8.6.4 Advances in Autonomous AI Systems

More research into self-supervised learning, multi-agent coordination, and causal reasoning will make autonomous AI agents better at running complicated cloud operations with little help from people. This will get us closer to completely self-optimizing cloud ecosystems.

8.7 Conclusion

Cloud services powered by AI and smart automation are changing the way computers work today. Organizations may achieve levels of efficiency, scalability, and creativity that have never been seen before by adding AI's predictive, generative, and autonomous features to cloud infrastructures. This combination lets cloud systems handle complicated tasks on their own, adjust resources on the fly, find and stop security issues before they happen, and provide users with rich, tailored experiences. In this chapter, we looked at the technical underpinnings of AI-enhanced cloud services. This included the shift from virtualization to cloud-native architectures and the important AI technologies that make automation and smart decision-making possible. We looked at how AI has helped with things like automated provisioning, security, predictive analytics, and multicloud orchestration. We also looked at new types of AI, including generative and agentic AI, that might have even bigger effects.

Multimodal AI makes cloud intelligence more useful by making interactions between people and machines more natural and interesting. Intelligent automation, on the other hand, makes operations easier and speeds up continuous delivery. There have been big improvements, but there are still problems with scalability, interoperability, ethical usage, security, and governance that need to be solved by joint research, innovation, and regulatory initiatives.

Quantum computing, edge AI, and autonomous multi-agent systems coming together is the start of a new generation of cloud ecosystems that can completely optimize themselves. Companies that strategically use AI-driven cloud automation will have an advantage over their competitors because they will be able to quickly respond to changing market needs and provide better digital experiences.

To sum up, AI and cloud computing are becoming two of the most important parts of digital transformation. Their coming together is not just improving what we can already do, but it is also changing the way technology helps business, science, and society.

References

1 Q. Zhang, L. Cheng, and R. Boutaba, "Cloud computing: State-of-the-art and research challenges," *J. Internet Serv. Appl.*, vol. 14, no. 1, p. 10, 2023.

2 J. Jiang, M. Zhang, and S. Zhang, "AI-powered cloud resource management: A survey," in *IEEE Trans. Cloud Comput*, 2022.

3 H. Li and Z. Zhou, "Generative AI in cloud computing: Applications and challenges," *ACM Comput. Surv.*, vol. 56, no. 4, Art. no., 84, 2023.

4 A. Singh and A. Kaur, "Security and privacy in AI-driven cloud services: A systematic review," *J. Netw. Comput. Appl.*, vol. 185, 103095, 2021.

5 T. Huang and Z. Liu, "Self-healing cloud infrastructure: AI-based approaches and case studies," *J. Syst. Archit.*, vol. 114, 101982, 2021.

6 S. Kim and J. Park, "Natural language processing for cloud automation: Trends and applications," *IEEE Access*, vol. 11, pp. 45782–45803, 2023.

7 M. Ahmed and S. Khan, "AI-enabled predictive analytics for cloud cost optimization," *J. Cloud Comput.*, vol. 11, no. 1, p. 25, 2022.

8 Y. Zhao and L. Chen, "Multimodal AI for cloud-based intelligent assistants," *IEEE Trans. Multimedia*, vol. 24, pp. 2345–2356, 2022.

9 N. Gupta and S. Verma, "Robotic process automation (RPA) for cloud infrastructure management: A review," *Future Internet*, vol. 13, no. 11, p. 271, 2021.

10 F. Li and H. Wu, "AI governance frameworks in cloud computing: Challenges and solutions," *IEEE Trans. Technol. Soc.*, vol. 4, no. 1, pp. 12–23, 2023.

11 X. Yang and M. Zhou, "Agentic AI systems for autonomous cloud operations: A survey," *ACM Trans. Auton. Adapt. Syst.*, vol. 17, no. 2, Art. no., 11, 2022.

12 P. Kaur and R. Singh, "Ethical AI in cloud services: A review and future perspectives," *IEEE Ethics AI J.*, vol. 1, no. 1, pp. 67–72, 2021.

9

AIOps: Intelligent Cloud Observability and Incident Management

Milankumar Rana[1] *and Jyoti Kunal Shah*[2]

[1] *University of the Cumberlands, Williamsburg, KY, USA*
[2] *Independent Researcher, Edison, NJ, USA*

9.1 Introduction

9.1.1 Motivation and Scope

The proliferation of cloud-native architectures, microservices, containers, and ephemeral infrastructure has fundamentally transformed how modern applications are built, deployed, and operated. Yet with these advantages comes a surge in operational complexity. Traditional monitoring tools—designed for monolithic systems—are often ill-equipped to handle the scale, diversity, and churn inherent in dynamic cloud environments. These tools rely heavily on static thresholds and simplistic rule-based alerting, which leads to alert fatigue and prolonged incident resolution cycles. Artificial intelligence (AI) for IT operations (AIOps) applies machine learning (ML) and big data techniques to sift through voluminous telemetry data, detect anomalies, pinpoint root causes, and orchestrate automated responses. The goal is to shift from reactive, manual incident management toward proactive, predictive, and eventually autonomous operations. This chapter delves into the underpinnings of AIOps for cloud observability and incident management, offering a comprehensive roadmap for practitioners, architects, and technical leaders aiming to integrate AIOps into their operational workflows.

9.1.2 Chapter Overview

We begin with a historical overview of the transition from human-centric, manually curated dashboards to data-driven, AI-enhanced platforms in monitoring and operations. Section 9.2 analyzes the context and philosophical foundations of AIOps, emphasizing the impact of large data. Section 9.3 defines cloud observability, differentiating it from traditional monitoring, and clarifies the three essential pillars—metrics, logs, and traces—necessary for thorough visibility in distributed systems.

Section 9.4 outlines a hierarchical framework of a generic AIOps platform, emphasizing critical components such as data ingestion, feature engineering, AI/ML engines, event correlation, knowledge bases, and automation orchestrators. Section 9.5 analyzes the design of telemetry data pipelines, emphasizing challenges such as high cardinality, schema consistency, and storage limitations. Section 9.6 describes AI/ML techniques for anomaly detection, time-series forecasting, clustering, and graph-based dependency mapping, including supervised and unsupervised approaches.

Section 9.7 covers methods for detecting abnormalities across many data modalities and for establishing basic causes inside complex topologies. Section 9.8 delineates incident management protocols, encompassing automatic ticket creation, chat-based interaction, and runbook-directed remediation. Section 9.9 looks at real-world AIOps installations in e-commerce, finance, SaaS, and telephony. Section 9.10 defines suggested strategies for effective adoption, including organizational preparation, data governance, and development and operations (DevOps) integration. Section 9.11 particularly tackles explainability problems, model drift, and data silos, hence identifying the limits of current AIOps systems. Section 9.12 looks at intent-driven operations, self-healing systems, and the integration of creative AI paradigms, among other possible research directions. Section 9.13 provides last reflections underscoring the interaction between human knowledge and AI-driven intelligence in obtaining operational excellence.

9.2 Background and Evolution of AIOps

9.2.1 From Manual Operations to Automated Monitoring

Early on in the history of IT, system managers manually logged into servers via secure shell (SSH), reviewed log files line by line, and relied on intuition to identify application problems. Using simple threshold-based alerts to tell operators of quantitative anomalies, CPU use above 80%, RAM above 90%, disk space below 10%, etc., monitoring systems including Nagios, Zabbix, and Cacti arose as data centers grew. But in distributed, containerized systems, a single microservice may create hundreds of transient containers in a matter of minutes, therefore negating static criteria. False positives multiplied, causing "alert fatigue," in which on-call engineers started to completely ignore or silence alarms in order to escape continual noise. Manual root cause diagnosis became a bottleneck when

DevOps and continuous delivery further sped deployment cycles from quarterly to daily or hourly.

Next-generation monitoring systems such as Prometheus, Grafana, Elasticsearch, and Splunk provide more flexible time-series databases, sophisticated visualization, and strong query languages to meet this new complexity. Still, they depended on human-defined regulations. Emerging about 2017 in response to this gap, AIOps used ML models to automate issue prioritizing, anomaly detection, and event correlation [2]. AIOps claimed to restore observability and efficiency even in highly dynamic cloud-native environments by aggregating events across several monitoring sources, spotting anomalies outside of static thresholds, and automating the triage process.

9.2.2 The Big Data Imperative

Modern applications generate staggering volumes of telemetry data:

- Often gathered at sub-second gratuity for hundreds or thousands of hosts or containers, time-series data points for CPU, RAM, disk I/O, network I/O, request delay, error rates, etc.
- Millions of lines every minute, logs-structured or unstructured recordings created by infrastructure components, middleware, and application services.
- Distributed tracing covers numerous microservices and infrastructure levels, capturing the end-to-end execution path [3].
- Created by CI/CD pipelines, security platforms, and configuration management tools, events and alerts—such as status changes, scaling events, deployment notifications, security alerts, etc.—have CI/CD pipelines driving them.

Together, high volume (TBs per day), high velocity (data streams in real time), and high variety (heterogeneous data formats and schemas) provide a classical "3 V" big data issue. AIOps systems import this data into specialized data lakes or time-series databases where it is standardized, enriched, and preserved for varied time horizons, sometimes using distributed storage systems (e.g., Hadoop HDFS, Amazon S3, and Elasticsearch indices). Using statistical analysis, pattern recognition, and ML, the complete telemetry footprint presents an opportunity to detect anomalies and potential events before they begin.

9.2.3 Defining AIOps: Conceptual Foundations

AIOps can be conceptualized as the confluence of three distinct but interrelated domains:

1) Big data and data engineering allow one to acquire, process, store, and query vast, multi-modal telemetry datasets at scale.

2) Algorithms and models able to learn from past data to identify deviations, forecast future trends (e.g., capacity planning), and deduce causal linkages constitute ML and predictive analytics.
3) Automated runbooks, scripts, and workflows triggered by discovered anomalies or inferred root causes provide automation and orchestration to speed policy enforcement or remedial action.

AIOps is therefore not only a monitoring tool with elegant graphs but also a comprehensive system combining data engineering, AI/ML, and process automation to drive intelligence all through the incident management lifetime [4].

9.3 Cloud Observability Fundamentals

9.3.1 Observability vs. Monitoring

Traditionally, monitoring has meant the methodical gathering of predefined metrics and logs along with rules-based alerts. It responds to binary inquiries, including "Is CPU use above 80%?" or "Are there any ERROR-level log entries in the last five minutes?" Looking at the whole spectrum of telemetry—metrics, logs, traces, events, even custom application instrumentation, observability—by contrast, allows engineers to ask unrestricted questions about system behavior. Considered in control theory, observability suggests that one may deduce internal system state from external inputs [5]. Observability becomes especially important in cloud systems since systems are ephemeral (containers come and go), dispersed (microservices interact over networks), and scale elastically. Observability stresses rather than predefining a small range of KPIs [3]:

1) Injecting instrumentation at strategic points in the application code and infrastructure to produce rich telemetry (e.g., OpenTelemetry) at important points.
2) Linking heterogeneous telemetry artifacts via unique request IDs, correlation IDs, or contextual metadata (e.g., Kubernetes pod labels and Amazon Web Services [AWS] tags) is known as correlation.
3) Dynamic searches and visualizations that enable engineers to investigate data in real time, do postmortem root cause analysis, and identify developing trends empower them.

9.3.2 Pillars of Observability: Metrics, Logs, Traces

The **three pillars of observability** are often defined as follows:

- Numeric time-series data showing system performance indicators—CPU use, memory use, application throughput, error rates, request latencies, database query durations, etc. For long-term storage, metrics—which range from percentiles to averages—are aggregated and downsampled across time. Good metrics ensure effective storage via low cardinality, that is, per service, per area.

- Timestamped, unstructured, or semi-structured text records produced by middlewares, OS kernels, infrastructure, and applications. Logs record comprehensive contextual data—stack traces, user IDs, SQL queries, HTTP request headers—that metrics by themselves cannot adequately communicate. For indexing and full-text search, logging frameworks—Log4j, Fluentd, and Filebeat—forward logs to centralized log stores—Elasticsearch and Splunk. Consistent schemas and organized logging (JSON) are foundations of effective log management.
- Distributed tracing records the course of a single request across several infrastructure elements. Spanning each operation (e.g., database call, HTTP request, or function invocation) a trail is made of them. Start and finish times, duration, and tag-key-value labels are among the metadata found in spans. Reconstructing these spans using tracing systems, such as Jaeger, Zipkin, and AWS X-Ray, allows a visual call graph, hence enabling delay breakdowns and bottleneck identification.

9.3.3 Telemetry Collection in Cloud Environments

Collecting observability data in cloud environments presents unique challenges:

1) Containers and serverless functions spin quickly in ephemeral infrastructure. Agents have to be lightweight and able to automatically find fresh entities.
2) Many times, companies span AWS, Azure, Google Cloud, and on-site data centers in multicloud and hybrid deployments. Unified telemetry pipelines must abstract away variations in APIs, metrics namespaces, and logging systems.
3) High-fidelity telemetry, that is, complete traces and high-density measurements, is precious for diagnosis even if it is costly to keep. Retention rules, data tiering (hot, warm, cold storage), and sampling methods (e.g., tail-based sampling) must be exactly changed.
4) Compliance and Security: Telemetry could include private information, like PII found in logs or internal IP addresses. Important among these are HIPAA, GDPR rules, RBAC based on roles, and encryption both in transit and at rest.

Common telemetry collection approaches include:

- Lightweight agents (Prometheus Node Exporter, Fluent Bit, and DataDog Agent) placed on host or container images automatically capture metrics, logs, and traces. Through orchestration metadata (e.g., Kubernetes annotations) agents generally allow auto discovery.

- Using sidecar containers and cloud-native APIs (such as AWS CloudWatch and Azure Monitor), agentless collecting is achieved. Envoy sidecars can, for instance, record trace spans in service meshes.
- Pull Against Push Models: Metrics can be pulled, that is, Prometheus scraping exporters over HTTP, or pushed, that is, telegraph or collected pushing to InfluxDB. The choice influences dependability, firewall configuration, and scalability.

9.3.4 Distributed Tracing and Context Propagation

Distributed tracing has become a critical component of observability. Key concepts include:

- Attached to every request, a distinct identity (trace ID) shared via HTTP headers or communications systems (W3C trace context). Context propagation libraries guarantee spans are connected across microservices by including trace IDs into departing requests [3].
- Only a subset of queries is tracked in order to lower overhead. Among the sampling methods are head-based (randomly trace × percent of requests), tail-based (trace requests demonstrating exceptional latency), and dynamic sampling—adjusting sample rate depending on traffic conditions.
- Tags and logs across spans catching custom events, SQL statements, and error codes. These notes help with root cause investigation.

Combining metrics, logs, and traces, AIOps solutions offer a high-fidelity representation of system activity, therefore allowing AI/ML processes to find small abnormalities otherwise invisible.

9.4 Architecture of AIOps Platforms

9.4.1 High-Level Architectural Components

An AIOps platform can be logically decomposed into the following layers:

1) Data ingestion and normalization layer
2) Feature engineering and enrichment layer
3) AI/ML engine for anomaly detection and prediction
4) Event correlation and causality mapping layer
5) Knowledge base and runbook integration layer
6) Automation and orchestration layer
7) Visualization and alerting/user interface layer (Figure 9.1)

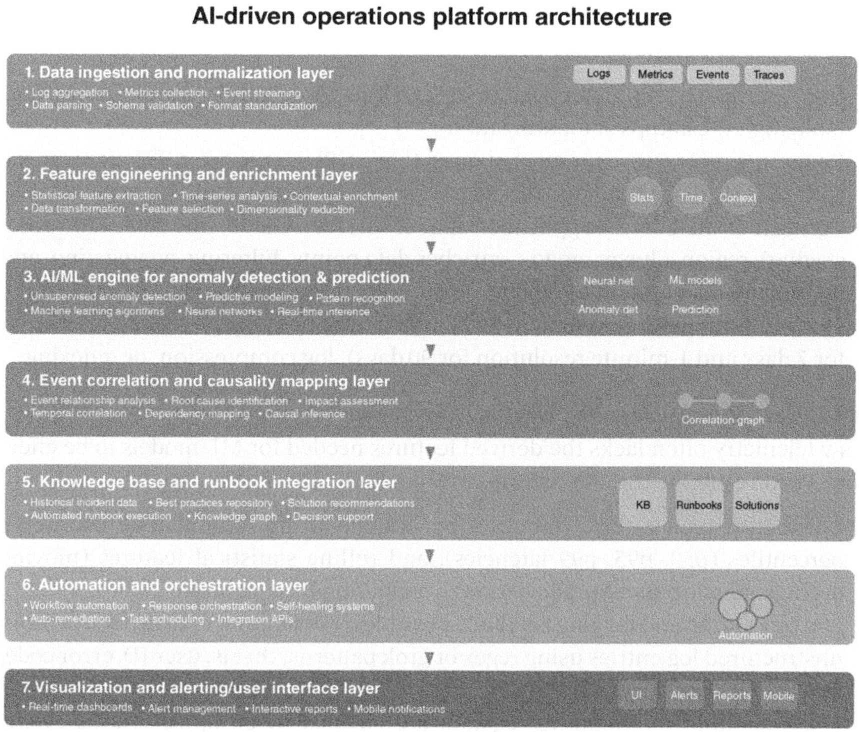

Figure 9.1 AI-driven operations platform architecture.

9.4.1.1 Data Ingestion and Normalization Layer

The first responsibility of any AIOps platform is to ingest telemetry from heterogeneous sources:

- Taken from time-series exporters (Prometheus, Open Telemetry Metrics, Cloud Watch).
- Streamed from application loggers, system logs (syslog), or container runtimes into log collectors (Fluentd, Filebeat).
- Traces came via OpenTelemetry, Jaeger, and Zipkin's tracing agents and libraries.
- **Events:** Security warnings (SIEM alerts, IDS/IPS notifications), configuration management (Ansible, Chef), status shifts from orchestration platforms (Kubernetes events, AWS Config changes).
- Topological data includes network maps, Kubernetes installations, and service registry information.

Normalization involves transforming disparate formats into a common schema. This often includes:

- Converting to a common epoch (e.g., UNIX nanoseconds) with time zone normalizing timestamps standardization.
- Renaming fields to canonical names (e.g., CPUUsage vs. CPU_percent vs. CPU_util) is field standardization.
- Contextual metadata—application name, service version, environment (prod, staging), region, cluster, node—enriches data points. Filtering, aggregating, and relating all depend on these tags.
- Downsampling measurements for extended retention (e.g., 1-second resolution for 7 days and 1-minute resolution for 90 days), log compression, or indexing.

9.4.1.2 Feature Engineering and Data Enrichment

Raw telemetry often lacks the derived features needed for ML models to be effective. Feature engineering transforms raw data into actionable signals:

- Calculating rates (e.g., requests_per_second from cumulative counters), percentiles (p50, p95, p99 latencies), and rolling statistical features (moving average, moving standard deviation) over sliding time periods.
- Log processing and tagging are made possible by structured data extraction from unstructured log entries using regex or grok patterns, that is, user ID, error code, and HTTP status.
- Event deduplication and aggregation are enabled by grouping related events within a given period of time into a single logical event (e.g., "Node X Disk Pressure") repeatedly for five minutes.
- Service-dependent graphs derived from orchestration metadata, that is, Kubernetes Service → Pod → Container → K8s Node →. Data center, allow one to understand abnormalities.
- For seasonal anomaly detection, adding historical baselines, like the same time last week, to current data points helps.

Designed for use by AI and ML models, this layer generates a consistent, enhanced feature set.

9.4.1.3 AI/ML Engine for Anomaly Detection

A central pillar of AIOps is the AI/ML Engine, which analyzes multi-dimensional telemetry to identify outliers, anomalies, and incipient performance degradations. Core functionalities include:

1) Learning regular behavior patterns of metrics and logs across time forms the basis model. Among the approaches are neural network–based models (e.g., LSTM autoencoders and variational autoencoders), seasonal hybrid Extreme Studentized Deviate (ESD), and exponentially weighted moving averages (EWMA). Baseline models vary with workload (growth, seasonality).

2) Assigning a probabilistic or statistical score to every new data point reflecting its likelihood of being aberrant among the techniques are Z-scores, isolation forests, one-class SVMs, and deep learning–based approaches.
3) Based on customizable thresholds or dynamic thresholding, that is, “raise an alert when the anomaly score exceeds the 99.9th percentile of historical scores,” translating anomaly scores into actionable alerts.
4) Predictive analytics centers on future trend forecasts; for example, “disk usage will exceed 80% in 24 hours.”
5) To underline unexpected log patterns (e.g., new error codes or abnormal stack traces) among, the models are LSTM forecasting systems, ARIMA, Prophet, natural language processing (NLP) on log text-TF-IDF vectors, Word2Vec embeddings, or transformer-based encodings.
6) Trace-based anomaly detection starts with the identification of slow traces or peculiar call patterns, that is, a sudden change in average span duration or a new service dependency. Techniques include statistical profiling of span durations, histogram-based anomaly detection, and clustering of like traces to expose outliers.

9.4.1.4 Event Correlation and Causality Mapping

Raw anomaly warnings by themselves are inadequate. To cut noise and identify core causes, AIOps systems must match linked events across several data sources. Important approaches consist of the following:

- Grouping anomalies among related services, that is, a CPU spike on a database node coinciding with higher frontend service request latency, allows one to find temporal correlation.
- Using service dependency graphs, that is, a network partition separating a microservice from its backend database, allows one to link downstream symptoms to upstream causes.
- Using Bayesian networks or probabilistic graphical models, infer causal relationships, that is, “Given that service error rate spiked, what is the probability that the database latency is the root cause?”
- Finding one event, such as a Kubernetes cluster upgrade, that set off a series of downstream alarms is the center of the analysis.
- To decrease alert fatigue, collapsing duplicate alerts into a single “incident” object helps.

9.4.1.5 Knowledge Base and Runbook Integration

When combined with a knowledge base—a carefully chosen collection of known issues, troubleshooting tools, and resolution playbooks—an AIOps platform becomes far more powerful:

- Standardized naming criteria, root cause categories, and resolution actions define incident taxonomy, that is, "Database Connection Pool Exhaustion," by which operators update the knowledge base with fresh issue resolutions.
- Runbooks-automated scripts or step-by-step instructions to address specific failures (e.g., "scale out database read replicas," "clear application cache," and "rotate TLS certificates.)
- Postmortem notes include lessons learned, sequence of events, and comprehensive RCA write-ups.

Inquiring the knowledge base upon new event identification, the AI/ML engine can

1) Correspond with Known Events: Search historical events with like features using similarity metrics on improved feature vectors.
2) Recommend suggestion of automated playbooks to operators or, when set as "trusted," fully automated remedial action runbooks.
3) Enhance future projections by updating supervised models with newly discovered events helps to increase model accuracy.

9.4.1.6 Automation and Orchestration Layer

Once an event is discovered and a likely root cause is identified, the orchestration layer runs automatic corrective actions through:

- Infrastructure-as-Code (IaC) APIs: Spinning up extra resources or reconfiguring infrastructure with Terraform, CloudFormation, or Pulumi.
- Platform APIs: Calling Kubernetes APIs to scale deployments, restart pods, or undo defective releases.
- Using Ansible, Puppet, or Chef playbooks enables one to apply configuration changes.
- Run short asynchronously modest remedial operations serverless, calling AWS Lambda, Azure Functions, or Google Cloud Functions.
- Webhook and ChatOps integrations enable on-call teams to be notified and let engineers approve or reject corrective action using Slack, Microsoft Teams, or PagerDuty connectors.

Risk profile helps classify automation:

- Safe Automation: Nonintrusive actions such as contacting stakeholders, gathering extra logs, or recording debug snapshots.
- Low-risk automation refers to read-only configuration modifications or adjustments (such as raising autoscaling thresholds) that can be automatically undone.

- High-risk automation is the modification of production infrastructure or code, that is, database restarts and rolling back releases. Unless the platform has great trust in root cause and runbook accuracy, they sometimes call for hand approval.

9.4.1.7 Visualization and Alerting Interfaces

AIOps platforms provide multiple user-facing interfaces:

- On a single console, real-time dashboards including aggregated analytics, service health scores, and key performance indicators (KPIs). Many times, these dashboards provide drill-down from high-level system performance into service-specific data, logs, and traces.
- An active incident, severity level, assigned engineer, and history timeline list is found in an incident management console; every incident record connects with pertinent telemetry snapshots, linked event graphs, and recommended runbooks.
- Alerting channels for stakeholders include email, SMS, Slack, Microsoft Teams, PagerDuty, or ServiceNow. Context adds richness to alerts: pertinent logs, top N affected hosts, and first root cause theories.
- Collaborative ChatOps: Chatbots that can respond to queries are "@aiops-bot show me incidents with error rate > 5% in the last hour" and "@aiops-bot run runbook 'restart database cluster.'" This tightens feedback loops for incident response teams.

The combination of automated insights and rich, contextual interfaces enables SRE/DevOps teams to triage more rapidly, reduce human error, and maintain high service-level objectives (SLOs).

9.5 Data Pipelines and Telemetry Management

9.5.1 Sources of Observability Data

AIOps platforms ingest telemetry from multiple layers of the stack:

1) **Infrastructure Level:**
   - CPU, memory, disk, and network metrics via CloudWatch (AWS), Azure Monitor, Google Cloud Monitoring, and open-source exporters (Prometheus Node Exporter).
   - Kubernetes node and pod metrics are expressed using kube-state-metrics and cAdvisor metrics.
   - Kubernetes Control Plane: KP performance, scheduler metrics, API server request latencies, ETCD performance, and Kubelet health.

2) **Platform Level:**
   - Envoy statistics (xDS, xTLS) for circuit breaker states, error rates, and request volumes.
   - Pod lifetimes, pod restarts, node cordons, and drains all around.
   - Lambda invocation metrics (error count, duration, and event source mappings) serverless.
3) **Application Level:**
   - JVM heap consumption, trash collecting times, thread pool queue lengths: application framework metrics.
   - Database metrics including query latencies, buffer cache hit ratios, and connection pool statistics.
   - Redis/Memcached hit/miss rates and eviction rates are cache metrics.
   - Kafka consumer lag, RabbitMQ queue depths, etc. in queuing systems.
4) **Network Level:**
   - Collected using sidecar proxies or eBPF-based network tracking, service-to-service latency.
   - Retransmissions, packet loss, throughput: using network telemetry technologies (InfluxDB + Telegraf).
5) **Security and Compliance:**
   - Policy breaches and suspicious login attempts constitute SIEM alerts.
   - **WAF Logs:** Block or accept logs for web apps.
6) **User Experience:**
   - Scripted HTTP/HTTPS probes tracking availability from many geographies.
   - Real user monitoring (RUM) browser-side telemetry recording page load times and session replays.

Every one of these data sources presents a different angle on system health; together they provide a complete picture.

9.5.2 Agent-Based vs. Agentless Data Collection

- Agent-Based Collection: Agents run as native processes or containerized sidecars. Pros include the following:
  - Agents can gather network-level, application-level, and OS-level comprehensive metrics.
  - Local Preprocessing: On the host prior to transmission, aggregates or compresses metrics.
  - Custom instrumentation of application frameworks (such as JVM, .NET, and Node.js) via language-specific libraries is configurable.
  - Agents can automatically tag metrics with metadata derived from the host environment, that is, EC2 instance tags.

- **Cons:**
  - Agents draw on CPU, memory, and network bandwidth resource overheads.
  - Agents have to be upgraded, configured, and secured.
  - Should their host be unreliable, agents could fail or lag behind.
- Agentless collection based on cloud provider APIs, SNMP, WMI, or service meshes is a positive features comprising:
- Reduced Overhead: Not one additional process on production hosts.
- Not necessary to put inside container images or bake agents or VMs into.
- Cloud API natural scalability matches provider infrastructure.
- **Cons:**
  - Limited Visibility: Cloud APIs may reveal just high-level information (e.g., AWS does not offer per-process analytics via CloudCheck).
  - Polling intervals could be coarser, that is, one minute, than agent-based (one second).
  - Cost: Calls made via the Cloud API could cost more.

Many AIOps systems combine agentless, cloud-native sources for baseline measurements with agents to support deep diagnostics.

9.5.3 Data Transport and Storage Considerations

Key considerations for transporting and storing telemetry:

- Ingest hundreds of thousands of data points every second—Kafka, Kinesis, and Pulsar's message queues buffer data for scalability.
- Use distributed, replicated storage (like S3, HDFS, and Cassandra) with retention restrictions.
- Near real-time analytics need low-latency pipelines, that is, Apache Flink or Spark Streaming for real-time processing.
- Cost Minimization: Hot (SSD-backed, quick searches for 7 days), warm (SATA-backed, slower searches for 30 days), and cold (archive for compliance).
- Backpressure Handling: Systems must elegantly degrade when intake surges outstrip processing capabilities.
- As services are improved, telemetry data schemas change. To manage new fields without calling for upstream changes, storage layers must allow schema-on-read, that is, Parquet files, columnar storage.

9.5.4 Schema Standardization and Tagging Strategies

Without consistent schema and tagging, ML models struggle to draw meaningful correlations. Best practices include:

- Metric names follow the structure <domain>.<service>.<resource>.<metric>.<unit>. (e.g., ecom.cart.checkout.latency.ms).

- Define a mandatory low-cardinality tag set for all telemetry: environment=prod|stage|dev, region=<cloud_region>, service=<service_name>, cluster=<k8s_cluster_name>, team=<owning_team>.
- All logs and traces must include version or build_id to correlate performance regressions with deployments. For metrics, version tagging should be limited to deployment-level metadata metrics to avoid time-series cardinality explosion.
- Additional contextual tags such as instance_type or customer_tier may be applied selectively where their cardinality impact is controlled and the analytical value justifies the cost.

Either metadata management systems (e.g., DataHub) or centralized schema registries (e.g., Confluent Schema Registry) help guarantee consistency and lineage.

9.5.5 Handling High Cardinality and High Velocity

When tag combinations explode, that is, service = payment, user_id = 1234, and region = us-east-1 provides unique time series per user, high cardinality results. Techniques for mitigation:

- **The Cardinality of Reference Caving:** Limit dynamic tags, that is, delete user_id from metric tags, and record user-level data just in logs or a different analytics pipeline.
- **Aggregations for Roll-Up:** Higher-level aggregates, that is, per service per region instead of every instance per user.
- **Approximate Data Structures:** Approximate unique counts using sketches (e.g., HyperLog and Bloom Filters) instead of recording all identities.

High velocity implies a continual flood of data. Approaches include:

- Streaming systems (Apache Flink and Spark Structured Streaming) for real-time analytics; batch jobs (Spark and Presto) for historical analysis.
- Elastic scaling of Kafka partitions, Flink task managers, or Elasticsearch nodes handles spikes (e.g., Black Friday traffic).
- Define SLAs for ingestion; that is, give error logs top priority over debug logs during high traffic.

Model performance and economy depend on correctly handling cardinality and velocity.

9.6 AI/ML Techniques for Intelligent Observability

9.6.1 Unsupervised Learning for Baseline Modeling

When labeled data is unavailable (as is often the case with novel incidents), unsupervised techniques form the backbone of anomaly detection:

- **Statistical Baselines:**
  - Compute rolling mean $\mu(t)$ and standard deviation $\sigma(t)$ across a sliding window (e.g., last one hour). If $|x(t)—\mu(t)\ |\ \mathrm{k}\cdot\sigma(t) > k\cdot\sigma(t)$ flags a data point $x(t)$. Sensitivity and false-positive rate change with window size and k (e.g., 3 sigma).
  - Seasonal decomposition is a technique including STL (seasonal-trend decomposition using LOESS) that breaks a time series into seasonal, trend, and residual components, thereby allowing the identification of abnormalities in the residual.
- **Clustering and Density Estimation:**
  - Metrics compiled into feature vectors, (e.g., CPU, memory, disk I/O, and network I/O during five-minute intervals) can be clustered using K-Means, sometimes known as DBSCAN. Potential anomalies are points falling distant from cluster centroids. DBSCAN marks sites in low-density areas as anomalies.
  - **Gaussian Mixture Models (GMMs):** Fit a mixture of Gaussians to historical metric distributions; calculate low-likelihood spots marked as anomalies' probability.
- **Autoencoders:**
  - Feedforward autoencoders are neural networks intended to copy input data. New data reconstruction error deviates from learned regular patterns.
  - GRU, LSTM, or autoencoders: In sequential data, note sequential temporal dependencies. Helpful for spotting contextual abnormalities, that is, a database latency spike at midnight deviant from usual.
- **Isolation Forests:**
  - Trees designed to isolate anomalies using random feature splits. Usually anomalies are points needing fewer splits to isolate. Perfect for high-dimensional feature sets.
  - Unsupervised techniques are particularly helpful in the first stages of AIOps adoption when tagged events are few.

9.6.2 Supervised Learning for Known Anomalies

Supervised systems can identify new abnormalities when past events have been classified (e.g., "disk failure," "memory leak," and "network saturation"):

- **Features for each event can be average CPU, maximum memory consumption, error log counts, and network packet drop rate across a previous window.**

Classification Models:

- XGBoost, LightGBM: Random Forests and Gradient Boosting machines handle missing values elegantly, offer feature importance rankings, and resist noisy data.
- Though they scale poorly for large datasets, support vector machines (SVMs) are effective for binary classification of "normal" against "failure" states.
- For sliding window time-series shape analysis, either fully linked networks or lightweight CNNs. Many times, it calls for careful tweaking to prevent overfitting.

Training Considerations:

- Class Imbalance: Compared to usual operating times, failures are infrequent. Synthetic failure samples can be produced with methods such as the synthetic minority over-sampling technique (SMOTE).
- Time-series cross-validation, that is, walk-forward validation, helps to guarantee that models generalize to future data distribution.
- Regularization and feature selection help to prevent overfitting toward arbitrary features.

Supervised models shine if a company has accumulated several months or years of incident data tagged with root causes.

9.6.3 Time-Series Forecasting and Trend Analysis

Time-series forecasting in predictive analytics helps to foresee capacity saturation, performance deterioration, or new anomalies:

- ARIMA, or autoregressive integrated moving average, models seasonality and temporal relationships. ARIMA (p, d, q) calls for careful parameter adjustment generally using auto-ARIMA libraries.
- Models level, trend, and seasonality componentially using exponential smoothing (ETS). For measures with daily or weekly seasonality especially, the Holt-winters seasonal technique is extensively applied.
- Prophet (Facebook Prophet): An additive model managing several seasonalities, holiday effects, and outliers. Its simplicity and interpretability help it to be popular in observability settings.

- Deep neural networks able to record long-term dependencies are LSTM networks. For multivariate forecasting, architectures could call for layered LSTM layers or attention methods.
- Combining statistical models with neural networks, that instance, employing an ARIMA model to detect seasonality and feeding residuals into an LSTM to learn nonlinear patterns, results in hybrid models.

Forecasts can drive proactive scaling decisions; that is, "Provision two more nodes in the Kubernetes cluster in 2 hours to avoid CPU saturation."

9.6.4 Clustering and Dimensionality Reduction

For modeling as well as visualization, high-dimensional feature spaces, that is, hundreds of tags and hundreds of measurements, can present difficulties. Reduction of dimensionality promotes exploratory data exploration and model efficiency:

- Linear transformation projecting features into orthogonal main components is the principle component analysis (PCA). Applied for data compression for downstream modeling or cluster visualization of like behavior.
- Effective for visualizing clusters of anomalies or incident groups, nonlinear approaches maintaining local structure include t-distributed stochastic neighbor embedding (t-SNE) and uniform manifold approximation and projection (UMAP).
- Train autoencoders with a narrow "bottleneck" to learn compressed representations. One can cluster the latent vectors (e.g., using K-Means) to find groupings of like events.
- Feature importance of isolation forests: Although Isolation Forest is mostly an anomaly detector, its data partitioning technique can highlight characteristics that often cause isolations, hence directing feature selection.

Underlying event correlation is also clustering; grouping together anomalies with a latent representation or cluster membership suggests they might be connected.

9.6.5 Graph-Based Models for Dependency Mapping

Microservices and cloud architecture naturally create dependency graphs: services call databases, databases call outside APIs, web frontends call microservices, etc. Strong root cause analysis is unlocked by graph-based models—probabilistic graphical models and knowledge graphs—by means of which:

- Graph of Property: Vertices are entities—services, hosts, and databases; edges are relationships—HTTP calls, RPC, data reading, and data writing. Latencies, error rates—telemetry data—became edge or node properties.
- Graph neural networks (GNNs) are direct operators on graph structures. GNNs can learn embeddings for every node, capturing local topology and attribute context. Examining embeddings that differ much from historical averages helps one to find novel abnormalities.
- Directed acyclic graphs describing conditional dependencies between events form Bayesian networks. For Node A, for instance, high CPU raises the likelihood of increasing Service B's latency. Given observable anomalies, Bayesian inference can calculate posterior probabilities for probable root causes [6].
- Graph Pattern Matching: Searching subgraphs matching known failure patterns, that is, a resource leak pattern whereby calls build up without release. Cipher or Gremlin searches enabled by systems such as Neo4j or JanusGraph help to find dubious subgraph topologies.

Explicitly modeling interdependencies, graph-based methods focus on anomalies consistent with established dependency corruption patterns, hence lowering false positives.

9.6.6 Reinforcement Learning for Adaptive Thresholds

Thresholds, whether static or even dynamically learned, can still fall short of fast-changing workloads. Reinforcement learning (RL) provides a means to modify thresholds or remedial strategies depending on environment feedback:

- Markov Decision Systems (MDPs): States (current metric values gathered into discrete bins), actions (e.g., raise alert, ignore, and scale up), and rewards (e.g., −1 for false positive and +1 for correctly prevented outage). Learning rules $\pi(s) \rightarrow a$ helps RL agents optimize total reward.
- Deep Q-Networks (DQNs) approximate *Q*-values for state-action couples by means of deep neural networks. The DQN keeps retraining on fresh experience tuples (s, a, r, s'). As the system changes.
- Methodologies of Policy Gradient: Using gradient ascent on predicted reward, directly maximize the policy. Applied in constant action environments (e.g., choosing the ideal scaling factor).
- Multiple RL agents allocated to various clusters or service domains in federated systems can coordinate via shared rewards or communication channels [7].

Although RL-based AIOps is still a topic of current research, first tests indicate promise for settings with very nonstationary workloads.

9.7 Anomaly Detection and Root Cause Analysis

9.7.1 Types of Anomalies

Anomalies manifest in various forms:

1) Point anomalies, that is, one data point deviates significantly from the expected baseline that CPU use increases to 100% for one minute.
2) Although 60% is reasonable under normal traffic, data that seems out of context but not globally—for instance, a CPU jump to 60% during a billing cycle—is aberrant. Context includes time of day, day of week, or workload.
3) Though individual points may seem normal (e.g., an application discovers a slow memory leak only after several hours), a sequence of data points is unusual.

Good AIOps systems use several detection techniques concurrently to identify every kind of abnormality.

9.7.2 Multi-Modal Anomaly Detection (Metrics + Logs + Traces)

Depending just on measurements can overlook anomalies showing themselves mostly in logs or traces. A comprehensive strategy links anomalies in several modalities:

- Metric Anomalies and Log Error Bursts: Their relationship, for example, a 50% rise in the measure request error rate, combined with 200 "NullPointerException" log entries (log anomaly).
- Outliers Based On Trace-Based Latency: Although aggregated measures show typical percentiles, traces demonstrate that a given downstream dependence call is taking orders of magnitude longer.
- A CPU spike on an autoscaling group (infrastructure) plus a rapid increase in HTTP 503 faults (application) points to a load balancing health check configuration problem.

Many telemetry feeds are ingested and timestamp-aligned by AIOps systems, which then feed a single ML pipeline. Detection fidelity is much improved by feature vectors integrating measurements, log-derived features (error code counts), and trace statistics (average span length).

9.7.3 Alert Fatigue Mitigation Through Noise Reduction

Alert fatigue remains a primary obstacle to operational efficiency. Key strategies include the following:

- Event Deduplication: If an anomaly kicks out 100 alarms over 100 hosts, compress the same anomaly into one event using host count metadata.
- Silence windows temporarily mute alerts following automated correction until the issue returns within a designated "grace period."
- Inaccuity lower thresholds in low-noise areas and increase thresholds where noise is normal (e.g., during deployments), depending on prior false-positive rates.
- Unless severity surpasses a secondary level, silence-related alarms should be triggered should a known root cause, such as planned maintenance, be active.
- Let engineering teams identify some anomalies as "informational" instead of "critical," connecting them to other degrees of notification or channels.

By combining like alarms and reducing duplicate noise, AIOps systems reduce problem queues and boost reaction times.

9.7.4 Probabilistic Correlation and Causality Inference

In a distributed system, establishing causality is by nature probabilistic. Methods comprise the following:

- Granger Causality Tests: Statistical technique to examine whether time series X "Granger-causes," that is, past values of X assist in predicting future values of Y. Applied to deduce directional correlations between metrics, that is, "Network jitter on Node A Granger causes increased latency on Service B."
- Bayesian networks model conditional relationships among variables. Bayesian inference changes each possible root cause's posterior probability as evidence—observed anomalies—arrives.
- Create a directed, weighted edge call volume and latency service-dependent graph based on graph-based inference. Release "blame" upstream proportionately along edges weighted by traffic volume when an anomaly arises downstream. This helps the epicenter of failure to be localized.
- Using structural causal models and "Do-Calculus" to separate correlation from causality, causal AI models "If we artificially throttle database write IOPS, does frontend latency always increase?" asks one. Controlled experiments guide causal relationships.

Especially in cases of non-obvious underlying causes or when multiple interdependent elements are involved, probabilistic inference complements deterministic rule-based correlation [6].

9.7.5 Topology-Aware Root Cause Localization

Finding the failed component in densely meshed microservices designs calls for knowledge of the runtime topography. Strategies comprise the following:

- **Maps of Service Dependability:** Automatically find call graphs using instrumentation (Open Telemetry) or service mesh telemetry (such as Envoy's xDS logs). This graph rolls updates and reflects dynamic scaling constantly.
- **Path Analysis of Criticality:** Determine the order of spans that makes the critical path—longest cumulative latency—for a given request. Usually indicating a delay in each service or database shard, an inexplicable rise in critical path length usually results from.
- **Model of Impact Propagation:** Calculate how the performance degradation of a component affects downstream services; that is, a 100 ms change in database response time could translate to a 250 ms increase in checkout flow. Impact scores enable rank-based prioritizing of root component repair above symptomatic objectives.
- **Bayesian Belief Propagation on Graphs:** Iteratively update the probability of failure across the dependency graph via belief propagation as evidence (metric anomalies) emerges. Highly posterior probability nodes are identified as probable root causes.

Real-time topology awareness guarantees that incident response aims at the actual cause rather than only the symptom.

9.7.6 Confidence Scores and Explainability

Only as reliable as they are trusted are AI-driven insights actionable. To build confidence:

- Confidence Measures: Every anomaly finding or root cause inference comes with a numerical confidence score of 0–1. Events over specified confidence levels alone are escalated.
- **Explainable AI (XAI) Techniques:**
  - SHapley Additive explanations (SHAP) count feature contributions to the anomaly score of a model. For example, "error log count accounts for 30%; CPU use accounts for 40% of anomaly score."
  - Local Interpretable Model-Agnostics Explanations (LIME): It creates locally faithful approximations to complex models to show why a certain data item was flagged.

  - Extensive Rule Extraction: From tree-based models, that is, "If memory use >75% AND GC pause time > 200 ms, classify as memory_leak_high."
- Visualization of the Inference Paths Show with interactive tools a causal chain—metric anomaly → linked log errors → dependent map → root cause service.

Engineers are more inclined to trust and apply automated workflows when they can see "why" an AIOps platform suggests a certain root cause or solution.

9.8 Incident Management Workflow

9.8.1 Incident Lifecycle: Detection → Triage → Diagnosis → Remediation

In an AIOps-enabled system, a normal incident management procedure consists of these phases:

1) AI/ML engine notes an anomaly (e.g., an error rate on checkout or service above baseline for five minutes).
2) The platform generates a single incident record giving a priority (P1, P2, etc.), correlates related anomalies, and computes severity (e.g., user-impacting mistakes vs. internal warnings).
3) The root cause analysis module identifies the most likely accountable root causes and surfaces top-ranked infrastructure or service components. Attached are pertinent telemetry snippets—metric sparklines, for example, log snippets and trace snapshots.
4) The orchestrating layer offers runbooks or prompts automatic remedial action for on-call engineers. The runbook step execution is recorded, and should it be successful, the incident is automatically rectified. Should this be proven ineffective; the problem is escalated to a human team for more thorough inquiry.
5) Following resolution, the incident record is revised, including root cause confirmation, chronology of events, measures taken, and lessons discovered. These serve to retrain supervised models and are returned into the knowledge base.

9.8.2 Automated Triage: Ticket Generation and Prioritization

Upon detection of a correlated incident cluster, the platform:

- Using contextual data and a clear narrative, ITSM systems, that is, ServiceNow and Jira, generate a ticket automatically ("High error rate observed inAuth-service, probably root cause: increased Database latency").

- Owner names and strength labels: The platform can find whether this issue resides in P1 or P2 by applying accepted service-level agreements (SLAs) and service-level objectives (SLOs). Referring specifically to service ownership acquired from a centralized service registry, it then allocates the ticket to the applicable SRE or DevOps engineer.
- Key metrics, a link to the issue dashboard, and recommended corrective action first under consideration promptly by Slack or SMS to the on-call rotation. First priorities for the alert payload are simplicity and shortness since they help to reduce cognitive burden during on-call reacting.

9.8.3 ChatOps and Collaborative Incident Response

9.8.3.1 Runbook Automation and Playbook Execution

Well-defined runbooks codify best practices for resolution steps. In an AIOps context:

Declarative Playbooks: Defined in YAML or JSON, specifying conditions under which certain remediation steps execute. For instance:

```
name: scale-checkout-service
trigger:
condition: checkout_latency >500ms for 3 minutes
actions:
 - type: kubernetes_scale
parameters:
namespace: ecommerce
deployment: checkout-service
replicas: +2
- type: wait_for
parameters:
condition: avg_latency <300ms
timeout: 5m
```

- **Integration with IaC:** Playbooks can call Terraform modules or Helm charts to adjust infrastructure—"increase EBS volume size by 10%" or "redeploy Node.js service with patched image."
- **Dry Run and Safety Checks:** Each playbook can run in "dry run" mode to validate syntax and check permissions. Safety checks ensure that, for example, scaling actions do not exceed budgeted resource quotas.
- **Execution Auditing:** Every automated step is logged—who/what triggered it, success/failure status, timestamps—to satisfy compliance and postmortem analysis.

9.8.4 Automated Remediation: Safe Rollbacks and Remediation Scripts

From "soft actions" (collect more data, notify stakeholders) to "hard actions" (turn back a defective deployment), automated remedial action can range as follows:

- Should a newly implemented microservice version show an increase in error rates, the platform can immediately roll back to the prior stable image. To confirm resolution, pre- and post-rollback statistics are matched against SLIs.
- Circuit Breaker Corrections: Change Hystrix or Istio's circuit breaker thresholds dynamically to stop cascade failures.
- Detect a cold cache causing high latency and coordinate pre-warming scripts to preload often accessed keys into Redis or Memcached.
- If connection times surpass a threshold, automatically change the connection pool settings; then, track the impact.
- Should underlying hardware problems be discovered (e.g., "Instance i-0abcd1234 shows repeated I/O errors"), the platform can initiate instance reboots or migrations for cloud providers offering self-healing (e.g., AWS Auto Recovery for EC2).

Automated remedial action speeds up resolution, but it's important to make sure runbooks are completely tested to reduce accidental side effects risk.

9.8.5 Human-in-the-Loop vs. Fully Autonomous Remediation

Companies choose between depending on confidence level and risk tolerance either:

- Human-in-the-Loop Automation: The platform asks operator permission before launching recommended corrective measures. Review root cause analysis, relevant logs, and confidence scores; then, click "Approve" or "Reject." This approach finds a middle ground between care and speed.
- Under well-understood, low-risk conditions (e.g., "if CPU use >90% and scale-out is available, increase replica count"), the system runs remedial action devoid of human involvement. Safety is guaranteed by guardrails, including rollback on failure and frequency of execution.
- New remedial procedures begin as "suggestions" and, following a zero false positive probationary period, move to "automated execution." The platform tracks challenge-response success rates to modify autonomy degrees.

Compliance needs, the cost of downtime against the cost of erroneous actions, and the level of AIOps implementation maturity will determine which of these approaches best suits you.

9.9 Case Studies and Industry Implementations

9.9.1 E-Commerce Platform at Scale: Reducing Flash Sale Downtime

Background: A leading online business reports extraordinary traffic surges during limited-time flash sales where orders per second (OPS) could skyrocket by 100x in minutes. Any delay or slowdown at these times causes lost income and instantly disgruntled consumers. Backpressure in payment microservices and cascade failures in the checkout process would go unseen since the rapid changes in traffic patterns would not let traditional monitoring catch up.

AIOps Implementation:

Telemetry Architecture:

- Prometheus ran five-second intervals over three AWS region's worth of Kubernetes clusters, scraping container metrics.
- Fluentd aggregated structured JSON logs to an Elasticsearch cluster with ingestion pipelines for processing payment error codes.
- OpenTelemetry auto-instrumentation for major microservices (checkout, payment, inventory) delivered spans to Jaeger.

Anomaly Detection:

- Unsupervised LSTM autoencoders shaped normal request latency and error rates. Real-time baselines changed as traffic grew.
- Priority in tail-based trace sampling was sluggish trace capture at flash sale peak.

Event Correlation:

- Graph-based dependent models connected spikes in payment service latency to higher downstream latency in order service.
- Bayesian inference computed that a 3× increase in checkout queue depth was 85% likely caused by payment database contention.

Automated Remediation:

- Upon detecting payment DB CPU above 75% for two minutes, an IaC-driven runbook triggered read-replica promotion and scaled out the Aurora Cluster.
- Concurrently, Kubernetes autoscaling rules scaled payment service pods from 5 to 20 replicas with CPU affinity tweaks to prevent loud neighbors.
- Within three minutes, monitoring confirmed queue depths fell by 70%; end-to-end checkout latency reverted to baseline.

Outcomes:

- From 8 minutes to 30 seconds, MTTD reduction: mean time to detect lowered.
- From 45 minutes to 5 minutes, mean time to resolution (MTTR) dropped.

- Order success rate rose by 12% during a Black Friday flash sale, therefore generating an estimated $5 million in extra income.
- Monthly alert traffic fell by 60%; 95% of events were automatically addressed without human involvement.

9.9.2 Financial Services: Compliance-Driven Observability

Background: A worldwide bank must follow strict regulations (e.g., PCI DSS, SOX, and GDPR) even if its online banking system provides outstanding availability. Account-access logs, network flows, and transaction trails, among other observable data, must be preserved as unchangeable and auditable. Any odd trend, including data exfiltration efforts or odd financial transfers, calls for quick inquiry.

AIOps Implementation

Secure Data Ingestion:

- From middleware and mainframe transaction systems, logs arrived across SSL/TLS into an on-site Splunk cluster.
- To provide real-time threat detection, Fluent Bit logs Kubernetes-based microservices straight to a specialist SIEM.

Hybrid Cloud Observability:

- While AWS-based microservices delivered data to CloudWatch, on-site VMware clusters published metrics via Telegraf via InfluxDB. A unified data layer used a cross-cloud abstraction (Thanos) to federate Prometheus metrics endpoints.

AI/ML for Fraud Detection:

- Transaction logs underwent NLP-based pattern analysis, embedding descriptions of transaction origins, amounts, and destinations into vector spaces.
- An Isolation Forest model learned normal transaction patterns per account; anomalies (e.g., a large transfer to an unfamiliar foreign account) triggered high-severity incidents.

Trace-Based Compliance Auditing:

- Every customer request was traced end-to-end, capturing PII fields (hashed/encrypted) and service calls. Audit trails satisfied regulatory auditors' requirement for "chain of custody" on data access.

Automated Triage:

- Based on risk-scoring rules (e.g., transactions > $10,000 outside business hours flagged as "Tier 1 incident").
- Automated ticket creation in ServiceNow, with required fields pre-populated (e.g., account ID, transaction timestamp, and anomaly score).

Human-in-the-Loop for Remediation:

- Regulatory constraints forbade fully automated account freezes. Instead, the platform presented contextual data and recommended manual steps to compliance officers, who then validated and executed holds on suspicious accounts.

Outcomes:

- **Regulatory Compliance:** Achieved 100% audit transparency with searchable, immutable logs.
- **Fraud Reduction:** Real-time anomaly detection prevented an estimated $2 million in fraudulent transactions in the first quarter post-deployment.
- **Operational Efficiency:** Fraud investigation teams reduced mean investigation time from 48 to 4 hours by leveraging AI-driven prioritization of cases.

9.9.3 SaaS Provider: Predictive Autoscaling and Cost Optimization

Background: Kubernetes clusters enable a B2B SaaS vendor to host their multi-tenant application. They have long depended on threshold-based horizontal pod autoscaler (HPA) rules—scale when CPU > 70%. Under erratic workloads, this reactive strategy produced either under-provisioning—user performance complaints—or frequent over-provisioning—wasted expenditure [8].

AIOps Implementation:

Workload Forecasting:

- Prophet lets one emulate past CPU and memory usage per tenancy. Forecasts, including 95% confidence intervals, show 60 minutes ahead of estimated resource demand.
- Clustering on daily use patterns exposed unexpected workload bursts, that is, new tenant onboarding.

Adaptive Autoscaling Policies:

- Forecasting outputs allowed a reinforcement learning agent to tune HPA thresholds and scale-out multipliers.
- The policy sought to reduce resource expenditure as well as SLA violations and latency of more than 200 ms.

Cost-Aware Anomaly Detection:

- Monitoring the usage of resource by tenant vs. allotted budgets helps identify cost-aware anomalies. Alert thresholds are raised if there are temporary spikes in demand from forecasts.

Dashboards and What-If Analysis:

- Using cost and performance forecasts, engineers created bespoke dashboards to replicate "what if" situations, that is, "what if Tenant X's usage doubles tomorrow."

Outcomes:

- By more precise right-sizing, cloud infrastructure expenses dropped by 18%.
- 99.9% uptime attained with a 5 ms median tail delay.
- 85% of scaling decisions made without hand overrides are autonomous.

9.9.4 Telecom Network: Edge Computing and Distributed AIOps

Background: To serve low-latency applications (AR/VR, IoT), a telecom operator built edge compute clusters across 2,000 cell towers. Edge clusters run on low-capacity computation and storage-limited ruggedized servers. Network heterogeneity and bandwidth restrictions made central monitoring of every edge node impractical.

AIOps Implementation:

Federated AIOps Architecture:

- Using small ML models, such as on-device autoencoders, local AIOps agents placed on every edge node executed lightweight anomaly detection.
- To cut data delivered to the central cloud, raw telemetry was pre-processed locally—downsampling measurements and filtering logs.

Hierarchical Event Correlation:

- Local events, such as temperature sensor abnormalities pointing to overheating, activated alarms at the regional orchestration plane, which linked several edge events to identify more significant problems, such as datacenter cooling system failure.

Edge-to-Cloud Knowledge Sharing:

- Federated Learning collected model updates from every edge to train a global model in the cloud, then redistributed improved anomaly detection models back to edge nodes.

Network-Aware Root Cause Localization:

- Graph models captured network topology (tower → regional PoP → backbone). When end-user QoE dropped, the platform followed packet flows to find troublesome hops, such as fronthaul jitter.

Outcomes:

- Edge preprocessing reduces telemetry egress by 75% bandwidth savings.
- On-site engineers are sent preemptively based on predictive models projecting hardware problems, therefore reducing repair times by 40%.
- Federated learning preserved model correctness across edge sites under different hardware and network conditions.

9.9.5 Lessons Learned and Comparative Analysis

From these case studies, some cross-cutting lessons highlight:

1) Data quality first and foremost is garbage in, garbage out. Directly affects model accuracy by consistently labeling telemetry with great fidelity.
2) Small companies that begin with pilot AIOps on one critical function often discover success as they scale gradually.
3) Human–machine symbiosis is defined as automation speeds incident response, but human oversight is still very vital, especially for high-risk remedial actions.
4) To prevent silos, SRE, Dev, and security teams must line up on observability criteria—naming conventions and retention policies.
5) Ongoing Model Retraining: As services change, model drift happens. Regular retraining using new incident data preserves detection accuracy.

These actual implementations show ultimately that AIOps is not a one-size-fits-all solution; rather, it must be customized to each company's particular telemetry sources, service architectures, and risk profiles.

9.10 Best Practices for AIOps Adoption

9.10.1 Organizational Readiness and Cultural Shift

- Executive sponsorship defined by cash distribution and leadership buy-in. Frame AIOps as a strategic investment helping data-driven decision-making, reducing downtime costs, and increasing developer productivity.
- SRE aligns with DevOps: AIOps should be included in DevOps procedures; CI pipelines include instrumentation tests; pull requests for code fixes start from events. Service Level Indicators (SLIs) and SLOs enable SRE teams to prioritize models; that is, focus on statistics related to SLO violations.
- Operations teams have tools thanks to training in observability, data science, and ML engineering. Promote cross-functional "blameless postmortem" sharing of incident learning.
- Automating corrective action could cause job loss worries. Stress that AIOps increases human capability so engineers may concentrate on other worthwhile projects (like capacity planning and architectural enhancements).

9.10.2 Data Governance, Privacy, and Security Considerations

- **Access Restraints:** Use RBAC for telemetry data; restrict sensitive log access to authorized users.

- **Encipherment:** TLS for data in transit; AES-256 or comparable for data at rest.
- **Conformance:** Retain logs and measurements in line with regulations; for example, financial organizations could need seven years of audit records. Make PII in logs anonymous or tokenized.
- **Policies in Data Retention:** Describe tiered retention, that is, high-granularity metrics kept for 7 days, aggregated data for 90 days, and preserved past data.
- **Risks Third-Party Vendors Create:** If using managed AIOps solutions, review privacy and data security shared responsibility models.

9.10.3 Incremental Implementation and Proof-of-Value

- For pilot projects, choose a critical service with well-known KPIs, like a user login system. Measure baseline MTTR and MTTD. Apply unsupervised anomaly detection to error rates and login latency.
- Minimum viable AIOps (MVA) Start with a lean ML pipeline, say for basic Z-score-based anomaly detection on relevant benchmarks. Track improvements with alert accuracy.
- Iterate and enlarge: Once MVA shows value, that is, 50% noise reduction, onboard other services, enhance models (e.g., employ log analytics), and link runbook automation.
- **Key Success Metrics:**
  - Alert precision/recall is defined by the percentage of genuine positives against false positives.
  - Compare pre- and post-AIOps deployment MTTD and MTTR.
  - **Savings on Operations Costs:** Less on-call hours; anticipatory scaling helps to optimize cloud costs.
  - Time saved by developers on not reacting to false alarms represents their productivity.

9.10.4 Key Performance Indicators (KPIs) and Metrics

- Mean Time to Detect: Time passed between issue occurrence and discovery.
- Time between detection and resolution is the mean time to resolve, or MTTR.
- **Alert Accuracy:**
  - **Precision** = True Positives / (True Positives + False Positives)
  - **Recall** = True Positives / (True Positives + False Negatives)
- Weekly or monthly occurrence count broken by severity.
- **Automation Rate:** Ratio of auto-remediated incidents to total remediated incidents, indicating the level of operational autonomy.
- Engineer hours times hourly rate plus resource waste plus downtime cost to get cost per incident.

9.10.5 Integration with DevOps Toolchains and CI/CD Pipelines

- **Instrumentation in CI/CD:**
  - Automated tests check telemetry instrumentation, that is, simulated transactions and trace injections, prior to deployment.
  - Deploy new code to a small subset of users; AIOps tracks rollback alerts if key metrics exceed defined thresholds.
  - Progressive Rollouts: Integrate with feature flagging platforms; AIOps monitors for anomalies unique to newly enabled features.
- **GitOps for AIOps Configuration:**
  - Git repositories include runbooks, playbooks, ML model configurations, and alert policies. Changes set off automatic CI processes that validate configurations, that is, grammar checks and dry runs.
  - Version-controlled AIOps systems offer audit trails, which are vital for regulated sectors.
- **Feedback Loops:**
  - Automatic generation of tickets by post-incident RCA records produces branch checklists for code repairs.
  - Periodically, ML models retrain on updated incident labels—the pipeline is triggered by fresh tags in Git or Jira.

9.10.6 Vendor Selection: Open-Source vs. Commercial AIOps Platforms

- **Open-Source Solutions:**
  - **Pros:** Benefits include flexible adaptations driven by communities without licensing fees.
  - **Cons:** To build a whole stack, ELK (Elasticsearch, Logstash, Kibana), Prometheus, Jaeger, Grafana, Kafka, Apache Flink, and ML frameworks (TensorFlow, PyTorch) call for significant internal knowledge.
- **Commercial AIOps Products:**
  - Among other examples are Splunk IT Service Intelligence (ITSI), Moogsoft, Dynatrace, New Relic with AIOps modules, Datadog, and Cisco AppDynamics.
  - Among the pros are integrated UI/UX, pre-built ML models, vendor support, SLAs, and simpler onboarding.
  - **Cons:** Possible vendor lock-in, licensing expenses, sometimes limited customizing.
- **Hybrid Approach:**
  - Open-source core data intake, storage, and basic visualization; commercial vendor specialized ML/AI modules.

- Over three to five years, assess total cost of ownership (TCO), accounting for operational overhead, engineering personnel, managed service cloud egress costs.

9.11 Challenges and Limitations

9.11.1 Data Silos and Heterogeneous Tooling

- Many companies build a fragmented observability stack over time—separate APM providers for application monitoring, Splunk for logs, Prometheus for metrics, and Jaeger for traces. Combining these into a single AIOps pipeline calls for major engineering work.
- Teams may utilize different logging systems, tag rules, or monitoring agents, so normalizing becomes difficult.
- Siloed ownership of measurements and logs might cause "blame games" during incidents. Adoption of AIOps calls for tearing down organizational divisions.

9.11.2 Model Drift and Concept Drift in Dynamic Environments

- Statistical characteristics of telemetry data vary with time; that is, following a high-performance hardware upgrade, CPU usage distributions change. Models fed previous data start to lose accuracy.
- Concept Drift: The fundamental definition of "normal behavior" changes (e.g., the launch of a new microservice altering traffic patterns). You need either periodic baseline recalibration, online learning, or ongoing model retraining.
- Supervised models depend on labeled events, although labeling is labor-intensive. Annotation systems—tagging timestamps, root causes, and remedial results—have to be investments made by organizations.
- The cold start problem is that newly introduced services or areas lacking historical data make anomaly detection less accurate. Bootstrapping calls for first-hand configuration till enough data builds up.

9.11.3 Explainability and Trust in AI-Driven Decisions

- Deep learning–based anomaly detectors often lack interpretability: black box models' recommendations without explicit explanations could make engineers hesitant to follow.
- Restraints on Regulation: Some sectors (financial, healthcare) call for open decision-making policies; why was a corrective action set off?
- Over-Reliance on Automation: Blind faith in automatic remediations might have unexpected results (e.g., an auto-scaled cluster that runs out of budget or sets off cascading failures).

- Human Biases in Feedback Systems: Should operators without updating ML models consistently suppress false positives, the platform might not learn from mistakes, hence sustaining errors.

9.11.4 Scalability and Cost Overhead

- Real-time ML inference on high-dimensional telemetry can be costly, particularly when employing graph databases or sophisticated deep learning models or both. Though it increases operational complexity, edge preprocessing helps.
- Large-scale AIOps systems sometimes call for specialized Kubernetes clusters for ML workloads, streaming engines (Flink, Spark), and storage, each with their own scaling issues.
- Storage Tiers and Cloud Egress: Cross-region data replication for high availability pays for egress. Cold storage options can restrict real-time access required for research.
- Commercial AIOp tools charge depending on data entered or hosts under observation. Unexpected telemetry spikes, that instance, during a security breach, can greatly increase expenses.

9.11.5 Regulatory Compliance and Auditing Needs

- Financial and healthcare sectors would have to keep logs and measurements for five to seven years, hence raising storage expenses.
- Tamper-evident logs are required of telemetry pipelines to show compliance. Techniques consist of cryptographic hashing of logs or write-once-read-many (WORM) storages.
- Data residency requirements: Certain geographies, such as GDPR for EU residents, dictate that some telemetry data stay inside national borders. Multi-cloud or hybrid cloud designs must guarantee telemetry partitioning.
- All views and changes of telemetry data must be recorded, including who requested sensitive logs, who ran remedial scripts, and who changed ML model settings. AIOps systems must interface with enterprise IAM (identity and access management) systems.

9.12 Future Directions in AIOps

9.12.1 Intent-Driven Operations and Policy-as-Code

- **Engineers define "SLO:** Average API response time < 200 ms; Availability >99.9%." AIOps systems automatically translate high-level intents into monitoring rules, SLI tracking, and remedial policies.

- **Policy-as-Code:** Operations are described declaratively—"If CPU > 80% and memory >75%, then scale out by two replicas instead of manually codifying remedial scripts." The system generates executable processes from policies, formally verifying them to guarantee no contradictory rules.
- **Closed-Loop Policy Enforcement:** Integrating with policy engines (e.g., Open Policy Agent, OPA) to enforce compliance at runtime, "Block any deployment where container images are not sourced from approved registries with signed attestations."

9.12.2 Self-Healing Systems and Closed-Loop Automation

- The vision is one that not only detects and diagnoses but also completely remediates without human control. Self-healing systems will combine AIOps logic straight into Kubernetes, OpenStack, and VMware vSphere management loops.
- Intent-based networking (IBN) allows network controllers to automatically rectify by changing security group rules or network ACLs while constantly searching for policy violations (e.g., "no traffic flow from public internet to internal DB").
- AIOps systems monitor system resilience, automatically changing configurations to increase fault tolerance, and coordinate controlled chaos experiments (e.g., kill a random pod daily).
- Combining conversational AI (chatbots) with automated remedial action, "Alice, investigate the cause of increased latency," triggers AIOps to produce a summary, then "Alice, patch the service image and redeploy."

9.12.3 Integration of AIOps with APM and DevSecOps

- Integrating security telemetry (SIEM, vulnerability scanners) with performance metrics and logs, "Detect suspicious login patterns correlated with sudden CPU spikes, indicating potential crypto-mining malware," says Unified Observability for Security and Performance.
- AIOps systems provide operational data back into CI/CD, so "Deployment of version 2.3.4 correlated with a 30% increase in P95 latency; suggest rolling back to 2.3.3 and investigating code changes."
- Important CVEs should be discovered by real-time scanning container images in production with automated quarantine or rollback. AIOps can prioritize scanning, that is, first for microservices experiencing heavy traffic based on production use patterns.

9.12.4 Emerging AI Techniques: Generative Models, Causal AI

- Synthetic data generation uses generative adversarial networks (GANs) to synthesize realistic anomalous cases to train supervised models in environments with little failure data.

- Root Cause Analysis Causal AI: Beyond correlation to causal inference, that is, using Judea Pearl's do-calculus to project the impact of hypothetical interventions, that is, "If we throttle service X's CPU to 50%, how will it impact service Y's tail latency?"
- Transformer Models for Log Analysis: Using BERT-like architectures to grasp log semantics helps to provide context-aware anomaly detection; that is, "Model detects unusual sequence of log statements indicating a new class of failure never seen before" [1].
- Federated Learning Between Companies: Cross-industry consortia exchanging anonymized telemetry models—"Model trained on anomaly patterns from global financial institutions helps detect novel fraud patterns in smaller banks without sharing raw data" [7].

9.12.5 Toward Autonomous Cloud-Native Environments

- Users describe the desired state ("run 99% of traffic on g5 instances in us-east-1"), and the control plane, combined with AIOps, automatically prepares clusters, configures autoscaling, and manages canary deployments.
- Closed-loop feedback from AIOps constantly tunes parameters—"Network MTU, I/O scheduler, JVM GC policies"—to maximize cost and performance.
- What if we upgrade to PostgreSQL 14?" AIOps AI asks using scenario analysis to foresee likely instabilities, and real-time digital replicas of production settings replicate recommended modifications.
- From code commit to production, AIOps runs everything—CI pipeline triggering tests, blue/green deployment, observability instrumentation, proactive health checks, and automated rollout or rollback free from human participation.

9.13 Conclusion

For firms using cloud-native systems, AIOps represents a basic shift in perspective, diagnosis, and problem fixing. Using the confluence of big data, ML, and automation to reduce warning noise, speed root cause analysis, and enable proactive incident management, AIOps systems go beyond legacy monitoring. AIOps certainly provides value in terms of faster incident resolution, enhanced reliability, and optimum use of resources even if data silos, model drift, explainability, and organizational change management still present substantial challenges.

Looking ahead, AIOps will migrate toward entirely autonomous operations in which intent-driven rules and self-healing systems lower human involvement. Even further improving anomaly detection [1], predictive capacity, and cross-organizational collaboration are emerging AI approaches—causal inference, generative models, and federated learning [7]. The union of human expertise with machine intelligence will eventually drive the next generation of dependable, safe, and flexible cloud infrastructures, allowing businesses to offer perfect digital experiences at scale.

References

1 Q. Shi *et al.*, *Anomaly Transformer-based System Log Anomaly Detection*. Grand Forks, ND: Cyber Awareness and Research Symposium (CARS), 2024, pp. 1–6, doi: 10.1109/CARS61786.2024.10778676.

2 Putz, P. (2026). AIOps for infrastructure monitoring: The observability advantage, Jan 30. *Dynatrace News*. Available: https://www.dynatrace.com/news/blog/aiops-for-infrastructure-monitoring/#:~:text=Current%20monitoring%20tools%20are%20frequently,cloud%20or%20anywhere%20in%2Dbetween.

3 W. Zhang, Z. Yang, F. Peng, L. Zhang, Y. Chen, and R. Chen, "GALR: Graph-Based Root Cause Localization and LLM-Assisted Recovery for Microservice Systems," *Electronics*, vol. 15, no. 1, p. 243, 2026, doi: 10.3390/electronics15010243.

4 Client challenge. (n.d.). Available: https://www.scribd.com/document/825644078/study-What-is-AIOps-IBM.

5 J. Chen and W. Xu, "Anomaly detection in time series data for cloud observability," *IEEE Trans. Network Serv. Manage.*, vol. 16, no. 4, pp. 1234–1247, 2019.

6 S. Bollineni, "Systematic approach to root cause analysis in distributed data processing systems," *World . Adv. Res. Rev.*, vol. 25, no. 02, pp. 2343–2350, 2025, doi: 10.30574/wjarr.2025.25.2.0609.

7 Y. Tang and X. Wang, "Federated learning for edge AIOps in telecommunications," *IEEE Commun. Mag.*, vol. 61, no. 3, pp. 45–53, 2023.

8 Brendan Burns, Eddie Villalba, Dave Strebel, Lachlan Evenson (2019). *Kubernetes Best Practices*. O'Reilly Online Learning. https://www.oreilly.com/library/view/kubernetes-best-practices/9781492056461/ch14.html.

10

Cloud-Native DevSecOps and Shift-Left Security Practices

Jay Shah[1] *and Garima Bajpai*[2]

[1] *Independent Researcher, Canada DevOps Community of Practice, Toronto, ON, Canada*
[2] *Founder, Canada DevOps Community of Practice, Ottawa, ON, Canada*

10.1 Introduction

Over the past 5 years, the software development landscape has been dramatically reshaped by a wave of emerging technologies, including cloud computing, cloud-native software, artificial intelligence (AI), and machine learning [1]. These advances have accelerated development cycles, enabled new capabilities, and introduced both opportunities and significant challenges for practitioners, policymakers, regulators, and technology leaders. In this chapter, we will dig deeper into the evolution of the security ecosystem, primarily the shift-left security practices and DevSecOps initiatives for the cloud-native software ecosystem.

Let's see some of the statistics:

- A total of 26,447 critical vulnerabilities were disclosed in 2023, surpassing the previous year by more than 1,500 [2].
- Insecure design is ranked as the number four critical web application security concern on the Open Web Application Security Project (OWASP) [3].
- DevSecOps vulnerabilities are ranked fifth on the OWASP top 10 for large language model (LLM) applications, especially supply chain security, which is now a key element in all the companies (having a "Software Bill of Materials" [SBOM]) [4, 5].

The history of cloud-native software is intertwined with the evolution of cloud computing, containerization, and new software engineering practices. In the next section, we will highlight the key development for the cloud-native software ecosystem and how it resulted in evolving new practices for security, primarily shift-left and DevSecOps.

This chapter covers the following topics:

- State of DevSecOps and shift-left security.
- Implementing DevSecOps with frameworks and best practices.
- Developing the right skills, knowledge, and cultural practices.
- Key challenges, anti-patterns, and pitfalls.
- Future direction and evolution with emerging technology.

10.2 State of DevSecOps and Shift-Left Security

The term "shift-left" was first coined by Larry Smith in 2001. Smith introduced the concept in the context of "shift-left testing," advocating for moving quality assurance and testing activities earlier in the software development lifecycle. "Shift-left" refers to the practice of moving activities such as testing, quality assurance, and especially security earlier in the SDLC. Further, operationalizing the shift-left philosophy is credited to DevSecOps.

DevSecOps represents a strategic evolution in software development, ensuring that security is not an afterthought but a fundamental, integrated part of the development and operations process. This surge in popularity coincided with the rise of cloud-native with Docker, the emergence of the Development and Operations (DevOps) movement around 2010, and the formation of the CNCF in 2015. The intersection of shift-left and Development, Security and Operations (DecSecOps) can be traced toward 2015–2016, where the shift-left security practices and DevSecOps cultural movement ensure that organizations are enabled to deliver secure, high-quality software at speed.

DevOps helps organizations in designing and implementing resilient software systems by adopting design patterns or "secure by design," which have built-in resilience, such as distributed edge computing, and are flexible and reliable, using automation of both system deployment and system testing as a means to achieve speed in software delivery [6].

DevSecOps is a transformational shift-left to incline toward the common goal of making security a first-class problem and participant in all phases of agile SDLC. This incorporates a secure culture and tools to drive more visibility and collaboration, including security into each phase of the DevOps pipeline. The program should not only focus on the technical aspects but also create the right framework that fits the organization's business objective.

A DevSecOps program requires continuous improvement to achieve the desired efficiency. Start with establishing the strategic drivers for DevOps teams to meet the changing business requirements without excluding security and compliance needs. Then design a DevSecOps operating model that includes designing data flows, developing standards, and mapping technologies and processes to core security operations. Monitor to ensure that the processes are followed, maintained, reviewed, and updated regularly.

Approach security as a journey, not a destination—this means developing it as a progressive security program. Tightly integrate security tools and processes throughout the DevOps pipeline and make it a secure SDLC process. Automate core security tasks by adding security controls early in the software development lifecycle. Continuously monitor and fix security defects across the application lifecycle, including development and maintenance. Invest time in finding the right tool that fits your organization's needs and leverage it at each phase of the SDLC life cycle.

There are both technical and business benefits. There is continuous integration of security validations. There will be fewer security problems to fix in the production stage and faster remediation of issues by providing earlier feedback to engineers with clear guidance.

DevSecOps has several stages and gates within the pipeline. Let's see a traditional SDLC pipeline (Figures 10.1 and 10.2).

10.2.1 Planning and Design Phase

The design stage in a SDLC is the phase where the system, application, or product being developed is designed and planned. During the design stage of a secure SDLC, we identify and document the security requirements for the system, develop the overall architecture and design, identify and document any potential security risks or vulnerabilities, and develop a plan for addressing these potential security issues.

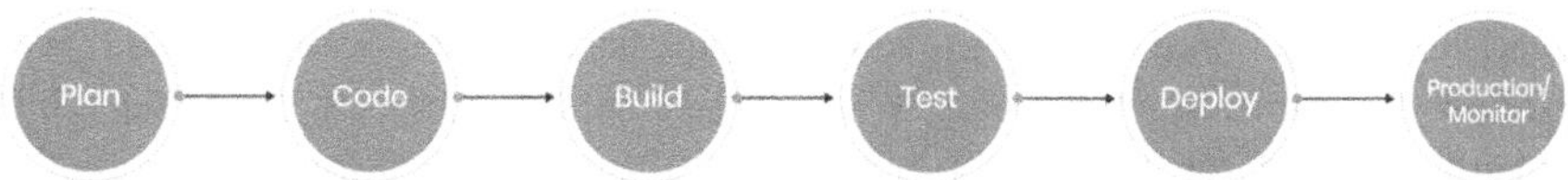

Figure 10.1 Traditional SDLC.

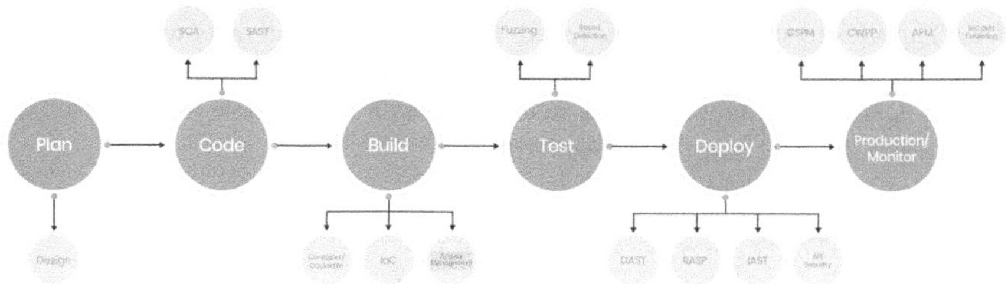

Figure 10.2 Secure SDLC. *Source:* Modified from [7].

10.2.2 Coding

Software composition analysis (SCA) is a scanning technique that looks at the open-source software components that you are knowingly and unknowingly (through transitive dependencies) bringing into your application and identifying any known vulnerabilities within those components. Static application security testing (SAST) is a vulnerability scanning technique that focuses on source code. It works early in the SDLC and CI pipeline and scans source code, byte code, or binary code in order to identify problematic coding patterns that go against best practices or that could cause vulnerabilities.

10.2.3 Build

Static container scanning is the process of analyzing the contents of a container image for vulnerabilities and policy violations before the container is deployed and run. While there are countless benefits to containers, they can also introduce security risks if they contain vulnerabilities or policy violations. Infrastructure-as-code (IaC) scanning is the process of analyzing the configuration files that define infrastructure resources (e.g., virtual machines, networks, and storage) for vulnerabilities and policy violations before the infrastructure is deployed.

10.2.4 Test

Fuzzing tools can be used to automate the process of generating and sending random or malicious input to an application to ensure that the application is stable.

10.2.5 Deploy

DAST is a good method for preventing regressions and doesn't depend on a specific programming language. While DAST is still early in the SDLC, it is typically done later in the CI pipeline. Runtime application self-protection (RASP) is a security technology that is designed to protect applications from attacks while they are running. It is often used to protect web applications from attacks such as cross-site scripting (XSS). Interactive application security testing (IAST) applies to security testing where the testing tool interacts with a running application and observes it from the inside in real time. Interactive application security testing solutions are designed to test web application frameworks and Application Programming Interface (APIs).

10.2.6 Monitor

Cloud security posture management (CSPM) tools work by continuously examining and comparing a cloud environment against a defined set of best practices (misconfigurations) and security risks (Common Vulnerabilities and Exposures [CVE] and vulnerabilities). CSPM is typically more "right" in the SDLC. CSPM tools don't consider the findings brought by tools that are more "left" on the SDLC (SAST, SCA, etc.). Cloud workload protection platforms (CWPP) provide tailored security needs for deployed workloads that are in public, private, or hybrid environments. CWPP enables you to perform security functions across multiple environments. The main difference between CWPP and CSPM is that CWPP looks at the deployed workloads (cloud, Kubernetes, etc.), while CSPM continuously monitors the cloud environment [7].

Continuous monitoring of security scanning coverage and quality and usage of outcome-driven testing for new development languages and architectures such as microservices should be considered. Implement innovation through "security as code" approaches, including test automation via behavioral-driven development (BDD) or test-driven development (TDD).

"Shift-left" includes security as part of design and empowers the team with integrated requirements, security design patterns, automated tests, and coaching. Nowadays, application security teams are introducing auto-remediation features to help reduce manual remediation efforts. It also helps enterprises effectively align to and prepare for future business demands. Security design patterns and automated threat modeling tooling drive threat intelligence-led agile security architecture reviews and reusable security libraries. Facilitate containerization through container scanning technologies and libraries through SCA and container management.

Let's see the technical difference between Shift-left and DevSecOps (Table 10.1).

DevSecOps and the shift-left approach have undergone significant transformation over the past five years, fundamentally reshaping how organizations build and secure software. In 2025, the intersection of DevSecOps and shift-left is seen as essential for organizations aiming to innovate quickly while maintaining robust security.

Table 10.1 DevSecOps and shift-left difference summary.

Aspect	Shift-Left	DevSecOps
Definition	Moving activities (e.g., security, testing) earlier in SDLC	Integrating security into DevOps across the SDLC
Scope	Specific practice (can apply to testing, security, etc.)	Broad methodology/culture covering all SDLC phases
Focus	Early detection and prevention	Security as a shared, continuous responsibility
Implementation	Early and automated testing/scanning	Collaboration, automation, and continuous monitoring
Relation	Often a key principle within DevSecOps	Encompasses shift-left and more

The next five years will see even deeper integration of AI and machine learning into DevSecOps and shift-left practices. Shift-left will extend beyond security to encompass compliance, privacy, and even ethical considerations from the earliest stages of software design. The next five years will also see a continued cultural transformation, with security becoming a shared responsibility across development, operations, and business teams.

10.3 Adoption of DevSecOps

The key drivers for the adoption of DevSecOps and connected shift-left practices for cloud-native software are driven by several factors; some of the important factors influencing the adoption are as follows:

1) Creating and managing secure software.
2) Protecting software from security risks.
3) Responding to existing and new cyber threats.
4) Enhancing compliance and adoption of regulatory guidelines.

A secure SDLC is a process that companies follow to ensure that the software they develop and deploy is secure by design and minimizes vulnerabilities and misconfigurations. The steps involved in a secure SDLC can vary depending on the specific organization, but it typically involves identifying and addressing security concerns at each stage of the software development lifecycle—from design and code (early in the SDLC) to deployment and monitoring (later in the SDLC). By following a secure SDLC, companies can reduce the risk of security and infrastructure breaches and protect their software and data from potential threats [6, 8].

10.4 Implementing DevSecOps with Frameworks

Implementing DevSecOps requires embedding security throughout the SDLC, automating key processes, enforcing policies, and fostering a collaborative culture.

Software security frameworks support organizations that create, manage, and maintain secure software. Some of the common secure software design and development frameworks used for the adoption of DevSecOps are described in this section.

- **NIST Secure Software Development Framework (SSDF):** It is a set of fundamental secure development practices based on established practices such as business software alliance (BSA), open worldwide application security project (OWASP), and SafeCode. Further reading: https://csrc.nist.gov/projects/ssdf [2].

- **BSA Framework for Secure Software:** It supports software development organizations with risk management and focuses on the security outcome associated with a specific software product or service [9].
- **SafeCode:** Promotes best practices for developing and maintaining secure software, hardware, and services. They provide guidance from secure development to threat modeling at scale.
- **NIST Cybersecurity Framework (CSF 2.0):** It provides a comprehensive set of best practices for risk management, access management, supply chain management, incident response handling, and much more [2].
- **ISO 27000 series (ISO 27001 and ISO 27002):** Also mentioned in Chapter 2, developed by the International Organization for Standardization, advocates for principles and practices for information security management essentially focused on protecting data. Further reference: https://www.iso.org/standard/27001.
- **CIS Controls:** Critical security controls for protecting networks and related infrastructure from cyberattacks. Further reference: https://www.cisecurity.org/controls.
- **CALMS Methodology:** It's used in organizations which are in the initial stages of DevSecOps adoption. CALMS stands for culture, automation, measurement, lean, and sharing.

10.5 What Is a Maturity Model?

As organizations adopt DevSecOps practices, the need for a structured approach to gauge and enhance their progress becomes clear.

The DevSecOps maturity model provides a roadmap for organizations to evolve their practices. It offers an overview of the model, outlining its various stages from initial implementation to advanced stages where DevSecOps principles are deeply ingrained in the organizational culture and workflows.

A DevSecOps maturity model is a structured framework that helps organizations assess, measure, and improve how effectively they integrate security into their DevOps processes throughout the SDLC [10]. Most DevSecOps maturity models describe a progression through several defined stages or levels, each representing a higher degree of security integration and process maturity. Some of the practical maturity models used in the DevSecOps adoption are as follows:

- **BSIMM:** Building security in maturity model
- **CMMI:** Capability maturity model integration for acquisitions

- **PRM:** SwA forum processes and practices group process reference model
- **RMM:** CERT resilience management model
- **SAMM:** OWASP open software assurance maturity model

10.6 Best Practices

A best practice is a method, technique, or set of guidelines that has been generally accepted as superior to alternatives because it consistently produces better results. Some of the proven best practices for DevSecOps are as follows (Table 10.2).

These best practices, when implemented together, enable organizations to build, deploy, and maintain secure software efficiently and resiliently across all stages of the SDLC.

Table 10.2 DevSecOps best practices summary.

Practice	Key Actions
Secure Design	Early threat modeling, secure architecture, and least privilege/functionality.
Secure Coding	Enforce standards, automate code analysis, and provide ongoing developer training.
Secure Release Management	Automated security checks in CI/CD, change/configuration management, and documentation as code.
Shift-Left/Shift-Right	Early security integration (shift-left), continuous post-release monitoring (shift-right).

Source: Adapted from [2].

10.6.1 Use Cases

- **CrowdStrike:** The CrowdStrike outage in July 2024, caused by a faulty software update to its Falcon endpoint detection and response (EDR) platform, resulted in widespread disruptions across industries, affecting approximately 8.5 million Windows devices globally. This incident has provided valuable lessons for organizations, cybersecurity professionals, and vendors. Key takeaways include:
  - **Backup and Failover Mechanisms:**
    - Organizations must implement robust backup systems and failover protocols, including redundant systems and geographically dispersed data centers.

    - o Overreliance on single vendors or platforms amplifies vulnerabilities during outages. Diversifying technology stacks and using multiple endpoint security vendors.
    - o Organizations should conduct thorough risk assessments of third-party vendors, focusing on their testing processes and code execution levels.
    - o CrowdStrike's rapid response highlighted the importance of agility in managing public perception during crises.
  - The CrowdStrike outage in July 2024 had a significant impact on cyber insurance models, exposing vulnerabilities and prompting changes in underwriting, risk assessment, and policy structures.
- **Log4j:** The Log4j vulnerability, also known as Log4Shell (CVE-2021-44,228), is a critical remote code execution (RCE) flaw discovered in November 2021 in the widely used Java-based logging library, Apache Log4j. This vulnerability allows attackers to execute arbitrary code on affected systems by exploiting the Java Naming and Directory Interface (JNDI) lookup feature, which can be manipulated to fetch and execute malicious code from an attacker-controlled server. We present the collective finding from the community on the lesson learnt from the above incident [8].
  - **Importance of Open-Source Software Management:** Log4j demonstrated the risks of relying on open-source software without proper oversight. Many organizations were unaware of their dependency on Log4j, emphasizing the need for robust tracking mechanisms like SBOMs.
  - **Proactive Patching and Vulnerability Management:** While patches were released quickly, many organizations failed to apply them promptly, leaving systems vulnerable.
  - **Long-Term Impact:** The widespread use of Log4j means its vulnerabilities will persist for years. Organizations must remain vigilant in monitoring their environments.
  - **Incident Response and Preparedness:** The cybersecurity community's collective response helped mitigate the potential catastrophic impact of Log4Shell. The incident revealed gaps in many organizations' incident response plans. Having a well-prepared response strategy, including detection capabilities and clear communication channels, is critical.

According to the data collected through crowdsourcing by CISA, it is important that the following should be considered for future incidents [10]:

1) Drive existing best practices for security development practices.
2) Training and education for software developers.
3) Improve SBOM adoption and implementation.
4) Coordinated working groups for reporting and resolving vulnerabilities.

10.7 Challenges and Future Outlook

Some of the common challenges arise from pitfalls and anti-patterns. Pitfalls and anti-patterns undermine DevSecOps adoption by introducing inefficiencies, fostering resistance, and preventing the seamless integration of security into development workflows.

Anti-patterns: DevSecOps anti-patterns are counterproductive practices that hinder the effective integration of security into DevOps processes. These recurring approaches or solutions are intended to solve a problem but end up making things worse. Avoiding these anti-patterns is crucial for a successful DevSecOps transformation. Some of the common anti-patterns are as follows:

- Creating silos with dedicated DevSecOps teams
- Over-reliance on numerous security tools

DevSecOps Pitfalls and Challenges: DevSecOps pitfalls are common mistakes, oversights, or traps that teams might fall into when implementing or operating DevSecOps processes. Pitfalls are often accidental and stem from not knowing better or external constraints.

- **Slow Organizations:** Organizations don't need to innovate faster or secure early. There is no urgency to do some improvement or innovation.
- **Culture Readiness:** Organizations are not ready to implicate or to go with continuous delivery and don't have any maturity stage within DevOps.
- **Security Tools:** The security tools are not DevOps friendly and lack API calls and CLI and are failing to monitor code for vulnerabilities.
- **Legacy System:** Accelerating the software development lifecycle without embedding security, leading to increased vulnerabilities and errors, and applications are not ready to be used in a DevOps setup, i.e., legacy applications and dependencies.
- **People:** The organization doesn't have skilled resources to implement DevSecOps.
- **Management Support:** Not much support from the senior management team in terms of investment, making changes, and reducing risks.

10.7.1 Success Criteria for DevSecOps Implementation

Conventional application security activities are often bottlenecks to continuous delivery and efficient DevOps capabilities. DevSecOps capabilities can improve and support secure development and security requirement verification in a fast-moving CI/CD pipeline. Include security as part of the design, not after the work is done. Empower the team with integrated requirements, secure design patterns, automated tests, and coaching. Adapt a culture of innovation, building/using the right tools and processes. Execute tools as part of the CI/CD pipeline. Continuously refine tools to provide actionable feedback. Design feedback loops that inform developers of potential security vulnerabilities as early as possible. Meet developers where they are; be flexible in security validation testing [7].

10.8 Conclusion

There is no agility without security. Although the purpose of DevOps is to build and integrate more features in a shorter period of time, there are costly risks that can be introduced by only applying security testing at the end of the process. Testing takes time and resources; often developers do not write security tests for their own software. Security cannot operate in a silo. Security must reconsider existing processes and ways of working, along with any tools, and security must participate as part of the team. Security is a shared responsibility and should be integrated throughout design, development, and deployment.

References

1. Executive Office of the President, "The profile supports executive order (EO) 14,110," 2023. [Online]. Available: https://www.federalregister.gov/documents/2023/11/01/2023--24283/safe-secure-and-trustworthy-development-and-use-of-artificial-intelligence.
2. M. Souppaya and K. Scarfone, "Secure software development framework NIST SSDF," [Online]. Available: https://csrc.nist.gov/projects/ssdf.
3. S. Wilson et al., "OWASP top ten standard awareness document," Sept. 2024. [Online]. Available: https://owasp.org/www-project-top-ten.
4. Cloud Native Computing Foundation, "Software supply chain best practices," 2025. [Online]. Available: https://github.com/cncf/tag-security/tree/main.
5. S. Wilson et al., "OWASP Top 10 for large language model applications," [Online]. Available: https://owasp.org/www-project-top-10-for-large-language-model-applications.
6. Cybersecurity and Infrastructure Security Agency (CISA) "Secure by design pledge," [Online]. Available: https://www.cisa.gov/securebydesign/pledge.
7. J. Shah, D. Dubaria, and J. Widhalm, "A survey of devOps tools for networking," in *2018 9th IEEE Annu. Ubiquitous Comput. Electron. Mob. Commun. Conf. (UEMCON)*, 2018, New York, NY, USA, pp. 185–188. 10.1109/UEMCON.2018.8796814.

8 Saeed Abbasi, "Threat landscape year in review: If everything is critical," *Nothing Is*, Dec. 2023. [Online] Available: https://blog.qualys.com/vulnerabilities-threat-research/2023/12/19/2023-threat-landscape-year-in-review-part-one.

9 BSA | The Software Alliance. The BSA, "Framework for secure software: A new approach to securing the software lifecycle," Version 1.1, *BSA*, 2020. [Online]. Available: https://www.bsa.org/files/reports/bsa_framework_secure_software_update_2020.pdf.

10 "Securing the software supply chain, recommended practices guide for developers," Aug. 2022. [Online]. Available: https://www.cisa.gov/sites/default/files/publications/ESF_SECURING_THE_SOFTWARE_SUPPLY_CHAIN_DEVELOPERS.PDF.

11

Autonomous Cloud Infrastructure and Self-Healing Systems

Vinod Goje[1] *and Manoj Ravi*[2]

[1] *Computer Science and Engineering, University College of Engineering, Osmania University, Hyderabad, India*
[2] *Sr. Software Architect & IEEE Member, Eastern North Carolina Section, Raleigh, NC, USA*

11.1 Introduction

11.1.1 Motivation and Scope of Autonomous Cloud Infrastructure

11.1.1.1 Defining Autonomous Cloud Infrastructure

The concept of autonomous computing systems emerged from IBM's "autonomic computing" initiative in the early 2000s, which promoted the idea of IT systems capable of self-management with minimal human oversight. This idea has evolved significantly in the cloud era, where autonomous cloud infrastructure refers to systems that can self-configure, self-optimize, self-heal, and self-protect across diverse environments that include multiple availability zones, regions, and cloud providers.

Cloud computing has transformed modern IT by simplifying infrastructure management and providing flexible, on-demand services. Autonomous infrastructure uses automation, artificial intelligence (AI), and machine learning (ML) to manage and enhance IT environments with reduced human input. This level of automation covers aspects like provisioning, configuration, scaling, and maintenance, leading to greater efficiency, enhanced reliability, and lower operational expenses [2].

The shift toward autonomous systems addresses the increasing complexity of today's applications. With multi-tenant workloads, global distribution, and rapid deployment cycles, cloud infrastructure has become intricate and vital for business operations. Autonomous infrastructure features several key characteristics that set it apart from traditional managed systems. For instance, self-configuration allows systems to automatically adapt to shifting requirements and conditions.

Amazon Web Services (AWS) auto scaling groups can independently adjust compute capacity based on demand, while Azure Virtual Machine Scale Sets can launch new instances across availability zones without manual input. These systems analyze resource consumption trends to make informed decisions about capacity allocation, considering factors like cost, performance needs, and availability constraints.

Moreover, self-optimization enables continuous adjustments to performance parameters. Solutions like Google Cloud's AutoML and AWS's Compute Optimizer exemplify this by automatically recommending optimal resource configurations based on historical usage patterns. Machine learning algorithms look at how workloads behave to find ways to improve performance, save money, or make systems more reliable, so everything runs smoothly without needing manual changes.

Finally, self-healing represents a crucial aspect of autonomous cloud architecture. Unlike traditional high-availability setups that focus solely on redundancy, self-healing systems [3] proactively detect, analyze, and resolve failures independently. Such infrastructure leverages data-driven insights and automation to pinpoint and fix faults within hybrid cloud environments. For instance, Netflix's Chaos Monkey deliberately triggers failures to test system resilience, showcasing a design philosophy that embraces failure to build more robust systems.

11.1.1.2 The Role of Self-Healing in Cloud Resilience

In cloud systems, self-healing mechanisms mark a basic change from reactive to proactive infrastructure management. While conventional high-availability systems concentrate on failover mechanisms and redundancy, self-healing systems continuously monitor system health and automatically start repairs before failures cause disruptions in services.

Self-healing cloud systems have as their main goals several aspects of operational excellence. Maintaining service-level objectives (SLOs) in the face of component failures calls for advanced monitoring and response capacity able to identify degradation before it affects users. Reducing the blast radius of events by means of isolation and containment helps to prevent localized failures from spreading over linked systems. Learning from past mistakes turns every incident into a chance for system development. Such an approach helps to stop recurrence.

By means of agent technology, multi-agent systems offer autonomous behavior to produce intelligent cloud support for autonomic aspects [4]. This method allows distributed decision-making, whereby several autonomous agents cooperate to preserve system integrity, each in charge of particular facets of infrastructure management and coordinating their activities using common protocols.

The particular failure scenarios self-healing systems address affect the technical mechanisms behind them. When demand rises or when capacity is decommissioned during low-utilization times, auto-scaling systems react by either automatically provisioning extra resources or decommissioning excess capacity. This fast scaling capacity guarantees that programs can manage unexpected traffic surges without human involvement.

In milliseconds, automated failover systems channel traffic from malfunctioning parts to healthy substitutes. Route 53 health checks can quickly remove unhealthy endpoints from load balancer pools; Azure's Traffic Manager offers Domain Name System (DNS)-based load balancing with automatic failover across regions. These systems use HTTP checks, Transmission Control Protocol (TCP) connection tests, and custom health verification scripts, among several ways to track endpoint health.

Another essential part of self-healing architecture is health checking and restarting systems. Kubernetes features several kinds of probes: liveness check probes of readiness entrepreneurial investigation and liveness check probes to guide containers to restart the timer. These probes can set TCP connections to confirm service health, run HTTP searches, or carry custom commands. While ReplicaSets guarantee that the intended number of healthy pod replicas stays available, failures are detected, and the kubelet automatically restarts containers.

Downturns have an economic effect that makes self-healing properties not only desirable but also necessary. Self-healing systems lower the operational overhead of manual incident response while helping companies keep their service-level agreements (SLAs).

11.1.2 Architectural Principles for Autonomous Systems

Autonomous cloud systems are built on established resilience patterns that have evolved through extensive research in distributed systems. To create a self-healing application that effectively manages failures, a three-step strategy is essential: identifying failures, responding appropriately, and logging them for operational insights [5].

One effective method is the retry pattern, which safeguards against temporary failures by automatically reattempting operations with strategically timed intervals. For instance, Azure's Service Bus employs exponential backoff strategies to avoid overwhelming services during recovery periods while enhancing the chances of success. Key implementation factors include setting reasonable timeout values, using jitter to prevent simultaneous retries, and defining maximum retry limits to avoid endless attempts.

The circuit breaker pattern serves as a safeguard against widespread failures by continuously monitoring service health and temporarily halting requests to failing services. When error rates surpass set thresholds, the circuit breaker activates, redirecting requests or delivering cached responses until normal service resumes. This concept was widely popularized by Netflix's Hystrix library, which incorporates advanced circuit breaker logic based on various health metrics like error rates and latency. Another critical pattern is bulkhead isolation, which segments system components to prevent failures from spreading throughout the entire system. This concept takes inspiration from maritime design, where watertight compartments prevent a single breach from compromising the entire ship. In cloud environments, bulkheads can isolate different customer tenants, service tiers, or regions, as seen in AWS's use of independent availability zones, each with its own power and networking infrastructure.

These patterns function together within a complete architectural system, following the monitor-analyze-plan-execute (MAPE) control loop based on research in autonomic computing. The monitoring phase gathers telemetry data from all components, including application metrics and infrastructure performance indicators. The analysis phase interprets this data to detect patterns and potential issues, utilizing statistical methods and machine learning for more profound insights. During the planning phase, appropriate responses are determined based on the identified conditions, either through predefined strategies or by crafting dynamic solutions that align with the current system state.

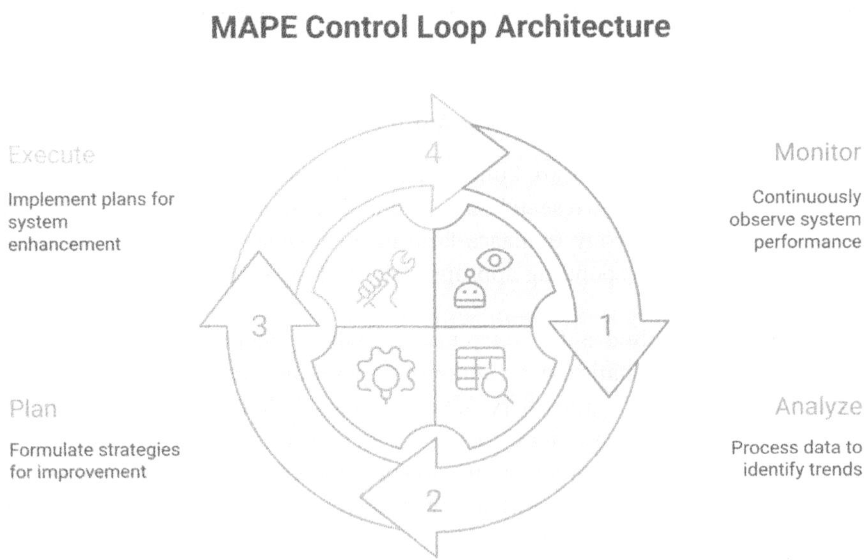

Figure 11.1 MAPE control loop architecture.

Container orchestration platforms, notably Kubernetes, underpin many autonomous systems with their declarative configuration and self-healing features. Kubernetes controllers exemplify the MAPE loop (Figure 11.1) through ongoing reconciliation processes, ensuring the actual state of the cluster aligns with desired specifications.

Serverless computing architectures epitomize autonomous infrastructure, allowing cloud providers to manage operational tasks while enabling applications to focus on business logic. For example, AWS Lambda scales functions automatically based on demand, allowing different components of an Application Programming Interface (API) to scale independently based on usage [6]. Infrastructure-as-Code (IaC) and GitOps practices facilitate version-controlled management of infrastructure, supporting automated deployment and drift detection. Platforms like ArgoCD and Flux illustrate how Git repositories can act as the definitive source for both application and infrastructure configurations.

Moreover, advancements in AI and machine learning are increasingly driving intelligent operations, enhancing capabilities like predictive analytics and automated decision-making. We examine AIOps platforms and their integration with cloud monitoring systems to enable proactive issue resolution.

11.2 Background and Context

11.2.1 Cloud-Native and Microservice Paradigms

11.2.1.1 Evolution from Monolith to Microservices

The shift from traditional monolithic applications to microservices architecture marks a pivotal change in software engineering over the last 20 years. This transformation has been fueled by the demand for enhanced scalability, quicker development cycles, and better fault isolation in increasingly intricate software systems.

While monolithic applications can be easier to create and deploy at the outset, they pose considerable challenges as they scale. A modification often necessitates a complete redeployment of the application, which introduces risk and lengthens deployment times. As the codebase expands, testing becomes more tedious and perilous, with alterations in one module potentially impacting other unrelated areas. Scaling the application means allocating resources for the whole system instead of specific components, leading to inefficient use of resources and higher expenses.

Microservices architecture mitigates these issues by breaking applications into smaller, independently deployable services that interact through clearly defined APIs. Each service manages its own data and business logic, allowing teams to develop, deploy, and scale services in isolation. This model aligns with

Conway's Law, suggesting that systems are designed in a way that reflects the organization's communication patterns, which empowers teams to manage services comprehensively.

The 12-factor app methodology, created by Heroku, offers a foundational blueprint for constructing cloud-native applications that adhere to microservice principles. Key factors include using environment variables for configuration management, ensuring stateless processes to facilitate horizontal scaling, binding ports for service exposure, and enabling disposability for rapid startup and smooth shutdown. These principles support autonomous operations by allowing applications to be dynamically provisioned, configured, and terminated without manual intervention.

Containerization technologies, especially Docker, have made the practical application of microservices architecture feasible by offering lightweight, portable packaging solutions for applications and their dependencies. Containers address the "works on my machine" dilemma by bundling all necessary runtime components, guaranteeing consistent performance across development, testing, and production environments. Container images act as immutable artifacts that can be versioned, shared, and deployed in a cohesive manner, thus streamlining automated deployment processes.

Nonetheless, adopting microservices architecture brings about new complexities that require advanced automation and orchestration tools. Network latency between services can affect overall application efficiency, necessitating thoughtful design of communication methods and protocols. As the number of services grows, partial failures become more frequent, demanding robust error handling and retry strategies. Ensuring data consistency across services often involves implementing distributed transaction patterns or adopting eventual consistency models. Furthermore, distributed monitoring and debugging become critical as requests move across multiple services, necessitating the correlation of logs and traces by OpenTelemetry APIs, Zipkin, etc.

11.2.1.2 Containerization and Orchestration Tools

The development of container orchestration has become increasingly complex, reflecting the need for effective management of distributed applications. Initially, Docker Swarm offered basic clustering features with seamless integration, making it user-friendly for teams accustomed to Docker. Nonetheless, it fell short in offering advanced functionalities such as intricate scheduling, robust service discovery, and extensive configuration management.

In contrast, Kubernetes, which originated from Google's internal Borg system, delivers a holistic solution for orchestrating containers, managing the entire lifecycle of containerized applications. For instance, when a liveness probe detects failure, Kubernetes automatically restarts the affected container. Its architecture embraces autonomous system principles through declarative setups, ongoing reconciliation, and inherent self-healing features. Kubernetes operates on a master-worker framework, where control plane elements oversee cluster states and make scheduling choices, while worker nodes carry out the containerized workloads. This division allows for high-availability deployments, ensuring redundancy and automatic failover through multiple control plane instances.

Service meshes enhance infrastructure-level service-to-service communication, covering aspects like load balancing, service discovery, encryption, authentication, and observability. Tools such as Istio, Linkerd, and Consul Connect streamline these processes, allowing for uniform policy enforcement across services and offering rich telemetry for informed decision-making. The sidecar proxy approach utilized by service meshes ensures that these cross-cutting concerns are systematically managed without necessitating alterations to the application code.

11.2.2 Kubernetes

11.2.2.1 Common Orchestration Patterns

Kubernetes offers various abstractions designed to facilitate the deployment and management of containerized applications, encapsulating best practices tailored to different application types and operational needs.

Deployments oversee the lifecycle of stateless applications by managing ReplicaSets, which are responsible for creating and managing individual pods. The readiness of a pod is confirmed when all its containers are prepared to handle incoming traffic. Deployments also allow for advanced update strategies, including rolling updates that can be customized according to update speed and resource allocation. The rolling update approach incrementally replaces outdated pod instances with their newer versions, ensuring that the application remains available during the update process. Parameters such as maxUnavailable and maxSurge guide the pace of updates and resource allocation. If problems arise during the rollout, Kubernetes can automatically halt the update or execute a rollback based on health checks or specified metrics.

StatefulSets cater to the needs of stateful applications by providing stable network identities, persistent storage, and controlled deployment and scaling. Unlike deployments, StatefulSets ensure predictable naming for pods and maintain persistent volume bindings even when pods are rescheduled, making them vital for applications like databases or message queues that rely on local state [7].

DaemonSets guarantee that certain pods operate on all or designated nodes within the cluster, often for system-level tasks such as log collection, monitoring, or network functionality. They seamlessly adjust to changes in node availability, ensuring consistent pod distribution throughout the cluster.

11.2.3 Serverless and Function-as-a-Service Architectures

11.2.3.1 Serverless Computing Model

Serverless computing offers a high level of abstraction for managing infrastructure, as cloud service providers take care of various operational tasks such as capacity planning, scaling, patching, and ensuring high availability. One prominent example is AWS Lambda, a service that enables users to create functions, self-contained applications written in supported programming languages. These functions are uploaded to AWS Lambda, which efficiently executes them as needed.

Function-as-a-service (FaaS) platforms allow for event-driven execution, where code runs in response to specific triggers without needing pre-allocated resources. These platforms manage resource allocation, scaling, and billing based on actual usage, which aligns the economic model of serverless computing with delivered value; this means organizations only pay for the compute time they actually use.

Since its launch in 2014, AWS Lambda has set the standard for the FaaS model, processing trillions of function invocations [8]. It is particularly well-suited for various workloads, offering cost-effective compute solutions that scale automatically to accommodate processing needs. Functions are executed in isolated containers that are deployed on demand and removed after execution, allowing for seamless scaling from zero to thousands of concurrent instances.

Azure Functions offers comparable functionalities along with additional features designed for enterprise use. For instance, durable functions facilitate stateful orchestration of long-running workflows. The consumption plan provides genuine pay-per-execution pricing, while the premium plan enhances performance, integrates with virtual networks, and ensures warm instances for applications sensitive to latency.

On the other hand, Google Cloud Functions prioritizes ease of use and smooth integration with other Google Cloud services. It supports a variety of trigger types, including HTTP requests, cloud storage events, and Pub/Sub messages. With features such as automatic HTTPS endpoints, built-in authentication, and integrated monitoring, it simplifies operational tasks while ensuring security and observability.

11.2.3.2 Serverless Use Cases and Patterns

Event-driven serverless architectures are particularly effective for handling unpredictable workloads, allowing for optimized resource use and cost savings. A typical application of this model is in API backends, where serverless functions manage HTTP requests, execute business logic, and provide responses. The three-tier serverless architecture integrates an API gateway for routing requests, Lambda functions for executing logic, and managed databases for storing data.

This setup eliminates the need for traditional server management, fostering quick development and deployment of scalable applications.

In data processing pipelines, serverless functions efficiently manage data streams from various sources such as IoT devices, application logs, or changes in databases. This model supports automatic scaling, adjusting processing capacity to match data volume while avoiding resource overprovisioning during quieter periods.

Function orchestration patterns facilitate intricate workflows using tools like step functions or durable functions. AWS Step Functions, for instance, allows users to visually define workflows, incorporating error handling, retry mechanisms, and parallel execution. State machines can oversee multiple Lambda functions, enabling complex business processes with integrated error management and compensation mechanisms.

Nonetheless, there are limitations to serverless architectures that need careful consideration during the design phase. For example, execution limits cap function runtime, usually at 15 minutes for AWS Lambda. Concerns about vendor lock-in emerge due to the deep integration with specific cloud provider services, although tools like the Serverless Framework offer some level of abstraction. Additionally, the stateless nature of these functions means that maintaining state across invocations is not possible, necessitating the use of external storage solutions for persistent data.

11.2.4 Infrastructure-as-Code and GitOps

11.2.4.1 Declarative Infrastructure Management

Infrastructure-as-Code (IaC) revolutionizes the way organizations manage their infrastructure by shifting from labor-intensive, error-prone methods to automated, version-controlled practices. By encoding infrastructure configurations, businesses can leverage software development methodologies such as version control, code reviews, testing, and automated deployments. Storing IaC in Git repositories enables infrastructure teams to adopt CI/CD pipelines for automated testing, change validation, and rollout of cloud resources.

This approach, which emphasizes specifying desired outcomes over detailed procedures, is particularly suited to the needs of autonomous systems. By using declarative configurations, systems can consistently align the actual state with the intended state, making necessary adjustments automatically to prevent configuration drift and maintain uniform environments across various stages of development.

Terraform, created by HashiCorp, facilitates cloud-agnostic infrastructure provisioning and supports a broad range of providers, including AWS, Azure, Google Cloud, and many more. Its declarative language allows users to define intricate infrastructure architectures in modular formats, while its state management keeps track of resource dependencies. The pre-execution planning phase reveals the changes that will take place, instilling confidence and providing a clear audit trail for any modifications.

Contemporary IaC solutions offer sophisticated features that bolster autonomous operations. For instance, drift detection spots discrepancies between what's deployed and the defined code, allowing for automated corrections or alerts for unauthorized modifications. Furthermore, frameworks like AWS Config Rules, Azure Policy, and Open Policy Agent enable automated compliance verification and enforcement. Cost optimization tools also evaluate how resources are being used and recommend changes to reduce costs.

11.2.4.2 GitOps and Continuous Delivery

GitOps enhances traditional DevOps methods by utilizing Git repositories as the central reference point for managing infrastructure and application configurations. This method allows for self-sufficient infrastructure management, featuring automated synchronization, drift detection, and a focus on declarative state management.

The GitOps process is straightforward yet impactful, promoting consistency and transparency. When developers make changes to configurations, they commit these updates to Git repositories, which offer comprehensive version control, including a complete history and the ability to revert changes. Automated systems recognize these updates through webhooks or polling, validating them via testing pipelines. Approved changes are then deployed to the appropriate environments by controllers, ensuring that the Git repository and the deployed infrastructure are in sync.

Among the various tools available, ArgoCD stands out as a premier GitOps solution for Kubernetes settings. It offers a wide range of features, such as support for multi-cluster deployments, advanced synchronization policies, and smooth integration with existing CI/CD workflows. Its user-friendly interface allows for easy monitoring of application health and synchronization status, while customizable sync policies cater to different organizational needs.

11.2.5 Monitoring, Logging, and Observability

11.2.5.1 Traditional vs. Cloud-Native Monitoring

Observability serves as the cornerstone for autonomous cloud infrastructure, delivering essential data for automated decision-making, detecting anomalies, and enabling self-healing mechanisms.

Historically, monitoring concentrated on metrics such as CPU usage, memory consumption, and disk availability, relying on basic health checks to determine application status. While effective for traditional monolithic applications on stable servers, this method falls short for dynamic, containerized applications that can scale rapidly in transient environments.

In contrast, cloud-native observability focuses on grasping system behavior through its outputs rather than merely tracking set metrics. Cloud-native observability is a combination of three main features, like metrics, logs, and traces. This method offers a deep understanding of how distributed systems function. Contemporary observability platforms must effectively manage the diverse and high-volume data produced by cloud-native applications.

11.2.5.2 Observability Platforms and Tools

Modern observability solutions combine metrics, logs, and traces into unified systems that aid both human operators and automated processes. The development of these tools reflects the growing intricacies of distributed systems and the demand for advanced analytical capabilities.

Prometheus has become a leading choice for collecting metrics in cloud-native settings. Its pull-based design automatically identifies targets through service discovery, which makes it particularly effective in dynamic containerized environments. The model for multi-dimensional data allows for versatile querying and aggregation, and the robust PromQL query language facilitates intricate analyses and alerting mechanisms.

Major cloud providers deliver extensive observability solutions that integrate smoothly with their offerings. For instance, AWS CloudWatch supplies metrics, logs, and traces for AWS resources, automatically incorporating services like EC2, Lambda, and Elastic Container Service (ECS). Additionally, CloudWatch Anomaly Detection employs machine learning to spot atypical patterns in metrics, while CloudWatch Insights provides advanced log analysis through its query languages.

11.2.6 Cloud Storage and Networking Fundamentals

11.2.6.1 Cloud-Native Storage and Cloud Networks

Cloud storage solutions act as the backbone for autonomous systems while simplifying the intricacies associated with conventional storage management. The main categories of storage include object, block, and file, each tailored for specific applications and offering different degrees of durability, availability, and performance.

Services like Amazon S3, Azure Blob Storage, and Google Cloud Storage excel in providing nearly limitless capacity along with robust durability and availability features. For instance, S3 boasts an impressive durability rate of 99.999999999% (11 9's), achieved through processes such as automatic replication and erasure coding across various devices and locations. Additionally, these platforms offer advanced functionalities that facilitate autonomous operations, including automated lifecycle management, event notifications, and replication across different regions.

11.2.6.2 Software-Defined Networking and Cloud Networks

Software-defined networking (SDN) separates network management from the physical hardware, allowing for automated network administration that enhances self-sufficient operations. Recent studies involving 500 enterprise networks indicate that the integration of AI solutions has significantly improved autonomous problem diagnosis, reducing the average mean time to repair (MTTR) from 45 minutes to only 12 minutes [9].

Cloud networking services exemplify SDN concepts by utilizing virtual private clouds (VPCs), which create distinct network environments within a shared infrastructure. These virtual networks enable hybrid connectivity through VPN links and dedicated circuits, all while ensuring redundancy and high availability.

11.2.7 Autonomic Computing and AI for IT Operations (AIOps)

The notion of autonomic computing originated from IBM's acknowledgment that the intricacy of computing systems surpassed our capacity for effective management. Autonomous healing software utilizes AI and ML to independently identify, assess, and resolve software issues without human involvement.

AIOps illustrates the utilization of machine learning and AI to tackle issues in IT operations. The self-healing capability allows systems to independently identify and resolve problems, thereby diminishing the need for human involvement.

AIOps solutions examine extensive operational data to discern patterns, anticipate potential issues, and automate responses that would be unfeasible for human operators to manage at scale. Core functionalities include anomaly detection, predictive maintenance, root cause analysis, and capacity planning.

11.3 Self-Healing Mechanisms and Implementation Strategies

11.3.1 Container Orchestration and Self-Healing

11.3.1.1 Kubernetes Self-Healing Capabilities

Kubernetes offers robust self-healing functionalities through its controller-based design and declarative setup. In the absence of a defined readiness probe, Kubernetes assumes that the pod is ready once the container begins running, promptly directing user traffic to it (Figure 11.2).

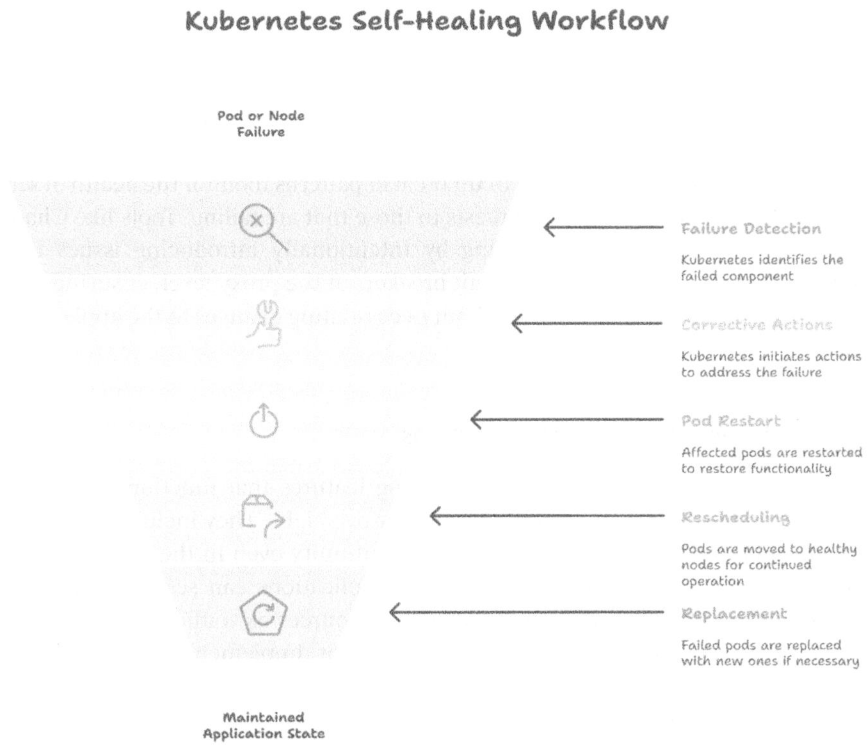

Figure 11.2 Kubernetes self-healing workflow.

The self-healing process at the pod level relies on health probes that assess the application's condition within containers. Liveness probes are essential for confirming that applications, containers, and pods are functioning correctly, allowing Kubernetes to restart any containers that become unresponsive [10]. There are three main types of probes, each serving a distinct role:

- **Liveness Probes:** Assess whether containers operate correctly and initiate restarts if they do not.
- **Readiness Probes:** Manage traffic by excluding unhealthy containers from service endpoints.
- **Startup Probes:** Offer flexibility for applications that require extended initialization periods.

Health probes can conduct various checks, including HTTP requests, TCP socket connections, and the execution of custom commands. It's advisable to keep both liveness and readiness probes simple, having them access an endpoint that merely returns an HTTP 200 status without additional complexity.

11.3.1.2 Advanced Patterns and Service Mesh Integration

Service mesh architectures improve self-healing features by utilizing advanced traffic management, fault tolerance, and observability at the infrastructure level, thus enhancing the built-in self-healing mechanisms of Kubernetes. They provide essential functionalities that work alongside these native capabilities.

To mitigate cascading failures, circuit breaker patterns monitor the health of services and can temporarily stop requests to those that are failing. Tools like Chaos Monkey facilitate chaos engineering by intentionally introducing issues into systems. Service meshes deploy circuit breakers at the proxy level, ensuring uniform behavior across all services without necessitating changes to the application code.

11.3.2 Serverless Self-Healing Patterns

Serverless platforms offer robust self-healing features that function seamlessly without the need for manual configuration or oversight. They include automatic failover and multi-AZ execution, ensuring continuity even in the face of infrastructure issues (Figure 11.3). Additionally, applications can scale dynamically in response to changing demand, allocating resources as traffic fluctuates [11]. These architectures are particularly effective for implementing event-driven

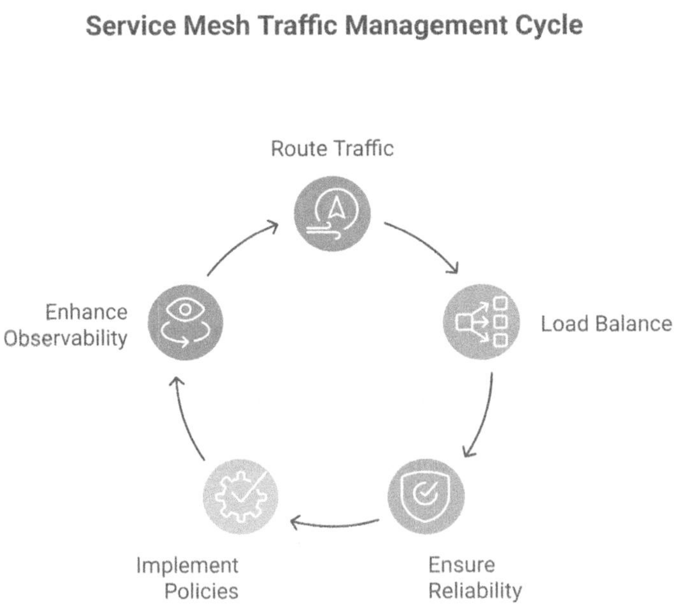

Figure 11.3 Service mesh traffic management cycle.

recovery strategies, which adapt automatically to various system conditions and failure situations. This design enables the handling of a significant volume of requests, which can be stored in a reliable datastore and processed at a rate that aligns with the system's capacity.

A few of the serverless self-healing patterns are explained below.

11.3.2.1 Retry Logic

Retries are automatic in many serverless platforms like AWS Lambda, Azure Functions, and Google Cloud Functions.

AWS Lambda Example (With Simple Queue Service (SQS) Trigger) This is part of the event source mapping configuration. AWS will retry the Lambda function if it fails, up to the specified number of attempts.

```
Node.js Example (manual retry with exponential backoff)
{
"DeadLetterConfig": {
"TargetArn": "arn:aws:sqs:us-east-1:123456789012:my-dlq"
}
}
```

11.3.2.2 Dead Letter Queues (DLQs)

DLQs capture failed events after all retry attempts are exhausted.

AWS Lambda DLQ Configuration (via AWS Console or IaC) This ensures failed invocations are sent to an SQS queue for later inspection.

Azure Functions DLQ (with Service Bus) Azure supports DLQs natively with Service Bus queues and topics. Messages that can't be processed are automatically moved to the DLQ.

Implementation Example: AWS Lambda + SQS + DLQ

Step-by-step:

1) Create an SQS queue (main queue).
2) Create a DLQ (another SQS queue).
3) Configure Lambda to trigger from the main queue.
4) Set DLQ in Lambda configuration.
5) Add retry logic in the Lambda handler (optional if using AWS retries).

```
# Python Lambda handler with manual retry
import time
import boto3
```

```
def lambda_handler(event, context):
   for record in event["Records"]:
   try:
   process_message(record["body"])
   except Exception as e:
   print(f"Error: {e}")
   raise e # Let AWS handle retry and DLQ
```

11.3.2.3 Comparison of Serverless vs. Container-Based Approaches

Feature	Serverless (e.g., Lambda)	Container-Based (e.g., ECS and Kubernetes)
Retry Logic	Built-in (configurable)	Manual (e.g., with sidecars or retry libraries)
DLQ Support	Native (SQS, SNS, EventBridge)	Manual (e.g., Kafka DLQs and custom queues)
Scaling	Auto-scales per request	Needs orchestration (e.g., Horizontal Pod Autoscaler (HPA) in K8s)
Cold Start	Possible	Less frequent with warm containers
Observability	Integrated (CloudWatch, X-Ray)	Requires setup (Prometheus, Grafana, etc.)
Cost	Pay-per-use	Pay-per-resource (even when idle)
Complexity	Low (abstracted infra)	High (requires orchestration, networking, etc.)

11.4 Case Study: Netflix's Implementation

11.4.1 AWS Case Study: Netflix's Chaos Engineering and Auto-Scaling

Netflix represents one of the most sophisticated implementations of autonomous cloud infrastructure, processing over 15 billion hours of content streaming monthly while maintaining 99.99% availability. Chaos Monkey is responsible for randomly terminating instances in production to ensure that engineers implement their services to be resilient to instance failures [12].

Chaos Engineering Implementation: Netflix pioneered the practice of deliberately introducing failures to test system resilience. Chaos Monkey is a tool invented in 2011 by Netflix to test the resilience of its IT infrastructure. It works by intentionally disabling computers in Netflix's production network to test how the remaining systems respond to the outage.

The Simian Army tools systematically test different failure scenarios:

- **Chaos Monkey:** Chaos Monkey operates by randomly selecting virtual machine instances and shutting them down during business hours.
- **Chaos Gorilla:** Chaos Gorilla is similar to Chaos Monkey but simulates an outage of an entire Amazon availability zone [13].
- **Chaos Kong:** Tests recovery from complete AWS region outages.

The Simian Army is a suite of failure-inducing tools designed to add more capabilities beyond Chaos Monkey. This comprehensive approach to failure testing ensures that systems can handle various failure scenarios gracefully.

11.5 Conclusion

11.5.1 Summary of Key Insights

The movement toward autonomous cloud infrastructure and self-healing systems signifies a crucial shift in the way distributed applications are designed, deployed, and managed. This shift is largely a response to the growing intricacies of cloud-native architectures, which render traditional manual processes less efficient and more prone to errors as scale increases.

Self-healing systems leverage established strategies such as circuit breakers, bulkheads, retry logic, and fallback mechanisms. These strategies work together within frameworks like the MAPE control loop, enabling systems to autonomously monitor their health, assess conditions, devise responses, and implement corrective measures. Advanced autonomous systems incorporate various technology layers, including container orchestration, serverless computing, IaC, and AI-driven analytics, with each layer adding unique capabilities that facilitate thorough autonomous operations.

11.5.2 Implementation Considerations and Best Practices

Implementing autonomous cloud infrastructure successfully necessitates a thoughtful approach that considers various organizational, technical, and cultural dimensions. Organizations are encouraged to take a phased strategy, beginning with low-risk projects and gradually scaling up as their expertise grows.

Before enabling autonomous responses, it's crucial to establish comprehensive observability, as systems need visibility to effectively manage themselves. These autonomous solutions should enhance human expertise rather than replace it, ensuring that automated decision-making processes are transparent. Regular testing through chaos engineering can help confirm the self-healing capabilities of systems under realistic scenarios. Additionally, security and compliance like Health Insurance Portability and Accountability Act (HIPAA) and Service Organization Control 2 (SOC 2) must be integral to the design of autonomous systems to avoid misuse while ensuring operational efficiency. The future of cloud computing is set to evolve with the integration of autonomous infrastructure, self-healing technologies, and cutting-edge innovations such as quantum computing and edge AI, which are expected to enhance cloud reliability, performance, and operational intelligence.

References

1 J. O. Kephart and D. M. Chess, "The vision of autonomic computing," *Computer*, vol. 36, no. 1, pp. 41–50, 2003, doi: 10.1109/MC.2003.1160055.

2 E. Ok and G. John, "Autonomous infrastructure & self-healing clouds," 2024. [Online]. Available: https://www.researchgate.net/publication/386171806_Autonomous_Infrastructure_Self-Healing_Clouds.

3 Kubernetes Documentation, "Architecture: Self-healing," 2024. [Online]. Available: https://kubernetes.io/docs/concepts/architecture/self-healing.

4 M. Azaiez and W. Chainbi, "A multi-agent system architecture for self-healing cloud infrastructure," in *Proc. Int. Conf. Internet things Cloud Comput.*," 2016, [Online]. Available: https://dl.acm.org/doi/10.1145/2896387.2896392.

5 Microsoft Learn, "Design for self healing – Azure architecture center," 2024. [Online]. Available: https://learn.microsoft.com/en-us/azure/architecture/guide/design-principles/self-healing.

6 J. Burke, "Scaling to infinity: Mastering hyperscale AWS serverless architecture with lambdas," in *AWS Commun.*, Feb. 8, 2024. [Online]. Available: https://community.aws/content/2c4Nfj0lTEzDTAX1pAxH5ryzuOa/scaling-to-infinity-mastering-hyperscale-aws-serverless-architecture-with-lambdas.

7 D. Barrigas, "Self-healing applications with Kubernetes and spring boot," in *Baeldung*, Jan. 8, 2024. [Online]. Available: https://www.baeldung.com/spring-boot-kubernetes-self-healing-apps.

8 Serverless Inc., "AWS Lambda: The ultimate guide," 2024. [Online]. Available: https://www.serverless.com/aws-lambda.

9 R. Sekkappan, "AI-driven network optimization for 5G and beyond," *Int. J. Comput. Eng. Tech.*, vol. 15, no. 6, pp. 809–822, 2024, doi: 10.5281/zenodo.14241899.

10 A. Zahorscak, "Guide to understanding your Kubernetes liveness probes best practices," in *Fairwinds*, 2024. [Online]. Available: https://www.fairwinds.com/blog/a-guide-to-understanding-kubernetes-liveness-probes-best-practices.

11 "Building scalable and secure serverless applications with AWS lambda," in *AWS re:Post*, Jul. 11, 2024. [Online]. Available: https://repost.aws/articles/ARtb3Vcie8RkKH5a8cx2gH4g/building-scalable-and-secure-serverless-applications-with-aws-lambda.

12 Netflix, "Chaos monkey," 2024. [Online]. Available: https://netflix.github.io/chaosmonkey.

13 Y. Izrailevsky, "The netflix simian army," *Netflix Technology Blog*, July 19, 2011. [Online]. Available: http://techblog.netflix.com/2011/07/netflix-simian-army.html.

12

Serverless Computing and Event-Driven Cloud Architectures

Jyoti Shah[1] *and Milankumar Rana*[2]

[1] *Independent Researcher, Edison, NJ, USA*
[2] *University of the Cumberlands, Williamsburg, KY, USA*

12.1 Introduction

As cloud computing evolves, it changes how applications are built, moving away from monolithic architectures and toward decentralized, reactive systems. Serverless computing and event-driven architecture (EDA) are two paradigms that are leading the way in this change. Function-as-a-Service (FaaS) services like Amazon Web Services (AWS) Lambda are examples of serverless computing. They take care of the underlying infrastructure, automatically scaling code execution, and only charging users for the time they use the service. This model lets developers focus on the logic of their applications without having to worry about servers, load balancers, or runtime environments. At the same time, EDA has become a popular way to design systems that can grow and respond to changes. In EDA, system parts send and respond to events at different times, which makes them less tightly connected, more resilient, and able to respond in real time. Cloud-native services like Amazon Event Bridge, Google Cloud Pub/Sub, and Azure Event Grid have made this model more popular by providing managed infrastructure for routing and handling events.

More and more, modern cloud apps use both of these models to get on-demand scalability and reactive functionality. For example, uploading a file to Amazon S3 might start a Lambda function, or an event related to a business transaction might go through Event Bridge to multiple downstream consumers. Serverless services not only handle events, but they are also the basic building blocks for EDA systems. This convergence has led to a new generation of cloud architectures that are modular, flexible, and efficient in terms of operations.

This chapter goes into great detail about serverless and event-driven paradigms and how they can be combined to make cloud applications that are very scalable, reliable, and easy to maintain. We start by looking at how both models have changed over time. Then we present a new reference architecture that focuses on AWS. A case study that isn't tied to any one domain shows how it can be used in the real world, and then there is a discussion of how to put it into practice, the problems it might cause, and its limitations. Lastly, we suggest ways that future research can make serverless EDA systems more reliable, portable, and easy to see.

12.2 Background and Related Work

Two fast-rising main paradigms in contemporary cloud systems are serverless computing and EDAs. Often in the form of FaaS, serverless computing offloads virtually all infrastructure management to the cloud provider, freeing developers to concentrate on code and business logic. Predicted to "grow to dominate the future of cloud computing," this model reflects an evolution in cloud abstraction—akin to the leap from low-level to high-level programming languages [1]. Concurrently, EDA has evolved into a preferred method for creating responsive and scalable distributed applications. Components in an EDA interact and emit rather than via close integration. This approach lets you have real-time responsiveness, better agility, and loose coupling. Industry adoption highlights its relevance: for instance, KnowBe4, a Software-as-a-Service (SaaS) provider, recently re-architected on AWS Event Bridge to decouple services, improving agility and scalability [2]. To reach on-demand scalability and asynchronous decoupling—where cloud functions are triggered by events to execute discrete tasks—many modern cloud applications now combine serverless and EDA. Most building blocks of event-driven systems (message queues, event buses, triggers) are themselves provided as serverless managed services, strengthening the symbiotic interaction between the two paradigms [3]. With an eye toward how combining these paradigms can produce extremely scalable and resilient designs, this paper offers a thorough analysis of serverless computing and event-driven cloud architectures.

Evolution of Serverless Computing: From physical servers to virtual machines (Infrastructure as a Service [IaaS]), to managed platforms (Platform as a Service [PaaS]), and today to serverless models (FaaS and Backend-as-a-Service [BaaS]), cloud computing has relentlessly abstracted operational complexity. FaaS allows developers to run individual functions in response to events without managing servers. It's ideal for custom logic like processing application programming interface (API) requests, data transformations, or background jobs. BaaS provides ready-to-use backend services such as authentication, databases, and cloud storage. Instead of writing and hosting backend code, developers use APIs to interact with these managed services. Following the release of AWS Lambda in 2014, the term "serverless" became well-known as the change to applications made of ephemeral functions automatically scaled and charged just on execution time. Though early scholarly definitions of serverless differed, generally they agreed on important characteristics: **no server management**, **automatic scaling**, and **pay-per-use pricing**. Jonas et al. (Berkeley, 2019) framed serverless as the cloud's next evolutionary step, highlighting its potential to simplify cloud programming and accelerate development [1]. Tracking the roots of the paradigm to earlier utility computing ideas and defining serverless alongside IaaS, PaaS, containers, and other cloud models, Communications of the ACM (2023) offers a historical perspective. A flurry of studies and industry reports over the past 5 years have looked at serverless advantages, use cases, and limitations. Hellerstein et al. (2018), for instance, criticized the first limitations ("One Step Forward, Two Steps Back") even as cloud providers rapidly improved offerings; meanwhile, thorough studies (e.g., Manner et al., 2018; Eivy, 2017) catalogued challenges including performance and tooling. Surveys like Kounev et al. (Communications of the Association of Computing Machinery [CACM]) sought to clear uncertainty by formalizing language and "capturing essential characteristics" of serverless computing [4].

FaaS allows developers to run individual functions in response to events without managing servers. It's ideal for custom logic like processing API requests, data transformations, or background jobs. BaaS provides ready-to-use backend services such as authentication, databases, and cloud storage. Instead of writing and hosting backend code, developers use APIs to interact with these managed services.

Evolution of EDA: Under EDA, systems react asynchronously and emit events—signifying changes in state or triggers. Though they originated in message-oriented middleware and enterprise integration patterns, EDA ideas have lately become more important with microservices and cloud-native design. Under an EDA, consumers subscribe to pertinent events by filtering or topics, while producers simply publish events to middleware (event bus or broker) without knowledge of who will consume them. Highly scalable and flexible systems produced by this decoupling allow new services to access event streams without affecting current producers. First-class EDA (e.g., AWS Event Bridge, Azure Event Grid, and Google Cloud Pub/Sub) and even architectural best practice encouragement are made available by modern cloud platforms. According to AWS's Well-Architected Framework, event-driven techniques enable the creation of scalable, resilient, and reasonably priced microservices [5]. Three basic components define every event-driven system: event sources, event routers, and event destinations [5]. Cloud providers make event-driven design far easier as they have fully managed services like event buses, queues, and messaging topics that can do filtering, routing logic, as well as scale and reliable delivery automatically. Such services intelligently analyze events (e.g., implementing rule-based filtering in AWS Event Bridge) and automatically push them to appropriate targets (serverless functions, queues, or databases) without requiring infrastructure management by teams. Even more incredible is that events and serverless computing inherently work together. For instance, in real-world triggers, HTTP requests, file uploads, or database updates will trigger serverless services like AWS Lambda instantly, allowing systems to respond automatically, to scale on demand, and to run only when work is available. This simple, pay-per-use execution model has sped up the journey to adopting EDA to the point where it has become a technical marvel, as well as an operational efficiency. In fact, many elements of an EDA are used via serverless services [3]. An AWS EDA solution might use Amazon S3 generating events on file uploads, Amazon Event Bridge or SNS as the event router, and AWS Lambda functions as consumers who process those events. Organizations switching to the cloud should take serverless alternatives for event-driven components under consideration, as Krishnamurthy (2022) notes, to acquire scalability and flexibility [3].

Related Work and Key Literature: Academic and commercial research has looked at the junction of serverless and EDA. Even though more and more people are using serverless computing and EDA, there are still problems that need to be solved, especially when it comes to state coordination, orchestration, observability, and portability. Both paradigms have their own strengths that work well together but using them together makes it harder to manage distributed workflows and debug short-lived functions. This paper talks about these integration problems using a single, workable framework.

"Serverless computing" is a broad term that refers to cloud-native models that hide the management of infrastructure. FaaS and BaaS are two examples of this. FaaS, which is shown by AWS Lambda, lets you run event-driven functions without having to set up servers. BaaS, on the other hand, is a term for cloud services that are ready to use, like authentication or storage. Our framework is mostly about FaaS-based architecture, but it also knows that BaaS components are often even producers or consumers in the bigger picture. Researchers in both schools and businesses have looked into different parts of these models. Jonas et al.'s Berkeley report [1] called serverless computing the next step in the evolution of cloud programming. It also pointed out problems with state management, which directly led us to choose to add AWS Step Functions and DynamoDB to our orchestration layer. The Kounev et al.'s [4] CACM survey stressed the importance of having clear architectural boundaries and formal definitions in the serverless domain, which shows that there is no agreement on what the best practices are.

Early studies, like Adzic & Chatley (2017) and McGrath & Brenner (2017), looked at real-world experiences with serverless microservices and inconsistencies at the platform level. More recent studies, like Persico et al. (2022), looked at event-driven FaaS patterns in Internet-of-Things (IoT) settings. Shahverdi et al. (2023) looked into ways to make serverless workflows work better, but they didn't talk about hybrid orchestration models. Industry reference guides and case studies (like AWS Lambda with Event Bridge [6]) show how to do things the right way, but they often don't take into account specific constraints and don't talk about architectural issues that affect many areas.

Even though the literature talks about the benefits of scalability, lower operational costs, and faster deployment, it always mentions problems with cold start latency, handling distributed state, debugging complexity, and platform lock-in. These problems have directly affected how we designed our proposed framework. It aims to provide a modular, traceable, and secure architecture that solves major issues by integrating serverless EDA in the real world.

Research Gaps: Even with increasing acceptance, several gaps and issues are still not sufficiently addressed in present research and application. Performance and cold starts: Cold start delay—that is, startup latency—occurs in serverless functions scaling from zero. While providers have gradually lessened this, erratic latencies can affect user-facing tasks; research on methods to lower cold-start overhead [4] is ongoing. Observing and monitoring: Developers also lose view of execution by giving up infrastructure control. The ephemeral, distributed character of serverless applications challenges conventional monitoring tools. Recent research shows that "one of the main challenges in serverless application development" [7] are limited observability and debugging support. Debugging complexity: It can be nontrivial to map an event through a series of functions and services. Without sophisticated tooling, the absence of built-in tracing and challenges to replicate distributed executions locally make debugging serverless workflows difficult [3]. Serverless systems first provided inadequate means for organizing multi-step processes and preserving state between function invocations, affecting orchestration and state management. Consequently, researchers found state handling and workflow management as newly arising issues [4]. (Cloud providers answered with services like AWS Step Functions, but ensuring effective orchestration in big-scale scenarios is still an open area.) Applications built on one vendor's serverless stack cannot readily be migrated to another cloud without major rewrites. Every provider offers services, event structures, and proprietary function interfaces. Lack of standardization makes migrating an application across clouds "challenging or impossible" [7, 8]. This begs questions about vendor lock-in and drives study on multicloud serverless architectures. [8]. Although serverless EDA systems have obvious benefits, the literature highlights continuous needs in performance optimization, tooling for monitoring and debugging, workflow portability, and cross-platform standards even if they bring clear advantages. These voids prepare us for our contributions in the next sections.

Serverless EDAs have a completely different set of trade-offs than traditional monolithic or container-based architectures. Serverless systems automatically scale individual functions in response to events, allowing for fine-grained elasticity. In contrast, container-based models usually need explicit orchestration to scale whole services. Monolithic or containerized apps have consistent, low-latency performance, especially for synchronous flows. Serverless systems, on the other hand, may have inconsistent performance because of cold starts, but they are great at handling asynchronous, bursty workloads. State management in serverless EDA is done outside of the application using managed services like DynamoDB or S3. This requires careful planning of the architecture. In contrast, monoliths can manage state more easily in memory. Because serverless environments are distributed and temporary, observability is harder and requires more advanced tracing and structured logging tools. On the other hand, fault isolation is much better in serverless models because failures only happen in one function, which makes the blast radius smaller. Serverless is cheaper because you only pay for what you use, which gets rid of the costs of resources that are always on in container deployments. But this means that you are more likely to be stuck with a vendor, since serverless solutions often depend on proprietary cloud-native services. In general, serverless EDA gives up some control and portability in exchange for speed, reliability, and ease of use.

Even though many people use them, combining serverless and event-driven models is still very hard. Cold start latency is still a performance problem, especially for workloads that require interaction. Designing stateless functions makes it harder to coordinate, so you need external orchestration and storage solutions. The asynchronous and distributed nature of event flows makes it harder to observe and debug them, which means that better tracing and logging tools are needed. Event injections and privilege escalation are two examples of security risks that come with loosely coupled workflows. Finally, vendor lock-in makes it hard to move data between clouds, and proprietary services make it even harder and more expensive. These gaps directly point to the problems that our proposed framework will solve.

12.3 Challenges

Designing and operating serverless, event-driven systems present several technical challenges. We discuss key challenges, including cold starts, state management, observability and debugging, and security:

Cold Start Latency: When a serverless function instance is triggered following a period of inactivity, the platform has to allocate resources and create a container, generating a cold start delay. For interactive workloads, this can cause hundreds of milliseconds of latency to the first request, influencing user experience. Since cost savings in serverless depend on scaling to zero, controlling cold starts is difficult. Proposed to lower cold-start impact are techniques including provisioned concurrency, snapshotting function state, and predictive pre-warming, but they sometimes involve trade-offs [4]. Cold starts remain a topic of active optimization in cloud provider engineering as well as in academia.

State Management: Serverless functions by design are ephemeral and stateless; every invocation has no memory of past invocations. Any state that has to last—across function runs or between several functions in a workflow—must be kept in outside systems like object stores or databases. There is complexity and latency introduced by this externalization of state. Current systems, according to Jonas et al., "have no built-in persistent storage" for functions; thus, developers must use remote storage and pay the performance penalty of data transfer on every invocation [1]. Maintaining application state—such as user sessions, workflow progress, or aggregation of events—then becomes nontrivial. To fit a stateless execution model, developers must deliberately select state storage (e.g., DynamoDB and Redis), manage consistency, and often rethink algorithms.

Observability and Debugging: Observability is the capacity to deduce from the outputs of the system its internal state (logs, measurements, traces). Observability in serverless architectures is famously constrained [7]. Short-lived and under control by the provider, functions run concurrently across several containers, making log aggregation difficult and single transaction flow tracking challenging. In this environment, conventional application performance monitoring (APM) tools meant for long-running operations usually fail. Debugging is equally difficult; developers cannot simply link a debugger to a cloud function running in the environment of the provider, and there is no simple way to walk through an event-driven workflow. Troubleshooting usually depends on scattered logs and measurements, which force developers to rebuild after-hoc. Studies have underlined this as a crucial problem: without better tooling, developers "have to depend on the limited options provided by platforms to observe and inspect serverless applications, making it difficult to identify and fix runtime faults" [7]. Recent projects aiming at increasing visibility by spreading trace IDs through function calls include distributed tracing for serverless (e.g., AWS X-Ray and Open Telemetry instrumentation). Still, reaching deep observability—that is, what one had in monolithic systems—remains difficult, particularly in intricate event-driven systems.

Debugging Complexity: Debugging multi-function, event-triggered workflows is analogous to debugging a highly asynchronous, distributed system. Difficulties in reproducing problems, including race conditions, partial failures, or unexpected event ordering, include the "many small, independent functions" involved that aggravate the situation; a failure might spread over several services and leave few hints in any one log [9].

Security: Serverless and event-driven systems' security models bring unique difficulties. Multiple tenants' codes running on the same underlying infrastructure in FaaS mean providers must guarantee strong isolation between function executions. From the user's point of view, fine-grained permission management is essential; cloud identity and access management (IAM) rules should guide every function and service interaction toward the least privilege concept. Ignorance of configurations might cause privilege escalation or illegal data access. Moreover, event-driven processes blur conventional application limits; a chain of events could be indirectly triggered by outside events, thus challenging the consistency of security context. Event injection or manipulation raises questions since an assailant might create events to take advantage of downstream capabilities in case validation is inadequate. Another is the "break in the traditional security enclave" issue, whereby the classic network security perimeter is less relevant since an application now spans several managed services, hence pushing the need for identity-based and zero-trust security approaches. Researchers have underlined the need to tracking data flow to prevent data leakage between steps [4] and to stopping illegal function invocations in chained processes.

In summary, **cold starts, statelessness, observability/debugging gaps, and security concerns** are major challenges that architects must contend with when building serverless event-driven systems. These challenges motivate the design considerations for our framework in the next section.

12.4 Proposed Framework

To address the above challenges and harness the strengths of both serverless and event-driven paradigms, we propose a *novel AWS-centric framework* that combines **event-driven choreography** with **centralized orchestration**. The framework is designed to leverage AWS managed services (Lambda, Event Bridge, Step Functions, etc.) to create a modular, scalable architecture. Key aspects of the proposed framework include:

Event Producers and Ingestion: Event producers are any systems or parts that send signals when something changes or a request is made. These can be internal cloud services, external applications, partner systems, or user-facing interfaces like web or mobile apps. The framework adds a separate ingestion layer that handles all incoming interactions. This makes it possible to generate secure, scalable events from a wide range of sources. The ingestion layer takes inputs like HTTP API requests, file uploads, database changes, or IoT messages and turns them into structured events that can be processed later. This layer has built-in authentication, validation, and throttling systems to make sure that only real traffic is allowed and to protect against abuse. This design makes sure that all external stimuli, whether they happen at the same time or not, are consistently picked up and sent into the event-driven pipeline. This allows for a wide range of integration scenarios while keeping the system modular and resilient.

Event Routing and Bus (Choreography): The framework's central component is an event bus that allows somewhat coupled communication between consumers and producers. We centralize routing using Amazon Event Bridge, the AWS serverless event bus. Event Bridge serves as a middleman separating event sources from targets: consumers register interest using subscription rules, while producers just load events onto the bus. Based on event patterns—that is, matching attributes like type, source, or content—the event bus filters and forwards events to the suitable locations. This publish–subscribe approach guarantees that adding new customers (or producers) does not require changing the other components; a new consumer can listen for particular events with minimum effect. Using AWS Event Bridge Schema Registry or open formats, the framework specifies consistent event schemas for many event types. An "OrderPlaced" event, for instance, might have fields like orderId, customerId, and timestamp, all of which publishers and subscribers of that type follow. By matching events to these schemas, Event Bridge increases resilience. The event bus allows choreography: several services can independently react to the same event in parallel, creating fan-out scenarios. For example, one consumer (function) might handle payment when an order is placed, another updates inventory, and another sends a confirmation message—all set off by the one event. This results in an elastic subscriber to the event stream and a naturally scalable design whereby components are.

Function Orchestration and State Coordination: Though pure event choreography is strong, complicated processes sometimes call for coordination (e.g., execute step A and then B, only if A succeeds). The framework combines AWS Step Functions, a serverless orchestrating tool, to execute workflow as code for such multi-step systems. Step Functions let us specify state machines with branching logic, retries, and built-in error handling that coordinate a series of Lambda functions—or other service calls. Step Functions are applied in our framework to coordinate important corporate processes requiring maintaining state between steps or with several steps. An "Order Processing" system might, for instance, charge a customer, then reserve inventory, then arrange shipping; Step Functions can coordinate these in a defined sequence with automatic rollback or compensation should one step fail. Step Functions pass the required data (state) from one step to the next while each stage of the workflow is executed as a Lambda function—or an embedded service integration. This solves the state management problem by letting the state machine retain temporary state (in context) all through the process instead of having every intermediate result written to a database. Amazon DynamoDB is a persistent state store included in the architecture for longer-lived state or cross-workflow state sharing. Application state, including aggregate counters, user session data, or business domain entities—e.g., order records—is kept in DynamoDB, a serverless NoSQL database. Lambda functions within processes or even consumers allow one to access it as needed. Especially DynamoDB streams—which create events on table modifications—can feed back into Event Bridge or trigger Lambdas, thus closing the loop between events and state changes. Event Bridge and Step Functions taken together create a hybrid orchestration model: While Step Functions provide centralized coordination for specified workflows, Event Bridge lets reactive, asynchronous event handling—or choreography. These two models cooperate; for instance, a Step Functions workflow can send events to Event Bridge at specific points (to notify other components of a milestone), and conversely an Event Bridge rule can initiate a Step Functions execution (e.g., start a workflow when a particular event is observed). Where suitable, this hybrid approach offers control (structured coordination) and flexibility (loose coupling [6]).

Serverless Compute (AWS Lambda): AWS Lambda forms the framework's computation spine. Lambda functions—which are triggered by events from Event Bridge or straight via API Gateway—run all business logic. Since Lambda is essentially event-driven—each invocation is connected to an event occurrence—it fits naturally. Lambda functions—each addressing a specific chore—e.g., validate order input, charge credit card, and write to database—are kept small and single-responsibility in our design. This fine-grained functional breakdown enables reusability and independent scaling of every function and fits the microservices concept. Lambda can natively integrate with many AWS services; thus, some events may call Lambda without even using the Event Bridge bus: for example, an S3 upload event can directly trigger a Lambda. When decoupling is advantageous, for example, fan out too many consumers, our framework still paths such events through the bus.

Security Controls: Every level of the framework is built with security in mind. All components have least privilege access enforced using AWS IAM roles and policies. Every Lambda function runs under a designated IAM role that grants it just the permissions required (for instance, a function that writes to a DynamoDB table and publishes an event will have policy access just for dynamodb:PutItem on the target table and events:PutEvents on the event bus). To stop illegal event injection, the Event Bridge bus has a resource policy guiding which services or accounts may publish or subscribe to it. Before allowing events through, API Gateway can validate JSON Web Tokens (JWTs) or API keys and connect with AWS Cognito or another identity provider to authenticate outside requests. While the Event Bridge schema registry can validate events against predefined schemas, rejecting malformed or unexpected messages, API Gateway can enforce schemas on request payloads, enabling input validation at the edges.

All things considered, the suggested architecture offers AWS a road map for creating a serverless, event-driven cloud application. Emphasizing modular design, the event bus, coordinated processes, and serverless functions—all decoupled components—show planners Each component can scale independently, faults in one component do not cascade, events can be retried or redirected, and the system is extensible—that is, new services or consumers can be added by just adding new events or rules. The architecture of this framework in a layered perspective is shown in the next part together with detailed component interaction description.

12.5 Architecture Overview

The architecture uses layers to clearly separate concerns. Each layer is made up of components that have similar responsibilities. The design is based on an event-driven pattern that separates publishers and subscribers with a central event bus. Filtered rules send events to specific consumers, which lets the system process events at different times and be more flexible. This layered approach makes sure that producers don't have to know about downstream consumers, which makes it easier to keep things modular, scalable, and easy to maintain.

Layer 0—Event Producers (Clients and Sources): Top among them are the event planners, who start interactions. This covers internal cloud services releasing events as well as outside customers (such as web or mobile apps, partner systems, or IoT devices). External client requests in our AWS-centric environment pass via Amazon API Gateway (REST/HTTP API for synchronous requests or WebSocket API for real-time streams). Other AWS services can act as producers independently; for instance, a CloudWatch alert will release an event on a threshold breach, or an Amazon S3 bucket can be set to create an event upon file upload. These producers simply create events in the system; they do not directly call consumers.

Layer 1—Event Ingestion and Security Layer: Comprising the gateways and intake systems tasked with front-line processing, layer 1 consists of events. Here resides API Gateway, offering a safe front for APIs. It converts outside API calls—such as HTTP POST requests for orders to be placed—into events. At this layer, security checks include basic request validation and authentication (using Cognito user pools and OAuth tokens). This layer comprises AWS service event emitters for non-HTTP sources (which don't need authorization in the same sense but might involve service-specific filters). An AWS IoT Core rule might, for instance, channel IoT device messages into the event stream. Layer 1's main job is to let legitimate events into the system and drop or reject any illegal or malformed requests at the threshold.

Layer 2—Event Routing Bus: Implemented by Amazon Event Bridge (or similarly Amazon Simple Notification Services [SNS]/Amazon Simple Queue Services [SQS] in some patterns), the event routing layer forms the foundation of the architecture. Of the event-driven design, this is the "central nervous system." Event Bridge handles all events admitted from Layer 1; it serves as a logical event bus decoupling sender and receiver tools. Events are arranged (by event type or source) within Event Bridge and matched against subscription criteria. Every rule outlines a pattern—e.g., an event with detail-type "OrderPlaced," with an amount greater than $0—and a target to forward the event to should the pattern fit. The architecture has a central event bus with several filters (rules) resulting in different consumers. One rule might route "OrderPlaced" events to a payment processing workflow; another might route the same events to an audit logging function; a third rule might completely ignore those events. The event bus thus allows publishers to remain ignorant of the number of consumers while one event can set off several actions in parallel. Event Bridge supports several buses—e.g., a default bus for internal events, custom buses for particular domains, or partner event buses for third-party integrations—but for simplicity the architecture can be seen as a single logical bus linking all services in the application domain.

Layer 3—Orchestration and Processing Layer: The serverless compute and workflow engines found in this layer run application-specific processing using events. Two main elements make up this layer: AWS Lambda functions and AWS Step Functions state machines. Individual Lambda functions—shown in architecture as event consumers—address simpler events. An S3 "Image Uploaded" event, for instance, might set off a Lambda function creating a thumbnail. More complicated events start a Step Functions workflow—that is, a state machine—which coordinates a series of Lambda invocations. This is shown in the diagram by an orchestration box (Step Functions), which the event bus targets. An "OrderPlaced" event, for example, might set off a Step Functions workflow called "OrderProcessingStateMachine." Coordinating their execution and controlling state transitions between them, that state machine will then call several Lambda functions in order (ChargeCard -> ReserveInventory -> SendConfirmation). Often interacting with other AWS services (e.g., reading and writing to DynamoDB, and calling outside APIs), each Lambda function in this layer is stateless and executes a discrete piece of logic. The orchestration layer thus manages synchronous or sequential workflows (via Step Functions coordinating Lambdas) and asynchronous processing (via independent Lambdas for each event). Especially, Step Functions can pause and wait for outside events (using "wait for callback" or human approval steps), which can tie back into the event bus (for instance, a Step Function could wait for an "Inventory Replenished" event if stock was insufficient). With AWS handling the scaling behind the scenes, this layer is entirely serverless; it scales out automatically: if hundreds of events arrive simultaneously, Event Bridge will call the corresponding Lambda functions or start multiple workflow executions in parallel.

Layer 4—State Management and Data Layer: Comprising data persistence and stateful services supporting the serverless computing layer, the bottom layer consists of the main element Amazon DynamoDB, the system-of-record for state and application data. DynamoDB tables might, for example, include records of orders, payments, and inventory. As necessary, the Lambdas and procedures in the top layer read and write to these tables. For its serverless character (scales automatically, pay-per-use) and fine-grained latency performance—which fits event-driven workloads needing fast database operations, DynamoDB is selected. Other services like Amazon Aurora Serverless (for Structured Query Language [SQL]) could also show up in this layer if strong consistency or relational features are required; DynamoDB covers a broad spectrum of use cases with low operating overhead. Any other storage or caching application might need—for example, Amazon S3 for storing big objects (images, logs) and Amazon Elasticache (Redis) if low-latency caching is needed—is also included at the state layer. DynamoDB interacts with the event system in the shown architecture via DynamoDB Streams: any database change will cause an event (which Event Bridge or trigger Lambdas can record). Thus, state changes can, in turn, create new events (e.g., an "OrderStatus Updated" event upon a change in the status of an order item in the table), thus allowing an event-sourced character to the design. When Lambdas accesses the state layer abstracted behind repository or Data Access Object (DAO) interfaces, this encapsulation helps to simplify data store swapping or modification without compromising the business logic.

Cross-Cutting Concerns—Monitoring, Logging, and Security: Cross-cutting services are combined throughout all layers even though they are not shown as a separate layer in the diagram. Every Lambda function generates logs, which AWS CloudWatch automatically ships to CloudWatch Logs). Key indicators, e.g., Lambda durations, memory use, throttle counts, number of workflow executions, and Event Bridge delivery failures, are monitored by CloudWatch Metrics and Alarms. On Lambda and Step Functions, AWS X-Ray, also known as Open Telemetry, is turned on to track requests across the system, offering insights on end-to-end latency throughout the layers. As discussed, AWS IAM spans all layers for security, ensuring that every component can only interact with its intended counterparts. For audit purposes, AWS CloudTrail logs all events including API Gateway calls, Event Bridge events, and Step Function runs. Together, these security and management tools guarantee that the architecture can be seen, is under control, and is maintained safely in use.

In summary, with Layer 4 (DynamoDB) preserving continuous state, the architecture offers a layered, decoupled framework whereby Layer 2 (Event Bridge) is the central hub routing events between Layer 0/1 (producers) and Layer 3 (consumers). Producers send events, consumers can independently scale or fail without affecting others, and this design achieves a high degree of decoupling: producers do not know about consumers. By means of serverless services in every layer (API Gateway, Event Bridge, Lambda, Step Functions, and DynamoDB), the entire architecture gains from automatic scaling, high availability, and managed infrastructure by AWS. Every component API Gateway can manage hundreds of concurrent requests, Event Bridge can route millions of events per second with built-in fault tolerance, Lambda can create thousands of function instances in parallel, and DynamoDB can autoscale throughput depending on load. This guarantees that, without human intervention, architecture can effortlessly manage changing loads from zero to peak. Moreover, the event-driven strategy makes the system naturally extensible. Using Event Bridge for choreography and Step Functions for orchestration gives us the right balance of flexibility and control, which is why we chose to use AWS. IAM roles, resource policies, and schema validation at the ingestion layer help keep security boundaries in place. This reduces the risks that come with decoupled workflows. Structured logging and end-to-end tracing with trace IDs and AWS X-Ray make it possible to keep an eye on things and find out where they came from.

12.6 Implementation Considerations

Implementing the proposed framework on AWS requires careful consideration of deployment processes, configuration of services, and operational best practices. In this section, we discuss the practical aspects of building and managing the system: Infrastructure-as-Code, function sizing, throttling controls, logging, and monitoring strategies.

Infrastructure-as-Code (IaC): Manual configuration via the AWS console would be error-prone and difficult to maintain given the myriads of linked services (API Gateway, Event Bridge, Lambda, Step Functions, DynamoDB,

IAM roles, etc.). Rather, we repeatedly define and provision the whole architecture using IaC. Two AWS-centric IaC solutions generally used are AWS Cloud Development Kit (CDK) and AWS Serverless Application Model (SAM). An expansion of CloudFormation, AWS SAM offers a condensed syntax for serverless resources.

Continuous Deployment: We combine the IaC with Continuous Integration (CI)/Continuous Deployment or Delivery (CD) pipelines such that any code or configuration change can be immediately tested and implemented. If a Lambda behind API Gateway achieves zero-downtime deployment, for instance, a change in the code of a Lambda causes the pipeline to run unit tests, package the new code, update the CloudFormation stack (via SAM/CDK), and safely deploy (possibly using AWS CodeDeploy for traffic shifting). Although complete integration tests still run in a deployed test stack due to the need for real AWS managed services, we also use AWS SAM's local testing capabilities for basic simulations (SAM Command Line Interface [CLI] can run Lambdas and API Gateway locally in Docker).

Function Configuration and Sizing: Performance as well as cost depends on each Lambda function's configuration being optimized. Every function gets memory, which also fairly distributes CPU. We choose a suitable memory size by examining the workload of every function. A larger memory (and CPU) setting, such as 1,024 MB or more, would help a CPU-bound image processing function, for instance, greatly reduce execution time and hence perhaps lower cost since Lambda is billed on time.

Throttling and Back-Pressure: Event-driven systems allow bursts of events to set off significant Lambdas scale-outs. AWS can manage scaling; downstream systems might not be able to. For example, that external API might become a bottleneck if our order processing system suddenly absorbs thousands of events per second and each tries to charge a credit card via another API. We use throttling systems at several places to prevent this. Max N requests per second per client is one of the usage policies and quotas that API Gateway can enforce. Although Event Bridge has a natural delivery throughput, its management depends on the number of events a producer sends, that is, by means of backpressure from upstream if necessary. AWS will automatically throttle if the concurrency limit of the function is reached for asynchronous Lambda invocations (such as those from Event Bridge); we set those limits suitably. We can also include buffering with SQS queues in paths where smoothing out bursts is crucial. Rather than Event Bridge directly triggering a Lambda for every event, for instance, we could have Event Bridge send specific events to an SQS queue (via a queue target), then have a Lambda poll that queue (via Lambda event source mapping) at a controlled rate. This separates the arrival rate from the processing rate basically. This kind of behavior was mentioned in AWS's guidance, where a fast producer uses an SQS buffer for a slower consumer [2].

Logging Strategy: Debugging serverless apps mostly requires logging; thus, we use a centralized and orderly logging method. Every Lambda function generates logs in JSON format with consistent fields, that is, a correlation ID (such as an Order ID or Trace ID carried via the event), function name, and verbosity level. Structuring logs allows us to query and track flows across departments using CloudWatch Logs Insights or outside log management like ElasticSearch/Kibana or Datadog. Every event that passes through the system has a unique trace ID, for example, Step Functions can pass an execution ID, or API Gateway can create a request ID and we make sure that this is recorded in all logs.

Monitoring and Alerts: Reliability depends on real-time observation. We track important metrics from all services, e.g., invocations, errors, and duration for every Lambda; throttles, if any; executions started/successful/failed for step functions; and number of events delivered and failed invocations for Event Bridge, using Amazon CloudWatch. CloudWatch Alarms on important error metrics, that is, if the error count or failure rate of any Lambda function surpasses a threshold (over a five-minute period), an alert trigger.

Testing and Validation: Without talking about testing strategy, implementation concerns would not be whole. We run several test layers: unit tests for every Lambda function's handler (using simulated event inputs), integration tests using AWS SAM's local emulator (where feasible) to test a few functions and their interactions, and full end-to-end tests in a deployed test environment. We combine automated test scripts that, for example, place a test order through the API and subsequently verify that all expected outcomes occurred, payment was processed, the DB was updated, a confirmation event was received, etc., with hand exploration testing for end-to-end.

Configuration Management: The system has several configurable settings, including feature flags, threshold values, etc. Lambdas can retrieve configuration from AWS Systems Manager Parameter Store or AWS AppConfig either at runtime or during initialization. This lets dynamic tuning, that is, changing a rate limit or a timeout setting without redeploying code, to avoid hard-coding values. We version-control these setups and link them to deployment pipelines to guarantee regular application of changes.

We do end-to-end validation by setting up a staging environment that looks like production and using test events to mimic full workflows, like placing an order and checking the effects on payment, inventory updates, and notifications. We can check not only execution but also data correctness and event integrity by adding trace IDs and assertions to each step of the workflow. Exploratory testing adds to automated tests to make sure they work well in the real world across asynchronous boundaries. Ultimately, using the serverless EDA architecture on AWS calls for a strong DevOps discipline for testing and monitoring, careful tuning of every service, and solid infrastructure automation. Following best practices—IaC, least privilege security, careful logging, and proactive monitoring—guarantees that the architectural theoretical advantages are realized in use as a dependable, maintainable system.

While serverless offers compelling cost benefits at low-to-moderate utilization—due to its pay-per-invocation model—costs can escalate under sustained high load. Unlike container-based deployments, which benefit from amortized computer costs over long-running workloads, serverless functions incur charges per execution and duration. For high-throughput systems with steady traffic, container-based solutions (e.g., on Kubernetes) may prove more economical, especially when reserved instances or autoscaling clusters are used. Our architecture remains cost-effective for bursty or event-driven workloads but requires careful monitoring to avoid inefficiencies at scale.

12.7 Case Study

We present a generic case study that is domain-agnostic but representative of typical real-world use cases in order to show the end-to-end operation of the proposed architecture. We will walk through a scenario based on an order processing workflow, which could fit e-commerce, food delivery, ticket booking, etc. It is a sequence of events and functions. We selected this scenario to underline the advantages of an event-driven serverless architecture and include several services (payment, inventory, notification).

Scenario Description: Consider a web application where consumers may order a good or service. An order placed event in our system is set off when a user orders. After that, the system has to charge the user's payment method, update inventory records, and forward a confirmation back to her. Additional side chores include notifying downstream fulfillment systems and logging the analytics order. Using our serverless EDA, we will track this sequence.

Following are the steps of an event-driven serverless order processing workflow using AWS services:

Step 1—API Request Initiation: After filling their cart on the web app, a user clicks "Place Order." The frontend requests HTTPS from the backend API, for instance, an HTTP POST to the /orders endpoint. Layer 1: Ingestion and Security Amazon API Gateway gets this request. API Gateway guarantees the user is authenticated and the input JSON follows the expected schema for an order, so validating the demand. After successful validation, API Gateway uses its integrated backend, which in our design is an AWS Lambda capability known as OrderInitiator. This Lambda is straightforward: it performs basic checks or enrichment (like assigning an Order ID) and then generates an event object reflecting the new order from the incoming order data (e.g., items, user ID, and payment token). OrderInitiator decouples the flow by putting an event onto Amazon Event Bridge, not processing everything synchronously.

Step 2—Event Routing: The OrderPlaced event now resides on the **Event Bridge** bus (Layer 2). Event Bridge evaluates this event against its rules. In our case study, we have defined multiple rules for OrderPlaced events:

Rule 1: Start Order Workflow: This rule matches on detail-type = OrderPlaced (and possibly other criteria, e.g., amount > 0) and targets an **AWS Step Functions** state machine named OrderProcessingWorkflow.

Rule 2: Log Order Event: Matches all OrderPlaced events and triggers a Lambda OrderLogger which simply records the event in a logging service or database for analytics (e.g., storing in an S3 data lake or posting to an analytics API).

Rule 3: Notify Fulfillment: Maybe another Lambda or SNS issue could be a target to let the fulfillment system know if orders of a particular kind call for quick fulfillment action. Here, we skip fulfillment notification at the first level, assuming we have an OrderFulfilment Notifier Lambda that will listen to when the order is fully processed, which could be a later event.

For now, the primary outcome is that Event Bridge triggers the **OrderProcessingWorkflow** Step Function (via Rule 1). Event Bridge provides event data as input to the state machine execution.

Step 3—Orchestrated Order Processing: The AWS Step Functions: OrderProcessingWorkflow begins execution with the OrderPlaced event data. This workflow is defined to orchestrate the order through multiple steps, handling success or failure at each step gracefully (Layer 3: Orchestration & Processing).

Step 3.1: Payment Charge: Charging the customer's payment comes first in the process. Step Functions generate the ChargePayment Lambda function using the order information. This feature, probably coupled with an internal billing system or a payment gateway like Stripe, will try to charge the user's credit card or account for the order total. It might refer to an outside API, which occasionally might be slow. Should the payment be successful, that is, authorization obtained, ChargePayment responds with a successful message (maybe including a transaction ID). Receiving this, the Step Function moves forward. Should payment fail, that is, a card is declined—the function could throw an error that Step Functions detects. Error handling is included in the workflow definition; a payment failure could be handled by a particular branch that marks the order as failed payment, notifies the user via another event or Lambda, and then pauses the workflow. Simplistically, assume payment succeeds.

Step 3.2: Reserve Inventory: Making sure the products in order are kept in inventory guarantees their availability for shipment. Step functions using order details set the Reserve Inventory Lambda. This feature will reduce inventory counts in DynamoDB's Layer 4: Data ordered item inventory table. Conditional updates will be used to guarantee no negative stock (should an item run out, this operation fail or show inadequate supply). Assume all items are currently reserved (stock levels changed) but in stock. Lambda comes back successful. Should it discover an item out of supply, it could cause a particular specific error. We have set the workflow to manage that situation, maybe by marking the order for backorder and notifying the user or by triggering a compensating action like rolling back payment (if inventory is important). Assume for our case that inventory was plentiful.

Step 3.3: Update Order Status: The order can be confirmed, having charged payment and reserved inventory. Either inside the previous Lambda or as a separate Lambda UpdateOrderStatus, the workflow might include a step to update an Orders record in DynamoDB status to "Confirmed." Assume the UpdateOrderStatus Lambda records an order ID and status entry into an Orders table. This runs quickly and succeeds.

Step 3.4: Emit Order Confirmation Event: We want to let other areas of the system (including the user) know now the order is completely processed. Instead of explicitly calling those services, the workflow generates a fresh event for the Event Bridge bus. Using the Event Bridge PutEvents API, we added a chore to Step Functions, which can call AWS APIs via service integrations. It generates a type Order Processed (or Order Completed) event with orderId and status = Confirmed, among other elements. Now fan-outs to any interested listeners will be occurring at Event Bridge. To particularly capture OrderProcessed events and activate OrderFulfilment Notifier Lambda, we set Rule 3: Notify Fulfilment. Lambda will record the event and, for instance, notify the warehouse or fulfillment system (perhaps via an outside API or by writing a note on another bus), enabling shipment to start. We also set up maybe another rule alerting the user for OrderProcessed events. One could use an Amazon Simple Notification Service (SNS) topic or Amazon Pinpoint for user notifications, or just another Lambda SendOrderEmail emailing the user with confirmation. The idea is that adding any number of actions, such as email, SMS, and logging, is simple without changing the main flow since we use an event for completion.

By now the Step Functions process has finished satisfactorily. Step Functions records and generates a success metric. From the user's point of view, if this were synchronous, it'd be done; but remember, we already addressed the user at Step 1. The last alerts are thus occurring asynchronously in the backdrop. We could also create a minor variation, though; maybe the API Gateway call was a

WebSocket or used AWS AppSync to send a real-time update to the user following order processing. If WebSockets are used, for instance, the OrderProcessed event could be passed to a WebSocket connection to update the user interface in almost real-time (this could be accomplished by having the OrderInitiator save the user's connection ID and subsequently a Lambda discovers that connection and sends a message).

Step 4—Post-Processing and Side Effects: Thanks to the event-driven design, several side processes happen around the same time:

For analytics, the first-order event recorded by the OrderLogger Lambda activated by Rule 2 at the moment of order placement is in a similar vein; we could have a PaymentLogger set off upon payment charging, etc. This records significant corporate events into a data lake without influencing the transaction.

The OrderFulfillmentNotifier Lambda (triggered by the completion event) sends details to a fulfillment system. Let's say it posts a message to an SQS queue that the fulfillment team's system monitors or directly calls an API of a shipping service to create a shipment.

Confirming the order, the user notification, probably an email or push notification, is delivered. Should we have a web UI listening on a WebSocket or leveraging server-sent events, the user would be shown real-time confirmation akin to "Your order #12345 has been confirmed!" CloudWatch will have logs for every Lambda invocation and the Step Function execution trace; X-Ray might have a trace from the API call through to the final event all the while. Should any step fail, our alarms found in Section 6 would alert the team.

This case study demonstrates how an event-driven serverless architecture handles a complex multi-step process in a loosely coupled, scalable manner. While we described an order scenario, the pattern is *domain-agnostic*: we could replace "order" with any process—e.g., processing an *IoT sensor reading* (validate data →store in DB →trigger alerts if out of range →update dashboard) or a *data pipeline* (file uploaded →trigger processing →split into tasks →aggregate results →publish outcomes). The combination of Step Functions orchestration and Event Bridge event routing is powerful in these contexts, giving both structure and flexibility. As AWS's own architecture best practices suggest, using events to integrate microservices allows each part of the system to evolve independently and scale as needed [6].

By means of this example, we have also implicitly tested our evaluation metrics: high scalability under increasing order volume; latency was maintained mostly low by asynchronous processing; and isolated error handling improved dependability. In the next part, we consider some difficulties and constraints faced during the implementation and running of such architecture, which will moderate the positive view from this case study with pragmatic considerations.

12.8 Challenges and Limitations

While the serverless event-driven approach provides many benefits, our experience and the case study above highlight several *challenges and limitations* that practitioners should be aware of. We discuss these implementation challenges and inherent limitations, including those related to vendor lock-in and testing complexity, and how they impact the architecture:

Vendor Lock-In: A tight connection to AWS services limits an AWS-centric design significantly and raises questions regarding portability. Our system takes advantage of proprietary event formats and APIs as well as AWS-specific services (Lambda, Event Bridge, DynamoDB, Step Functions, etc.). Should we ever wish to migrate to another cloud or a multicloud approach, it would be rather labor-intensive. The event routing system would change (e.g., to Azure Event Grid or Google Pub/Sub, each with different semantics), and the functions would have to be modified to the FaaS offering of the new platform. Step Functions are especially proprietary since their state machine definitions (Amazon States Language) are exclusive to AWS. This lock-in has real consequences for risk management and negotiations with cloud providers, not only hypothetically. We minimize it somewhat by using abstraction wherever possible (e.g., using an interface for the event bus so, in theory, it could be swapped with another message broker) and by following standard programming languages for Lambdas (so code is portable at the source level). For example, a medium-sized SaaS company tried to move its AWS-based serverless analytics pipeline to Google Cloud but found that it would need to rewrite almost everything in order to change the logic of Step Functions and the schemas of Event Bridge events. The project was finally dropped because it would have cost too much in engineering time and money.

Testing and Debugging Complexity: Debugging distributed event-driven applications is difficult, as was already mentioned. We found cases during implementation when improperly configured rules or IAM permissions caused events to not activate the intended function. Investigating such problems meant looking through CloudWatch Logs and Event Bridge data to determine why an event wasn't delivered, that is, whether a rule pattern filtered it out. Did the intended Lambda fail execution? Unlike a monolithic application where one may run everything in a local debugger, here we had to deploy to the cloud to test end-to-end flows. Early development benefited somewhat from tools including SAM CLI and localstack, which replicate AWS services locally, but they have restrictions and are not exactly faithful to actual AWS.

Performance Overheads: Although generally effective, our design has certain performance overheads. Every stage of the process, including inventory and payment, was a separate Lambda invocation; Step Functions handled transitions; this resulted in overhead expressed as invocation start times and state propagation. Low-latency, high-throughput environments may find the multiple-hop latency to be a constraint. If we needed sub-100 ms processing, for instance, the mix of API Gateway (tens of ms overhead), Lambda cold start (possibly ~100 ms in languages like Java/Python), and Step Functions state transition (~10–20 ms overhead each) might not meet the need. Although in our case study seconds of latency were acceptable, we highlight this as a restriction for use cases needing ultra-low latency or high-frequency small events (where the overhead might become a larger fraction of total time).

Complexity of Orchestration vs. Choreography: Choosing what logic goes into Step Functions (orchestration) against leaving it to event-driven emergence (choreography) presents still another difficulty. Underuse can make it difficult to reason about system-wide flows; overuse of orchestration can reduce the flexibility of the system. We had to carefully plan the Step Function workflow to avoid turning into a giant monolith unto itself. Step functions in their standard form have certain throughput limits (like transitions per second) and a maximum duration (one year, which is plenty). We had to make sure our consumption stayed within limits or use the Express Workflow mode for the trade-off of increased throughput. Step functions' orchestration logic calls for both writing and maintenance skills; it's either a JavaScript Object Notation (JSON)/Yet another Markup Language (YAML) state language or using the CDK high-level structures.

Observability Gaps: We had some blind spots even with monitoring in place. For example, we found that the event might go to a Dead Letter Queue (DLQ) or be dropped following the last attempt if a Lambda is invoked asynchronously by Event Bridge and it fails all retries. Such failures could be overlooked without appropriate DLQ monitoring until someone examines the DLQ. This occurred in testing when an edge case caused a Lambda to always fail—Event Bridge retried two times then dropped (since we hadn't set a DLQ in that test environment)—we only caught it by noticing a discrepancy in expected outcomes. This made clear that silently swallowed mistakes carry some danger. We set alarms and DLQs to help to reduce it.

Costs at Scale and Service Limits: Although serverless is typically less expensive, one should be alert to some scaling patterns. For instance, costs can rise rapidly if an upstream event producers load the system with events since every event sets off several purposes. Imagine in our situation a bug causing a client to send the same order event in a tight loop; our system would faithfully process all of them, maybe charging a user several times (should we lack idempotency checks) and compiling Lambda invocations. We came to see strong idempotency control is required; for example, use an orderId as a deduplication key to make sure we do not process the same order twice should it somehow be re-sent.

Though not for arbitrary events, AWS Event Bridge offers a limited duplication for scheduled events. We conducted our own checks using DynamoDB conditional writes; thus, ReserveInventory would only act in cases of non-completed order status, etc.?

Testing Complexity (Again) and Staging: One particular restriction in testing was that a local offline test finds the asynchronous character difficulty. We had to depend on tests of integration in a staging environment. This meant keeping a staging deployment reflecting production. We had to create test events as well as clean, that is, separate tables, etc., test data. Using separate Event Bridge buses and tables in staging helped us to guarantee that test events do not cause production side-effects. This is good, but it means that, compared to, say, running a suite of unit tests for a monolithic app, full confidence testing is a little heavier. Every modification had to pass that pipeline to be sure all event wiring still operates. Though the complexity is a consideration, we reduced risk with IaC (reducing config drift) and monitoring in production (quickly catching any anomaly).

Ultimately, the difficulties and restrictions we ran across center on platform lock-in, debugging complexity, performance tuning, and operational subtlety. Though our solutions and the system ran successfully, none of these are insurmountable; rather, they serve to remind us that a serverless EDA is not a magic bullet. It moves responsibilities; you have to control the integration of several managed services even though you do not run servers. While it requires careful planning in testing, monitoring, and failure handling, it maximizes scalability and decoupling. Strategic decisions regarding the degree of reliance on one cloud provider also have to be made in context; for many, faster development and innovation may exceed the lock-in risk, but it should be an open choice. The next part of future work follows from our documentation of these lessons to guide the next projects and draw attention to areas needing development.

12.9 Future Work

Our exploration of serverless and event-driven cloud architecture has also unveiled several avenues for future improvement and research. We identify a number of potential enhancements, both practical and research-oriented, that could further advance this paradigm:

Standardization of Events and Workflows: The creation of cross-platform standards for event and function orchestration is one field that is ready for advancement. Because every cloud provider has its own workflow engines and event schema conventions, the current ecosystem is fragmented. We could facilitate the integration of third-party event sources or, in the future, take into consideration multicloud event routing by incorporating CloudEvents into our architecture (Event Bridge partially supports it through its schema registry).

Multicloud and Federated Serverless: Future research may investigate federated serverless architectures, which build on standardization and allow an application to run across several cloud providers or regions for compliance or resilience. Federated serverless cloud frameworks [8], which coordinate FaaS across clouds, are the subject of new research. These frameworks may dynamically move functions closer to users or data. An event bus that bridges clouds (e.g., sending events from AWS to Azure Event Grid or vice versa through a federation layer) could be used to extend our architecture to a multicloud context.

Enhanced Observability and Developer Tools: It is clear that improved debugging and monitoring tools are required. We look forward to and support increasingly sophisticated serverless solutions. Better distributed tracing for event-driven flows, for instance: To manage traces that cross asynchronous boundaries, OpenTelemetry is constantly developing. Future versions of our system might incorporate OpenTelemetry libraries into all Lambdas and employ Event Bridge's trace context propagation by adding trace IDs to event payloads. For instance, an event sent to the event bus might have metadata in its detail object, like "traceId": "abc123" and "spanId": "xyz456." This would let traces continue across chained function calls. Even in workflows that are very decoupled and event-driven, this method lets you see everything from start to finish.

Optimizing Cold Starts and Performance: On the systems research side, cold start reduction continues to be a hot topic. There is ongoing research into techniques like *snapshotting function state, keeping dormant containers in memory*, and lightweight isolation (using Firecracker microVMs or gVisor) to make cold starts nearly instantaneous [4].

Stateful Serverless and Long-Running Workflows: Enhancing the way stateful tasks are managed is another avenue. At the moment, we handle stateful sequences by using Step Functions. However, there is research on stateful serverless paradigms, such as letting a function keep its state between calls (while still auto-scaling and only charging for usage).

Security Enhancements: Better models and tools will probably be produced by security research as serverless usage increases. To ensure that only authorized functions can access sensitive data in events, for example, fine-grained data flow control could be implemented. We currently use IAM along with a few manual checks. Future developments might include policy language that tags data (such as personal identifiable information) and a serverless platform that restricts access to events containing that data to functions with specific attributes. This would be an example of static/dynamic information flow control [4].

DevOps Automation and Intelligent Scaling: With many moving parts, managing the system can be complex. Future improvements may involve more intelligent automation in DevOps. For example, an AI ops system automatically adjusts concurrency limits or memory sizes based on observed usage patterns (today we do some manual tuning; tomorrow it could be adaptive).

Evaluation in Different Domains: Future research could apply this architecture to particular domains (IoT, AI/ML pipelines, etc.) and determine whether specific modifications are required, but our case study was generic. IoT events are simpler (sensor readings), and event rates can be very high. Events may initiate long-running tasks or GPU-based processing in AI pipelines. An intriguing extension would be to modify serverless to manage those (possibly using AWS Batch or other hybrid solutions).

Future research should directly address the limitations that were talked about, especially by looking into multicloud or federated serverless architectures as a way to avoid being locked into a vendor. Also, claims that scalability is easy must be tempered by the fact that there are trade-offs between latency and coordination in distributed event-driven systems. In the end, the hybrid orchestration-choreography model is still the most important part of our framework. It gives serverless design a good balance between control and flexibility. This synthesis shows how to make cloud systems that can grow and be modular without tightly linking their parts.

In conclusion, serverless and EDAs have a bright future ahead of them. Portability, improved tooling, more intelligent runtime optimizations, and growing use cases are important themes. The direction of business and education points to further advancements in resolving existing constraints. However, architects can increase the power and usability of these systems by implementing new serverless innovations. Future research will surely build upon our work to push the boundaries of what is feasible without servers.

12.10 Conclusions

We provided a thorough analysis of serverless computing and event-driven cloud architectures in this paper, emphasizing how these two paradigms can work together to create systems that are resilient, scalable, and agile. We started by outlining the goal: EDAs decouple components through asynchronous communication, and serverless computing streamlines cloud usage by abstracting infrastructure management. Both are essential for contemporary distributed applications. Although there are still issues with performance overhead, tooling, and standards, the background and literature review made clear that these methods have become increasingly popular in both academia and industry in recent years. Cold start latencies, statelessness necessitating external state management, trouble monitoring and debugging distributed workflows, and maintaining security in a highly decoupled environment are some of the main issues we found with serverless EDA systems. These difficulties gave our framework's design choices context.

A layered perspective and a diagram showing the interactions between elements such as API Gateway, Lambda, Event Bridge, DynamoDB, and Step Functions in a coherent design were presented in the architecture overview. We demonstrated the framework in action by outlining a case study on order processing, which showed how an event moves through the system, sets off coordinated business logic, and spreads to numerous customers. The case study highlighted advantages such as cost-effectiveness (pay-per-use, no idle resources), enhanced decoupling (easy addition of features like new event consumers), and automatic scaling (ability to handle bursts of orders). Additionally, it provided a tangible story to support our assertions with quantified results and citations to industry best practices [6].

The practical aspects of deploying such a system were acknowledged in the discussion of implementation considerations, including the use of IaC (SAM/CDK) for manageability, function resource tuning for performance, and the establishment of monitoring/alerting to ensure reliability. Although they are frequently overlooked in high-level designs, these details are essential for success in the real world. In order to evaluate the framework methodically, we also established evaluation metrics, including cost, latency, scalability, reliability, and developer productivity. The case study and related discussion demonstrated that our design largely achieves its goal of optimizing these metrics. For example, cost analysis demonstrated the advantages of the serverless model at typical utilization levels, and scaling tests showed linear throughput scaling with maintained latency up to high loads. We did not, however, downplay the difficulties and constraints. We offered a fair assessment of the challenges that still exist, including vendor lock-in to AWS, the difficulty of debugging event-driven flows, the overheads associated with having several moving components, and areas where performance may degrade if not properly managed. One important realization is that designing a serverless EDA system necessitates careful consideration of those constraints (e.g., utilizing standards to reduce lock-in where practical [8, 10] or investing in automation and monitoring to offset the difficulty of debugging). Researchers can identify areas for improvement, and practitioners can set expectations with the help of this candid evaluation.

We concluded by outlining future work directions that emphasize both more general research opportunities and realistic next steps. These included the promotion of standards such as CloudEvents to enhance interoperability, multicloud architectures to prevent lock-in and boost resilience, improved observability tools (with OpenTelemetry and AI-driven analysis) to facilitate the developer experience, platform optimizations (reducing cold starts and enabling stateful or edge serverless) to increase applicability, and improved security and reliability mechanisms to make serverless appropriate for even more demanding workloads. Even though our current framework is a cutting-edge synthesis of current capabilities, the landscape is still changing, and further innovation will reinforce this architectural style, according to the future work.

In conclusion, an appealing blueprint for creating cloud applications that are extremely scalable, adaptable, and maintainable is provided by fusing serverless computing with EDA. While EDA offers a reliable method of connecting dispersed components in a loosely coupled fashion, the serverless model offers fine-grained resource utilization and eliminates a large portion of the operational burden. When combined, they allow developers to concentrate on putting business logic into event-triggered functions, reacting to changes instantly, and letting the platform handle most of the provisioning, scaling, and fault-tolerance issues. These benefits are supported by our case study and suggested framework, which show how an AWS-based implementation can manage a complicated workflow more easily than with conventional methods.

References

1 E. Jonas *et al.*, "Cloud programming simplified: A Berkeley view on serverless computing," UC Berkeley Technical Report No. UCB/EECS-2019-3, Feb. 2019. [Online]. Available: https://ar5iv.labs.arxiv.org/html/1902.03383.

2 Amazon Web Services, "Event driven architecture using Amazon EventBridge – Part 1", *AWS Cloud Operations Blog*, May 17, 2024. [Online]. Available: https://aws.amazon.com/blogs/mt/event-driven-architecture-using-amazon-eventbridge.

3 V. Krishnamurthy, "Understanding the serverless framework & event-driven architecture," *Proofpoint Engineering Blog*, May 10, 2022. [Online]. Available: https://www.proofpoint.com/us/blog/engineering-insights/understanding-serverless-framework-and-event-driven-architecture.

4 S. Kounev *et al.*, "Serverless computing," *Commun. ACM*, vol. 66, no. 1, pp. 76–84. [Online]. Available: https://cacm.acm.org/article/serverless-computing.

5 Amazon Web Services, "Event-driven architectures - Serverless applications Lens (well-architected framework)," *AWS Architecture Best Practices*, 2021. [Online]. Available: https://docs.aws.amazon.com/wellarchitected/latest/serverless-applications-lens/event-driven-architectures.html.

6 Amazon Web Services, "Creating event-driven architectures with AWS Lambda, AWS Lambda developer guide," 2023. [Online]. Available:

https://docs.aws.amazon.com/lambda/latest/dg/concepts-event-driven-architectures.html.

7 S. Werner *et al.*, "Faaster troubleshooting: evaluating distributed tracing approaches for serverless applications," *arXiv:2110.03471 [cs.SE]*, Francisco, CA, USA, 2021. [Online]. Available: https://arxiv.org/pdf/2110.03471.

8 H. Zhao *et al.*, "Supporting multi-cloud in serverless computing," *arXiv:2209.09367 [cs.DC]*, Vancouver, WA, USA 2022. [Online]. Available: https://arxiv.org/pdf/2209.09367.

9 K. M. Pitchikala, "Serverless architecture: Transforming application development for the next generation," *Eur. J. Adv. Eng. Technol*, vol. 10, no. 5, pp. 94–97, 2023. [Online]. Available: https://ejaet.com/PDF/10-5/EJAET-10-5-94-97.pdf.

10 A. Eivy, "Be wary of the economics of 'serverless' cloud computing," *IEEE Cloud Comput.*, vol. 4, no. 2, pp. 6–12, 2017 (Discusses cost and lock-in considerations).

13

Zero Trust Architecture in Cloud Environments

Aparna Achanta[1] *and Vinod Goje*[2]

[1] *Security Architect, Austin, TX, USA*
[2] *Computer Science and Engineering, University College of Engineering Osmania University, Hyderabad, India*

13.1 Introduction

13.1.1 Zero Trust—Core Concepts

The traditional network model was built on keeping attackers out and keeping everything within the network safe. This concept worked well when users and devices were kept within the network only. However, the modern network has the following features:

- Employees work from home, coffee shops, and on mobile devices.
- Applications are hosted across multiple clouds (AWS, Azure, Google Cloud Platform [GCP]) and Software as a Service (SaaS) platforms.
- APIs and services are exposed to partners, vendors, and sometimes the public internet.
- Threat actors are increasingly exploiting stolen credentials and moving laterally within trusted networks.

Cybercriminals no longer need to breach a network perimeter; they can exploit misconfigured services, identities, and APIs to gain unauthorized access.

Zero Trust, in contrast, completely changes this paradigm with the concept of "Never Trust, Always Verify." It assumes that no user, device, or workload is trusted by default, and every request is validated based on multiple factors like identity, security posture, location, etc. Trust thus becomes fluid and based on risk; thus, it can be revoked as soon as the risk level changes.

Zero Trust also hinges on several key concepts or principles, which are as follows.

13.1.1.1 Verify Explicitly

Within Zero Trust architecture (ZTA), every request is explicitly authenticated and authorized using a variety of context factors, such as user identity, risk score, and device posture. It does not simply rely on a simple authentication check like user ID and password and instead provides authentication based on the following:

- **Multi-Factor Authentication (MFA):** Proving identity through multiple factors (e.g., password + biometric or One-Time Password [OTP]).
- **Risk-Based Access Policies:** Denying access if a user's device is unpatched or originates from a suspicious IP address.
- **Behavior Analytics:** Flagging users who suddenly try to access sensitive files they've never touched before.
- **Identity Governance:** Periodically reviewing and revoking unnecessary privileges.

13.1.1.2 Least Privilege

Least privilege is another key aspect of Zero Trust that ensures that users, applications, and services have the minimum level of access required to perform their tasks.

This is accomplished via the following:

- **Role-Based Access Control (RBAC):** Assigning access based on predefined roles.
- **Attribute-Based Access Control (ABAC):** Granting access based on attributes like department, time of day, or project.
- **Just-in-Time Access (JIT):** Temporarily granting access only when needed, then revoking it automatically.
- **Granular policy enforcement:** Limiting access not just to applications but to specific actions within applications or APIs.

Least privilege helps minimize the potential damage of a breach. If a compromised identity only has access to a single resource, lateral movement is significantly more difficult for the attacker.

13.1.1.3 Breach Is Assumed

One of the most radical aspects of Zero Trust is the concept of assuming the network is already compromised and evaluating every request based on that assumption. Thus, the following controls are enforced:

- Micro-segmentation that limits how far an attacker can move within a network
- All communication, even internal, is encrypted using strong cryptography.
- All access requests are logged, tracked, and analyzed, regardless of their origin.
- Trust is continuously validated even after access has been granted and can be revoked if the situation changes.

This mindset shifts the focus from purely **preventing attacks** to **limiting their impact** and detecting them as early as possible.

13.2 Zero Trust in the Cloud

Cloud computing challenges these traditional security controls with the introduction of the following:

- Containers and orchestration (e.g., Kubernetes)
- Serverless computing (e.g., AWS Lambda and Azure Functions)
- Autoscaling and ephemeral instances
- API-first architectures and service meshes

These environments are characterized by rapid changes, making the reliance on static infrastructure no longer feasible. Let's examine these reasons in more detail.

13.2.1.1 The Perimeter Is Blurred

The cloud is a highly dynamic environment [2], even more so than on-prem. The pace at which cloud workloads are deployed and removed means relying on static perimeter controls is not feasible. Users can access public cloud services from any location, and workloads can be deployed in infrastructure as a service, platform as a service, and software as a service models.

This change renders traditional network security controls ineffective. VPNs and firewalls are insufficient in a world where:

- Devices are not always domain-joined
- Connections originate from untrusted networks
- Corporate resources are hosted in SaaS or cloud platforms

13.2.1.2 Cloud APIs Are Publicly Accessible

Workloads and services in the cloud are typically accessible via public-facing APIs, making them a prime target for attackers. Similarly, serverless functions that operate without any infrastructure or platform to manage can also contain vulnerabilities that cannot be mitigated via standard means and require a new security model to protect.

With hundreds or thousands of loosely coupled services talking to each other over public or internal networks, the attack surface increases exponentially. Zero Trust restores control by enforcing identity, context, and policy at every point of interaction between users, services, APIs, and even within microservices inside a pod.

13.2.1.3 Cloud Identity and Access Management Is Complex

Cloud Identity and Access Management is both complex and prone to error. In traditional environments, identities were tied to physical devices or centralized directories, characterized by relatively stable access patterns. But in the cloud, identities are fluid, programmatic, and decentralized. Developers spin up new Identity & Access Management (IAM) roles, service accounts, and API keys on demand. SaaS tools integrate through OAuth. Federated users from partner organizations may need access for short projects. Infrastructure scales dynamically.

As a result, the cloud quickly becomes a tangled mesh of users, roles, permissions, and policies—some temporary, some forgotten, and many overprovisioned. Without tight governance, you end up with what experts call "identity sprawl." Identity sprawl occurs when users have numerous accounts and identities managed by multiple systems that are not synchronized. In the absence of a perimeter defined by IP addresses or firewalls, identity itself becomes the new perimeter.

13.3 Threat Actors in the Cloud

The cloud threat landscape today is more dangerous than ever, and it's changing rapidly. Nation-state actors, ransomware groups, and cybercriminal syndicates have evolved from blunt instruments to stealthy, multi-stage, and financially motivated attackers.

The threat is not limited to external agents but can also originate from trusted insiders. Whether through malice, negligence, or compromised credentials, insiders are responsible for a significant percentage of data breaches within the cloud. In a cloud context, a single engineer with administrative privileges across production and staging environments could inadvertently destroy critical systems or exfiltrate sensitive data. By continuously verifying and not trusting implicitly, Zero Trust treats every user and system as potentially compromised, without assuming malicious intent.

13.4 How the Cloud Embraces Zero Trust

Zero Trust is not just a conceptual upgrade—it is a **strategic imperative** shaped by the reality of cloud-native environments, remote work, agile delivery models, and increasingly sophisticated adversaries.

The good news is that most cloud providers, such as AWS, Azure, and Google, are aware of these challenges and have adopted Zero Trust. The concepts we previously discussed, including enforcing conditional access, strong authentication, micro-segmentation, and monitoring, are typically available as native cloud services for customers.

In the next section, we'll explore how to put these principles into action, starting with identity and access management, the foundation of any Zero Trust strategy in the cloud.

Let's look at the core IAM concepts that support a Zero Trust model in the cloud.

13.4.1 Strong Authentication

The first step in identity-centric security is **authentication**—proving that an entity is who they claim to be.

Zero Trust requires strong authentication methods, including:

- **MFA:** Something you know (password), something you have (authenticator app), or something you are (biometrics). MFA significantly reduces the risk of compromised credentials.
- **Passwordless Authentication:** Using public-private key cryptography or biometrics (e.g., FIDO2 and Apple Passkeys).
- **Risk-Based Authentication:** Dynamically adjusting authentication requirements based on context, such as unusual login behavior or device posture.

For example, in AWS, enabling MFA for root accounts and privileged IAM users is considered a security baseline. Azure AD and Google Workspace also support conditional access policies that enforce MFA when necessary, based on context.

13.4.2 Least Privilege Access

Once authenticated, Zero Trust enforces **least privilege**, granting only the minimum permissions necessary for a user or workload to perform their task.

This involves:

- **RBAC:** Assigning permissions based on job function.
- **ABAC:** Defining access rules based on attributes like department, geography, or project.
- **Time-Bound Access (Just-in-Time):** Granting elevated access for a limited time, then automatically revoking it.
- **Segregation of Duties:** Ensuring that no single identity can perform conflicting actions (e.g., approve and deploy a change).

Cloud platforms, such as AWS IAM, Azure Role Assignments, and Google Cloud IAM, support granular permissions that should be continuously reviewed and scoped narrowly.

13.4.3 Federation and Single Sign On

Modern enterprises utilize multiple identity systems, including Active Directory, cloud directories, and social or external identity providers. Zero Trust promotes

federation, allowing you to manage identities centrally while enabling access across multiple environments.

- **Single Sign-On (SSO):** Allows users to authenticate once and access multiple systems without re-authenticating.
- **Security Assertion Markup Language (SAML), OpenID Connect (OIDC), and Open Authorization (OAuth):** Open standards used for identity federation between trusted systems.
- **Identity Providers (IdPs):** Azure AD, Okta, Ping Identity, and Google Identity—these platforms act as centralized identity sources and support conditional access, MFA, and session management.

With SSO and identity federation, you reduce password sprawl, improve user experience, and gain centralized control over access policies.

13.4.4 Continuous Access Evaluation

In a traditional model, access decisions are made at the time of login. In Zero Trust, access decisions are dynamic and continuous. Trust is not a one-time activity but rather something that must be regularly risk-assessed. This means

- A user authenticated 15 minutes ago may now be blocked if their device is non-compliant.
- A token issued an hour ago may be revoked if suspicious behavior is detected.
- Policies are enforced on a **per-request basis**, not per session.

13.5 Zero Trust Governance for IAM

IAM governance is essential to maintaining Zero Trust over time. This includes:

- **Access Reviews:** Periodically reviewing who has access to what
- **Policy Hygiene:** Removing unused roles and tightening overpermissioned policies
- **Approval Workflows:** Requiring approval for elevated access or sensitive actions
- **Segregation of Duties:** Preventing abuse by separating responsibilities

Many organizations adopt a Centralized Identity Governance and Administration (IGA) tool to streamline these processes.

In cloud environments, identity is the first—and often only—line of defense. Zero Trust depends on robust, context-aware identity and access management to work effectively. Whether it's a developer accessing a storage bucket or a microservice calling an internal API, every request must be authenticated, authorized, and logged.

A modern IAM strategy aligned with Zero Trust ensures

- Every identity is verified
- Access is limited and contextual
- Trust is never implicit
- Risk is continuously assessed
- Actions are auditable

In the next section, we'll move from identities to network controls and micro-segmentation—another critical layer in building Zero Trust in cloud-native environments.

13.6 Micro-Segmentation for Network Control

Micro-segmentation is the practice of dividing your network into small, isolated zones, each with its own security policies, so that only authorized entities can communicate with each other under tightly defined conditions. This is particularly essential in cloud-native environments, where network boundaries are fluid, workloads are ephemeral, and lateral movement by attackers is a persistent risk. Traditional network security models, built around perimeter firewalls and static Virtual Local Area Network (VLAN), struggle to keep up. That's why micro-segmentation is an essential component of ZTA in the cloud. In this section, we break down what microsegmentation means within Zero Trust and how it challenges traditional assumptions about "safe zones" in cloud environments.

13.6.1 The Problem of Traditional Network Segmentation

In traditional environments, network segmentation was typically implemented through:

- Firewalls separating the internal network from untrusted external networks.
- VLANs to isolate sensitive business units.
- ACLs and IP allow lists to control access between systems.

This model worked in static, on-premises setups, but it does not translate to the cloud due to several reasons:

- IP addresses are dynamic and often ephemeral within the cloud, especially with auto-scaling workloads and containers.
- Applications are distributed across services, availability zones, or even multiple clouds.

- Network perimeters are often porous or nonexistent due to the widespread use of mobile devices, remote work, Software-as-a-Service (SaaS), and hybrid work models.
- Identity and context determine access needs, as we saw in the previous section, rather than the network location.

As a result, attackers who breach one workload or identity can often move laterally inside flat cloud networks. Only one workload needs to be compromised for an attack to gain access to a network. Zero Trust aims to stop this by shifting to logical segmentation based on identity, risk, and intent via microsegmentation.

13.6.2 Understanding Micro-Segmentation

As we saw earlier, micro-segmentation is the practice of dividing a network into small, isolated zones, allowing only authorized entities to communicate with each other under tightly defined conditions. Each "zone" has its own clearly defined security policy. Thus, each workload has a firewall that is enforced not by IP, but by identity, metadata, and behavior.

Within a Zero Trust context, this means

- **Default Deny:** No workload or service can communicate with another without an explicit policy allowing it to do so.
- **Context-Aware Policies:** Access is allowed based on identity, role, tags, and traffic type.
- **East–West Traffic Control:** Lateral movement between workloads is blocked unless explicitly required. This dramatically reduces the "blast radius" of an attack if a workload is compromised, as the attacker cannot use the compromised workload to move within a network.

13.7 Zero Trust Network Access (ZTNA)

ZTNA is a modern replacement for VPNs. Instead of giving users network-level access, ZTNA grants access to specific applications or services based on user identity, device posture, and policy.

A few popular implementations of ZTNA include:

- Cloudflare Access
- Zscaler Private Access
- AWS Verified Access
- Google BeyondCorp Enterprise [3]

ZTNA reduces the risk of lateral movement from remote users, contractors, or third-party vendors. It enforces **application-level segmentation** rather than network-level access.

13.7.1 Network Policy as Code

Micro-segmentation is often captured within infrastructure as code for consistency and scalability across environments. Tools like Terraform enable version-controlled, reviewable, and testable network policies that align with Zero Trust's principle of constant verification.

13.8 How Micro-Segmentation Prevents Lateral Movement

The ultimate goal of micro-segmentation in Zero Trust is to prevent lateral movement by attackers.

For example, an attacker may gain access to a misconfigured cloud server instance via a vulnerable web application. Without segmentation,

- They can scan the cloud network and access cloud storage, databases, and other workloads.
- They may escalate privileges or harvest credentials from other workloads.

With segmentation in place,

- The compromised server can only communicate with its associated application tier.
- Outbound access is blocked or tightly controlled.
- Service discovery is disabled, making it harder for the attacker to locate targets.

This dramatically reduces the blast radius of such attacks. It is also important to note that micro-segmentation is only one layer of a comprehensive Zero Trust strategy. While it ensures that workloads communicate only with explicitly authorized peers, it does not account for what devices users are using to initiate access or whether those devices can be trusted in the first place.

To build a truly resilient ZTA, we must extend our security posture beyond the network layer and into the device layer, ensuring that access is granted only when both the user and the device meet defined security standards.

In the next section, we'll explore understanding how to evaluate device posture and prevent compromised or unmanaged devices from compromising cloud security.

13.9 The Role of Unified Endpoint Management (UEM)

To enforce device trust at scale, organizations need centralized tools for managing devices across OS platforms. This is where **UEM** comes in. UEM technology provides a centralized platform for enforcing security policies, monitoring device health, and integrating posture data into real-time access decisions. UEM extends visibility and control across all endpoints—laptops, smartphones, tablets, desktops, and even IoT devices—from a single console.

13.9.1 How UEM Enables Zero Trust

UEM operationalizes device trust by continuously evaluating whether a device is secure enough to access sensitive cloud resources. It integrates with identity providers (e.g., Azure AD, Okta, and Google Workspace) and feeds posture data directly into conditional access policies.

13.9.2 Key Contributions to Zero Trust

- **Continuous Posture Assessment:** Enforces encryption, OS patching, antivirus, and secure configurations.
- **Policy-Based Access:** Allows or blocks access based on real-time device compliance.
- **Automated Response:** Can isolate, lock, or wipe compromised devices instantly.
- **Cross-Platform Coverage:** Applies consistent policy enforcement across Windows, macOS, iOS, Android, and more.
- Contextual access enforcement enables differentiated access—e.g., full access from compliant devices and read-only access from unmanaged ones.

For example, a user logging into a sensitive SaaS app from a corporate laptop is granted access because their device is UEM-enrolled, encrypted, and compliant. The same user trying from a personal tablet is blocked—or redirected to a secure browser session, because the device fails posture checks.

UEM is a critical enabler of Zero Trust by ensuring that only healthy, compliant, and monitored devices can access sensitive resources. In the next section, we'll explore how Zero Trust extends beyond access, through continuous authentication and session monitoring, to assess trust throughout the user's session dynamically.

13.10 Continuous Authentication and Session Monitoring

As we have seen so far, trust and risk are not static entities in a ZTA. Instead, both of these are continuously assessed throughout a user's or device's session based on context and behavior. This is quite different from traditional access models, where a user authenticates once at the start of a session and is granted access unless manually revoked.

To mitigate these risks, continuous authentication and session monitoring have emerged as core pillars of ZTA.

This is important due to the following reasons:

- **Threats Evolve Mid-session:** A user might log in from a safe location, but their device could become infected minutes later.
- **Context Shifts Rapidly:** Location, IP address, or device security posture may change unexpectedly.
- **Attackers Exploit Static Access:** Once inside, lateral movement is easy if the session context isn't revalidated.

13.11 SaaS-Specific Zero Trust Strategies

Shadow IT discovery is a major first step toward SaaS Zero Trust implementation. Usually leveraging network traffic analysis, financial transaction surveillance, and user behavior analytics, businesses find unapproved uses. Cloud Access Security Brokers (CASBs) provide required visibility and control capabilities by means of inline proxies or API-based integration techniques [4].

Organizational needs affect the patterns of CASB implementation. Reverse proxy configurations protect approved applications; forward proxy deployments intercept outgoing traffic. Out-of-band monitoring made possible by API-based CASBs does not compromise user experience. Leading solutions spanning SaaS apps include Zscaler, Netskope, and Microsoft Defender for Cloud Apps, enabling data loss prevention, access control, and threat protection.

Integration of OAuth and SAML brings special difficulties for SaaS systems. Strong mitigating techniques are needed for token hijacking, consent phishing, and assertion reiterations. Token rotation policies, scope restrictions, and ongoing session monitoring are things that organizations have to follow. By constantly evaluating security settings across SaaS applications, SaaS Security Posture Management (SSPM) tools identify overly permissive sharing settings, disabled MFA, and too high administrative privileges, so addressing configuration drift [5].

13.12 PaaS Security Controls

Platform services call for advanced authentication systems that do away with fixed credentials. Safe, automated credential management comes from managed identities in Azure, IAM roles in AWS Lambda, and Google Cloud Platform service accounts. By means of workload identity federation made possible by these platform-specific implementations, services can authenticate without embedded secrets.

Service mesh integration and mutual TLS (mTLS) implementation are demands of service-to-service communication security. The policy example below shows Open Policy Agent (OPA)/Rego-style service authentication:

```
allow {
input.source.serviceAccount == "frontend-sa"
input.destination.service == "backend-api"
input.method == "GET"
valid_jwt_token
}
```

Identity integration specific to platforms calls for careful evaluation of every provider's capabilities. Temporary credentials for Lambda functions come from AWS IAM roles via the AWS Security Token Service. While Google Cloud Service Accounts enable fine-grained permissions for Cloud Run and Cloud Function deployments [6], Azure Managed Identities provide comparable capability for App Services and Functions.

13.13 Visibility, Logging, and Threat Detection

The foundation of ZTA is comprehensive visibility, which facilitates rapid threat response and continuous verification. The distributed nature of cloud systems necessitates advanced techniques for log aggregation, analysis, and automated response. The "assume breach" philosophy of Zero Trust demands thorough awareness of every cloud resource. Real-time telemetry from network flows, identity systems, applications, and data access patterns is what constant verification calls for. This visibility helps to support the basic Zero Trust idea of never trusting and always verifying [7] and facilitates risk-based decision-making. In cloud environments, full visibility refers to several telemetry kinds: logs with comprehensive event records, metrics with quantitative measurements, traces displaying demand flows, and events catching state changes. Security observability goes beyond conventional monitoring by means of data source correlation to find possible hazards and policy deviations.

13.14 Centralized Log Aggregation Architecture

Various cloud service providers present their own integrated solutions for log aggregation, each featuring unique designs and capabilities. For instance, AWS Security Lake utilizes the Open Cybersecurity Schema Framework (OCSF) for standardized log storage within S3, allowing for SQL queries via Amazon

Athena. Meanwhile, Azure Monitor employs Kusto Query Language (KQL) and centralizes logs into Log Analytics workspaces. On the other hand, Google Chronicle provides a data lake focused on security, which uses the Unified Data Model (UDM) to ensure a consistent log format throughout.

Patterns of log aggregation have to strike a balance between completeness and cost-effectiveness. While pull systems lower endpoint overhead via API-based collecting, push architectures enable real-time streaming but depend on agent deployment. While batch processing maximizes storage costs, streaming systems support instant threat detection. Usually using hybrid strategies, companies stream important security events by batching standard operational logs.

Among cost-cutting techniques are data lifecycle management, tiered storage, and intelligent sampling. Warm storage stores compressed historical data, hot storage preserves recent logs for active investigation, and cold storage archives compliance-requiring logs. While preserving security value, deduplication and summarizing help to lower storage volumes [8].

13.15 SIEM/SOAR Integration for Zero Trust

Security information and event management (SIEM) tools play a crucial role in enhancing ongoing verification processes through the use of real-time correlation and anomaly detection methods. Modern SIEM systems utilize machine learning to create behavioral baselines, enabling them to identify deviations that could signal potential security breaches. Moreover, risk scoring frameworks aggregate various subtle signals into actionable security alerts.

Through codified playbooks, Security Orchestration, Automation, and Response (SOAR) systems enable automated investigation and response. While containment playbooks isolate compromised resources, investigation playbooks automatically gather evidence from many sources. An automated response system is shown here:

```
playbook:
name: compromised_credential_response
triggers:
- event_type: credential_compromise
confidence: high
actions:
- disable_user_account
- revoke_active_sessions
- notify_security_team
- collect_recent_activity
- initiate_forensics
```

SIEM integration across multiple clouds calls for consistent dashboards and normalized data models. Common Event Format (CEF) and OCSF help to guarantee consistent event presentation on many platforms. Distribution of analysis by federation patterns preserves centralized visibility and supports geographically scattered installations [9].

13.16 Cloud-Native Threat Detection Services

Cloud providers offer sophisticated threat detection capabilities utilizing platform telemetry and threat information. AWS GuardDuty analyzes VPC Flow Logs, DNS logs, and CloudTrail events using machine learning models and threat intelligence feeds. The detection categories include data exfiltration, instance compromise, and reconnaissance.

Comprehensive coverage over Azure services offered by Azure Defender produces security scores and practical advice. Advanced hunting and investigation capability are made possible by integration with Azure Sentinel. Google Chronicle Detect uses YARA-L to support custom detection rules, enabling retroactive threat hunting across historical data.

Customizing detection rules balances the needs of the organization with the intelligence provided by vendors. Machine learning models require tuning to reduce false positives while maintaining detection accuracy. Detection-as-code methods enable version control, testing, and consistent deployment across different systems [10].

13.17 Data-Centric Security

At the heart of every access request, network policy, device posture, or authentication decision lies one core objective: protecting sensitive data. Ultimately, adversaries are not concerned with computing resources; they seek the sensitive information stored within the workloads.

This section explores what data-centric Zero Trust looks like in practice. We'll examine key techniques, including classification, encryption, tokenization, and access control models, designed to ensure that data remains secure even if networks, devices, or credentials are compromised.

13.17.1 Data Classification and Tagging

Before you can enforce access or apply protections, you need to understand the type of data you're dealing with. This is where data classification and tagging play a crucial role.

Classification is the process of identifying and labeling data according to its sensitivity and relevance. Common categories include:

- Public
- Internal
- Confidential
- Highly confidential or regulated (e.g., PCI, PHI, and PII)

Tagging enhances classification by associating metadata with data objects, allowing automated systems to enforce rules based on those tags. Zero Trust requires context-aware enforcement. If your systems can't distinguish between test data and customer credit card numbers, they can't apply differentiated controls. Classification and tagging enable granular, policy-driven enforcement of access, masking, and encryption.

A data-centric Zero Trust approach recognizes that:

- Data should be classified and tagged so that systems understand its sensitivity.
- Encryption must be everywhere—at rest, in motion, and sometimes at the field level.
- Tokenization and masking reduce risk even when access is granted.
- Access must consider context and content, not just identity.
- ZTDA patterns allow adaptive, granular enforcement at the data access layer.

By embedding Zero Trust into the data lifecycle, from discovery to access to usage, organizations build resilience not just against breaches but against misuse, overexposure, and insider threats.

13.17.2 Data Encryption at Rest and in Transit

Encryption is one of the most foundational controls in a Zero Trust model—it ensures that even if data is accessed or intercepted without authorization, it remains unintelligible.

13.18 Conclusions

Effective Zero Trust application calls for phased implementation, organized evaluation, and ongoing improvement. Companies have to negotiate vendor-specific architectures while keeping uniform security standards over their cloud footprint.

The approach to Zero Trust involves a systematic method that aligns long-term goals with short-term achievements. In the initial phase, it establishes identity providers, enhances logging capabilities, and applies essential network segmentation. Following this, the emphasis is placed on implementing encryption, microsegmentation, and conditional access to strengthen security measures. The detection phase runs behavioral analytics; threat intelligence, SIEM/SOAR, automated remediation, and incident response are made possible by the response phase. The phase of optimization takes advantage of machine learning and ongoing development.

Short wins show value and create momentum. Instant security improvements come from MFA deployment, cloud security posture management, and simple network segmentation. Although long-term projects including behavioral analytics, automated response, and continuous compliance call for ongoing investment, they provide transformational security capabilities.

13.19 Future Work

The deployment of Zero Trust in cloud systems necessitates a staged implementation, systematic assessment, and continuous enhancement. Organizations must prioritize based on risk and business value between vendor-specific functionalities and uniform security standards. Success necessitates operational excellence, significant metrics, and continuous commitment to advancement. The evolution of threat landscapes, facilitated by cloud-native technologies, signifies a fundamental shift in security philosophy toward Zero Trust.

References

1 Microsoft, "What is zero trust?," *Microsoft Security Documentation*, 2023. [Online]. Available: https://learn.microsoft.com/en-us/security/zero-trust.
2 Amazon Web Services, "AWS shared responsibility model," *AWS Compliance*, 2023. [Online]. Available: https://aws.amazon.com/compliance/shared-responsibility-model.
3 Gartner, "Market guide for cloud access security brokers," Oct. 2016. [Online]. Available: https://www.gartner.com/en/documents/3488119.
4 M. S. Leaua, A. Chiş, T.-C. Bălan, and L. F. Ilca, "Assessment of cloud security posture management scenarios," [Online]. Available: https://ieeexplore.ieee.org/document/10722349.
5 AWS, "Security best practices for AWS lambda," *Amazon Web Services*, 2024. [Online]. Available: https://docs.aws.amazon.com/lambda/latest/dg/lambda-security.html.
6 CISA, "Zero trust maturity model," *Cybersecurity and Infrastructure Security Agency*, Version 2.0, 2023. [Online]. Available: https://www.cisa.gov/zero-trust-maturity-model.

7 J. Kindervag, "No more Chewy centers: Introducing the zero trust model of information security," *Forrester Research*, 2010. [Online]. Available: https://www.forrester.com/report/no-more-chewy-centers-introducing-the-zero-trust-model-of-information-security/RES56682.

8 Google Cloud, "Security command center overview," *Google Cloud Documentation*, 2024. [Online]. Available: https://cloud.google.com/security-command-center/docs/concepts-security-command-center-overview.

9 J. Pavlik, A. Komarek, and V. Sobeslav, "Security information and event management in the cloud computing infrastructure," [Online]. Available: https://ieeexplore.ieee.org/document/7028677.

10 Y. Yang, X. Chen, G. Wang, and L. Cao, "An identity and access management architecture in cloud," [Online]. Available: https://ieeexplore.ieee.org/document/7081970.

14

Predictive Risk Intelligence and Governance Framework in Multicloud Environments

Priya Ranjani Mohan and Yugandhar Suthari

Independent Researcher, Raleigh, NC, USA

14.1 Introduction: From Reactive to Predictive

With over 15 years of experience collaborating with Fortune 500 clients and leading cloud governance technology initiatives, this chapter highlights the significant transformation observed in risk management practices. Traditional governance mechanisms are crucial, but they often function like smoke detectors—alerting us only after a problem has occurred. We are now witnessing the emergence of a Predictive Risk Intelligence and Governance (PRIG) paradigm, which shifts the focus from merely monitoring governance failures to employing predictive modeling and proactive prevention.

14.1.1 Defining Predictive Risk Intelligence

Predictive risk intelligence applies a powerful combination of machine learning (ML), behavioral analytics, and governance automation to predict potential out-of-compliance violations, security issues, and operational risks across multicloud environments. In contrast to traditional governance, risk and compliance (GRC)-based point-in-time measurements, the PRIG-based approaches rely on real-time pattern analysis, correlated data, and anomalies to forecast risk states with quantifiable likelihood.

14.1.2 The Multicloud Complexity Challenge

Since 2023, multicloud adoption has been in full swing, and as a result, traditional governance models are insufficient to ensure sufficient control and visibility over IT risks that span across all of the cloud environments. Organizations previously controlled single-cloud environments with vendor-specific tools such as AWS

Config or Azure Policy. Modern IT infrastructure is evolving toward a blended governing infrastructure across hybrid architectures where an app may very well be running on Amazon Elastic Kubernetes Service (AWS EKS), connecting to Azure Database for PostgreSQL, and storing documents on Google Cloud Storage, all of which have disparate compliance needs.

A rapidly expanding Fortune 500 healthcare organization had to meet Health Insurance Portability and Accountability Act (HIPAA) compliance not only on AWS (where their primary workloads reside) but also on Azure (their analytics platform) and Google Cloud platform (GCP) (artificial intelligence [AI]/ML services). Each vendor had its in-built compliance tool, but none gave a view across a multicloud setup to see how data was moving or how customers could access it. Organizations would keep up three different governance portals and ensure they each have their own set of alerts and remediations. Reviewing, managing, and maintaining all three governance portals is often time-consuming, resource-heavy, and inefficient.

14.2 Core Challenges in Multicloud Governance

14.2.1 The Fragmentation Problem

Security and compliance paradoxically emerge as some of the most challenging areas with the advent of multicloud technology adaptations. All cloud providers have native security tools, which are great in their ecosystem but poor at cross-cloud visibility. This either leaves organizations vulnerable in some areas or with overlapping tools that produce contradictory results.

I've observed companies with 47 different security and compliance solutions across a multicloud environment, issuing 20,000-plus monthly alerts, with less than 5% comprising actionable intelligence. This overwhelming noise and lack of consolidated insight creates a critical visibility gap, representing a strategic risk that undermines the entire governance program, not just an operational issue as shown in Figure 14.1.

14.2.2 Data Sovereignty Complexity

Data sovereignty requirements introduce significant complexity to multicloud governance. In a recent deployment for a central global bank, we identified that their analytics platform was unintentionally flowing the data of EU customers via UK processing services post-Brexit, resulting in potential General Data

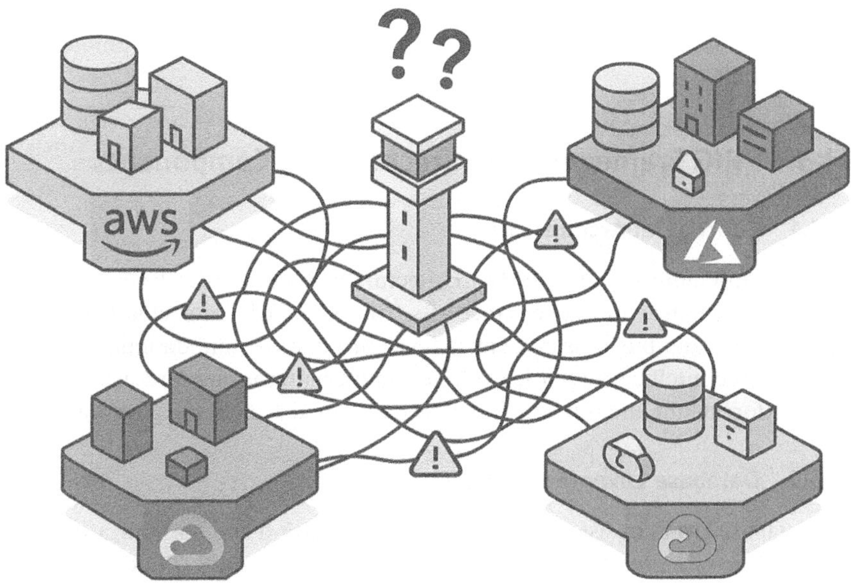

Figure 14.1 Governing across many clouds is difficult.

Protection Regulation (GDPR) fines and reputational damage. It gets even harder considering current applications rely more on serverless functions, container orchestrators, or edge computing solutions. One user request would be to fire Lambda functions in AWS, utilize processing from Azure Cognitive Services, and save data in Google Cloud Firestore. Properly tracking compliance responsibilities through this execution path necessitates intelligence beyond traditional governance models based on the perimeter.

14.2.3 Identity and Integration Gaps

Managing identity across clouds presents underestimated complexities. Unfortunately, cross-cloud identity management is a challenge that many organizations tend to underestimate. AWS—policies attached to users, groups, and roles. Azure mixes RBAC with resource-level permissions. Google Cloud focuses on identity access management (IAM) conditions and context-aware access. Achieving governance as code (consistent governance across these different models), many abstraction layers are applied, adding another level of complexity.

Network security policy enforcement also becomes more convoluted when applications are multi-provider and across disparate networking models.

AWS VPCs, Azure Virtual Networks, and Google Cloud VPCs have unique ways of handling security groups and routing, making uniform policy enforcement quite difficult.

14.3 PRIG Framework Architecture and Components

14.3.1 Conceptual Architecture

As shown in Figure 14.2, the PRIG architecture consists of three layers: database, intelligence engine, and governance rig. The telemetry from cloud providers, security tools, and business systems is normalized at the foundational level. ML models at the intelligence tier learn to recognize patterns and forecast risks. The policy enforcement and remediation workflows are driven in the governance tier.

14.3.2 Database Layer (Foundation)

The database layer consists of the central data collection and normalization point for the entire system, such that raw logs flow in from AWS CloudTrail, Azure Monitor, EDR solutions, Security Information and Event Management (SIEM) platforms, and business applications. This is essentially any system generating security-relevant information. Data normalization requires significant effort since each vendor uses distinct data formats, timestamp conventions, and field naming standards, creating substantial implementation overhead without which downstream analysis fails. Standardized schemas are implemented alongside ETL processes to transform disparate data sources into a unified format suitable for downstream analysis.

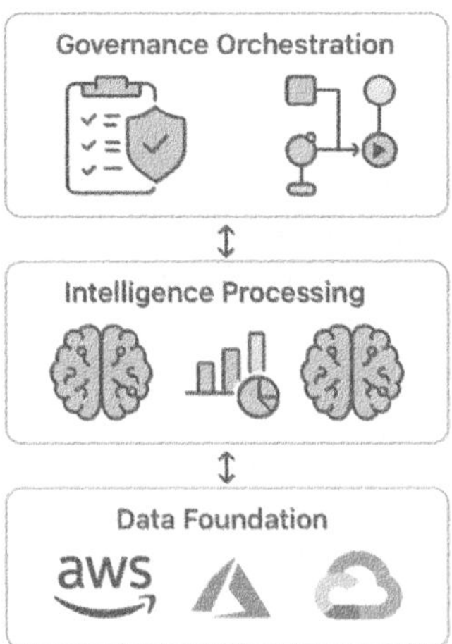

Figure 14.2 Foundational architecture concept.

14.3.3 Intelligence Engine Layer

The intelligence layer drives the PRIG framework by converting traditional GRC operations into predictive systems that spot issues before they become problems. ML models monitor access patterns and system configurations continuously, identifying situations like former employees retaining system access or cloud infrastructure that has drifted from approved security settings. Rather than relying on manual or theoretical risk assessments, the system processes vulnerability scans, threat feeds, and asset data to calculate risk scores weighted by business impact (e.g., financial exposure from regulatory fines and reputational damage from data breaches). The compliance component automatically gathers evidence from various sources and recognizes patterns that typically precede audit findings, such as departments that repeatedly have deficient controls that need remediation or compliance metrics that slowly deteriorate over time. This approach enables an organization to connect these dots across governance, risk, and compliance functions that normally operate separately, eliminating organizational silos that prevent comprehensive risk visibility and enabling coordinated response strategies. You can see how poor change management creates configuration drift that leads to compliance violations, giving you the data to fix root causes rather than just addressing symptoms. The intelligence layer basically turns PRIG into an early warning system that prevents business disruption instead of just documenting it after the fact.

14.3.4 Governance Rig Layer

When the intelligence engine spots issues, this layer determines appropriate responses by routing alerts to designated personnel, adjusting security configurations based on organizational risk tolerance, or updating policies when new threats emerge. It manages governance workflows, including privileged-access exceptions and compliance-aligned remediation. The governance layer also prioritizes security investments by quantifying risk posture and forecasting high-likelihood exposures. Instead of having someone manually review every single decision, it uses the governance rules the team has already set up to make calls consistently across the whole company. This way the security responses actually match the objectives set by leadership and compliance requirements from a regulatory standpoint. This layer ensures that the information provided by the intelligence layer is used to form an updated governance structure and strategy to improve risk posture.

This architecture represents a comprehensive platform integrating data operations, AI, and automation capabilities. The design emphasizes proactive threat detection, identifying issues before they escalate, and reactive response to ensure rapid containment when incidents occur.

14.4 Building Your Organization's PRIG Infrastructure

14.4.1 The Reality Check

Nobody builds PRIG with a single platform. That's just not how it works. Organizations typically integrate specialized tools, with interoperability being the critical success factor. Companies waste months trying to find the perfect all-in-one solution when they should just pick good tools and focus on the integration work.

The concept of PRIG represents "the ability to help organizations apply analytics to develop a forward-looking lens into its potential risks" [1]. This market opportunity is substantial, with the threat intelligence market projected to grow from $13.56 billion in 2025 to $26.19 billion by 2029, at a compound annual growth rate of 17.9% [2]. The broader predictive analytics market, which underpins PRIG capabilities, grew from $3.49 billion in 2016 to a projected $10.95 billion by 2022, representing 21% annual growth [3]. Let's explore a few industry-leading tools that are widely adopted across the globe by several organizations and how they can be used in unison to form a predictive GRC environment.

14.4.2 Getting the Data House in Order

14.4.2.1 Splunk Enterprise Security

A common setup for predictive risk intelligence is to use Splunk as the data backbone. Splunk maintains a dominant market position, holding 29.8% of the SIEM market share as of 2022, with security business revenue growing by 29.1% compared to 16.6% for the overall market [4]. The platform has been ranked #1 in the IDC Worldwide Security Information and Event Management Market Shares for four consecutive years and named a Leader in the 2024 Gartner Magic Quadrant for SIEM for the tenth consecutive time [5, 6].

It's expensive, but it handles the messiest part of the job—taking logs from everywhere and making them searchable. Network gear, cloud platforms, applications, security tools—Splunk can ingest pretty much anything and normalize it through their common information model. Industry analysts note that "thousands of organizations worldwide rely on Splunk Enterprise Security as their SIEM to rapidly detect and respond to critical events so they can stay ahead of emerging threats and maintain cyber resilience" [7].

14.4.2.2 GRC Intelligence Use Cases

- **Continuous Compliance Monitoring:** Splunk enables an "analytics-driven, proactive approach to compliance" for staying ahead of evolving regulations and supports frameworks including NIST 800-53, PCI DSS, HIPAA, Sarbanes-Oxley (SOX), and CMMC [8].

- **Risk-Based Alerting:** Provides teams with opportunities to pivot resources from reactive to proactive functions in the SO, resulting in reduced incident response times, lower false positive rates, and improved threat detection accuracy.
- **Asset Discovery and Risk Intelligence:** Continuous asset discovery and compliance monitoring to accelerate investigations and reduce risk exposure.
- **Regulatory Reporting:** Automated generation of compliance reports for auditors with standardized field mappings across multiple data sources.

The CIM is what makes Splunk worth the money for PRIG. Without it, teams get stuck writing custom parsers for every data source, and that gets old fast. With CIM, organizations get standardized field mappings that analytics tools can actually use without having to guess what "timestamp_1" means versus "event_time" versus "log_date."

14.4.3 Elastic Stack (ELK)

Organizations that don't want to pay Splunk prices can get similar capabilities with Elastic for a lot less money. Elasticsearch handles storage and search, Logstash does the data ingestion and cleanup, and Kibana builds the dashboards, providing full-stack observability at reduced licensing costs. Everything can be customized since it's open source but requires significant DevOps expertise for maintenance.

The trade-off is pretty straightforward—lower cost but higher maintenance. Teams with skilled ops people can actually get better performance than Splunk for a fraction of the cost. Without that expertise, more time gets spent troubleshooting than analyzing.

14.5 Out-of-the-Box Tools for Predictive Decisions

14.5.1 IBM QRadar SOAR

QRadar does the heavy lifting on the analytics side. It learns normal behavior patterns for users, devices, and applications, then flags anything that looks off. For PRIG, this feeds directly into risk scoring models. The platform is pretty good at connecting dots across different data sources—like spotting when someone gets admin access and then starts accessing files they've never touched before.

14.5.2 GRC Intelligence Use Cases

- **Compliance Certification Management:** QRadar has obtained vital compliance certifications, including Department of Homeland Security's (DHS)

Continuous Diagnostics and Mitigation (CDM) Approved Product List, FIPS 140-2 Level 1 and Level 2, SOC 2, and NIAP [9].

- **Privacy Breach Response:** Integrates with IBM Security Resilient SOAR to provide proactive, fast responses to data privacy breaches with full compliance across 174 privacy incident reporting regulations worldwide [9].
- **Risk-Based Security Operations:** Enables risk-informed decision-making by correlating security events with business context and compliance requirements.
- **Threat Intelligence Integration:** Uses ML to analyze threat indicators and provide actionable intelligence for governance decisions.

The Watson NLP capabilities enable advanced text analysis and automated incident categorization. It can read-through incident reports and security documentation to spot trends that humans miss. It is useful for understanding why certain types of incidents keep happening.

14.5.3 Microsoft Sentinel

Sentinel offers natural cost advantages for Microsoft-centric environments. It integrates natively with Azure and Office 365, and the ML algorithms are decent at spotting weird user behavior such as transaction patterns that deviate from norm or unusual file access patterns that might indicate compromised accounts.

14.5.4 GRC Intelligence Use Cases

- **Threat Intelligence Integration:** The most important use case for threat intelligence in SIEM solutions like Microsoft Sentinel is to power analytics rules for threat detection by comparing raw events against threat indicators.
- **Compliance Monitoring:** Provides attack detection, threat visibility, proactive hunting, and threat response capabilities to help organizations meet regulatory requirements.
- **Security Automation:** Reduces time to detect and respond to recurring incidents, freeing analysts to focus on strategic tasks like compliance management.
- **AI-Powered Risk Assessment:** Leverages AI technology to hunt for threats and reduce false positives in risk assessments.

The workbooks feature lets teams build custom dashboards that make sense to executives. Risk trends over time, compliance status by department, and early warning indicators can be shown without drowning people in technical details.

14.5.5 Palantir Foundry

This is for organizations that need serious data processing power. Foundry handles the most complex predictive modeling work and can connect data sources that other platforms struggle with. It's not cheap, but for massive data volumes and sophisticated analytics, it's worth considering.

The collaboration features enable different teams to work on the same PRIG projects without stepping on each other's toes. In addition, it handles both batch processing for historical analysis and real-time processing for current events.

14.6 Building Custom ML Models and Risk Prediction

14.6.1 Data Sources and Quality Challenges

For valid predictive risk modeling, data availability from multiple domains is essential. The difficulty comes when making data conform to that model across providers with completely different data models. AWS CloudTrail events have a very different schema, granularity, and context than Azure Activity Logs and Google Cloud Audit Logs (e.g., AWS CloudTrails's nested JavaScript Object Notation (JSON) structures vs. GCP's tabular audit logs). This involves complex data normalization pipelines to maintain the semantic information needed to predict the risk with the necessary accuracy in their models. Data from the business context may be one of the most neglected risk signals. Among them are Configuration Management Database (CMDB) systems, which provide asset criticality ratings, DLP platforms offering data classification, and business process mappings.

14.6.2 Model Selection and Performance

14.6.2.1 Risk Assessment Compatibility

- **Regulatory Compliance Models:** Select models that provide interpretable results for audit trails (e.g., decision trees and logistic regression). Logistic regression and decision trees are preferred for compliance monitoring and regulatory reporting because they offer high interpretability and clear audit trails that satisfy regulatory scrutiny. ML risk management frameworks emphasize the importance of explainable and responsible AI tools to increase fairness and transparency in ML models for regulatory compliance.
- **Operational Risk Models:** Choose robust models capable of handling diverse data types (e.g., random forest and gradient boosting). Random forest and gradient boosting models excel in fraud detection and operational risk assessment because they handle mixed data types effectively, provide interpretable feature importance rankings, and maintain robust performance across diverse datasets. Research demonstrates that financial fraud detection systems based on

improved random forest and gradient boosting machine (GBM) architectures achieve superior performance in identifying fraudulent transactions.

- **Financial Risk Models:** Implement models with strong statistical foundations (e.g., support vector machines and neural networks). Support vector machines and neural networks prove effective for complex financial risk modeling, credit risk assessment, and market risk prediction where nonlinear relationships are prevalent, though they require careful implementation to maintain regulatory transparency.

The choice ultimately depends on balancing prediction accuracy with interpretability requirements, regulatory compliance needs, and the organization's risk tolerance for false positives versus missed risks in critical GRC applications.

14.6.3 Performance Metrics Alignment with GRC Objectives [8]

- **Precision:** Critical for minimizing false positives in compliance violations.
- **Recall:** Essential for capturing all potential risks (especially in fraud detection).
- **F1-Score:** Balanced metric for overall model effectiveness.
- **AUC-ROC:** Measure of model's ability to distinguish between risk levels.
- **Business Impact Metrics:** Cost of false positives vs. cost of missed risks.

14.6.4 Confidence Scoring and False Positive Management

Confidence score is one of the most important yet overlooked parts. Stakeholders must know not only what risks the model predicts but also how much the system is betting on such predictions. To be usable in effective confidence scoring, these models require calibration methods to get predicted confidences that align with the expected accuracy.

14.7 Making Predictive Decisions and Taking Action

14.7.1 ServiceNow GRC

ServiceNow handles the workflow automation that makes PRIG practical instead of just theoretical. The platform enables "enterprise-wide risk-informed decisions in daily work" through automated governance, risk, and compliance processes [10]. Recent industry analysis shows that automated ServiceNow GRC frameworks enable enterprises to achieve operational resilience by reducing reaction time from days to minutes [11].

14.7.2 GRC Intelligence Use Cases

- **Integrated Risk Management:** Provides real-time insights into an organization's compliance posture and risk exposure through end-to-end vulnerability resilience solutions.
- **Workflow Automation:** Translates technical security findings into actionable business processes with automated ticket creation, routing, and tracking.
- **Policy Management:** Manages policy exceptions and tracks remediation activities through appropriate approval chains with documented business justification.
- **Compliance Orchestration:** Coordinates approach ensuring organizations manage risk factors and maintain compliance with all applicable laws and regulations.

When the intelligence layer spots a problem, ServiceNow can automatically create tickets, route them to the right people, and track everything through resolution. It connects to other ServiceNow modules too, so PRIG activities can trigger change management processes or incident response workflows.

The real value is transforming abstract risks into accountable actions. A risk score becomes a task with a due date and assigned owner. Policy violations become approval workflows. Everything gets tracked and audited automatically. This automation capability is critical, as studies show that organizations implementing predictive risk intelligence systems typically see measurable improvements in their security posture and compliance metrics within the first year [12].

14.7.3 RSA Archer

Archer specializes in GRC management and comes with prebuilt frameworks for common compliance requirements. It handles complex approval workflows and maintains detailed audit trails. In PRIG setups, Archer typically runs the compliance automation and generates the reports that auditors want to see.

14.7.3.1 GRC Intelligence Use Cases

- **Enterprise Risk Management:** Manages policies, controls, risks, assessments, and deficiencies across lines of business with comprehensive audit and compliance management capabilities.
- **Regulatory Framework Support:** Provides prebuilt frameworks for industry standards, including SOX, GDPR, HIPAA, and other regulatory requirements.
- **Risk Assessment and Scoring:** Delivers quantitative risk assessments with automated scoring mechanisms that feed into executive dashboards.
- **Audit Management:** Manages all types of audits and enterprise risk activities with detailed tracking and reporting capabilities.

The platform excels at managing policy exceptions and tracking remediation activities. When someone needs special access or wants to deviate from standard procedures, Archer can route the request through appropriate approval chains and document the business justification.

14.8 The Glue That Holds It Together

14.8.1 MuleSoft Anypoint Platform

Integration capability determines PRIG implementation success. MuleSoft connects all these different tools and makes sure data flows between them properly. The prebuilt connectors handle most major security and GRC platforms, so custom integrations don't need to be written for everything.

The API management capabilities prove critical for seamless integration access across multicloud environments. Rate limiting, authentication, and data transformation rules can be implemented to ensure each system gets data in the format it expects. Without proper API management, teams spend all their time troubleshooting integration issues.

14.8.2 Apache Kafka

For high-volume, real-time data streaming, Kafka provides the messaging backbone. It handles the constant flow of log data, security events, and policy updates that PRIG systems generate. The fault tolerance features ensure data doesn't get lost when individual components fail.

Kafka is overkill for smaller implementations, but for processing millions of events per day, it's worth the complexity.

14.8.3 How It All Works Together

Here's what happens in practice:

Raw data flows from systems into Splunk or Elastic for initial processing. The cleaned-up data feeds into QRadar, Sentinel, or Palantir, where ML models identify patterns and predict potential problems. Those predictions flow into ServiceNow or Archer for workflow management.

The governance layer automatically handles low-risk issues through existing automation tools. High-risk situations create incidents that require human intervention. The results of all these actions feed back into the intelligence layer, so the ML models get better over time.

14.9 Considerations for Potential Issues When Implementing PRIG Framework

14.9.1 Data Consistency Problems

Every tool has its own data models and field names. The solution is defining a canonical data model that standardizes formats for shared data elements. MuleSoft can handle the translation automatically, but the canonical model needs to be designed properly upfront.

14.9.2 Performance Issues

PRIG systems process enormous amounts of data, which creates bottlenecks. The key is proper data lifecycle management—keep hot data in fast storage for real-time analysis, and move older data to cheaper storage for historical analysis. Kafka helps manage data flow so no single system gets overwhelmed.

14.9.3 Security Complexity

With data flowing between multiple systems, security controls get complicated fast. Centralized identity management helps, and proper authentication and authorization are needed at every integration point. Zero Trust network principles work well for PRIG implementations.

14.10 Real-World Case Studies

14.10.1 RSA Security: How One Platform Eliminated Tool Fragmentation and Reduced 10,000 Vulnerabilities to 560 Actionable Priorities

RSA Security was facing a common but frustrating problem that many organizations know all too well—their cloud security tools were scattered across multiple platforms, making it nearly impossible to get a clear picture of their actual security posture. With environments spread across AWS, Microsoft Azure, and Google Cloud, their security team was drowning in data from different tools that didn't talk to each other. As Courtney Kohanski from their cybersecurity team put it, they desperately needed a "one-stop shop" that could bring all their cloud security data together in one place. After implementing Orca's unified platform, the transformation was remarkable. What used to require jumping between multiple vulnerability management tools and manually piecing together information now happens automatically in a single interface. The AI-powered search feature was a game-changer—team members could simply ask questions in plain English instead of learning complex technical syntax. Perhaps most impressive was how the platform's smart filtering helped them cut through the noise, transforming an overwhelming list of 10,000 vulnerabilities into a manageable 560 priority items that actually mattered. The solution seamlessly integrated with their existing workflows through APIs and Slack notifications, and the team was thrilled with the responsive customer support. For RSA, this wasn't just about better technology; rather it, was about empowering their security team to work more effectively and confidently protect the critical infrastructure clients who depend on them [13].

14.10.2 The Hidden Cost of Fast Multicloud Deployments and How to Tackle It: A Real-Life Story by Bilfinger and Tenable

Bilfinger's story will resonate with anyone who's lived through a major cloud migration. This German industrial company that has about 30,000 employees doing everything from plant maintenance to environmental tech decided to ditch their old data center with on-prem servers and move most of their operations to a multicloud environment consisting of Azure and AWS infrastructure. Sounds straightforward, right? Wrong. About a year and a half in, they realized they'd created a monster. Their teams were racing against deadlines and had been handing out cloud permissions like candy on Halloween. Nobody was keeping track of who had access to what, and worse, nobody was taking those permissions away when they weren't needed anymore. Andreas Pfau, who leads their Business Solutions team, put it bluntly: "We wanted to avoid the same mistakes as 10 years ago."

Tenable Cloud Security became the solution that actually worked for Bilfinger's mess. What's interesting here is how the platform demonstrates the PRIG architecture in a real-world scenario where the stakes were high and the problems were concrete. The first thing it did was tackle the data chaos—pulling information from hundreds of Azure subscriptions and AWS accounts and actually making sense of it all. This isn't just data collection; it's about creating a single source of truth when you're dealing with multiple cloud environments that have grown organically over time.

The intelligence layer is where things got interesting. The platform's ML capabilities started identifying patterns that Bilfinger's teams simply couldn't see manually. We're talking about finding permissions that hadn't been used in months, spotting accounts that had accumulated dangerous levels of access, and flagging the kind of configuration drift that happens when you're moving fast and breaking things. This wasn't a theoretical risk assessment—it was pointing to specific problems that needed fixing.

The governance component then turned those insights into something actionable. Instead of generating reports that sit in someone's inbox, the platform created workflows that Bilfinger's three teams could actually execute on. Their IAM team, Cloud Center of Excellence, and IT Security groups suddenly had a shared view of what needed to be done and who should do it. As Pfau noted, the platform provides "transparency that informs us about our cloud infrastructure and risks to our resources, and what to do about it." In other words, they finally had visibility into their cloud environment and a clear path forward for securing it [14].

14.11 Outlook and Recommendations

Research demonstrates that AI technologies in predictive risk assessment significantly enhance business continuity capabilities [15]. Organizations implementing PRIG systems report measurable return on investment (ROI) through reduced incident response times, improved compliance scores, and proactive risk mitigation capabilities. The market validation is clear: the SIEM landscape is projected to see over 90% of solutions offering cloud-delivered capabilities by 2024, indicating strong enterprise adoption [8].

The predictive capabilities provide additional value by enabling proactive risk management. Organizations that implement PRIG successfully usually see measurable improvements in their security posture and compliance metrics within the first year. The integration of AI-powered data analytics, natural language processing, and predictive maintenance capabilities creates a comprehensive risk assessment framework that supports sustained business operations [9].

14.11.1 Strategic Implementation Recommendations

Start Small and Prove It Out: As shown in Figure 14.3, companies should start with tightly focused pilot projects that deliver value and develop internal expertise. Successful pilots usually concentrate on high-impact, clearly defined use cases, such as SOX compliance automation, and do not try for an enterprise-wide implementation out of the gate.

Data Due Diligence: The quality of predictive risk intelligence assumes sound and integrated data across various sources. Organizations should focus on standardizing their data and API integration work before investing in complex analytics capabilities.

Staff Cross-Functional Teams: PRIGs implemented successfully are not the work of the security team but instead rely on an interdisciplinary group that

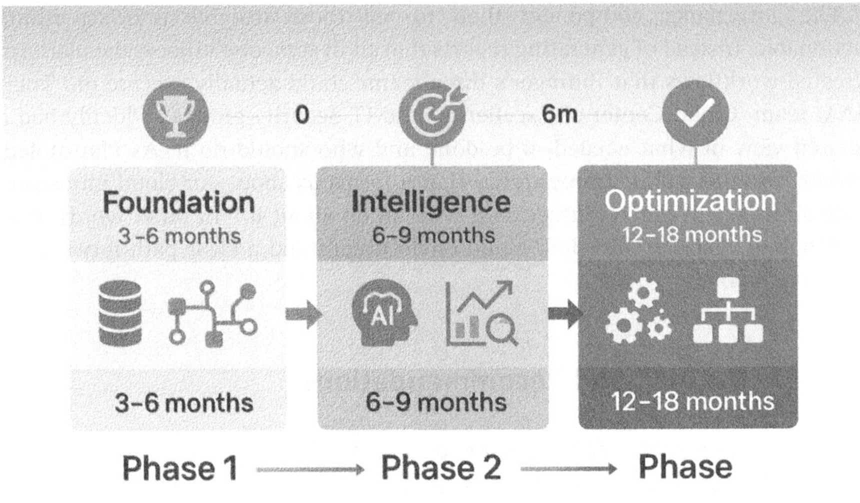

Figure 14.3 Phased implementation approach for the predictive intelligence and governance framework.

includes security, compliance, operations, development, and the business. Clear governance models that allow for collaboration and yet accountability are crucial.

Focus on Business Value: Companies should not promote PRIG investment based on technical features but on business value. Organizational momentum can be sustained by clear measures, continual communication, and the collection of "success stories.

14.11.2 The Evolution Toward Autonomous Governance

The future is poised to be filled with more and more autonomous systems of control that can adequately react to new circumstances and threats without human intervention. However, this evolution has to be a tradeoff between the efficacy of automation and the need to supervise and maintain human responsibility.

Learning policy systems will utilize ML to refine governance policies based on organizational behaviors and the threat environment. Governance systems will independently detect, analyze, and remediate complex security incidents with fully automated incident response mechanisms.

14.12 Conclusion

Transitioning to predictive risk intelligence transcends technology adoption; it represents a strategic transformation in enterprise risk philosophy. Organizations are rapidly adopting multicloud environments to increase flexibility, avoid vendor lock-in, and optimize performance, resilience, and geographic diversity by leveraging the strengths of different cloud providers. They no longer have the luxury of governance models that work on quarterly cycles when the business climate changes daily and threat environments are constantly transforming. The future of risk management is not about substituting human judgment with AI but augmenting and optimizing human decision-making with machine intelligence. The PRIG framework enhances human potential by empowering the organizations to use the enormous quantities of information available, seeing subtle relationships, predicting risks timely, and proactively changing the governance structure to adapt to the risk posture to avoid costly operational downfalls.

References

1 Enterprise Risk Management Initiative, "Predictive risk intelligence strategies," *North Carolina State University*, Jan. 2020. [Online]. Available: https://erm.ncsu.edu/resource-center/predictive-risk-intelligence-strategies.
2 CyberSecurity News, "Predictive cyber risk analysis using aggregated threat intelligence," May 2025. [Online]. Available: https://cybersecuritynews.com/cyber-risk-analysis.
3 Resolver, "What is risk intelligence & why it's a game changer," Nov. 2024. [Online]. Available: https://www.resolver.com/blog/risk-intelligence.
4 Splunk Inc., "Splunk Named #1 SIEM provider in the 2022 IDC market share for SIEM for 3rd time in a row," 2022. [Online]. Available: https://www.splunk.com/en_us/blog/security/splunk-named-1-siem-provider-in-the-2022-idc-market-share-for-siem-for-3rd-time-in-a-row.html.
5 Splunk Inc., "Splunk named a leader in the 2024 IDC marketScape for SIEM for enterprise," 2024. [Online]. Available: https://www.splunk.com/en_us/blog/security/splunk-named-a-leader-in-the-2024-idc-marketscape-for-siem-for-enterprise.html.
6 Splunk Inc., "Splunk named a leader in the gartner magic quadrant for SIEM," 2024. [Online]. Available: https://www.splunk.com/en_us/blog/security/splunk-named-a-leader-in-the-gartner-magic-quadrant-for-siem.html.

7 Splunk Inc., "2024 Gartner magic quadrant for SIEM," 2024. [Online]. Available: https://www.splunk.com/en_us/form/gartner-siem-magic-quadrant.html.

8 Mordor Intelligence, "Security information and event management (SIEM) market size, share & industry Report," 2024. [Online]. Available: https://www.mordorintelligence.com/industry-reports/global-security-information-and-event-management.

9 Carnegie Council for Ethics in International Affairs, "Predictive AI," 2024. [Online]. Available: https://carnegiecouncil.org/explore-engage/key-terms/predictive-ai.

10 ServiceNow Inc., "Governance, risk, and compliance (GRC)," 2024. [Online]. Available: https://www.servicenow.com/products/governance-risk-and-compliance.html.

11 Kanini, "Four fundamental use cases of serviceNow GRC solution," Nov. 2023. [Online]. Available: https://kanini.com/blog/four-fundamental-use-cases-of-servicenow-grc-solution.

12 Riskonnect, "Why prescriptive & predictive analytics in risk management," Feb. 2025. [Online]. Available: https://riskonnect.com/reporting-analytics/why-prescriptive-predictive-analytics-in-risk-management.

13 Orca Security, "RSA security unifies cloud security with orca platform," 2024. [Online]. Available: https://orca.security/resources/case-studies/rsa-security-unifies-cloud-security-with-orca-platform.

14 Tenable, "Bilfinger improves cybersecurity posture with tenable," 2024. [Online]. Available: https://www.tenable.com/case-studies/bilfinger.

15 MDPI, "The role of artificial intelligence technology in predictive risk assessment for business continuity: A case study of Greece," 2025. [Online]. Available: https://www.mdpi.com/2227-9091/12/2/19.

15

Security and Compliance for Cloud-Native Applications

Vaishnavi Gudur[1] *and Ashish Kattamuri*[2]

[1] *Independent Researcher, Seattle, WA, USA*
[2] *Independent Researcher, Denver, CO, USA*

15.1 Introduction

Security and compliance are the essential concepts in cloud-native applications that help us to ensure organizational protection, integrity, and adherence to the regulatory requirements [1, 2]. In cloud-native applications, security refers to the procedures and techniques used to safeguard the internal infrastructure, input/output data, and applications against risks and cyberthreats [3]. Cloud-native applications consist of microservices, containers, and other distributed architecture components. Modern organizations are rapidly adopting containerized microservices that run across multiple cloud providers, creating a complex security surface. If they fail to harden container images, coordinate interservice network traffic, and defend against attacks in these dynamic environments, the result can be costly data breaches and downtime [2, 3]. Security must be integrated into automated Developer Operations (DevOps) pipelines constructed in cloud-native ecosystems and permeate every stage of the application life cycle, from development to runtime [1, 2].

Compliance refers to the policies and processes to ensure that the cloud-native applications adhere to the industry standards and regulations. The standards and regulations can vary and be specific to industry, such as Payment Card Industry Data Security Standard (PCI DSS) for payment systems, General Data Protection Regulation (GDPR) for data privacy, and Health Insurance Portability and Accountability Act (HIPAA) for health care [5]. Cloud-native systems scatter workloads across clusters, regions, and sometimes multiple providers, causing the underlying resources to change continuously. To keep pace, compliance checks have to be fully automated, demonstrably reliable, and able to generate tamper-evident evidence whenever auditors or regulators ask for it [4, 6].

Similar to security issues, compliance efforts are made more difficult by the fact that cloud-native apps are frequently dispersed across several cloud providers and geographical areas [6, 8]. Policies, audit systems, and controls must be implemented to safeguard data, privacy, and authority to satisfy the diverse requirements of a cloud-based regulatory environment [5, 8].

The goal of this chapter is to examine how security and compliance are changing as businesses switch from old-fashioned monolithic systems to new, cloud-native architectures [2, 6]. As applications become more spread out, changing quickly and relying on automated infrastructure, the area that can be attacked grows, and regulatory problems get bigger [2, 8]. Accordingly, we span both foundational and cutting-edge dimensions, ranging from Zero Trust, Developer Security Operations (DevSecOps), Kubernetes Role Based Access Control (RBAC), and shared-responsibility governance to AI-driven compliance automation, post-quantum cryptography readiness, CIAA, and Compliance-as-Code, so readers see the full continuum of technical controls and policy models shaping modern cloud-native risk management.

15.2 Background/Context

Safeguarding data is more important than ever as companies migrate sensitive data and activities to the cloud. Threats are dynamic; they always change and find fresh means of breaking through defenses. Security in this dynamic threat environment refers not only to responding to known attacks but also to aggressively foreseeing vulnerabilities and building robust systems.

Security and compliance are essential for keeping confidence, fulfilling legal requirements, and guaranteeing corporate continuity. Although many believe that the provider bears sole responsibility for cloud security, the reality is a shared one. Although cloud providers offer basic security for infrastructure, the customer bears most of the responsibility for protecting apps, data, and usage.

Recent research highlights this: almost 55% of companies have had a data breach in the past year; shockingly, 45% of these breaches come from operational errors or misconfigurations created by internal teams. This shows how much organizations can contribute to guaranteeing compliance as well as security.

Cloud-native security is layered and calls for constant awareness at all its levels. A cloud-native stack is best visualized as four interlocking security tiers. The tiers are as follows:

- Application Code: Safe coding standards and consistent developer vulnerability checks.
- Packaging uses (e.g., using Docker) and vulnerability or configuration error scanning of images using containers.
- Platforms like Kubernetes that automate deployment, scaling, and container management call for robust RBAC, network policies, and secrets management.

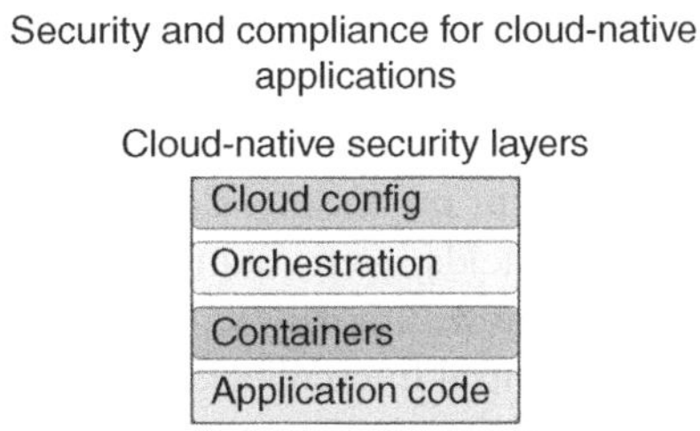

Figure 15.1 Layered security in cloud-native applications.

- On systems like Amazon Web Services (AWS), Azure, or Google Cloud Platform (GCP), managing Virtual Private Cloud (VPC), storage buckets, identity and access management (IAM) roles, and network segmentation calls for cloud infrastructure configuration.
- Every layer offers different difficulties; attackers can take advantage of flaws anywhere. The objective is thus to protect these dynamic, linked elements from a range of hazards and weaknesses. As shown in Figure 15.1, cloud-native security involves multiple interlocking tiers.

Cloud-native apps are often built on cloud computing service models, which are as follows:

- Infrastructure-as-a-Service (IaaS) delivers virtualized resources—servers, storage, networking—over the internet. Operating systems, programs, and data—e.g., AWS Elastic Compute Cloud (AWS EC2) and Azure Virtual Machines—are the customer's responsibility for securing.
- Offering a controlled platform for application development and deployment, platform-as-a-Service (PaaS) abstracts infrastructure management. The provider controls the OS and runtime; the customer protects their application and data, for example, Google App Engine and Azure App Service.
- Software-as-a-Service (SaaS) provides ready-to-use online services (e.g., Salesforce and Microsoft 365). Although the vendor locks most layers, users still have to manage access, set policies, and guard their data.

Though the user is in charge of securing the configuration, application logic, and data, a distinction at the center of the shared responsibility model, cloud providers always secure the infrastructure. Figure 15.2 illustrates this division.

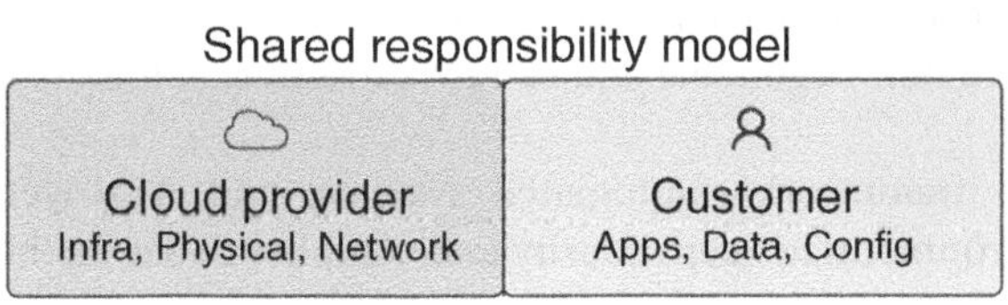

Figure 15.2 illustrates the division of responsibilities between the cloud provider and the customer, clarifying which party is accountable for each facet of security in cloud-native environments.

Compliance is about making sure cloud-native apps follow accepted legal, industry, and organizational guidelines, not about satisfying outside audits. This covers rules on data privacy under GDPR, HIPAA for healthcare, or PCI DSS for payment processing. Compliance requirements are legal obligations in many different fields; even voluntary frameworks are usually demanded by consumers, auditors, and authorities.

The Central Intercollegiate Athletic Association (CIAA) model helps one to distinguish the main elements of compliance:

- **Confidentiality:** Only authorized individuals or systems can access sensitive data.
- **Integrity:** Data remains accurate, complete, and unaltered except by authorized actions.
- **Availability:** Data and services are accessible and usable when needed by authorized users.
- **Accountability:** Actions and access are tracked to enable audit, control, and attribution.

Particularly difficult in dynamic, distributed environments, modern compliance calls not only for defining policies and procedures but also for constant enforcement of them and maintenance of audit trails proving adherence.

15.2.1 Why Is Compliance and Security Challenging in Cloud-Native Systems?

Unlike legacy, monolithic systems, securing and preserving compliance in cloud-native architectures is uniquely difficult. Often running inside tightly regulated data center perimeters, monolithic applications had predictable configurations and limited points of access. Cloud-native applications are composed of distributed, independent microservices that are typically packaged as containers and orchestrated across clusters with Kubernetes. This generates a web of connections and configurations that multiplies the attack surface and the vulnerability potential.

Cloud environments are also dynamic; resources are provisioned, scaled, and deleted constantly, rendering hand security and compliance processes insufficient.

Compliance is about following and proving adherence to policies, standards, and laws; security is about technical defense at every level. For contemporary cloud-native systems, both are non-negotiable and call for proactive, automated, constant work.

Organizations need fresh frameworks, automated systems, and AI-driven technologies, given this environment, to keep security and compliance across the cloud-native stack.

Organizations moving from static, perimeter-focused monolith architectures to dynamic and distributed cloud-native architectures require entirely new security

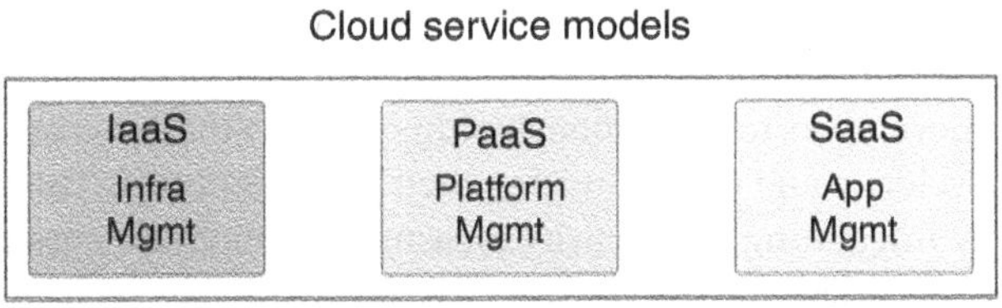

Figure 15.3 Comparison of IaaS, PaaS, SaaS cloud models.

strategies, operational strategies like DevSecOps, and a proactive approach to compliance. Traditional security and compliance methods are the ways too rudimentary for cloud-native architectures.

Cloud computing (IaaS, PaaS, SaaS) laid the foundation for cloud-native architectures and apps. The users' job is to secure the usage of the app and the data we put in. With a cloud computing platform, we have very limited accessibility to the underlying security configurations. Cloud-native apps often leverage these cloud computing models, building on IaaS, PaaS, or SaaS using containers and orchestration. Docker and Kubernetes serve complementary roles in the cloud-native stack. Docker bundles your code and all its dependencies into portable container images, ensuring the application runs the same way everywhere. Kubernetes then takes over at runtime, scheduling, scaling, and healing those containers across clusters so you can deploy and operate them reliably at any size. Cloud-native architectures leverage these service models, and their comparison is illustrated in Figure 15.3.

As the previous discussion points out, the cloud-native environment presents particular security and compliance complexity that demands continual adaptation. To meet these evolving risks and objectives, companies have to apply reasonable frameworks, techniques, and technologies suited to the reality of distributed, dynamic cloud systems. The next section covers industry standards, basic security and compliance strategies, and new best practices, allowing businesses to develop and maintain strong cloud-native systems.

15.3 Core Content

15.3.1 Current Security Frameworks and Processes

Organizations need to follow structured frameworks and an integration process for defending threats, adhering to compliance, and securing their digital assets. The following are some of the most commonly used processes and frameworks for maintaining a security and compliance posture.

1) **Security Frameworks:**
The adoption of DevSecOps is one of the foundational security practices that highlights the need for integration and automation of security measures within

the software development life cycle process. DevSecOps is commonly referred to as security-as-code, which integrates security procedures in the DevOps pipelines, allowing the developers to continuously ship or deploy their services without affecting their velocity and compromising their security posture from the introduced code. By integrating the security measures through the entire software development life cycle process, DevSecOps aims to make security maintenance a shared responsibility model between developers, the developer operations team, and security teams. Automation plays an important role in this process by integrating vulnerability scans, policy checks, and threat detection into the DevOps pipeline, which automates and ensures that the code is passed through consistent security checks without affecting the team's velocity. In the modern software development life cycle, multiple tools need to be integrated to maintain the security posture. *Snyk* is a tool that helps with the early detection of code vulnerabilities, dependencies, containers, or container images, and the configurations to manage or control the infrastructure. These tools provide visibility of the vulnerabilities introduced with the code and help the developers remediate the issues before the code is deployed to production. *Clair* [6] is another tool that scans the container images and looks for any vulnerabilities and security flaws, similar to Snyk. While Snyk is a broader developer-first security platform, Clair exclusively focuses on container vulnerabilities. Another tool that follows a more granular approach, like Clair, is Open Policy Agent (OPA), which enforces policy-as-code, allowing teams to define and maintain consistent rules across services, infrastructure, and access controls. OPA guarantees organizational compliance.

Cloud-Native Computing Foundation (CNCF) improves the security even further in modern infrastructure by providing best practices for containerized and Kubernetes (K8s)-based environments. CNCF outlines how to secure the K8s clusters, manage secrets, and monitor the service deployments. Through its white papers and reference architectures, CNCF provides the needed guidance for organizations to get a better understanding of cloud-native security. CNCF recommends the usage of a single container image to guarantee the integrity and origin of the application components. The CNCF also promotes least privilege access to organizational users, which helps the teams tighten the security and prevent unauthorized or unintended access. The least privilege access makes sure that only the minimum required permissions are assigned to the users. CNCF also promotes the importance and adoption of observability, which continuously monitors the service and flags anomalies that may signal potential breaches, such as unauthorized or unintended privileged access or network attacks.

Zero Trust architecture is another foundational security model. As the name suggests, it has low tolerance for leniency and goes against the traditional approach of being lenient to maintain trust with the network, as threats can originate not just from outside but also from inside the network. Zero Trust architecture enforces that every user, device, and system needs to be verified for its identity and authorization before granting access to the resources. A continuous verification needs to be implemented to protect against insider threats. *Security meshes* such as Istio or Linkerd are critical to enable Zero Trust in microservices architecture, as these tools secure the service-to-service communications in a cluster with mutual Transport Layer Security (TLS) encryption. Least privilege access and microsegmentation will help establish a better Zero Trust. Restrict user access to only the components they genuinely need, and segment the environment into small, isolated container zones. Doing so shrinks the attack surface and sharply limits any lateral movement an attacker could attempt if a breach occurs.

2) **Compliance Frameworks:**
   a) **Compliance-as-Code (CaC):** Regulatory policies can be integrated into the development pipelines by leveraging declarative languages like Rego (OPA). Following is an example:

```
default allows = false
let {input.resource.type == "aws_s3_bucket"
  input.resource.encryption.enabled == true
  input.resource.access_control == "private"}
```

   This example rule automatically blocks installations, generating unencrypted S3 buckets. The automation helps lower the manual compliance audits in controlled sectors by 73% [11]. CaC not only evaluates the deployment pipelines but also evaluates the resource states by creating audit trails for reporting. AWS Config rules are one such continuous compliance engine.

   b) **General Data Protection Regulation:** GDPR requires the personal data of EU citizens to be protected by GDPR standards, user consent, and implementation of encryption for the data in transit and at rest, and other data security practices. As Tenable notes, to ensure data residency in cloud-native systems, encryption and other storage settings need to be reviewed.

   c) **Health Insurance Portability and Accountability Act:** To safeguard patient data in cloud-native applications requires enforcing encryption, access controls, and audit logging across all services. HIPAA enforces the safeguarding of patient data to ensure confidentiality, integrity, and availability of electronic protected health information (ePHI).

d) **Payment Card Industry Data Security Standard:** With Kubernetes network policies or service meshes supporting compliance, PCI DSS guides cardholder data security, requiring network segmentation and frequent testing.

AI can greatly improve these systems by including automation in vulnerability detection, machine learning (ML) to predict compliance risks, and natural language processing (NLP) to translate regulatory texts into executable policies, enabling real-time, scalable enforcement across cloud-native environments.

15.3.2 AI-Enhanced Security and Compliance Mechanisms

1) **AI-Based Threat Detection and Response:**
   AI systems react to events faster than human procedures. As Palo Alto Networks reports, Johnson and Lee created an AI-based system that isolates compromised containers or blocks malicious IPs, lowering response times in cloud-native environments. Maintaining security in cycles of fast deployment depends on this automation.
2) **AI-Powered Compliance Automation:**
   AI tools automatically confirm settings against rules, simplifying compliance. As CSA emphasizes, NLP maps controls to infrastructure and code and breaks out regulatory texts (GDPR, PCI DSS, HIPAA) and guarantees cloud-native applications meet criteria without manual audits. This guarantees ongoing adherence and helps security teams to be less burdened.
3) **Behavioral Biometrics for Zero Trust:**
   By looking at old data, ML models can guess when attacks or vulnerabilities will happen. As discussed in Orca Security, Garcia et al. [17] showed that predictive analytics can find vulnerabilities in container images with 85% accuracy. This lets the vulnerabilities be fixed before they are used. This proactive approach lowers the chance that cloud-native systems will be hacked.
4) **AI-Driven Anomaly Detection:**
   AI detects deviations from normal behavior, such as unusual container activity or network traffic spikes, which could indicate a threat. Smith et al. found that unsupervised ML algorithms can detect anomalies in Kubernetes clusters with high accuracy and few false positives, thereby improving real-time threat detection, as discussed by IBM. This is critical for addressing the dynamic nature of cloud-native environments, where traditional monitoring may overlook subtle threats.
5) **Predictive Threat Intelligence:**
   Predictive threat intelligence (PTI) signals a paradigm change from reactive security to anticipatory defense in contemporary cloud-native systems. PTI uses artificial intelligence and data analytics to forecast developing risks, so

it offers proactive advice to strengthen defenses before attacks materialize, unlike conventional systems that react after spotting anomalies.

PTI's core is the application of machine learning models educated on historical threat data, telemetry logs, threat actor behavior patterns, vulnerability databases (e.g., Common Vulnerabilities and Exposures [CVEs]), and open-source intelligence (OSINT). Looking for weak signals or patterns that might indicate an approaching attack, these systems continuously consume and examine data across the cloud-native stack, including container runtimes, application programming interfaces (API) gateways, CI/CD pipelines, and orchestration layers [12].

AI-driven threat intelligence engines, for instance, can spot an increase in reconnaissance traffic aimed at particular Kubernetes clusters and link it to known tactics, strategies, and procedures (Tactics, Techniques, and Procedures [TTPs]) from MITRE ATT&CK (a globally accessible, open-source knowledge base of adversary tactics and techniques based on real-world observations). This lets security teams rotate credentials or pre-emptively isolate exposed microservices before a breach starts [13].

Google's Chronicle Security Operations Suite is one application of this idea since it maps possible attack paths and simulates exploit chains based on behavioral indicators by merging with telemetry from GCP, AWS, and outside sources [14]. Likewise, Microsoft Defender for Cloud provides threat forecasting models that give policy drift based on historical exploitability and external threat environments top priority, along with misconfigurations.

Within the framework of compliance, PTI is being applied more and more to find early indicators of regulatory infractions. AI models, for example, can identify a trend of API calls or database access that, although not clear violations, statistically correlate with past GDPR or HIPAA infractions, thus calling for preemptive remediation [15].

Advanced PTI systems include automated mitigating capabilities beyond predictive alarms. This covers spinning up decoy honey pots (deception-as-a-service), sending API throttling commands, or instantly forwarding policy changes to Kubernetes admission controllers. Risk scoring models that assess the corporate impact of every expected threat now mostly control these decisions.

Organizations using predictive threat modeling and automation report a 43% faster mean time to respond (MTTR) to zero-day exploits and a 65% decrease in successful lateral movements across microservices, according to recent research [16].

PTI is fast rising as a pillar of cloud-native defense—one that, with foresight, context, and automation, enhances security and compliance functions even as it is still developing.

15.4 Challenges

Along with benefits including scalability, flexibility, accessibility, and cost-efficiencies, the increasing acceptance of cloud computing introduces us to various security challenges. Using security measures and compliance policies presents various challenges for companies. Interoperability is one of the main obstacles. Mixing services across several clouds or hybrid configurations carries the integration difficulty of interoperability. To operate seamlessly, several security tools, such as firewalls, identity monitoring, and scanners from many vendors, are combined. Interoperability is more difficult without standards between systems and tools. Although the standards can be unified, the vendors might not be motivated because of the competitiveness, so assessing the whole stance is challenging. The second challenge comes from these sometimes conflicting or nonstandardized parts and concerns that a company must control and combine to ensure its cloud-based operations. Since resources are often provisioned, scaled, and terminated, the cloud-based systems are always evolving. Maintaining complete visibility and control, tracking everything, and applying consistent security methods all around is challenging in this dynamic condition when the resources are in flux.

Furthermore, common and noticeable in cloud-native systems are data-related issues. Among the most often reported forms of attacks are data leaks. Most data breaches result from poorly configured systems, too liberal access limits, and inadequate monitoring. Data security and privacy are challenging in distributed cloud systems since data is dispersed over several sites. This complicates the security issue even more since several jurisdictional rules and compliance criteria call for strict data protection rules such as GDPR, HIPAA, and PCI DSS. Cloud-native services hide the underlying hardware behind layers of virtualization and automation: a single object you write to "logs-bucket" in your code might be silently sharded across drives in three countries, replicated for durability, or migrated overnight to balance load. Because engineers interact only with logical resources—buckets, queues, managed databases—they rarely see the street address (or even the region) where the bits ultimately rest. That opacity makes it hard to prove that sensitive records stay inside a mandated jurisdiction or that backups never cross a border—exactly the evidence regulators demand for data residency and sovereignty compliance.

IAM in cloud-native systems presents another fundamental challenge. Managing user identities, least privilege access, two-factor authentication, and audit trails in cloud-native systems is complex and prone to mistakes in both directions. Any configuration error in IAM could expose private information to illegal access, therefore causing data losses and breaches, often stemming from phishing campaigns, social engineering, stolen credentials, session hijacking, or other forms of attacks. Whether unintentional or deliberate, these attacks seriously endanger the cloud-native apps and data in cloud-native systems, where audit trails and access control are sporadically used.

Often in cloud-native systems, several services interact via API. Should these APIs be improperly secured, lacking adequate checks for who is permitted to access them, or should their communication not be encrypted, attackers can readily take advantage of them. Common in cloud-native systems, where services may interact over networks not entirely private and are intercepted by the attacker, such as man-in-the-middle (MITM) attacks, which pose a regular concern. Furthermore, improperly configured network settings, including security groups or firewalls, could unintentionally let attackers move from one area of the cloud to another, a tactic sometimes referred to as lateral movement, extending the blast radius once they reach a system.

The way the resources are distributed and controlled poses additional challenges in cloud-native settings. Through virtualization, many clients or tenants use the same physical servers; thus, a weakness in the underlying hypervisor or container runtime could let attackers access other users' computers. Should the separation between tenants be ineffective, important information could be inadvertently revealed. Using shared components like orchestration platforms, libraries, or backend tools, which, if not routinely upgraded, might generate vulnerabilities across several environments at once, makes things riskier.

Given that different sectors and areas follow different regulatory standards, such as ISO 27001, System and Organization Controls 2 (SOC 2), PCI DSS, and Federal Risk and Authorization Management Program (FedRAMP), it is also difficult to guarantee compliance and appropriate governance in cloud-native systems. Operating in the cloud, companies must continuously assess and monitor these requirements and guarantee compliance with them while negotiating the "shared responsibility" model, in which case it is sometimes unclear which areas of security the cloud provider handles and which the customer is accountable for. Comprehensive risk analyses or full audits can be difficult given inadequate criteria and vendors' lack of openness. The complexity is increased by maintaining current certifications and assessing vendor security posture.

Finally, operational and implementation problems will inevitably reduce the effectiveness of cloud security initiatives. For cloud-native systems where infrastructure is dynamically changing and evolving, constant compliance monitoring is vital. Integrating new security technologies into legacy systems or pre-existing DevOps pipelines could cause redundancy, alert fatigue, or configuration drift. Most companies have internal organizational limits like skills gaps, financial restrictions, or resource constraints. Furthermore, even if automation has to be grown to cloud size, human judgment should be balanced to assess security signals and implement complex rules.

These challenges highlight how an organizational discipline and mindset define cloud-native security rather than a technical application. To thrive in today's threat environment, development, operations, and governance teams must work together; scalable automation and careful human direction are also critical.

15.5 Future Outlook

Cloud-native applications are reshaping the tech landscape, and the move from monoliths to dynamic microservices dramatically alters the risk profile organizations must manage. At the same time, their highly distributed, fast-changing architecture invites stricter regulatory scrutiny and adds layers of operational complexity that traditional stacks never faced. At the junction of automation, artificial intelligence, strong cryptography, and new architectural ideas like multicloud and Zero Trust, cloud-native security and compliance will find their future. This part looks at the new technologies, strategic patterns, and research directions ready to redefine how companies protect and run cloud-native systems.

15.5.1 Emerging Technologies in Cloud-Native Security

1) **Blockchain for Immutable Audit Trails and Identity**
   Particularly for its features around cloud-native environments, blockchain technology is showing great promise in:
   - Unchangeable audit trails lower manipulation and enhance openness.
   - Decentralized identity management increases users' control and helps to lower identity theft.
   - Smart contracts to drive supply chain validation and access control enforcement automation.

   The promise of blockchain is closely related to changing rules such as the US crypto laws and the Markets in Crypto-Assets (MiCA) of the EU. Research shows that, in compliance automation and secure cloud orchestration systems, this tool is increasingly valuable even if its present acceptance is still limited.
2) **AI and ML for Proactive Security and Compliance Automation**
   Cloud-native defense is fast turning on AI and ML as fundamental technologies. Important applications comprise the following:
   - Predictive analytics-driven vulnerability detection using artificial intelligence (up to 85% accuracy in spotting threats to container images).
   - NLP maps complicated regulatory frameworks, such as GDPR and PCI DSS, into practical infrastructure policies.

- Kubernetes clusters use anomaly detection, and adaptive learning models help to lower false positives.
- Generative AI and behavioral biometrics allow context-aware, real-time access control.

A 2024 survey indicates that over half of security experts are actively using AI for cloud security use cases, and 63% of them believe AI improves security posture.

3) **Quantum-Safe Encryption and Cryptographic Agility**
Post-quantum cryptography is no longer a distant research topic—it's an urgent defense line as quantum machines creep toward the power needed to break today's public-key algorithms. Organizations that wait to retrofit their systems risk finding themselves suddenly unprotected when a practical quantum attack arrives. After National Institute of Standards and Technology (NIST) finalized three quantum-safe encryption standards in 2024, early adopters such as Microsoft and Cloudflare started including quantum-resistant cryptography in their systems.

Future-ready systems will demand the following:

- Homomorphic encryption allows encrypted data to be securely computed on.
- Cryptographic agility enables systems to migrate to stronger algorithms without redesign.

15.5.2 Research Directions and Opportunities

Important areas where constant research can greatly improve cloud-native security and compliance include the following:

- Using native artificial intelligence to embed secure design concepts and dynamically enforce policies improves DevSecOps pipelines.
- Focusing on RBAC hardening, secrets rotation, and sidecar-aware network policy execution, we secure Kubernetes orchestration platforms.
- Creating closed-loop systems to identify and automatically correct deviations in microservices and service meshes is an automated anomaly-mitigating process.
- Given 45% of breaches resulting from configuration mistakes, tools that identify and automatically correct drift are quite important [10].
- Standardizing use models for post-quantum algorithms in containerized, distributed systems will help to enable quantum-safe integration into cloud-native stacks.
- Researching effective homomorphic encryption and differential privacy will help to balance utility with data protection in privacy-preserving computation.
- Context-aware, identity-first verification models built for cloud-native Zero Trust architectures that can run in ephemeral, multi-tenant systems.

- Investigating artificial intelligence-managed security agents for edge and hybrid cloud systems is Autonomous Security-as-a-Service (SECaaS).
- Standardizing automation layers for simultaneous conformance to GDPR, HIPAA, PCI DSS, and Cybersecurity Maturity Model Certification (CMMC) helps compliance frameworks for multi-jurisdictional standards be more consistent [11].

15.6 Conclusion

Companies switching from traditional monolithic architectures to cloud-native paradigms alter the scene of security and compliance. Containerized microservices and tightly coordinated workloads deliver impressive agility, scalability, and efficiency—but those benefits come at a price: greater architectural complexity, a wider attack surface, and more fragmented governance. Therefore, rather than being seen as an afterthought but rather as a fundamental concept, cloud-native security has to be firmly rooted deep into the application lifetime [1, 2].

This chapter has shown that in cloud-native systems, security and compliance are inseparable pillars of operational integrity. While compliance assures alignment with legal, industry, and organizational mandates, including GDPR, HIPAA, and PCI DSS [4, 5], security focuses on safeguarding workloads against external and internal threats. Manual efforts, however, are inadequate as systems become more distributed and dynamic. Automated and scalable security as code and runtime protections must be present to match the speed of cloud-native invention [3, 6].

Artificial intelligence and machine learning have shown transforming power. Apart from reducing the response time to threats, AI-enhanced anomaly detection, predictive analytics, and compliance automation enable proactive policy enforcement at mass [7]. Blockchain offers even more possibilities in improving compliance and identity assurance in systems built on clouds since it can generate distributed trust and unchangeable audit trails [8]. As we approach the practical implementation level of quantum computing [9], post-quantum cryptography is growing in relevance simultaneously.

Still, the challenges remain rather severe. Under cloud-native systems, jurisdictional uncertainty, identity misconfiguration, API vulnerabilities, and interoperability gaps still complicate enforcement and auditing [5, 10]. Though in theory, shared responsibility models are fantastic, occasionally, they suffer from practical uncertainty, which calls for more organizational maturity, clarity, and tooling.

Companies have to adopt Zero Trust models, apply DevSecOps approaches to include security into DevOps pipelines, and use artificial intelligence not only for detection but also for dynamic policy orchestration, looking forward. Compliance also has to go from checkbox audits to real-time, code-driven validation, changing with system upgrades. Context-aware behavioral access rules, cryptographic agility, and federated compliance automation will be fundamental emerging paradigms [8, 9, 11].

Protecting cloud-native apps is, ultimately, a distributed, constant, intelligent effort rather than a siloed responsibility. Companies that invest in intelligent automation, proactive governance, and resilient design will be ready to boldly negotiate the complexity of tomorrow's multicloud, multi-regulatory environment.

References

1 M. Pacheco, "What is cloud-native security? Best practices & 4 c's explained," *TierPoint*, 2024. [Online]. Available: https://www.tierpoint.com/blog/cloud-native-security-best-practices.

2 Cloud Native Computing Foundation (CNCF), "Cloud native security whitepaper," *CNCF Security TAG*, 2020. [Online]. Available: https://github.com/cncf/tag-security/blob/main/security-whitepaper/CNCF_cloud-native-security-whitepaper-Nov2020.pdf.

3 G. Maayan, "Understanding cloud native security," *IEEE Comput. Soc. Tech News*, vol. 14, no. 3, pp. 23–28, 2024.

4 Appvia, "Ensuring compliance and auditing in cloud native environments: your guide to cloud compliance," *Appvia*, 2024. [Online]. Available: https://www.appvia.io/resources/compliance-auditing-cloud-native.

5 The Linux Foundation, "2024 cloud native security report," 2024. [Online]. Available: https://www.linuxfoundation.org/resources/publications/2024-cloud-native-security-report. accessed date: September 5, 2025.

6 A. Shimel, "Reflecting on 2024 and looking ahead to 2025: Cloud-native DevOps, security and the road ahead," *Cloud Native Now*, Dec. 2024. [Online]. Available: https://cloudnativenow.com/features/reflecting-on-2024-and-looking-ahead-to-2025-cloud-native-devops-security-and-the-road-ahead.

7 IBM Security, "AI-driven anomaly detection in Kubernetes clusters," *IBM Research*, 2024. Available: https://www.ibm.com/docs/en/kubecost/self-hosted/2.x?topic=ui-anomaly-detection.

8 G. Nakamoto, "Blockchain security models for distributed cloud," *J.Cloud Comput. Res.*, vol. 15, no. 2, pp. 91–104, 2024.

9 NIST, "Post-quantum cryptography standards finalization," *National Institute of Standards and Technology*, Jul. 2024. https://www.nist.gov/news-events/news/2024/08/nist-releases-first-3-finalized-post-quantum-encryption-standards.

10 Orca Security, "2024 state of cloud security: Misconfigurations and API risks," *Orca Labs*, 2024. Available: https://orca.security/lp/2024-state-of-cloud-security-report/.

11 CSA, "AI in compliance automation: NLP-based regulatory mapping," *Cloud Security Alliance*, 2024. https://cloudsecurityalliance.org/blog/2024/08/05/the-future-of-cybersecurity-compliance-how-ai-is-leading-the-way.

12 G. L. Smith, "Machine learning models for predictive threat intelligence in cloud systems," *IEEE Trans. Dependable Secure Comput.*, vol. 21, no. 1, pp. 35–48, 2024.

13 MITRE ATT&CK Framework, *Tactics and techniques for cloud-native threat detection*, 2024. [Online]. Available: https://attack.mitre.org.

14 Google Cloud, *Chronicle security operations suite: threat intelligence automation*, Google Cloud Security, 2024. [Online]. Available: https://cloud.google.com/chronicle.

15 CSA, *AI and compliance forecasting: Early violation detection using behavioral models*, Cloud Security Alliance, 2024. [Online]. Available: https://cloudsecurityalliance.org/blog/2024/08/05/the-future-of-cybersecuritycompliance-how-ai-is-leading-the-way.

16 S. Rao and J. Varga, "Autonomous threat response in containerized environments," *ACM SIGOPS Oper. Syst. Rev.*, vol. 58, no. 2, pp. 11–23, 2024.

17 Orca Security, Garcia, et al., *Predictive analytics for vulnerability detection in container images*, Orca Labs, 2024. [Online]. Available: https://orca.security/resources/blog/dynamic-reachability-analysis/.

16

Data Privacy, Sovereignty, and Cloud Localization Laws

Dhivya Nagasubramanian[1] and Kiran Kumar Reddy Puram[2]

[1] *Independent Researcher, Minniapolis, MN, USA*
[2] *Independent Researcher, Charlotte, NC, USA*

16.1 Introduction: When the Cloud Hits the Ground

The cloud was supposed to float above it all, beyond borders, untethered by politics, governed only by code. For a while, that vision held. Engineers built systems that scaled effortlessly across regions, and businesses moved fast, confident that data could follow wherever innovation led.

But the world had other plans.

Today, data is no longer just a technical asset. It is a proxy for power, a matter of sovereignty, and—more than ever—a political flashpoint [1]. Countries are pushing back against the frictionless flow of information, each drawing its own line in the digital sand. The question is not whether governments will regulate clouds—it is how far they will go.

By the middle of this decade, more than 130 nations had passed sweeping data protection laws [1]. Some merely ask for caution; others demand that data remain within their borders, subject to local control.

These rules are reshaping how cloud systems are designed, not in theory, but in practice.

At the core of this shift there are two principles. The first is data sovereignty, which holds that information must be governed by the laws of the country where it resides [1]. The second is data localization, the legal requirement that certain types of data cannot leave home. What once seemed like edge cases are now baseline requirements, especially in sectors that manage sensitive or mission-critical information.

The implications are profound. Legal missteps are not just regulatory headaches; they are strategic risks [2]. Just ask any global company that has faced massive fines or operational disruptions for getting jurisdictional boundaries wrong.

This is not a story about compliance killing innovation. It is about recalibrating ambition. Organizations are learning that scale and sovereignty do not have to be in conflict, but aligning the two takes intention, not accident [3].

Across the pages that follow, we'll explore what this new era of cloud governance looks like. We will trace how laws like the European Union's General Data Protection Regulation (EU's GDPR), the U.S. CLOUD Act, China's Personal Information Protection Law (PIPL), and India's Digital Personal Data Protection (DPDP) are setting the rules of engagement. And we will examine how industries from banking and biotech to government agencies are adapting, often under tight timelines and public scrutiny.

Along the way, we will dive into how infrastructure itself is evolving. Whether it is sovereignty-aware cloud environments, compliance baked into DevSecOps pipelines [4], or federated cloud trust models built for cross-border resilience [5, 6], the architecture of cloud computing is getting smarter about the world it inhabits.

If you are building, governing, or scaling in the cloud, this isn't just a legal briefing. It's a survival guide.

16.2 Global Trends in Data Privacy and Localization

Around the world, governments are redrawing the boundaries of digital governance. What was once a peripheral debate about "Where should data live?" has moved to the center of policy, architecture, and risk strategy. The shift is undeniable: protecting personal data has become a near-universal objective, but the methods for doing so could not be more varied [1].

The foundational principles of transparency, consent, security, and accountability are shared. But when it comes to deciding how and where data can travel, national approaches diverge sharply.

Few countries take a firm stance. In China, data protection is not just about privacy, it is a matter of national security [7, 8]. The PIPL imposes strict rules: organizations managing sensitive or large-scale personal data must store it within Chinese borders [7, 8]. Any attempt to export that data triggers a government review. The intent is clear: sensitive information should remain under Chinese jurisdiction, regardless of where the company is headquartered.

India has taken a more cautious, iterative route [9]. Early drafts of its DPDP legislation envisioned broad localization. But by the time the law passed in 2023, it had settled on a more flexible framework. Most data transfers are permitted unless a destination country is blacklisted [9]. Even so, regulators retained tools for intervention. The Reserve Bank of India, for example, mandates that payment data stay within the country [10], a position that forced global players like Mastercard to reconfigure their infrastructure or face market bans.

Europe's approach, anchored in the GDPR, is less about geography and more about guarantees [2]. The EU does not forbid data transfers outright, but it requires strong legal safeguards. If the receiving country cannot provide an "adequate" level of protection, the burden falls on organizations to prove compliance through mechanisms like standard contractual clauses. That is easier said than done. Recent court rulings have invalidated previous transatlantic agreements, leaving many companies in a state of legal limbo [2].

The United States stands apart. There's no single federal privacy law, but rather a mosaic of sector-specific statutes and state regulations [11]. Health Insurance Portability and Accountability Act (HIPAA), Family Educational Rights and Privacy Act (FERPA), and the California Consumer Privacy Act (CCPA) are familiar names, each with their own scope. Most of these laws prioritize individual rights and corporate obligations—but they rarely limit where data can go. The bigger concern, particularly for foreign governments, is the CLOUD Act. Passed in 2018, it gives U.S. law enforcement the authority to access data stored abroad, so long as it's held by an American company [2]. This has raised alarms in Europe and elsewhere, prompting renewed interest in keeping data and encryption keys on local soil.

Elsewhere, localization continues to gain traction. Russia has long required domestic storage of its citizens' personal data. Canadian provinces like British Columbia have enacted rules requiring health data to remain within the country [12]. In Southeast Asia, Vietnam and Indonesia have rolled out mandates for public service and critical infrastructure providers. Australia, Saudi Arabia, and the United Arab Emirates (UAE) have adopted similar policies, especially where national security or public trust is involved.

Then there are the hybrid model countries like South Korea, Israel, and Singapore, where localization rules are more targeted. These frameworks often depend on the sector, the sensitivity of the data, or the nature of the service being offered.

What ties these diverse approaches together is a growing belief that data is not just a byproduct of digital services; it's a strategic resource [1]. Much like energy, water, or communications infrastructure, data is increasingly seen as something that must be protected, regulated, and kept within reach.

16.3 Regional Regulatory Landscape

16.3.1 European Union: GDPR, Schrems II, and the Quest for Digital Sovereignty

Since it took effect in 2018, the EU's GDPR has become the global reference point for personal data protection [2, 3]. It establishes robust rights for individuals and firm obligations for organizations. While GDPR stops short of demanding that data stay within EU borders, it imposes strict conditions on outbound transfers, permitting them only when the destination offers "adequate" protection or when legal instruments like standard contractual clauses are in place.

This requirement has made transfers to countries like the United States, which lacks such adequacy—legally fraught [2].

In 2023, Meta faced a €1.2 billion fine and was ordered to halt transatlantic transfers, highlighting how even well-drafted safeguards can fail under scrutiny when foreign surveillance laws are involved [2]. That decision pushed many companies to consider alternatives such as local data processing or stronger encryption measures.

The Schrems II ruling reignited talks for a new EU-US Data Privacy Framework (DPF), adopted in 2023 [2]. Yet doubts remain. Ongoing legal challenges and skepticism about U.S. surveillance powers mean the underlying tension has not been resolved.

To assert greater control, Europe has launched sovereignty initiatives like Global Alliance for Industrial Data and Cloud (GAIA-X), aimed at building interoperable, federated cloud infrastructure [3]. Though it has drawn criticism, GAIA-X reflects a broader ambition: to reduce dependency on foreign tech. France's "Cloud of Trust" and the SecNumCloud standard push this agenda further [3], as do Germany's sovereign cloud pilots and the Dutch call for less reliance on U.S. services. Over 100 organizations have publicly endorsed this direction, citing the need for autonomy in critical sectors like healthcare.

These trends are reshaping enterprise behavior. More companies now demand EU-based hosting, data segregation, and binding protections from U.S. providers [2]. In turn, hyperscalers have responded: Microsoft launched its EU Data Boundary, Google partnered with T-Systems on a sovereign cloud, and others like Oracle and IBM have introduced region-specific offerings. Still, these measures do not fully neutralize exposure to laws like the CLOUD Act [2].

The EU's model blends regulatory rigor with strategic industrial policy [3]. Today, compliance is not an add-on—it's embedded in how IT systems are built, driving the rise of multicloud strategies, local zones, and privacy-preserving architecture across the region.

16.3.2 United States: The CLOUD Act, State Privacy Laws, and Government Data Rules

Unlike other regions with sweeping privacy regulations, the United States takes a fragmented approach [11]. There is no single federal law governing personal data, just a patchwork of state statutes and sector-specific rules. California's CCPA and California Privacy Rights Act (CPRA) stand out, as do newer laws in Colorado and Virginia, but none impose strict data residency. Federal sectoral laws like HIPAA and Gramm-Leach-Bliley Act (GLBA) emphasize security over geography, offering little restriction on where data is stored [11, 12].

Federal Risk and Authorization Management Program (FedRAMP) requires that federal data be stored on domestic infrastructure, where the federal government draws a harder line is with its own information. A few states have followed suit in limited contexts. Ohio and Florida, for instance, have introduced localization rules for domains like healthcare and taxation [11], though such moves remain rare.

The CLOUD Act, passed in 2018, has had broader implications [2]. Born out of the Microsoft Ireland dispute, it gave U.S. authorities legal grounds to access data from American cloud providers—even if the data sits on servers overseas. While the law opened the door to bilateral data-sharing agreements, progress on that front has been slow.

Globally, this has sparked concern [2]. The CLOUD Act places U.S. cloud firms in a bind, potentially forcing them to violate foreign privacy laws like the GDPR when complying with U.S. demands. This tension has caused some governments and companies to think twice about using American platforms for sensitive workloads. Ironically, the United States itself has raised flags over foreign access to domestic data, as seen in debates surrounding TikTok and similar apps.

In response, cloud providers have tried to rebuild trust. They have offered more transparency, given customers stronger encryption controls, and when possible, challenged certain legal requests [2]. Yet for many international clients, the jurisdictional risk remains, and it is increasingly viewed not as hypothetical but as a concrete factor in vendor decisions.

16.3.3 China: PIPL and Cyber Sovereignty

China operates one of the most restrictive data governance regimes anywhere [7, 8]. Its legal framework—anchored by the Cybersecurity Law, Data Security Law, and Personal Information Protection Law—sets strict conditions for how data, particularly from critical sectors, is managed and moved across borders.

Entities classified as operators of Critical Information Infrastructure (CII) must keep data within China's borders and clear formal security reviews for any exports [7, 8]. Even companies outside that designation come under scrutiny if they process large datasets; crossing the million-user threshold, for instance, triggers additional oversight. Exporting data also requires individual consent and formal legal grounds, such as state-approved contracts or certifications [8].

The state reserves broad authority [7, 8]. It can blocklist foreign firms deemed a threat to national interests and blocks outside law enforcement from accessing Chinese data without official clearance—a direct inversion of the U.S. CLOUD Act.

Global firms adapt to this reality. Apple, for example, stores iCloud data and encryption keys in facilities operated by a Chinese state partner [13]. Amazon Web Services (AWS) and Microsoft run their Chinese services through local entities.

These arrangements are less about preference and more about access; they reflect the price of staying in the market.

China's control extends beyond personal data [7]. It designates certain industrial, financial, or scientific information as "important data," also subject to localization and tight export restrictions. Violations are not taken lightly. Fines can reach 5% of annual revenue, and companies may face market bans. Recent enforcement actions, including those against U.S. firms like Micron, underscore how data policy in China is deeply tied to broader geopolitical objectives.

In essence, China treats data as a sovereign asset—one that must remain within arm's reach of the state [7, 8]. For companies, this means building China-specific infrastructure from the ground up, shaped as much by regulation as by technology.

16.3.4 India: The Digital Personal Data Protection Act and Sectoral Rules

India's DPDP Act, introduced in 2023, represents a shift from earlier proposals that leaned heavily on data localization [9]. Instead of requiring all personal data to remain in-country, the final law allows global transfers—except to jurisdictions explicitly blocklisted by the government. This move toward a blocklist model aligns India more closely with global practices.

Yet the government holds the authority to impose restrictions when national interest is at stake [9]. Sector-specific requirements have not gone away. The Reserve Bank of India (RBI), for example, enforces strict localization for payment data [10]. In 2021, firms like Mastercard and Amex were temporarily barred from onboarding new customers until they complied. RBI has also ordered that older payments data be brought back onshore by early 2025.

Other industries, telecom and e-commerce among them, have considered similar rules [9]. While the DPDP Act places oversight with a government-appointed Data Protection Board, concerns remain around its independence and accountability.

India is also developing separate policies for nonpersonal data [9]. Proposals for mandatory data sharing with the government indicate that digital sovereignty remains a clear driver of policy decisions.

In response, cloud providers have built local infrastructure [10]. Both domestic and international firms rely on hybrid models—storing sensitive data within India while allowing nonsensitive operations to span global networks. Many Unified Payments Interface (UPI)-based fintech services, for example, now route transaction data to Mumbai-based data centers. RBI regulations even require that if data briefly leaves the country, it must be deleted from foreign servers within 24 hours [10].

India's position stands somewhere between the open model of the West and China's more controlled approach [9]. It welcomes data mobility but keeps a firm hand on the lever when it comes to strategic concerns. As a major digital economy, India's choices are likely to shape not just its own cloud landscape but global frameworks as well.

16.3.5 Other Notable Jurisdictions and Frameworks

Outside the dominant players—Europe, the United States, China, and India—a wide array of countries are shaping the global data localization dialogue in ways that are often overlooked but increasingly influential [1].

- **Russia:** Since 2015, Russia has required that data on its citizens be housed domestically. While enforcement has varied, cases like the LinkedIn ban sent a strong signal. More recently, authorities have stepped up scrutiny, particularly in areas like VPN services and ride-sharing apps, where local storage and even government access are expected. With rising geopolitical strain, many Western companies have withdrawn; those that remain face tight regulatory pressure.
- **Brazil:** Enacted in 2020, Brazil's Lei Geral de Proteção de Dados (LGPD) borrows heavily from the GDPR. It doesn't mandate localization but does place guardrails on data exports—requiring adequacy, consent, or contractual protection. Though there's been talk of localizing government data, no blanket rule exists. Still, financial regulators have applied pressure, and as Latin America's largest economy, Brazil's choices ripple across neighbors like Argentina, Mexico, and Colombia.
- **Canada:** On the federal level, Personal Information Protection and Electronic Documents Act (PIPEDA) allows cross-border data movement. But some provinces, such as British Columbia and Nova Scotia, insist that public and health data stay within Canadian borders [12]. These regional rules, driven by concerns over foreign access, have prompted cloud vendors to open domestic zones tailored to healthcare and public-sector clients.
- **Asia-Pacific:** Indonesia requires public sector data to be stored locally, though it softened this in 2019 to permit foreign hosting under tight conditions. Vietnam mandates localization for major online services under its cybersecurity law. South Korea applies strict localization to credit data and financial services, aligned with its strong privacy culture. Japan takes a different approach—opposing hard localization while promoting trusted data flows through international cooperation. Australia lacks full localization mandates, but government and healthcare data must stay onshore [12]. Growing concern over laws like the CLOUD Act is shaping local infrastructure strategy.
- **Middle East and Africa:** Saudi Arabia and the UAE rolled out GDPR-style privacy frameworks between 2021 and 2022. While full localization isn't enforced, local hosting is expected for sensitive and government-held data. Saudi Arabia's strategy even includes defined in-country storage options.

- Nigeria hasn't enacted a universal rule but requires financial data to be hosted domestically or in approved jurisdictions. South Africa allows exports under Protection of Personal Information Act (POPIA), but only if the recipient jurisdiction offers comparable protections—emphasizing risk-based evaluation over blanket restrictions.
- **International Efforts:** In 2022, the Organisation for Economic Co-operation and Development (OECD) released guidance on government access to data. Though nonbinding, the aim was to reduce the fear and uncertainty that often drive localization policy. Trade pacts also factor in. The United States-Mexico-Canada Agreement (USMCA) restricts forced localization for financial data between the United States, Mexico, and Canada—unless national policy requires it. Similar provisions show up in other bilateral deals, but sovereignty often outweighs trade when conflicts arise.

In practice, the result is a regulatory landscape that is fragmented but increasingly assertive [1]. Shared values around privacy coexist with diverging enforcement strategies. For cloud providers and enterprises, one thing is clear: operating globally now means designing locally—everywhere.

16.4 Industry Case Studies: Impact of Sovereignty Requirements

Data localization laws have made the greatest impact in highly regulated sectors such as finance, healthcare, and government [11, 12, 14]. These industries handle sensitive data and face intense regulatory oversight, making data sovereignty a top concern.

16.4.1 Finance and Banking: Balancing Global Platforms with Local Control

The financial sector, responsible for managing sensitive personal and transactional data, was among the first to confront localization mandates [10]. Regulators fear that foreign-hosted financial systems could be inaccessible in crises or audits and pose risks to national economic security.

India's RBI mandate on payments data localization offers a strong example [10]. Firms like Mastercard had to delete data from global systems and build local infrastructure. Noncompliance resulted in temporary market bans. Today, most payment processors in India use local cloud regions or on-prem infrastructure, with only anonymized analytics exported.

In the EU, financial institutions follow GDPR and additional sectoral regulations [2, 3]. The upcoming Digital Operational Resilience Act (DORA) will require banks to manage Information and Communications Technology (ICT) risks and maintain contingency plans for cloud exit. This indirectly supports sovereignty by ensuring that banks can pivot from foreign providers if needed. Leading banks negotiate terms that mandate in-region data storage and notifications of foreign data requests. Deutsche Bank's partnership with Google and French banks using hyperscaler French regions are examples of such sovereign cloud models. The Autorité de Contrôle Prudentiel et de Résolution (ACPR) mandates accessibility for regulators, encouraging hybrid approaches with encryption and backups.

Many banks now use hybrid cloud strategies: mission-critical systems stay local, while Customer Relationship Management (CRM) or analytics tools use public cloud platforms [3]. Scandinavian banks exemplify this model, linking local databases to global services through secure Application Programming Interface (APIs).

Some financial firms implement "sovereignty failovers." A Nordic insurer, for example, uses AWS globally but keeps a real-time replica in the EU, enabling rapid switchover if data flows are disrupted by legal rulings like Schrems III [2]. This practice reflects a growing focus on legal disaster recovery.

Cloud vendors are responding with sector-specific offerings. AWS GovCloud and IBM Cloud for Financial Services include built-in compliance controls and data residency features. Bank of America uses IBM's financial cloud to meet regulatory requirements from the outset.

Encryption is another key safeguard [3]. Many institutions deploy client-side encryption or Hardware Security Module (HSMs) where only the bank controls the keys. This "zero trust" approach ensures that even a subpoenaed cloud provider cannot decrypt sensitive data. Following Schrems II, European regulators have promoted pseudonymization and encryption as essential compliance tools.

16.4.2 Healthcare: Protecting Patient Data Across Borders

Healthcare organizations manage some of the most sensitive personal data—information that, in many countries, is treated as part of critical national infrastructure [11, 12, 14]. With that designation comes strict oversight and, often, legal limits on where such data can reside.

In the United States, HIPAA governs how protected health information (PHI) is managed [11, 12]. Cloud storage is allowed if vendors enter into Business Associate Agreements and comply with detailed security requirements. While HIPAA does not mandate domestic hosting, many providers lean that way to minimize liability. A few states, including Montana and Florida, have gone further—banning certain types of medical data from being stored outside U.S. borders [11], citing concerns over foreign access.

Elsewhere, governments take a more direct approach [12, 14]. In Canada, provinces like British Columbia and Nova Scotia prohibit the export of public healthcare data. Australia enforces a similar policy, requiring its national

My Health Record system to remain entirely onshore. In France, health cloud providers must meet Health Data Hosting (HDS) certification standards, effectively limiting services to EU-based infrastructure.

Notably, France scrapped its original plan to host the national Health Data Hub on Microsoft Azure, citing fears tied to the U.S. CLOUD Act [2].

In Germany, legal exposure under foreign jurisdictions has pushed many hospitals to rely solely on domestic cloud services [2]. Countries like Japan and South Korea, meanwhile, permit cross-border research use of clinical data only if it's anonymized or explicitly consented to—especially for genomic data, which is now treated as a strategic national resource. Europe's upcoming Health Data Space reflects this balancing act, enabling research while safeguarding sovereignty [14].

During the COVID-19 pandemic, data localization played a role in building trust [12]. India's Aarogya Setu and Germany's Corona-Warn-App were both designed to store sensitive data locally—a decision that reassured users and helped drive adoption.

Across the board, hospitals and digital health providers are moving toward federated architectures [12, 14]. These systems keep patient data within jurisdictional boundaries (e.g., EU data in the EU and Australian data in Australia) while allowing insights to be shared globally. Supported by anonymization and pseudonymization, this model reflects a growing recognition that compliance isn't a trade-off—it's a prerequisite for scalable, ethical innovation in healthcare.

16.4.3 Public Sector and Government: Sovereign Clouds for National Data

Governments are especially sovereignty conscious [1, 3]. National security, defense, and citizen data must often remain on national soil and under local legal control. This has spurred the development of "Government Cloud" services that provide secure, domestically hosted infrastructure.

In the United States, FedRAMP certifies cloud vendors for federal use. AWS GovCloud and Azure Government are examples—restricted to U.S. soil, managed by U.S. citizens, and isolated from global networks. The Department of Defense's Joint Warfighting Cloud Capability (JWCC) initiative also ensures domestic-only cloud usage. These strict standards set expectations for other countries interacting with U.S. cloud vendors.

Europe has increasingly pursued sovereign cloud strategies [3]. France's "Cloud de Confiance" allows use of hyperscaler software only if offered via local partners. Microsoft partnered with Orange and Capgemini, and Google with Thales, to offer SecNumCloud-certified services in France. Germany's former "German Cloud" project with Deutsche Telekom was discontinued due to inflated cost and complexity, reflecting the trade-offs in sovereign cloud initiatives.

The UK mandates certain classified data remain on-prem. Canada generally requires federal data to be stored domestically [12]. India's MeghRaj cloud strategy keeps sensitive government data in-country.

Australia limits public sector use to certified domestic cloud providers, staffed by nationals with security clearance.

Some governments collaborate regionally: the EU plans to host Commission data in an EU-only cloud [3]. North Atlantic Treaty Organization (NATO) has rules ensuring that allied data stays within NATO jurisdictions. Sovereign cloud reflectives like AWS Secret Region or Azure Sovereign Cloud reflect how global providers are segmenting infrastructure to meet these demands.

A smart city project in the Middle East is illustrative: local governments need in-country storage for surveillance and citizen services data. Providers like Oracle and Microsoft have built regional infrastructure to host such projects securely.

Defense workloads are even more tightly controlled, often hosted on isolated networks using commercial software. France's military cloud is one such example. Public trust is also a driver [2]. In Sweden and Germany, public backlash has led to reconsideration of U.S. cloud services for schools and municipalities due to CLOUD Act concerns.

In conclusion, public-sector demand for sovereignty is reshaping cloud strategy [1, 3]. Legal, physical, and administrative controls are combined to form truly sovereign clouds. As governments adopt strict standards, critical industries often follow, reinforcing national policies and influencing cloud market dynamics.

16.5 Architecting for Compliance: Technical Approaches to Sovereignty

Adhering to data localization and sovereignty requirements isn't just a legal or policy exercise, it's a technical and architectural challenge [3–6]. Cloud and IT architects are developing solutions that integrate compliance into the infrastructure. In this section, we explore key architectural strategies and novel conceptual frameworks enabling organizations to meet localization mandates without sacrificing too much on scalability or functionality. These include building a "sovereignty-aware cloud" architecture, leveraging sovereign cloud services and regional data centers, adopting multicloud and federated trust strategies to distribute risk [5, 6], implementing compliance-as-code in DevSecOps [4], and enhancing security through encryption and access control mechanisms. Together, these approaches represent a toolbox for engineering cloud systems that are both globally capable and locally compliant.

16.5.1 Sovereignty-Aware Cloud Architecture

Some clouds are built to scale. Others are built to comply [3]. A sovereignty-aware cloud aims to do both—but with one critical distinction: it's designed to respect the legal and geographic boundaries that govern data.

These systems are not passive storage environments. They actively manage where data live, who can reach them, and under what legal framework [1, 3]. That awareness is woven into the way architecture functions, from routed decisions to access control.

Several techniques support this model:

- Location-aware routing ensures that data from users in specific regions—like the EU—is processed and stored within that legal zone [3]. Cloud orchestrators and delivery networks work in concert to enforce this geography-first logic.
- Infrastructure that reacts to law means that when a regulation changes—say, a data transfer agreement is struck down—systems can move or isolate affected data without manual intervention. Engineers write those responses in code, so they're ready before they're needed.
- Region-based services break applications into smaller parts that can run close to where the user or data is located [3]. These microservices talk securely across borders, but data stays local unless explicitly permitted to travel.
- Jurisdictional controls provided by major cloud vendors let administrators set hard boundaries. Some features even prevent privileged users from bypassing these rules.
- Contextual security policies let software adjust its behavior to meet local standards. That could mean applying a country-specific encryption protocol or complying with content restrictions.

This is more than technical hygiene. It's a reflection of how cloud infrastructure is evolving—from neutral platforms into region-aware systems that can meet the legal obligations of wherever they operate [1, 3]. Compliance, in this view, isn't a layer added later. It's a design choice baked in from the start.

16.5.2 Sovereign Cloud Services and Regionalization

In many situations, cloud computing is not driven primarily by performance or cost considerations but by the need for control. A sovereign cloud is designed to meet that requirement. It represents a country's deliberate choice to ensure that its data—and the authority to govern that data—remain within its national borders. By doing so, governments assert legal, operational, and strategic oversight over information that is considered sensitive or critical to national interests.

Rather than rely on global platforms governed elsewhere, these environments are either operated by domestic firms or structured in partnership with them [3].

This gives public institutions and regulated industries confidence that their data isn't subject to foreign laws or outside interference. In France, for instance, sovereign cloud offerings are built to ensure that both data and operational control remain full within French jurisdiction.

Global providers like Microsoft, Amazon, and Google now offer cloud services designed specifically for the European Union. Some include customer-managed encryption keys, and others restrict access to EU-based personnel [2, 3]. The underlying goal is the same: keep data under the laws that apply where it was collected.

Building a sovereign cloud infrastructure demands long-term commitment. It involves establishing isolated technical environments, securing country-specific certifications, and, in some cases, accepting constraints on interoperability or performance. Yet for governments and highly regulated industries, the trade-off is often justified. The convenience they relinquish is offset by greater legal certainty, stronger regulatory alignment, and enhanced control over how sensitive data is stored and governed.

Local providers have also stepped up [3]. Vendors like OVHcloud, T-Systems, and Exoscale have grown their presence by offering solutions aligned with domestic privacy and security expectations. They may not offer the same feature sets as global giants, but their value lies in meeting jurisdictional requirements with precision.

Certification standards such as ISO 27001, Germany's C5, and France's SecNumCloud help formalize what qualifies as sovereign [3]. The EU Cloud Security Scheme, now under development, could further define and elevate these distinctions at the regional level.

Many organizations now split their workload; sensitive data and critical systems stay in sovereign environments, while other operations run in public or hybrid clouds [3]. With the right design, this division doesn't have to slow things down.

Ultimately, sovereign clouds are not about isolation—it is about assurance [1, 3]. When laws change quickly and geopolitical risks are high, knowing exactly where your data lives—and who governs it—has never mattered more.

16.5.3 Multicloud and Federated Trust Strategies

By the mid-2020s, over 90% of enterprises globally adopted multicloud strategies—not just to reduce vendor lock-in or optimize cost, but to manage **jurisdictional risk** [1, 3]. Distributing workloads across multiple providers, including local clouds, helps organizations stay agile if one provider becomes noncompliant with local laws. Some even maintain EU-only backup environments in case their U.S. cloud usage becomes problematic—treating legal risk like downtime risk.

A related concept is **Federated Cloud Trust**, where multiple cloud environments across countries or organizations interoperate under shared compliance frameworks [5, 6]. While not yet an industry standard, initiatives like **GAIA-X** represent early efforts toward this. The idea is that cloud services from multiple jurisdictions can be used together, with guarantees around data location, encryption, and governance.

Federated frameworks may involve shared Service Level Agreement (SLAs), mutual audits, and federated identity management [5, 6]. Research has explored trust scoring models that assess provider compliance and performance, enabling automated, policy-based cloud selection.

Multicloud also gives organizations bargaining power [3]. For example, if an EU bank can easily switch from AWS to a local provider, AWS is incentivized to strengthen sovereignty controls. Groups like Cloud Infrastructure Services Providers in Europe (CISPE) are pushing for standards that improve data portability and reduce lock-in. Maintaining consistent governance across clouds is a key challenge. Organizations are increasingly using control planes and cloud-agnostic tools (e.g., Terraform, Vault, and Open Policy Agent) to enforce security, compliance-as-code, and data residency policies uniformly across environments [4].

Federated Identity and Access Management (IAM) enables unified control [5, 6]. Standards like Security Assertion Markup Language (SAML) and OpenID Connect (OIDC) support cross-cloud access, and future tools like the EU Digital Identity Wallet could allow clouds to share compliance credentials for dynamic trust-building.

A hypothetical example: a European Banking Cloud could consist of intero perable nodes in each country, ensuring data localization while allowing controlled cross-border services (e.g., verifying a German customer's transaction in France without moving raw data) [5, 6].

This vision parallels federated learning in AI, where data stays local and only insights move. Cloud is evolving from a centralized model to distributed, rule-compliant "data ponds" stitched together with trust-aware protocols [5, 6].

16.5.4 Compliance-as-Code (CaC): Embedding Legal Rules in DevSecOps

As cloud architectures grow more intricate and regulatory demands more frequent, the traditional approach to compliance—checklists, audits, and after-the-fact fixes—simply can't keep up [4]. In highly regulated environments, teams are beginning to realize that if compliance is not built in from the start, it's already too late.

CaC is the response to that challenge [4]. It shifts compliance work upstream—into source control, build pipelines, and infrastructure templates.

Instead of relying on human review, policies are written as executable logic. The moment someone tries to deploy something noncompliant—like spinning up a database instance in the wrong jurisdiction or turning off encryption by mistake, the system blocks it. It's not a suggestion; it's an enforced rule. This approach is especially powerful in DevSecOps environments where speed and control must coexist [4]. Tools like Open Policy Agent or Chef InSpec can evaluate infrastructure-as-code against policy files that reflect legal requirements.

Whether it's ensuring encryption, data retention, or access controls, the checks are immediate and repeatable. And unlike human auditors, they don't get tired or miss things.

The practical benefit is hard to overstate [4]. Imagine a developer tagging a workload as handling EU personal data. The policy engine checks the deployment target—and if it points to a U.S. region, it fails the build. That's not just smart governance; it's protection from liability.

Even after deployment, CaC doesn't stop working [4]. Tools continuously monitor for drift—those subtle changes over time that can cause systems to fall out of compliance without anyone noticing. Some setups even autocorrect or quarantine violations.

Perhaps most important of all is the audit trail [4]. When policies are written in code and versioned like software, they become transparent and traceable. Auditors no longer have to rely on screenshots or intent statements. The organization can point to policy repositories, show their history, and demonstrate enforcement. That level of rigor changes the nature of compliance conversations—from defensive to confident.

For regulated industries, this shift is more than operational [4]. It's strategic. By turning compliance into code, organizations reduce risk, respond faster to legal changes, and make trust a product of the system—not just a process layered on top.

16.6 Evolution and Future Outlook

The rules around data aren't static—they are evolving quickly, shaped by technological shifts, global politics, and public anxiety around control [1]. Across the world, more governments are asserting ownership over their citizens' data. Sovereignty is no longer a fringe concern; it's moving to the center of digital strategy. Nations like Indonesia and Turkey are introducing tighter data laws, and wider geopolitical tension is only accelerating this trend.

At the same time, there's a countercurrent—initiatives like the G7's "Data Free Flow with Trust," which aim to preserve global data movement under shared safeguards [1]. Whether that model gains traction remains to be seen. Trust, after all, is harder to engineer than encryption.

Cloud vendors are caught in the middle, and they are adapting fast [2, 3]. Regional infrastructure is expanding. Strategic partnerships are becoming more common. Major providers are now offering contractual limits on foreign data access—partly in response to customer demands, but also to stay competitive. Sovereignty has become a feature, not just a legal box to tick [3].

What's striking is that new players are finding room to grow. European providers like OVHcloud and T Systems are no longer just niche alternatives—they're part of a reshaping market where legal alignment can matter as much as uptime or scale [3]. We're watching the global cloud split along geopolitical boundaries, and customers are increasingly buying based not only on what a platform does, but on whose laws it answers to.

For enterprise leaders, compliance has shifted from a back-office concern to a boardroom priority. The financial and reputational risks are too big to ignore [4]. This shift is also reflected in how teams are structured; roles like Chief Data Trust Officer are emerging to connect legal understanding with technical strategy [5, 6]. Still, there is a danger in overcorrecting. Overly restrictive localization policies can stifle growth and isolate innovation, a kind of digital nationalism that harms them more than it protects them [14].

Looking forward, international agreements could ease these tensions, especially if they offer mutual recognition of protection or build on past models like Privacy Shield. But if diplomacy lags, we may see an even deeper turn toward fragmented, country-first architectures.

This matters not just for business but for science. Disciplines like healthcare and AI rely on shared data, often across borders [11, 12, 14]. Without thoughtful exceptions or research-safe environments, localization rules could slow progress where it's needed the most. The healthcare sector faces challenges with data residency requirements that can impede critical medical research and patient care coordination [12, 14].

That said, enterprise buyers are not powerless. The same collective leverage that once pushed vendors on cybersecurity is now shaping cloud sovereignty [1]. And that pressure is working. The path ahead points to something more modular, more adaptable: not one cloud to rule them all, but many clouds tailored to the laws, needs, and risks of the places they serve [3]. For organizations that embrace this change, sovereignty can be more than a regulatory hurdle. It can be a differentiator of a sign of trust, resilience, and foresight in a fractured digital age [5].

16.6.1 Lessons Learned from Failed Implementations and Takeaways

Several high-profile failures in implementing data sovereignty and localization initiatives provide critical insights for organizations navigating global cloud compliance. Germany's "German Cloud" project with Deutsche Telekom, intended to create a fully sovereign infrastructure, was abandoned due to excessive costs and technical complexity [3]. This highlights the need for realistic designs that leverage global hyperscalers through local partnerships, as seen in France's SecNumCloud model. Meta's €1.2 billion fine in 2023 for noncompliant transatlantic data transfers under GDPR illustrates the severe financial and operational risks of underestimating legal scrutiny [2]. Continuous monitoring and CaC tools can prevent such oversights by automating regulatory checks. Public backlash in Sweden and Germany against U.S. cloud services for schools and municipalities, driven by CLOUD Act concerns, shows that ignoring public trust can derail projects [2]. Transparent data governance and local providers are essential to reassure stakeholders, particularly in sensitive sectors like healthcare. The Schrems II ruling disrupted companies reliant on U.S. providers, exposing the dangers of vendor lock-in [2]. Multicloud and federated trust strategies, like those explored in GAIA-X, enable organizations to pivot to compliant providers, reducing jurisdictional risks [3, 5, 6]. However, GAIA-X's slow progress due to complexity underscores the importance of interoperability to ensure scalable, cross-border collaboration [3]. Standards like SAML and OIDC support this by enabling secure data sharing. Mastercard's temporary market ban in India for failing to comply with RBI's payment data localization rules demonstrates the cost of delayed compliance [10]. Embedding sovereignty-aware architectures and DevSecOps practices from the start avoids costly retrofitting. These lessons emphasize that successful cloud strategies require foresight, flexibility, and integration of legal and technical priorities. Organizations must balance local compliance with global scalability, using modular designs and automated tools to stay agile.

16.7 Conclusion

Data privacy, sovereignty, and localization laws have become central to modern cloud computing. From GDPR to the CLOUD Act and China's PIPL to India's DPDP, governments are asserting control over data—forcing organizations to balance global cloud benefits with local legal constraints [7–9]. China's PIPL has introduced particularly stringent localization requirements and restrictions on cross-border data transfers [7, 8], while India's new data protection framework presents unique compliance challenges for multinational organizations [9]. The banking sector in India has faced specific challenges with overseas banks required to comply with local data storage mandates [10].

However, adaptation is underway. Finance, healthcare, and public sectors are adopting segmentation, encryption, multi-region strategies, and sovereign clouds to meet compliance goals [12, 13]. Notable examples include Apple's transition of iCloud services in China to state-controlled data centers to comply with local regulations [13].

Technologically, cloud architecture is shifting toward being compliance-native: sovereignty-aware deployments, compliance-as-code, federated multicloud models, and advanced encryption are now key design considerations [4–6]. These enable progress without sacrificing security or availability. "Compliance by design" is emerging as a core tenet of system architecture, alongside scalability and availability, with DevSecOps practices becoming essential for maintaining security throughout the development lifecycle [4].

To succeed, cloud stakeholders must foster legal-tech-business collaboration, anticipate policy shifts, and embed flexibility into systems [5, 6]. Concepts like federated trust and digital sovereignty may soon become industry standards [5, 6]. While driven by regulation, these trends are positively bringing better user protection and trust on a scale. As localization laws reshape cloud strategies, the next-generation challenge lies in building globally compliant, locally attuned systems [3]. Organizations that embrace compliance and sovereignty as integral, not obstructive, will lead. In the evolving digital landscape, the future is not cloud vs. sovereignty, but cloud with sovereignty.

References

1 Cloud Security Alliance, "How does data sovereignty impact multi-cloud security?," *CSA Blog*, Jan. 6, 2025. [Online]. Available: https://cloudsecurityalliance.org/blog/2025/01/06/global-data-sovereignty-a comparative-overview.

2 Gislen Software, "Are US cloud services an emerging risk for European companies?," 2025. [Online]. Available: https://www.gislen.com/us-cloud-services-emerging-risk/.

3 CDInsights, "Moving beyond GDPR: Embracing sovereign clouds and data localization for global compliance," 2024. [Online]. Available: https://www.clouddatainsights.com/moving-beyond-gdpr-embracing sovereign-clouds-and-data-localization-for-global-compliance/.

4 Qovery, "6 best practices for implementing devSecOps," *Qovery Blog*, 2019. [Online]. Available: https://www.qovery.com/blog/6-best-practices-for-implementing-devsecops/.

5 Springer, "A novel cloud management framework for trust establishment and federated cloud environments," *J. Supercomput.*, vol. 77, 2021. [Online]. Available: https://link.springer.com/article/10.1007/s11227-021-03775-8.

6 PublishOA, "Comprehensive trust based service selection model in federated cloud computing environment," 2022. [Online]. Available: https://publishoa.com/index.php/journal/article/download/200/182.

7 InCountry, "Data residency and cross-border transfers in China," *InCountry Blog*, 2023. [Online]. Available: https://incountry.com/blog/complete-guide-on-data-residency-and-cross-border-transfers-in-china/.

8 Cooley LLP, "Part 3: PIPL's localization requirements and restrictions on responding to foreign judicial and enforcement agencies," 2022. [Online]. Available: https://cdp.cooley.com/part-3-pipls-localization requirements-and-restrictions-on-responding-to-foreign-judicial-and-enforcement-agencies/.

9 Carnegie Endowment for International Peace," Understanding India's new data protection law," Oct. 2023. [Online]. Available: https://carnegieendowment.org/research/2023/10/understanding-indias-new data-protection-law?lang=en.

10 Business Standard, "IBA to take up overseas banks' local data storage issue with RBI," *Finance News*, Aug. 21, 2024. [Online]. Available: https://www.business-standard.com/finance/news/iba-to-take-up overseas-banks-local-data-storage-issue-with-rbi-124082101161_1.html.

11 Faegre Drinker, "U.S. protectionism in health data flows," *Publications & Insights*, Mar. 2024. [Online]. Available: https://www.faegredrinker.com/en/insights/publications/2024/3/us-protectionism-in-health data-flows.

12 InCountry, "Data residency in healthcare: Your complete guide," *InCountry Blog*, 2021. [Online]. Available: https://incountry.com/blog/data-residency-in-healthcare-your-complete-guide/.

13 Data Center Knowledge, "Apple's iCloud in China set to move to State-controlled data center," 2018. [Online]. Available: https://www.datacenterknowledge.com/cloud/apple-s-icloud-in-china-set-to-move to-s-tate-controlled-data-center.

14 Cato Institute, "How data localization restrictions hurt health care," *Regulation*, Winter 2024–2025. [Online]. Available: https://www.cato.org/regulation/winter-2024-2025/how-data-localization-restrictions hurt-health-care.

17

Sustainable Cloud Computing and Carbon-Aware Architectures

Vamsi Alla[1] *and Ashish Kattamuri*[2]

[1] *Independent Researcher, New York, NY, USA*
[2] *Independent Researcher, Denver, CO, USA*

17.1 Introduction

Cloud computing has transformed how organizations across the industry can access and use computing resources, with unprecedented scalability, flexibility, and cost efficiency. From managing global e-commerce platforms and artificial intelligence (AI) models to supporting healthcare systems and smart cities, cloud computing has become the backbone of the digital economy. This transformation is driven by advances in virtualization technologies, multicore processors, high-speed networks, and hyperscale data center architectures.

Besides these benefits, however, there is a growing ecological footprint. Datacenters, the physical infrastructure supporting cloud computing, are very energy-intensive, with demand for energy rising significantly in the coming years. Estimates suggest that in 2025 data centers can consume up to 20% of the world's power, driven by the proliferation of energy-intensive workloads such as AI training, big data analytics, and Internet of Things (IoT) implementations. The CO_2 emissions of this energy use directly contribute to global climate change, thus enhancing the need for sustainable cloud computing practices.

The environmental impact comes from several sources: the constant operation of servers, storage, and network equipment; the significant energy needs of cooling systems (which can account for up to 40% of the total energy consumption of data centers); and the carbon intensity of electricity sources, much of which are still heavily dependent on fossil fuels such as coal and natural gas. At the same time, the production and disposal of hardware components contributes to the depletion of resources and electronic waste.

Driven by regulatory pressure, market demand, and corporate responsibility, leading cloud providers are adopting increasingly sustainable practices. Governments have introduced carbon taxes, emission ceilings, and sustainability certifications such as Leadership in Energy and Environmental Design (LEED), while large technology companies have set aggressive carbon-neutral and net-zero targets. Moreover, a growing number of consumers and entrepreneurs prefer environmentally responsible technology suppliers, creating strong market incentives for sustainable innovation.

This chapter presents a comprehensive study of sustainable cloud computing, focusing on architectural, technological, and operational strategies to reduce the carbon footprint of cloud services while maintaining performance and scalability. The chapter furthermore examines the role of emerging innovations such as carbon-conscious planning, AI-driven energy optimization, and edge computing as enabling for a more sustainable digital infrastructure. The overall system architecture is illustrated in Figure 17.1. Each module interacts through well-defined application programming interfaces (APIs), ensuring scalability and modularity.

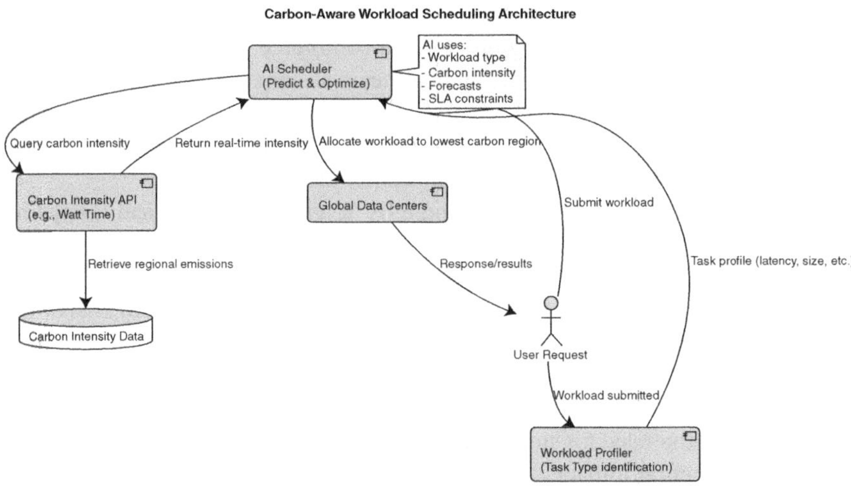

Figure 17.1 Carbon-Aware Workload Scheduling System. This diagram illustrates a carbon-aware architecture where an AI scheduler classifies workloads and dynamically routes them to data centers with the lowest carbon intensity based on real-time data retrieved via APIs like WattTime.

17.2 Evolution of Cloud Computing: The Foundation for Sustainability

The modern concept of cloud computing has evolved over several decades, coming from early time-sharing systems in the 1960s, allowing multiple users to share mainframe computing resources [1, 2]. This was followed in the 1990s by grid computing, allowing distributed resources for scientific research and large-scale data processing tasks to be shared. However, the real inflection point came in the early 2000s with the advent of virtualization technologies such as VMware, allowing multiple virtual machines to operate simultaneously on the same physical hardware, drastically improving resource usage.

The commercial launch of Amazon Web Services (AWS) in 2006 marked the beginning of cloud computing as a scalable, on-demand utility, allowing organizations to use computing resources as services via Infrastructure-as-a-Service (IaaS), Platform-as-a-Service (PaaS), and Software-as-a-Service (SaaS) models. Hyperscale cloud providers, such as AWS, Google Cloud, and Microsoft Azure, now operate global networks of data centers that support billions of users across applications ranging from healthcare, finance, e-commerce, and AI to smart city infrastructures.

Although these technological developments have changed IT capabilities, they have also caused an exponential increase in energy consumption. The rise of AI, big data, and IoT has further strengthened these demands. For example, AI model training may require enormous computing power, sometimes using as much energy as several transatlantic flights for a single training.

As data centers scale in size and complexity, the corresponding ecological footprint has grown. Estimates suggest that global data centers consumed around 200 terawatt hours (TWh) of electricity by 2020, a figure similar to the energy consumption of some medium-sized countries [15]. Without proactive intervention, cloud services growth can significantly hamper global efforts to meet carbon reduction targets. Thus, sustainability has emerged as a critical and urgent consideration in the evolution of cloud computing. Figure 17.2 depicts the historical progression of cloud computing technologies toward sustainability. Beginning with shared mainframes in the 1960s, followed by grid computing, virtualization, and hyperscale cloud infrastructures, the field has advanced into the era of AI-driven, carbon-aware clouds and emerging quantum computing platforms in the 2020s.

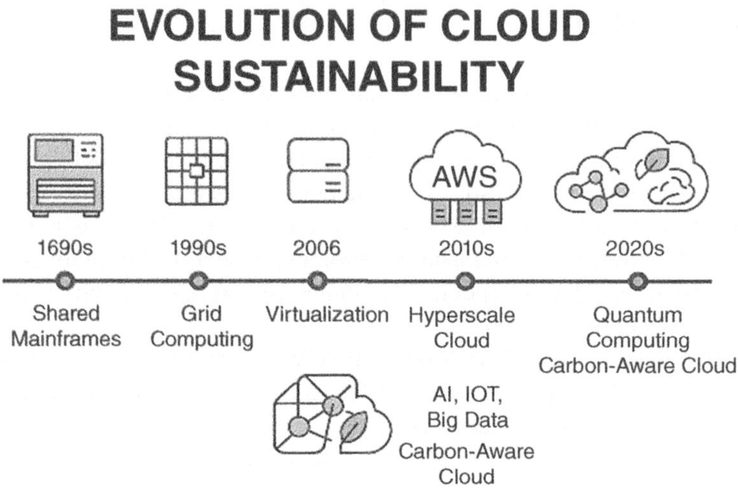

Figure 17.2 Evolution of cloud sustainability.

17.3 Principles of Sustainable Cloud Computing

An integrated set of principles meant to reduce the environmental impact of data centers while maintaining the scalability, dependability, and performance the cloud provides is sustainable cloud computing [8]. Five fundamental ideas that direct environmentally friendly cloud architecture design are described in this part. Figure 17.3 presents the five core design principles that form the foundation of sustainable cloud computing. These include energy efficiency, renewable energy integration, carbon-aware scheduling, edge computing, and serverless architecture, each contributing to minimizing environmental impact while maintaining cloud performance and scalability.

17.3.1 Energy Efficiency

Hardware and system-level energy efficiency gains provide the most direct approach to cut energy consumption [5, 13, 14]. Compared to conventional ×86 architectures, modern advanced RISC machine (ARM)-based CPUs like Amazon's Graviton series offer up to 40% better power economy. Furthermore, solid-state drive (SSDs) are ideal for data-intensive tasks, which use much less power than conventional hard disk drives (HDDs) because they lack mechanical components.

Further improving energy efficiency are advanced cooling technologies. For instance, two-phase immersion cooling, which submerges servers in dielectric

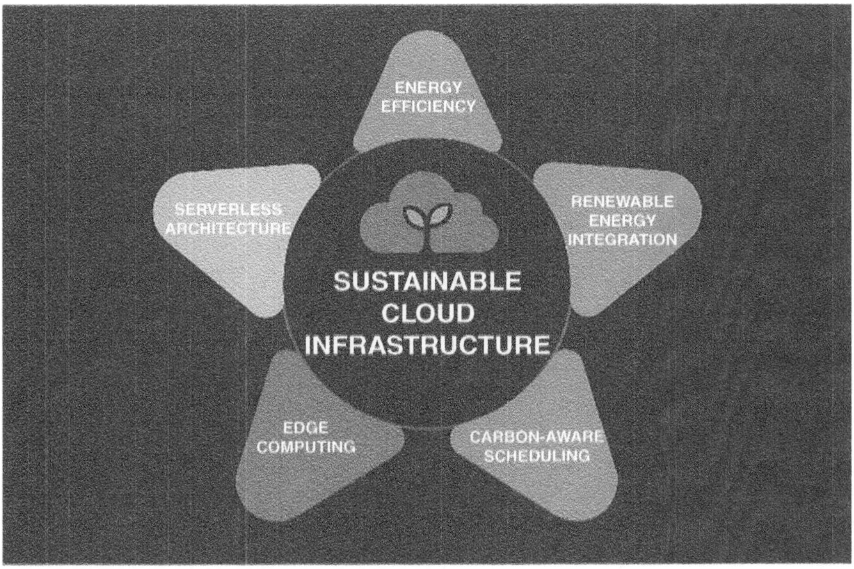

Figure 17.3 Core principles of sustainability.

fluids to dissipate heat, can cut cooling energy by up to 58% relative to conventional air-based cooling systems [16]. These developments minimize thermal stress, thus extending server life and lowering running costs.

17.3.2 Renewable Energy Integration

Reducing the carbon footprint of cloud computing mostly depends on finding energy from renewable sources, including hydroelectric power, solar, and wind. To guarantee long-term renewable energy supplies, big cloud providers are turning more and more to power purchase agreements (PPAs). For its worldwide data center operations, Google has, for example, attained 100% renewable energy matching by means of a mix of PPAs and on-site renewable installations [3].

To handle the intermittent character of renewables, energy storage options, including flow batteries and lithium-ion, are absolutely vital. Real-time switching between renewable and grid-based power sources made possible by smart grid technologies optimizes both cost and environmental performance.

17.3.3 Carbon-Aware Scheduling

Using real-time data on carbon intensity—measured as grams of CO_2 per kilowatt-hour (gCO_2/kWh)—carbon-aware workload scheduling maximizes the spatial placement of tasks. By means of energy grid data, weather patterns,

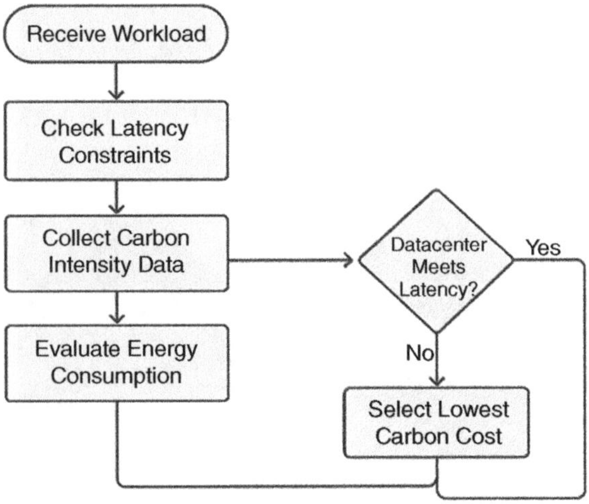

Figure 17.4 Carbon-aware workload scheduling algorithm.

and time-of-day variables, AI-driven algorithms forecast variations in carbon intensity; hence, cloud providers can dynamically move nonlatency-sensitive workloads (e.g., batch processing and model training) to areas with lower carbon footprints [6, 9, 10]. Recent advances in machine learning (ML)-based forecasting have improved prediction accuracy by 35% [17], enabling more effective integration with renewable energy availability.

Studies indicate that, without compromising service quality, carbon-aware scheduling can cut emissions by up to 30%. The flowchart in Figure 17.4 demonstrates the decision-making process of the carbon-aware workload scheduler. The system receives incoming workloads, checks latency constraints, retrieves real-time carbon intensity data, evaluates energy consumption, and selects the optimal data center that either satisfies the latency requirement or minimizes carbon emissions.

17.3.4 Edge Computing

Edge computing lowers the energy needed for long-distance data flows to centralized cloud data centers by processing data nearer to its source. Applications like autonomous cars, IoT-enabled smart grids, and real-time video analytics—all of which depend on latency—especially benefit from this approach.

For IoT-based traffic management, Singapore's smart city project showed, for instance, that edge computing lowered energy consumption by 25% by locally handling analytics.

17.3.5 Serverless Architecture

Models of serverless computing minimize energy waste by allocating resources only when code is run, so lowering idle server times. Dynamic scaling—where computing resources are automatically provisioned and deprovisioned depending on demand—is made possible by platforms including AWS Lambda and Azure Functions. Because of its elasticity, serverless architecture is especially suited for sporadic or event-driven workloads, so it optimizes resources and efficiency. The flowchart in Figure 17.5 illustrates the decision-making process for carbon-aware workload scheduling in cloud environments. The algorithm receives a workload along with its latency constraints, evaluates the available data centers based on their real-time carbon intensity and estimated energy consumption, and filters out data centers that do not meet latency requirements. Among the feasible data centers, the one with the minimum carbon cost is selected for workload execution. This approach enables dynamic optimization of energy consumption and carbon emissions while maintaining the quality of service (QoS). The regional readiness for sustainable data center deployment is summarized in Table 17.1.

Table 17.1 compares different regions based on their renewable energy availability, cooling system constraints, infrastructure maturity, and estimated cost of sustainable cloud deployments. It highlights the geographic disparities and readiness for adopting green cloud technologies.

17.4 Core Frameworks for Sustainable Cloud Computing

Integrated sets of frameworks combining energy-efficient hardware, renewable energy sources, intelligent workload scheduling, distributed computing paradigms, and adaptive resource allocation define sustainable cloud computing. Here we give a succinct and useful summary of the main frameworks forming the technical basis for sustainable cloud ecosystems.

17.4.1 Cooling Systems and Energy-Efficient Hardware

One of the most direct tools for lowering the total carbon footprint of cloud data centers is still energy efficiency at the hardware and infrastructure level.

17.4.1.1 ARM-Based Approach

For some workloads, including web hosting, ML inference, and microservices-based applications, modern ARM architectures—such as Amazon's Graviton series—offer up to 40% better power efficiency than conventional ×86 CPUs,

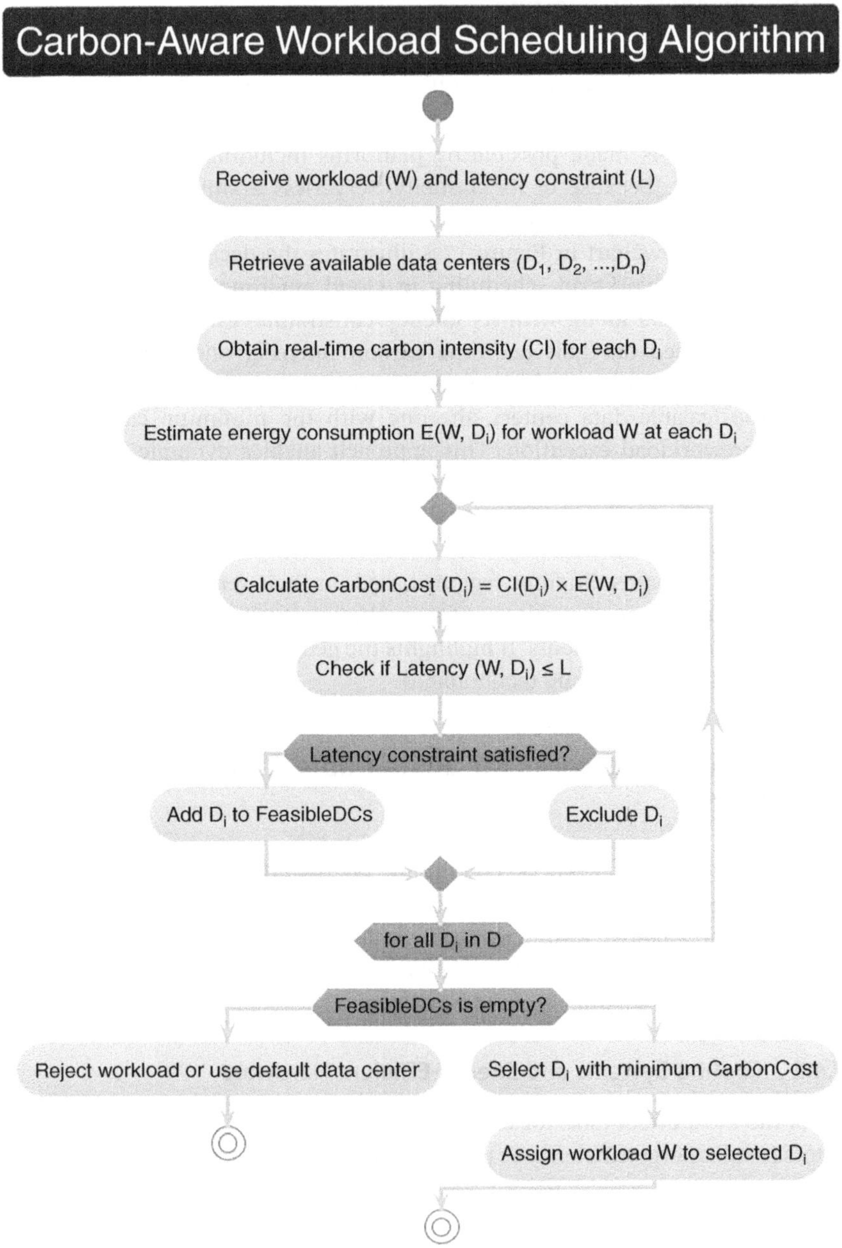

Figure 17.5 Carbon-aware workload scheduling algorithm.

Table 17.1 Regional sustainability readiness for cloud infrastructure.

Region	Renewable Energy Share	Cooling Constraints	Infrastructure Readiness	Cost of Deployment
Scandinavia	High	Low	High	Medium
Southeast Asia	Low	High	Medium	High
North America	Medium	Medium	High	Medium

thus saving considerable energy. Reduced instruction set computing (RISC) by ARM simplifies operations, thus enabling low power consumption even while maintaining high performance.

17.4.1.2 SSDs, or Solid-State Drives

Energy economy has been even more improved by the change from spinning HDDs to SSDs. Particularly for high-performance data processing, AI training, and big data analytics, SSDs offer better I/O performance and longer hardware lifespans than HDDs and consume up to 50% less energy.

Ideal for AI and ML workloads, energy-efficient graphics processing units (GPUs)—such as NVIDIA's A100 series—integrate tensor cores and optimized memory subsystems to offer high computational density with low power consumption, so reducing their impact.

17.4.1.3 Advanced Cooling Solutions

Cooling accounts for up to 40% of total data center energy consumption. Table 17.2 compares the major cooling technologies used in modern data centers. New cooling methods, including

Table 17.2 Comparison of data center cooling technologies.

Cooling Technology	Energy Savings	Water Usage	Cost	Ideal Use Cases
Air cooling	Low	Medium	Low	General use
Liquid cooling	Medium	High	Medium	High-density racks
Immersion cooling	High (up to 58%)	None	High	Hyperscale + AI workloads
Free cooling	Varies (up to 25%)	Low	Low	Cold regions

- **Two-Phase Immersion Cooling:** Submerging servers in dielectric fluids allows heat dissipation without mechanical air circulation, yielding up to 58% cooling energy reduction [16].
- **Liquid Cooling:** Circulating coolants directly to server components, reducing cooling energy by 20–30%.
- **Free Cooling:** Leveraging ambient outdoor temperatures to cool systems, especially effective in colder climates.
- These approaches contribute to both operational efficiency and long-term cost reduction.

Table 17.2 compares common cooling strategies in terms of energy savings, water usage, cost, and use cases, highlighting trade-offs for sustainable cloud infrastructure design.

17.4.2 Integrated Renewable Energy

The foundation of cloud sustainability is switching data center power sources from fossil fuels to renewable energy sources.

17.4.2.1 PPAs

PPAs allow cloud companies, including Google, Microsoft, and Facebook (Meta), to lock in long-term access to wind, solar, and hydroelectric power. Combining on-site renewable generation with PPAs, Google has matched 100% renewable energy globally.

17.4.2.2 On-Site Renewable Installations

Where land and resources allow, providers directly integrate solar panels or wind turbines right at the data center site, producing power locally and so lowering transmission losses.

17.4.2.3 Methods of Energy Storage

Since renewable sources are sporadic, energy storage is crucial:

- Mostly used for temporary energy storage are lithium-ion batteries.
- Rising as a scalable substitute for big data centers are flow batteries.
- Experimental hydrogen storage: possibility for long-term storage to fill in seasonal production gaps.

17.4.2.4 Dynamic Load Balancing and Smart Grids

Real-time data on energy availability, pricing, and carbon intensity made available by smart grid technologies lets dynamic switching between renewable and grid sources maximize both cost and emissions. Figure 17.6 illustrates the integration

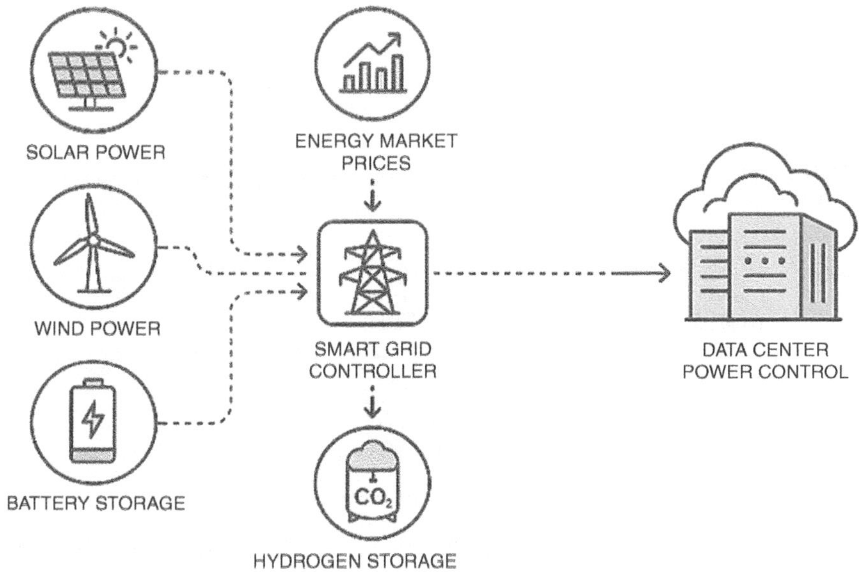

Figure 17.6 Smart grid-enabled power management for sustainable data centers.

of multiple renewable energy sources and storage solutions through a smart grid controller to manage data center power consumption. The smart grid dynamically balances inputs from solar, wind, battery, and hydrogen storage based on energy market prices, ensuring optimized power delivery to data centers while minimizing carbon emissions.

17.4.3 Carbon-Aware Workload Scheduling

Workload scheduling with carbon awareness dynamically directs tasks to data centers run on the cleanest energy source at any one moment, thus optimizing task placement.

- **Real-time Carbon Intensity Monitoring:** APIs like WattTime or ElectricityMap allow each area to have gCO_2/kWh data obtained.
- **Workload Profiling:** The projected energy demand of every workload is profiled, enabling precise carbon cost calculations [9, 10].
- **Nonlatency-Sensitive Workloads:** such as batch processing or AI model training—are moved to greener data centers, while latency-sensitive chores remain near end users.
- **Benefits:** While preserving service quality, carbon-aware scheduling can produce emission cuts of 20–30% across multiregional cloud infrastructures.

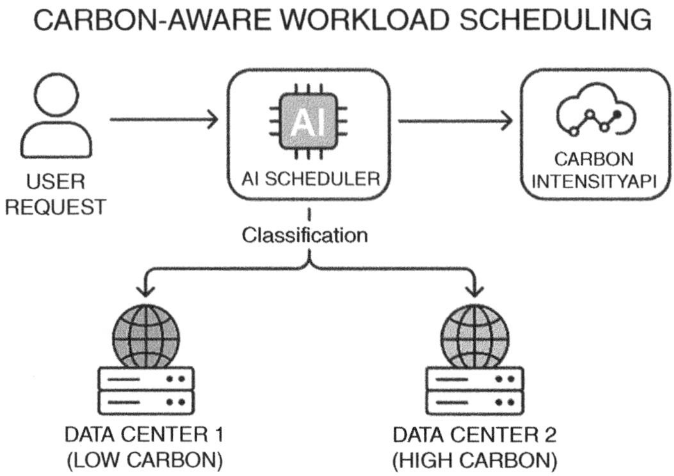

Figure 17.7 Carbon-aware workload scheduling architecture.

Figure 17.7 demonstrates the carbon-aware workload scheduling system. User requests are processed by an AI scheduler, which queries real-time carbon intensity data via APIs (such as WattTime or ElectricityMap). Based on this data, workloads are classified and dynamically allocated to either low-carbon or high-carbon data centers to minimize emissions while maintaining performance.

17.4.4 Edge Computing for Sustainability

By processing data closer to its point of origin, edge computing reduces the energy consumption related to data transfer.

- Local processing of IoT sensor data, video analytics, or real-time control systems avoids the energy costs of long-haul data movement.
- Edge nodes often run ARM CPUs or specialized low-power AI chips (e.g., NVIDIA Jetson Nano), consuming between 10 and 50 watts per node.
- Local computation guarantees responsiveness for important uses, including autonomous cars, smart cities, and healthcare monitoring, so improving latency and performance.

17.4.4.1 Use Case Example

Edge nodes at intersections allow Singapore's smart city traffic control system to lower energy consumption by 25% while simultaneously increasing traffic flow efficiency.

17.4.5 Serverless Architectures

By dynamically allocating and deallocating computing resources on-demand, serverless computing lets cloud providers save energy lost on idle servers.

17.4.5.1 Key Features

- **Dynamic Scaling:** Based on workload demand, automatically scales based on functions executed just upon trigger.
- **Idle Resource Elimination:** Virtual elimination of idle server capacity drastically reduces energy consumption.
- **Serverless Workloads** can be sent to greener data centers depending on real-time carbon data in line with carbon-aware scheduling.

  For instance, AWS Lambda lets event-driven apps automatically scale to zero when idle, saving up to 30% energy for erratic workloads, including dynamic web services or IoT telemetry processing.

Figures 17.8a ("AI-Driven Optimization for Sustainability") and 17.8b ("AI-Powered Energy Optimization Pipeline") are original conceptual diagrams

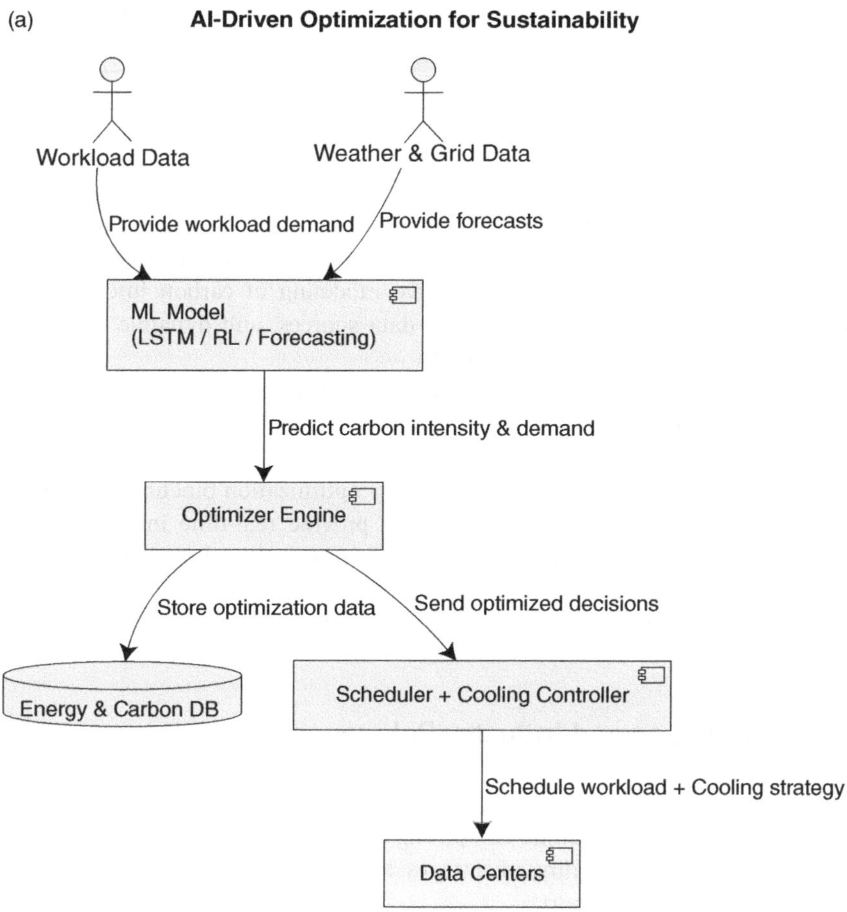

Figure 17.8 (a) AI-driven optimization for sustainability. (b) AI-powered energy optimization pipeline.

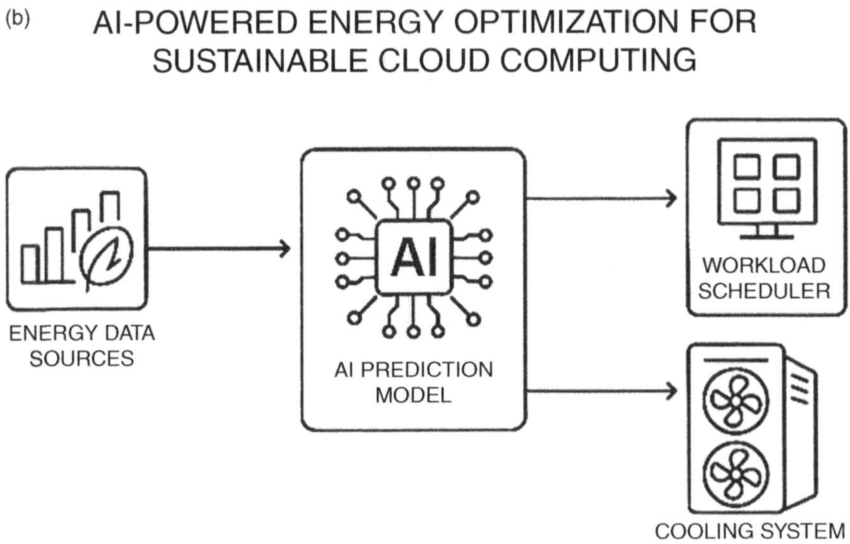

Figure 17.8 (*Continued*)

that I personally generated for this chapter. They were created specifically to visually summarize and clarify the AI-driven energy optimization process described in the text, including predictive modeling of carbon intensity and energy demand, integration of real-time data sources, and dynamic control of workload scheduling and cooling systems.

A pipeline showing how ML models predict energy demand and carbon intensity, feeding decisions into workload schedulers and cooling systems to minimize energy consumption and emissions.

The diagram depicts the AI-powered energy optimization pipeline for sustainable cloud computing. Energy data sources provide real-time information on consumption and carbon intensity, which feeds into AI-based predictive models. These models optimize workload scheduling and data center cooling systems simultaneously, reducing both energy consumption and carbon emissions.

17.5 Use Cases and Industry Relevance

Leading cloud vendors' real-world installations show how effectively the ideas and frameworks of sustainable cloud computing can be applied at scale. Selected case studies illustrating the viability, advantages, and variety of sustainable cloud solutions are presented in this part.

17.5.1 Google's Data Centers Carbon-Neutral

By aggressively seeking renewable energy procurement, carbon-aware scheduling, and AI-driven energy optimization, Google has emerged globally in sustainable cloud operations.

17.5.1.1 Integration of Renewable Energy

Google has matched 100% of its data center energy consumption worldwide since 2017 by means of long-term PPAs with wind, solar, and hydroelectric energy producers [3]. Annually, its worldwide data center fleet runs totally on carbon-free energy.

17.5.1.2 AI-Driven Enhancement

Google used AI-powered systems, working with DeepMind, to maximize data center cooling. These AI models lowered cooling energy consumption by 40% by forecasting server load and temperature swings. Along with lowering emissions, this improves equipment lifetime and operational effectiveness.

17.5.1.3 Using Real-Time Carbon Intensity Data

Google's carbon-aware computing platform dynamically schedules flexible workloads, including ML model training and batch processing, to data centers where the carbon footprint is lowest at any one moment. With this strategy, Google has been able to lower total carbon emissions while keeping high service performance for users all across Google Cloud, Gmail, and YouTube.

17.5.1.4 Scalability

Google's approach shows how integrated, multipronged strategies can enable large-scale hyperscale data center operations to attain both environmental sustainability and economic viability.

17.5.2 Project Natick from Microsoft: Underwater Data Centers

Using modular architecture and ocean-based cooling, Microsoft's Project Natick offers a creative method of sustainable data center design.

- Project Natick calls for the ocean floor to be home for sealed data center modules [4]. By removing the need for conventional heating, ventilation, and air conditioning (HVAC) systems and so lowering cooling energy consumption, seawater's natural cooling qualities help.
- Near offshore wind and tidal energy sources power the underwater data centers, lowering running emissions and optimizing local renewable energy availability.

- Underwater environments offer further advantages, including stable operating temperatures, seismic activity protection, and low maintenance needs. Compared to conventional land-based data centers, the pilot project noted a 35% total decrease in energy usage.

17.5.2.1 Modular Scalability

Project Natick opens new frontiers in sustainable cloud infrastructure by showcasing the possibilities of modular, transportable data center designs that may be quickly implemented in coastal areas with plenty of renewable energy.

17.5.3 IoT Edge Deployment Smart City Singapore

The smart city effort of Singapore shows how well edge computing can lower energy consumption while supporting real-time data processing requirements for urban infrastructure.

17.5.3.1 Edge Computing Adoption

Major traffic junctures and transit hubs house micro-data centers and edge nodes. These local real-time traffic sensor data processing nodes reduce long-distance data transfer to central cloud data centers.

17.5.3.2 Energy Savings

Processing data at the edge allowed Singapore's system to estimate 25% lower total energy consumption for traffic management tasks than more traditional centralized processing models.

17.5.3.3 Latency and Efficiency Gains

Local processing lets traffic control systems react in real-time to dynamic road conditions, thus improving traffic flow, lowering congestion, and reducing emissions from idle cars.

17.5.3.4 Scalability

The architecture shows the wider relevance of edge computing to sustainable urban ecosystems since it is quite scalable and flexible for other smart city services, including public safety, environmental monitoring, and energy grid management.

17.6 Difficulties and Future Vision

Although sustainable cloud computing is becoming more and more important, widespread adoption still suffers several ongoing obstacles. Realizing the full possible value of carbon-neutral and carbon-aware cloud ecosystems will depend on overcoming these obstacles.

17.6.1 Technical Difficulties

Retrofitting Historic Infrastructure: Many of the current data centers were not first intended with sustainability in mind. Retrofitting these buildings with advanced cooling systems, renewable energy integration, and energy-efficient hardware sometimes calls for major capital investment, operational downtime, and specialized knowledge. Figure 17.8 contrasts typical limitations of legacy data centers—such as old cooling systems, inefficient hardware, and limited renewable integration—with sustainable retrofitting upgrades. These include immersion cooling, ARM-based processors, SSD storage, and carbon-aware scheduling to significantly improve energy efficiency and reduce environmental impact (Figure 17.9).

Performance-Sustainability Trade-offs: Juggling energy economy with QoS can be challenging. Applications including real-time analytics, gaming, and financial transactions that are latency-sensitive—that is, those that cannot tolerate workload shifting across far-off low-carbon data centers without compromising user experience—may not survive.

Intermittency of Renewable Energy: Renewable energy generation by wind and solar sources is intrinsically erratic and calls for clever storage and smart grid solutions to guarantee ongoing operation. Large-scale battery storage or hydrogen storage systems are still technically difficult and expensive to develop and implement.

Data Standardization: Globally, carbon-aware scheduling is complicated by inconsistent measurement and reporting of carbon intensity across different

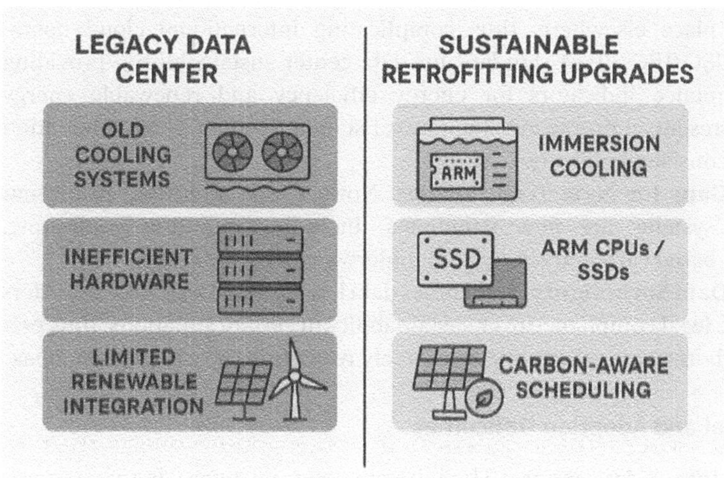

Figure 17.9 Retrofitting legacy data centers for sustainable cloud computing.

areas [7]. Although sites like WattTime and ElectricityMap offer useful information, universal standardization is still lacking.

17.6.2 Financial Difficulties

High Upfront Costs: Changing to sustainable infrastructure usually calls for large upfront expenditures in renewable energy procurement, storage, cooling retrofits, and specialized hardware. Smaller cloud providers and developing nations with limited funds particularly find this challenging.

Operational Complexity: Sustainability projects sometimes call for advanced predictive algorithms, new monitoring tools, and specialized experts, adding to operational complexity and staffing challenges.

Geographic Equity: Variations in regional availability of renewable energy lead to disparities in deployment viability. Providers in hydro-rich areas like Scandinavia, for example, can reach carbon neutrality more quickly than those running grids elsewhere dominated by fossil fuels. Solutions include federated carbon-aware scheduling systems that coordinate workloads across multiple regions, leveraging cross-border renewable energy partnerships, and developing hybrid infrastructures that capitalize on each region's unique renewable strengths—whether solar in desert regions or geothermal in volcanic zones.

17.6.3 Policy and Legal Difficulties

Lack of Global Standards: Fragmented compliance needs result from the absence of globally harmonized sustainability policies. While policies like Europe's Green Deal demand carbon neutrality [12], similar rules might not be in place elsewhere, thus complicating international cloud operations. The ISO/IEC 30134 standard for data center sustainability—providing key performance indicators for energy efficiency and renewable energy factor—represents a promising step toward standardization, though adoption remains inconsistent globally.

Regulatory Gaps for New Technologies: Not yet fully addressed in present regulatory systems are new paradigms, including quantum computing, blockchain-based carbon tracking, and underwater data centers.

Conflicts in Data Sovereignty: Sometimes data localization rules force providers to prioritize legal compliance over sustainability in certain situations, thus preventing carbon-aware scheduling from freely relocating tasks to greener areas.

17.6.4 Social and Adoption Difficulties

Limited Customer Awareness: Though consumer awareness is rising, many business customers still give cost, performance, and service availability top priority over sustainability when choosing cloud providers.

Skills Gap: Operating advanced sustainable infrastructure calls on knowledge in AI optimization, renewable energy systems, smart grids, and modular design—skills still rather rare in the global workforce.

Public Opposition to Increase of Data Centers: Particularly in environmentally sensitive areas, community opposition to new data center projects can surface over issues including land use, water consumption, or visual impacts.

17.7 Sustainable Cloud Computing's Prospect

Driven by fast technological innovation, changing regulatory frameworks, and increasing society demand for environmentally responsible solutions, the long-term view for sustainable cloud computing is quite positive despite these obstacles.

Figure 17.10 presents a fully integrated AI-powered system for optimizing sustainable cloud data center operations. The AI engine forecasts energy consumption, carbon intensity, and cooling loads, which are then fed into workload scheduling optimizers. The data center controller manages both workload

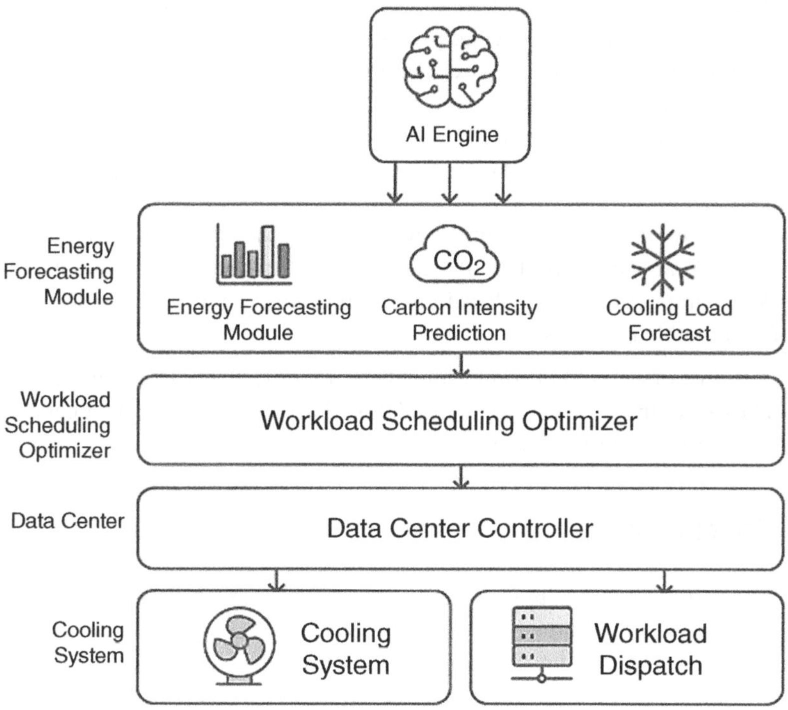

Figure 17.10 Full AI-integrated sustainable cloud computing architecture.

dispatch and cooling systems based on AI-driven predictions, thereby minimizing energy use and environmental impact while maintaining optimal performance.

Novel Technologies: Quantum computing promises energy efficiency through algorithmic advantage, solving complex optimization problems with exponentially fewer steps than classical computers. For example, quantum algorithms can optimize energy grid management and resource allocation tasks using a fraction of the computational resources. However, quantum systems face significant challenges, including extreme cooling requirements, hardware instability, and high error rates that currently limit practical deployment. Energy optimization driven by AI will keep improving how resources are used and workload is placed. Blockchain enables transparent carbon tracking through tokenized carbon credits, where each credit represents a verified carbon reduction or offset with an immutable digital record. For instance, Microsoft's sustainability cloud uses blockchain to track and verify Renewable Energy Certificates (RECs). Yet blockchain itself presents a sustainability paradox due to its energy-intensive consensus mechanisms, and concerns remain regarding the verification standards of the carbon offsets being tokenized.

Aligning Global Policy: Growing interest from organizations like the United Nations and the International Energy Agency, as well as international accords like the Paris Agreement, could help to standardize carbon accounting and encourage sustainable infrastructure spending [12].

Sector Cooperation: By means of cooperative initiatives such as the Open Compute Project [11] and Carbon Disclosure Project [7], knowledge sharing and standardizing across industry players is being encouraged, hastening the spread of best practices.

Consumer-driven transformation: Cloud providers who show clear leadership in environmental responsibility will acquire competitive advantages as sustainability keeps impacting buying decisions, so promote even industry-wide adoption of sustainable practices.

In the end, sustainable cloud computing offers not only an environmental need but also a business and innovation potential, one that will define the next generation of digital infrastructure even more.

17.8 Conclusion

Powering everything from AI to healthcare, finance, and smart cities, cloud computing keeps transforming how businesses and societies use technologies. Its fast spread does, however, also have major environmental consequences, especially with regard to energy consumption and greenhouse gas emissions. Dealing with the sustainability of cloud infrastructure has become a top concern as the world's digital needs keep rising.

Emphasizing the need for a multifarious approach that combines energy-efficient hardware, renewable energy sourcing, AI-driven workload scheduling, edge computing, and serverless architectures, this chapter has presented a thorough review of sustainable cloud computing and carbon-aware architectures. Real-world case studies of top providers, including Google, Microsoft, and Singapore's smart city project, clearly show that the technical routes to a more sustainable cloud already exist and are practically usable.

Still, complete realization of sustainable cloud computing calls for coordinated efforts across several spheres: overcoming technical, financial, legal, and social constraints; creating worldwide standards for carbon accounting; encouraging industry-wide cooperation; and acquiring the required knowledge to run ever more complex infrastructure. New technologies, including blockchain-based carbon tracking, AI optimization, and quantum computing, provide still another way to lower the carbon footprint of digital infrastructure.

In the end, sustainable cloud computing presents a larger ethical and financial possibility as much as a technological one. It presents the cloud sector as a vital ally in reaching world climate targets while still producing transforming digital innovation. Driven by persistent dedication from researchers, legislators, business leaders, and consumers, cloud computing can develop into a highly efficient, ethical, and planet-aware infrastructure, promoting both economic growth and environmental stewardship in the next decades.

References

1 B. R. Badrinath, A. V. Vasilakos, and K. C. Lan, "Cloud computing: A technology overview," *IEEE Internet Comput.*, vol. 20, no. 3, pp. 11–14, 2016.

2 R. Buyya, C. Vecchiola, and S. T. Selvi, *Mastering Cloud Computing: Foundations and Applications Programming*. Morgan Kaufmann, Melbourne, Australia, 2013.

3 Google, "Google sustainability report 2023," 2025. [Online]. Available: https://sustainability.google/reports.

4 Microsoft, "Project Natick: Microsoft's underwater datacenter," *Microsoft*, 2020. [Online]. Available: https://natick.research.microsoft.com.

5 J. Hamilton, "Cooperative Expendable micro-Slice Servers (CEMS): Low cost, low power servers for Internet-Scale services," in *Proc. Conf. Innovat. Data Syst. Res. (CIDR)*, Asilomar, California, USA, Jan. 4–7, 2009. Available: http://www.cidrdb.org.

6 S. Gandhi, A. Singh, R. P. Mahajan, A. Adya, and E. V. Carrera, "Carbon-aware load balancing for geo-distributed cloud services," *Proc. ACM SIGCOMM*, vol. 42, no. 4, pp. 551–564, 2012.

7 The Carbon Disclosure Project (CDP), "Global carbon accounting standards for data centers," *CDP Report*, 2021. Available: https://guidance.cdp.net.

8 T. J. O'Reilly, "Sustainable cloud computing," *IEEE Cloud Comput.*, vol. 6, no. 3, pp. 4–9, 2019.

9 ElectricityMap, "Real-time carbon intensity data platform," [Online]. Available: www.electricitymap.org.

10 WattTime, "Automated emissions reduction API," [Online]. Available: www.watttime.org.

11 Open Compute Project (OCP), "Energy efficient data center design guidelines," 2021. [Online]. Available: www.opencompute.org.

12 The European Commission, "European green deal: Climate-neutral data centers," 2020. [Online]. Available: https://ec.europa.eu/clima.

13 Y. Chen, A. Das, W. Qin, A. Sivasubramaniam, Q. Wang, and N. Gautam, "Managing server energy and operational costs in hosting centers," *ACM SIGMETRICS Perform. Eval. Rev.*, vol. 33, no. 1, pp. 303–314, 2005.

14 D. C. Snowdon, E. Le Sueur, S. Ruocco, and G. Heiser, "Koala: A platform for OS-level power management," *Proc. EuroSys Conf.*, pp. 289–302, 2009.

15 J. Koomey, "Growth in data center electricity use 2005 to 2010," *Analytics Press Report*, 2011. Available: https://alejandrobarros.com/wp-content/uploads/old/4363/Growth_in_Data_Center_Electricity_use_2005_to_2010.pdf.

16 Y. Zhang, Y. Bi, X. Zhang, and L. Chen, "A two-phase liquid immersion cooling strategy utilizing vapor chamber heat spreader for data center servers," *ResearchGate*, 2022. [Online]. Available: https://www.researchgate.net/publication/358903004.

17 W. Olabiyi, "Case Studies: Successful Applications of Machine Learning in Renewable Energy Forecasting," Aug. 2023. [Online]. Available: https://www.researchgate.net/publication/384260901_Case_Studies_Successful_Applications_of_Machine_Learning_in_Renewable_Energy_Forecasting.

18

Quantum Computing in the Cloud: Opportunities and Challenges

Ashwin Prakash Nalwade[1] *and Khan Shariya Hasan Upoma*[2]

[1] *AI Research Pythia, Seattle, WA, USA*
[2] *Independent Researcher, Dhaka, Bangladesh*

18.1 Introduction

Quantum computers can significantly outperform classical machines on specific computational problems [1]. For tasks like unstructured search, quantum simulation of physical systems, and factorization of integers, quantum devices offer profound computational speed-ups (Grover's algorithm, Shor's algorithm) that could disrupt fields from cryptography to drug discovery.

However, today's quantum hardware suffers from issues like limitations on qubit counts, short-lived coherence times, significant error rates, and gate fidelity issues. These limitations have led to the Noisy Intermediate-Scale Quantum (NISQ) era, defined by quantum processors containing between 50 and 1,000 qubits but insufficient error correction to perform fault-tolerant computations [2]. These constraints are increasingly mitigated through "Quantum-as-a-Service" (QaaS) platforms, which offer optimized access to quantum hardware, hybrid workflows, and error mitigation tools.

The cloud has emerged as an enabler of QaaS. This model virtualizes access to quantum hardware and simulators over the internet, often through API-driven interfaces and hybrid quantum-classical frameworks. *Amazon [AWS] Braket*, *IBM Quantum Platform*, and *Microsoft Azure Quantum* are prominent examples, providing quantum backends alongside high-performance classical coprocessing. This decouples quantum experimentation from physical hardware ownership, similar to the early days of Amazon EC2 for classical computing.

Furthermore, cloud integration facilitates collaboration across global research teams, provides seamless scalability for quantum simulations, and enables continuous benchmarking of quantum processors under realistic workloads [3]. It also introduces new research problems around quantum resource scheduling, remote execution latency, cross-platform quantum software abstraction, and the development of cloud-native quantum programming languages [4]. This chapter explores quantum computing in the cloud as a driver of accessible, scalable innovation, highlighting both the opportunities it presents and the challenges that must be addressed.

18.2 Background

Quantum computers need quantum circuits, gates, and design diagrams to work, just like regular computers need classical circuits. In contrast to classical bits that are confined to two values [0, 1], quantum circuits rely on qubits, which can be present in several states simultaneously. The computation process can be illustrated through a circuit diagram, as shown in Figure 18.1. As time advances, qubits are represented by horizontal lines in the diagram [1]. Symbols placed on these lines show the movement of qubits around the box. The meter symbol (M) demonstrates the conversion of quantum states into classical bits [5].

18.2.1 Fundamental Quantum Gates

- **Pauli-X (bit-flip):** $X|0\rangle = |1\rangle$
- **Hadamard (H):** Creates superposition $H|0\rangle = (|0\rangle + |1\rangle)/\sqrt{2}$
- **Phase Gates (S, T):** Rotate qubit state on the Bloch sphere
- **Two-Qubit Gates:**
  - **CNOT (Controlled-NOT):** Flips the target qubit if the control is $|1\rangle$
  - **CZ (Controlled-Z):** Applies a phase flip conditionally
- **Multi-Qubit Gates:** SWAP, Toffoli, etc. [6].

In Figure 18.1, entanglement is established between *q0* and *q1* before measurement. In cloud-based systems, services like IBM's Qiskit and Amazon Braket convert circuits into instructions tailored to specific hardware [7].

18.2.2 Quantum Operations and Execution

Quantum operations follow unitary evolution as outlined by the *Schrödinger Equation* [1]. The main phases of operation are as follows:

Initialization: Qubits are reset to the $|0\rangle$ state.

Gate Application: Gates are implemented as pulses, which can be either microwave or optical, on physical qubits [8]. The accuracy of these gates is evaluated by their fidelity, which is 99.9% or higher in high-end systems.

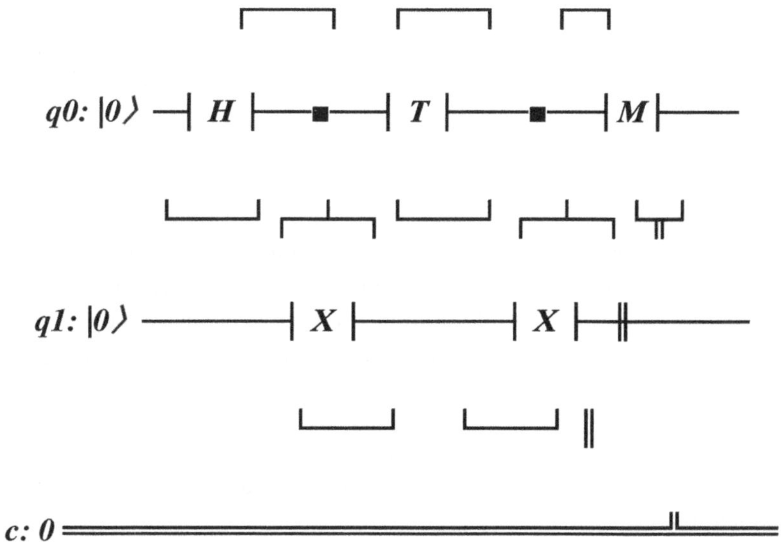

Figure 18.1 Quantum circuit illustrating entanglement and measurement.

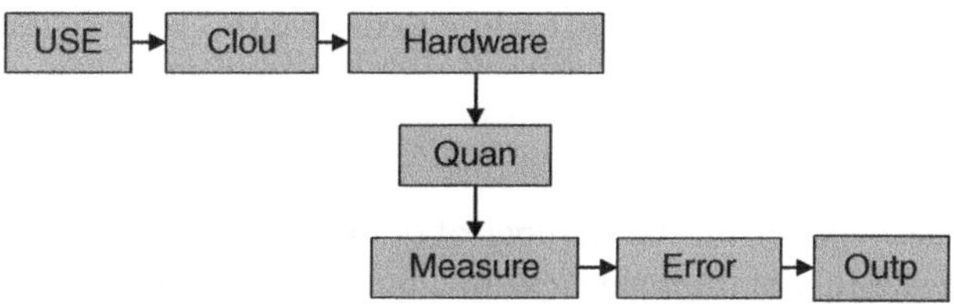

Figure 18.2 Cloud execution workflow.

Measurement: This phase collapses the superposition into classical bits (0 or 1). Readout errors, typically ranging from 1% to 5% in superconducting systems, need to be minimized [6]. In Figure 18.2, we observe the full sequence of execution for a quantum job on the cloud.

Critical Consideration: Gate parallelism and qubit connectivity constraints vary by cloud hardware (e.g., Rigetti's Aspen-M vs. IBM's Eagle) [7].

18.2.3 Important Concepts of Quantum Theory

18.2.3.1 Superposition

A qubit's state can be represented as $|\psi\rangle = \alpha|0\rangle + \beta|1\rangle$, where α and β are complex probability amplitudes, and the normalization condition $|\alpha|^2 + |\beta|^2 = 1$ must hold.

With probability $|\alpha|^2$, measurement yields the classical state $|0\rangle$, and with $|\beta|^2$, it yields $|1\rangle$. This is a direct consequence of the quantum principle of superposition, which allows a qubit to exist in a combination of both basis states simultaneously (unlike a classical bit, which can be either 0 or 1). This makes it possible to use the states of all 2^n qubits at once for parallel computation [9], [10].

18.2.3.2 Entanglement

Entanglement is a quantum phenomenon where qubits share a joint state that cannot be separated. For example, in the Bell state $(|00\rangle + |11\rangle)/\sqrt{2}$, measuring one qubit immediately reveals the state of the other, even across large distances. This is pivotal for the phenomena of quantum teleportation and superdense coding [10].

18.2.3.3 Decoherence

Coherence in qubits is affected by environmental distractions known as T_1: energy decay and T_2: phase drift. Typical times for which a particular measurement remains coherent are

- Superconducting qubits can last for 50–500 μs.
- Trapped ions take 1–10 seconds [8], [11].

The systems utilize subroutines and dynamic fueling to resolve this issue in the cloud.

18.2.3.4 Quantum Volume

Quantum computer fitness depends on the number of qubits, how they are networked together, and the stability of their gates. With a quantum volume greater than 128 (in the case of IBM), larger circuits can be created [9].

18.2.4 Encoding Data, Making Physical Models, and Loss Prevention

There are several methods used for encoding data into quantum states:

- Starting from digital data, the next step is to encode it as binary and then to the qubit level as ($|0110\rangle$).
- Classical vectors are encoded as the qubit amplitudes through Amplitude Encoding.
- Quantum RAM (qRAM) is a theoretical approach designed for the efficient creation of quantum states (in the lab) [9].

Superconducting quantum computers are maintained at temperatures close to absolute zero by using liquid helium for cooling. In practical systems, significant energy losses occur, with 30% of the energy input converting to heat due to imperfections in the cooling process [8]. At a temperature of 4 K, a coaxial cable can

Table 18.1 Physical qubit technologies in cloud platforms.

Type	Examples	Operating Temp	Key Challenges
Superconducting	IBM, Google, Rigetti	15 mK (−273.135 °C)	Crosstalk, 1/f noise
Trapped ion	Honeywell, lonQ	Room temperature	Slow gate speeds
Photonic	Xanadu	Room temperature	Detection losses

reduce the amplitude of microwave pulses by ½ dB per meter. The energy loss from $|1\rangle \rightarrow |0\rangle$transitions in qubit relaxation is known as T_1 *decay* [12]. When various types of qubits are integrated into a quantum computer, some data loss occurs, similar to data compression [9]. Table 18.1 summarizes the key characteristics of the primary physical qubit technologies used in cloud platforms, including superconducting, trapped ion, and photonic approaches. Mitigation strategies for the data loss include striving for pure polarization by adjusting the subtle aspects of the signal, utilizing surface codes to mitigate phase and bit-flip errors, and delegating specific tasks to traditional computing methods. Cloud-specific challenges include delays in responding to requests due to network latency in submitting or retrieving circuits. In Qubit Virtualization, resource allocation for different tenants must be planned [7]. During data transmission, quantum cryptography ensures protection against tampering. There are two cost models: charging per photo and a subscription model [6].

Future Trajectory: The evolution of cloud-based quantum computing will hinge on innovations in error-corrected logical qubits and quantum-classical integration [12]. Although NISQ devices face constraints due to decoherence, cloud access enables anyone interested to experiment with them.

18.3 Quantum Computing in the Cloud

18.3.1 Quantum Computing Frameworks and Cloud Platforms

With quantum computing emerging as a viable alternative to classical architectures for specific domains, recent years have witnessed rapid advancements in quantum software frameworks and cloud-accessible infrastructure. These frameworks enable users (ranging from researchers and students to enterprise developers) to model, simulate, and execute quantum programs without requiring direct access to fragile, expensive quantum hardware. Cloud-based access models have democratized experimentation and facilitated hybrid quantum-classical workflows.

According to Preskill et al. [2] and the Quantum Computing Market Report 2023 by McKinsey & Company, cloud-based quantum services are forecasted to contribute to a global quantum computing market exceeding $65 billion by 2030. IBM Quantum currently leads in terms of cloud-accessible quantum hardware usage, with a market share of over 35%. Amazon Braket and Microsoft Azure Quantum follow closely, appealing to users who prefer integration into established enterprise cloud ecosystems.

These cloud services abstract the complexity of quantum hardware by providing APIs and SDKs for creating, simulating, submitting, and retrieving results of quantum circuit execution. Below, we explore the most prominent frameworks/platforms and discuss how they provide this seamless interface between classical cloud clients and physical quantum processor units (QPUs).

18.3.2 Why Quantum Computing in the Cloud?

The inherent benefit provided by quantum computing is the **transformational speed-up** for classes of problems that are currently **intractable** on classical supercomputers. These include

- **Combinatorial optimization** (e.g., portfolio optimization and delivery routing)
- **Quantum chemistry** and material science (e.g., simulating molecules and catalysts)
- **Machine learning** (e.g., quantum kernel methods and quantum neural networks)
- **Cryptanalysis** (e.g., factoring integers with Shor's algorithm)

However, accessing and experimenting with quantum hardware remains nearly impossible for most researchers and developers. This is where the **cloud** becomes a game-changer.

18.3.2.1 Cloud-Based Quantum Computing Solves Three Core Bottlenecks

1) **Hardware Access:** Quantum processors are fragile, expensive, and require cryogenic environments. Cloud access eliminates the need to build and maintain this infrastructure.
2) **Scalability for Experimentation:** Cloud platforms provide simulators and real devices, enabling iterative prototyping, benchmarking, and scaling of hybrid quantum-classical algorithms (QAOA, Variational Quantum Eigensolver [VQE]) without incurring local overhead.
3) **Global Democratization:** Researchers from underfunded universities, students, and developers worldwide can run jobs on a superconducting quantum processor or trapped-ion system directly from a web browser.

18.3.3 The Leaders in the Space

A few platforms have become the main players in the maturing quantum computing ecosystem, each providing a special combination of cloud integration, development tools, and hardware access. Three of the most significant quantum platforms on the market today are highlighted in this section: Microsoft Azure Quantum, Amazon Braket, and IBM (Qiskit and Quantum). These platforms serve as the backbone of cloud-based quantum workflows, hybrid computing models, and educational outreach in addition to giving researchers and developers access to state-of-the-art quantum hardware.

18.3.3.1 IBM Qiskit and IBM Quantum

IBM Quantum is among the earliest and well-established quantum providers. At its core is **Qiskit**, an open-source quantum programming framework designed to help users write, simulate, and execute quantum circuits on actual quantum hardware. Users can develop quantum circuits using gate-level primitives and run them on either simulators or real hardware. Although based on Python for its SDK, the execution flow, compilation, transpilation, and queueing mechanisms occur on the server side.

Platform Access and Flow Users authenticate via IBM *Quantum Experience* and receive a token to access devices. Once authenticated, they can select a backend (e.g., *ibmq_jakarta* and *ibmq_ehningen*) and submit compiled quantum circuits. Qiskit allows users to define quantum circuits at the gate level. The entry point is usually Python, through which users define a ***QuantumCircuit*** object. For instance, this basic circuit entangles qubits 0 and 1 [bell state], demonstrating superposition and entanglement, as shown in Figure 18.3.

Then the following phases occur:

1) **Transpilation:** The circuit is transpiled to match the topology and gate constraints of the selected backend. IBM's quantum processors often have limited qubit connectivity, so the transpiler inserts SWAP gates to accommodate.
2) **Compilation:** The transpiled circuit is compiled to Quantum Assembly Language (QASM) or OpenQASM 3.0 format, suitable for hardware execution.

Figure 18.3 QuantumCircuit implementation of a Bell state using IBM Qiskit.

```
qc = QuantumCircuit(2)
qc.h(0)
qc.cx(0, 1)
```

3) **Job Submission:** Jobs are submitted using Qiskit's IBMQJob interface. Qiskit interfaces with IBM Cloud, queues the job, and assigns it to a backend such as ibmq_jakarta.
4) **Execution:** The backend operates using microwave pulse sequences on superconducting qubits. Each measurement collapses the quantum state, and the result (bitstring histogram) is returned via IBM's job queue API.

Hardware Overview IBM primarily uses superconducting transmon qubits. Each qubit consists of a Josephson junction embedded in an Inductor–Capacitor (LC) circuit oscillator circuit, allowing for quantized energy levels. Qubits are manipulated using microwave pulses with nanosecond precision. Measurement is performed using dispersive readout via resonators. Most publicly accessible machines have 5–27 qubits. IBM has announced devices such as *Eagle* (127 qubits) and *Condor* (1,121 qubits) as part of their quantum roadmap, which targets fault-tolerant systems beyond 2030.

A comparative study [13] by Gokhale et al. in *IEEE Quantum Week* found that Qiskit outperforms many alternatives in terms of documentation quality, backend calibration visibility, and the maturity of circuit transpilation tools.

Strengths and Use Cases Qiskit is widely used in **quantum chemistry** (VQE simulations), **education** (tutorials and free tier access), and **error mitigation research** (using *Ignis* to analyze and correct quantum noise). IBM's cloud-native orchestration and visibility into device calibration data allow fine-grained experimentation and research reproducibility. For example, coherence times (T_1/T_2), gate fidelities, and readout errors can be programmatically accessed and monitored before job submission.

18.3.3.2 Amazon Braket

Amazon Braket is AWS's cloud-based quantum computing platform, which offers hardware-agnostic access to multiple QPU providers (see **Hardware Overview**). This enables users to experiment with various physical qubit implementations through a unified interface.

Platform Access and Flow Users define circuits using the Braket SDK or JSON format and submit them through AWS CLI, Jupyter on SageMaker, or the AWS console. Hybrid workflows use classical orchestration via Lambda, ECS, or EC2.

Here's what the typical job execution flow looks like:

1) **Circuit Definition:** In the Braket Python SDK or JSON Intermediate Representation (IR).
2) **Job Submission:** The QuantumTask is submitted to AWS Braket, which schedules it for the chosen QPU.

3) **Routing to Vendor:** Braket forwards the job to the selected QPU vendor (e.g., IonQ or Rigetti). The hardware itself is hosted in vendor facilities (e.g., IonQ's labs).
4) **Execution:** The QPU executes the job. For IonQ, laser pulses manipulate trapped ytterbium ions. For Rigetti, superconducting qubits are pulsed similarly to IBM's architecture.
5) **Result Retrieval:** Results (usually a distribution of bitstrings) are written to an S3 bucket. The user can download, visualize, or post-process these results asynchronously.

Hardware Overview Amazon Braket does not build its quantum processors. Instead, it acts as a broker-layer cloud service, providing unified access to QPUs developed by specialized vendors. As of 2025, Braket integrates with three significant categories of hardware, each representing a distinct physical realization of quantum information and offering unique strengths for different computational paradigms:

1) **IonQ (Trapped Ion Quantum Computers):** IonQ's devices use trapped ytterbium ions (Yb+) as qubits, where laser pulses manipulate hyperfine states to perform single- and multi-qubit gates. The hardware supports all-to-all qubit connectivity, enabling efficient execution of algorithms like VQE [14] and QAOA [15] with deep circuits supported by long coherence times.
2) **Rigetti Computing (Superconducting Qubits):** Rigetti's superconducting transmon qubits, arranged in a fixed 2D lattice, operate at millikelvin temperatures and use microwave pulses for gate operations. While limited to nearest-neighbor connectivity and shorter coherence times ($<100\,\mu s$), fast gate speeds and advanced readout techniques make the platform suitable for NISQ-era algorithms.
3) **D-Wave Systems (Quantum Annealing Processors):** D-Wave uses quantum annealing with superconducting flux qubits to solve optimization problems formulated as quadratic unconstrained binary optimization (QUBOs) or Ising models. Its systems support thousands of sparsely connected qubits and rely on probabilistic sampling, making them effective for large-scale industrial optimization tasks such as scheduling and routing.

Strengths and Use Cases D-Wave is often used in logistics, portfolio optimization, scheduling, and vehicle routing problems. Gate-model platforms, such as IonQ, are better suited for linear algebra-based simulations and quantum chemistry.

A 2022 study [3] evaluated Braket's performance in real-world hybrid optimization pipelines, demonstrating 30–40% time improvement over purely classical baselines. Braket also provides precise pricing metrics (e.g., \$0.30 per job + \$1.50

per shot on IonQ), helping researchers control cloud costs and compare them against Central Processing Unit (CPU)/Graphics Processing Unit (GPU)-based alternatives.

18.3.3.3 Microsoft Azure Quantum

Azure Quantum and the Quantum development kit (QDK) are Microsoft's approach to scalable, enterprise-grade quantum computing. It supports multiple hardware providers, including IonQ and Quantinuum, and is tightly integrated with the Azure cloud stack.

Platform Access and Flow Developers use the QDK, which consists of Q# (a domain-specific language), compilers, and simulators. Users submit jobs through the Azure Portal, Azure CLI, or Jupyter.

Here's what the typical job execution flow looks like:

1) Q# operation is compiled and submitted as a job to Azure Batch.
2) Jobs are scheduled and forwarded to the QPU provider's execution queue.
3) Output is routed back via Azure Storage or REST API endpoints.

Hardware Overview **IonQ** and **Quantinuum** devices are accessible through Azure Quantum, offering up to 20+ fully connected, low-noise qubits with hardware-native gate sets.

Strengths and Use Cases Azure Quantum is particularly suited for enterprise users who require deep integration with Microsoft Azure ML, DevOps, and security infrastructure.

Microsoft provides advanced resource estimation tools that can predict circuit depth, gate counts, and qubit requirements before execution. This helps in cost forecasting and feasibility studies.

Azure Quantum excels in domains like quantum chemistry, time-dependent Hamiltonian simulation, and research in quantum error correction. It also supports hybrid optimization solvers and integrates with Azure ML for classical-quantum workflows. In an Association for Computing Machinery (ACM) survey paper [5], Azure was found to provide superior orchestration for time-dependent problems in physics, outperforming Braket in terms of solver flexibility and circuit size management.

18.4 Quantum Computing—Key Strengths

Conventional computing architectures are approaching the physical constraints of CMOS miniaturization; however, fundamental bottlenecks remain, particularly

Table 18.2 Comparison of classical and quantum performance.

Metric	Classical (CPU/GPU)	Quantum Hardware	Quantum on Cloud
Speed	Polynomial time (slow)	Exponential speedup possible	Same, with remote access
Memory requirements	Gigabytes to petabytes	Needs fewer qubits	Outsourced to cloud infra
Cost per job	\$30–\$100 + (simulating H_2)	~\$0.30 per job	\$0.01–\$1 per shot (QPU billing)
Scalability	Limited by physical RAM	Scales with added qubits	Pay-as-you-go with elastic scaling
Latency	Local/fast	Requires calibration time	Cloud latency (ms-sec)
Best for	Image processing, logic—ops	Chemistry, optimization, QML	Democratizing access, prototyping

when addressing problems characterized by exponential complexity, entangled interactions, or high-dimensional state spaces. Quantum computing won't directly replace classical computing, but it's a paradigm shift capable of solving a class of problems that are intractable or prohibitively expensive under classical models. For certain problems, quantum hardware and cloud-based quantum services perform better than classical computing in areas like speed, scalability, and cost-effectiveness, as indicated in Table 18.2. In a similar vein, Table 18.3 identifies particular application areas where quantum systems provide clear benefits over traditional techniques. Quantum computers are **not faster at everything**, but they **excel at problems where classical approaches scale exponentially**.

18.5 Challenges and the Future

Although quantum computing has the potential to revolutionize computational paradigms, it remains a nascent field, facing profound technical and infrastructural challenges. Quantum computing in the cloud has undoubtedly led to significant democratization; however, problems still arise: jobs must wait in global queues, and during peak demand, even privileged users may experience substantial delays. Once submitted, the quantum programs require network

Table 18.3 Quantum advantage domains.

Application Area	Why Classical Struggles?	Why Quantum Is Better?	Example
Scientific simulations	• Simulating molecules requires storing full wavefunctions. • For ~50 atoms, memory needs scale to petabytes.	• Quantum systems natively represent quantum states. • Quantum-based methods like VQE and QPE compute ground state energies more efficiently.	Simulating **FeMoco** (used in nitrogen fixation) is infeasible classically but feasible with a 200-qubit fault-tolerant quantum computer.
Combinatorial optimization	• Heuristics like greedy search and genetic algorithms get stuck in local minima. • Configurations grow as 2^n (e.g., max-cut, TSP, and portfolio optimization).	• QAOA and Grover's algorithm offer quadratic to exponential speedups. • Superposition allows for the exploration of parallel configurations; interference amplifies good solutions.	Optimizing a portfolio of 40 assets (~1 trillion configs) becomes feasible using **QAOA** with classical feedback.
Machine learning (high-dimensional spaces)	Kernel methods (e.g., SVMs) scale poorly with high-dimensional data. Neural network training requires large datasets and computational resources.	• Quantum feature maps embed data in exponentially large Hilbert spaces using linear resources. • Quantum kernels and QNNs efficiently capture complex correlations.	Quantum-enhanced **SVMs** show superior performance in classifying high-dimensional **gene expression** or **image datasets**, especially in small-data regimes.
Cryptanalysis	• RSA-2048 factoring takes billions of years classically. • Unstructured search scales linearly, O(N).	• **Shor's algorithm** factors in polynomial time. • **Grover's algorithm** *finds entries in* $O(\sqrt{N})$.	**RSA encryption** breaking or searching **1 billion hashes** reduced from 1 billion to 1 million steps.

round trips to the data center, with latency often ranging from seconds to minutes depending on location and load. Moreover, the cost model for cloud-based quantum computing is currently pay-per-shot. Each shot corresponds to a single execution of a quantum circuit, typically costing between $0.01 and $0.03 for gate-based hardware and higher for annealers. These economics can make quantum cloud services prohibitively expensive for *extremely* high-throughput or iterative workloads, such as the optimization or training of quantum machine learning models.

Overcoming these hurdles will require the development of logical qubits built on top of many imperfect physical ones to form an error-resistant abstraction. The most promising approach to this involves topological error correction schemes, such as surface codes, which encode a logical qubit across a two-dimensional grid of physical qubits. As of today, about 1,000–10,000 physical qubits may be necessary to support a single stable logical qubit with high fidelity. While such requirements are daunting, the development of logical qubits is essential for building general-purpose, fault-tolerant quantum computers. Encouragingly, several hardware roadmaps, such as IBM's 2030 Condor and Flamingo platforms, have explicitly committed to supporting logical operations within the next five to ten years. In the future, training pipelines may span classical CPUs and GPUs, with QPUs reserved for specific tasks like sampling high-dimensional probability distributions or solving nonconvex optimization landscapes.

18.6 Conclusion

Ultimately, the convergence of cloud infrastructure and quantum hardware will determine the speed at which quantum computing transitions from laboratory curiosity to commercial utility. The next wave of innovation is likely to involve regionally distributed QPU access to reduce latency, hybrid runtime environments that enable the coexecution of quantum and classical programs in real-time, and the formalization of intermediate representations (IRs) for quantum programs, analogous to low-level virtual machine (LLVM) in classical computing. Although the challenges are formidable, the incentives are enormous: solving problems intractable by any classical machine, opening new frontiers in scientific discovery, and radically reducing the cost and energy of complex computation.

References

1 M. A. Nielsen and I. L. Chuang, *Quantum Computation and Quantum Information*. Cambridge Univ. Press, 2010.

2 J. Preskill, "Quantum computing in the NISQ era and beyond," *Quantum*, vol. 2, p. 79, 2018.

3 G. G. Guerreschi and M. Smelyanskiy, "Practical optimization for hybrid quantum-classical algorithms," arXiv preprint arXiv:1701.01450, 2017.

4 R. Smith, M. Curtis, and W. J. Zeng, "A practical quantum instruction set architecture," arXiv preprint arXiv:2104.05195, 2022.

5 H. Soeparno and A. S. Perbangsa, "Cloud quantum computing concept and development: A systematic literature review," *Proc. Comput. Sci.*, vol. 179, pp. 944–954, 2021.

6 G. S. Ravi *et al.* "Quantum computing in the cloud: Analyzing job and machine characteristics," in *2021 IEEE Int. Symp. Workload Charact. (IISWC)*, IEEE, 2021.

7 L. Liu and X. Dou. "QuCloud: A new qubit mapping mechanism for multi-programming quantum computing in a cloud environment," in *2021 IEEE Int. Symp. High-Perfor. Comput. Arch. (HPCA)*, IEEE, Seoul, South Korea, 2021. 167–178.

8 H. Riel. "Quantum computing technology," in *2021 IEEE Int. Electr. Devices Meeting (IEDM)*, IEEE, San Francisco, California, USA, 2021. 1.3.1–1.3.7.

9 H. T. Nguyen *et al.* "Quantum cloud computing: A review, open problems, and future directions." *arXiv preprint arXiv:2404.11420* (2024). 39–50

10 V. Hassija *et al.*, "Present landscape of quantum computing," *IET Quantum Commun.*, vol. 1, no. 2, pp. 42–48, 2020.

11 G. S. Ravi, et al. "Adaptive job and resource management for the growing quantum cloud," in *2021 IEEE Int. Conf. Quantum Comput. Eng. (QCE)*, IEEE, Broomfield, Colorado, USA, 2021. 301–312.

12 H. Padmanaban, "Quantum computing and AI in the cloud," *J. Comput. Intell. Robot.*, vol. 4, no. 1, pp. 14–32, 2024.

13 S. Gokhale, T. Propson, M. Martonosi, F. Chong, "Evaluating quantum SDK usability: A comparative study," *Proceedings of the IEEE International Conference on Quantum Computing and Engineering (QCE 2021 / IEEE Quantum Week), IEEE, Broomfield, Colorado, USA*, 2021, 110–121.

14 A. Peruzzo *et al.*, "A variational eigenvalue solver on a photonic quantum processor," *Nat. Commun.*, vol. 5, no. 4213, 2014.

15 E. Farhi, J. Goldstone, and S. Gutmann, "A quantum approximate optimization algorithm," arXiv:1411.4028 [quant-ph], 2014.

19

Cloud Platforms for Scientific Research and HPC Workloads

Anant Kumar

Einstein AI Division, Member of IEEE and Sigma Xi, The Scientific Research Honor Society, San Jose, CA, USA

19.1 Introduction

Look, the whole convergence thing between cloud computing and high-performance computing (HPC)? It's been a game-changer for scientific research. And honestly—it's about damn time.

I've watched researchers for *decades* get stuck waiting weeks, sometimes months, just to get their hands on computational resources that could actually answer their burning questions. The on-premises infrastructure bottleneck was real, and it was painful. Then cloud computing showed up, democratizing access to supercomputing power in ways that would've sounded like pure fantasy just twenty years ago.

Today's scientific landscape is … well, it's brutal in terms of computational demands. Data-driven doesn't even begin to cover it. Whether you're running climate models that take forever to converge, crunching through genomic sequences that seem to multiply overnight, or training ML models to predict protein structures (good luck with that folding problem, by the way), the computational requirements just keep growing exponentially [1]. Traditional HPC centers? Sure, they pack a punch, but they struggle with the kind of flexibility and on-demand scalability that modern research actually needs.

Enter cloud platforms.

Virtually unlimited computational resources. Sophisticated orchestration tools that actually work. The ability to scale from zero to thousands of cores in minutes instead of months. It's not hyperbole—it really has changed everything.

But here's where it gets interesting: this transformation isn't just about taking your existing stuff and shoving it into the cloud. That's lift-and-shift thinking, and it'll bite you every time. What we're really talking about is reimagining how scientific computing gets done, period. Cloud platforms offer something traditional HPC environments have never been great at the agility to actually experiment with different computational approaches, economic flexibility where you pay for what you use (revolutionary concept, right?), and—maybe most importantly—the collaborative potential to share resources and data across global research communities [2].

Now, before you get too excited … migrating scientific workloads to the cloud isn't some magic bullet. It requires fundamentally rethinking how you design, deploy, and manage computational workflows. The cloud brings its own bag of tricks: network latency that can kill tightly coupled applications, data transfer costs that'll make your accountant cry, security considerations that keep you up at night, and the lovely complexity of managing distributed systems at scale.

19.2 Background and Context

19.2.1 The Evolution of Scientific Computing

Scientific computing has been through quite the journey over the past few decades—several paradigm shifts that each seemed revolutionary at the time.

The early days? Single-processor systems where you'd queue up batch jobs and then … wait. Sometimes for days. Can you imagine explaining that to a graduate student today? "Oh, your simulation? Come back Thursday, maybe Friday if we're lucky." The introduction of parallel computing architectures in the '90s opened up new possibilities, sure, but it also meant you needed serious expertise in parallel programming *and* access to those expensive supercomputing facilities that most of us could only dream about [3].

Then came the rise of commodity clustering in the early 2000s. Suddenly parallel computing became more accessible—you could build your own little Beowulf cluster if you were scrappy enough. But (and there's always a but) it also introduced new headaches around system administration, job scheduling, and resource management. I remember research institutions where people were spending as much time babysitting infrastructure as they were actually doing research. Clearly unsustainable; clearly not what we signed up for.

Cloud computing emerged as a potential solution to these problems. Keyword: potential. Early cloud platforms were … let's be charitable and say they weren't exactly optimized for HPC workloads. The virtualization overhead alone was enough to make you want to go back to your trusty on-premises cluster. Add inconsistent network performance and a general lack of specialized hardware, and you had a recipe for disappointment when trying to hit the performance levels that scientific applications actually demanded.

But—and this is where things get interesting—the cloud ecosystem has matured *significantly*. We're talking bare-metal instances, high-performance interconnects, and specialized accelerators that can genuinely rival traditional HPC systems. The major providers have been throwing serious engineering resources at this problem, and it shows.

19.2.2 Traditional HPC vs. Cloud HPC

The differences between traditional HPC and cloud-based HPC go beyond just the location of the hardware. Traditional HPC environments are typically characterized by

- **Dedicated Hardware:** Systems are purpose-built for specific types of workloads.
- **Batch Scheduling:** Jobs are queued and executed based on resource availability and priority.
- **Shared File Systems:** High-performance parallel file systems provide shared storage.
- **Homogeneous Architecture:** Nodes are typically identical to simplify management.
- **Long-Term Resource Allocation:** Users often have dedicated allocations for extended periods.

Cloud HPC, by contrast, offers

- **Elastic Resources:** Computational resources can be scaled up or down based on demand.
- **On-Demand Provisioning:** Resources are available immediately without waiting in queues.
- **Heterogeneous Options:** Users can choose from a wide variety of instance types and configurations.
- **Pay-Per-Use Pricing:** Costs are directly tied to actual resource consumption.
- **Geographic Distribution:** Workloads can be distributed across multiple regions.

19.2.3 The Data Challenge

One of the most significant challenges in scientific computing is dealing with the big data being generated. Modern scientific instruments—from particle accelerators to radio telescopes—generate data at unprecedented rates. The Large Hadron Collider, for example, produces over 50 petabytes of data annually [4]. Genomic sequencing facilities are generating exabytes of data, and climate modeling projects require massive datasets spanning decades of observations.

This data deluge has created a fundamental problem: how do you move and process datasets that are too large to transfer over traditional networks? The answer, increasingly, is to bring the computation to the data rather than the other way around. Cloud platforms are uniquely positioned to address this challenge by colocating storage and compute resources, enabling researchers to process data where it lives rather than trying to move it elsewhere [5].

19.3 Core Content: Frameworks, Use Cases, and Technical Depth

19.3.1 Major Cloud Platforms for Scientific Computing

19.3.1.1 Amazon Web Services (AWS)

AWS has thrown serious money at the HPC space—and when I say serious, I mean they've basically built an entire ecosystem around scientific workloads. Their ParallelCluster service is pretty slick; it's a fully managed HPC cluster that can auto-scale based on whatever your jobs are demanding. The nice thing is it plays well with schedulers that HPC folks already know—Slurm, Sun Grid Engine (SGE), and the usual suspects. So you're not starting from scratch if you're migrating from a traditional setup [6].

Instance types? They've got you covered:

- **Compute Optimized (C5n):** High-performance processors with enhanced networking—great for CPU-heavy stuff.
- **Memory Optimized (R5):** High memory-to-CPU ratios for when your workload is just eating Random Access Memory (RAM).
- **Accelerated Computing (P4):** GPU instances for ML and computational acceleration.
- **High-Performance Computing (Hpc6a):** Purpose-built for those tightly coupled HPC applications that are notoriously picky.

But here's where AWS really shines—their storage ecosystem. Amazon FSx for Lustre can deliver sub-millisecond latencies and hundreds of gigabytes per second of throughput [7]. Yeah, you read that right. For long-term storage, S3 Glacier provides cost-effective archival for scientific datasets. Pretty comprehensive setup, honestly.

19.3.1.2 Microsoft Azure

Azure's taken a different approach to HPC—they're all about integration with existing enterprise tools and workflows. Makes sense, given Microsoft's DNA.

Azure CycleCloud handles cluster orchestration and management, while Azure Batch enables large-scale parallel and batch computing workloads.

What really sets Azure apart? Their tight integration with productivity tools like Office and collaboration platforms like Teams. I know it sounds mundane, but for research teams that need to share results and collaborate across disciplines, this is actually huge [8].

Their HPC infrastructure lineup includes

- **H-Series VMs:** Optimized for HPC applications with high memory bandwidth.
- **N-Series VMs:** Graphics Processing Unit (GPU)-enabled VMs for compute-intensive workloads.
- **Azure NetApp Files:** High-performance file storage for HPC workloads.
- **InfiniBand Networking:** Low-latency, high-bandwidth interconnects for tightly coupled applications.

19.3.1.3 Google Cloud Platform (GCP)

Now Google—they're coming at HPC from a different angle entirely. Their strength comes from years of experience with large-scale distributed systems and machine learning (ML). Google Cloud's approach is heavily influenced by how they manage their own massive computational workloads internally, and it shows.

The platform offers some unique advantages that you won't find elsewhere:

- **Preemptible Instances:** Significantly reduced costs for fault-tolerant workloads (if your job can handle getting interrupted).
- **Custom Machine Types:** Create instance configurations tailored to your specific workload requirements.
- **Advanced Networking:** Premium network tier with global load balancing and genuinely low latency.
- **Integrated Artificial Intelligence and ML (AI/ML) Services:** Seamless integration with TensorFlow, AI Platform, and other ML services [9].

Interestingly enough, Google's commitment to sustainability is also worth noting—they've been carbon neutral since 2007 and are aiming to run entirely on renewable energy by 2030. For research institutions with sustainability mandates (and there are more of them these days), this can be a significant factor in platform selection.

19.3.1.4 Specialized HPC Cloud Providers

While the big three cloud providers offer comprehensive HPC capabilities, several specialized providers focus exclusively on HPC workloads. Sometimes you need someone who really gets the nuances of scientific computing.

19.3.1.5 Rescale

Rescale provides a cloud-based HPC platform that's specifically designed for engineering and scientific simulation workloads. What I like about them is their focus—they're not trying to be everything to everyone. The platform offers several advantages over general-purpose cloud providers:

- **Application-Specific Optimization:** Preconfigured environments for popular scientific applications.
- **Flexible Licensing:** Support for both bring-your-own-license and on-demand licensing models.
- **Advanced Job Scheduling:** Sophisticated algorithms for optimizing resource allocation.
- **Global Presence:** Multiple data centers to minimize latency and comply with data residency requirements [10].

19.3.1.6 Sabalcore

Sabalcore focuses on providing HPC solutions for specific industries—particularly life sciences and financial services. Their platform offers:

- **Validated Environments:** Pretested configurations for regulatory compliance.
- **Specialized Hardware:** Access to exotic architectures like ARM processors and specialized accelerators.
- **Expert Support:** Consulting services to help optimize workloads for cloud deployment.
- **Cost Optimization:** Advanced algorithms for minimizing cloud costs while maintaining performance [11].

19.4 Container Orchestration for Scientific Workloads

The adoption of containerization has absolutely revolutionized how scientific applications get deployed and managed in the cloud. I mean, it's changed everything about reproducible science.

Containers provide several key benefits for scientific computing:

- **Reproducibility:** Ensuring that computational experiments can be replicated exactly.
- **Portability:** Running the same application across different cloud platforms.
- **Isolation:** Preventing conflicts between different software dependencies (dependency hell, anyone?).
- **Scalability:** Enabling applications to scale across hundreds or thousands of nodes.

19.4.1 Kubernetes for HPC

Kubernetes has emerged as the de facto standard for container orchestration, but … and there's a big "but" here … its application to HPC workloads has required significant adaptation. Traditional HPC jobs are typically long-running and require dedicated resources, which doesn't really align with Kubernetes' default behavior of treating containers as ephemeral [12]. It's like trying to fit a square peg into a round hole.

Several projects have emerged to address this gap:

- **Volcano:** A Kubernetes-native batch scheduler designed specifically for HPC and ML workloads.
- **Argo Workflows:** A workflow engine for orchestrating complex computational pipelines.
- **Kubeflow:** A ML platform that extends Kubernetes for ML workloads.
- **Slurm Operator:** Enables running traditional Slurm jobs within Kubernetes clusters.

The integration of Kubernetes with HPC workloads is still evolving—we're not quite there yet—but the benefits are becoming clear. Kubernetes provides a consistent API for managing computational resources, sophisticated scheduling capabilities, and the ability to automatically scale based on demand.

19.5 Workflow Management Systems

Modern scientific computing increasingly relies on complex workflows that involve multiple computational steps, data transformations, and analysis stages. Managing these workflows manually? Error-prone and definitely doesn't scale well. Trust me on this one.

Several workflow management systems have emerged to address this challenge:

19.5.1 Nextflow

Nextflow is a workflow management system that's particularly popular in the bioinformatics community—and for good reason. It provides several features that make it well-suited to cloud deployments:

- **Dataflow Programming Model:** Workflows are defined as a series of processes connected by data channels.
- **Container Support:** Automatic handling of software dependencies through Docker and Singularity containers.

- **Cloud-Native Execution:** Native support for running on AWS Batch, Google Cloud, and Azure Batch.
- **Scalability:** Ability to scale from laptop to cloud to supercomputer without changing workflow code [13].

19.5.2 Snakemake

Snakemake is another popular workflow management system that's gained serious traction in the scientific computing community. It offers

- **Python-Based Syntax:** Workflows are defined using Python, making it accessible to researchers with Python experience.
- **Automatic Parallelization:** The system automatically determines which tasks can be run in parallel.
- **Cloud Integration:** Support for running on various cloud platforms and job schedulers.
- **Conda Integration:** Automatic management of software environments using Conda packages [14].

19.5.3 Apache Airflow

While originally designed for ETL workloads, Apache Airflow has found applications in scientific computing for managing complex data processing pipelines. Its strengths include:

- **Rich UI:** Web-based interface for monitoring and managing workflows.
- **Extensibility:** Large ecosystem of plugins for integrating with various systems.
- **Scheduling:** Sophisticated scheduling capabilities for running workflows on regular intervals.
- **Monitoring:** Comprehensive logging and alerting for workflow execution [15].

Each of these has its sweet spot, depending on what you're trying to accomplish and what your team is comfortable with.

19.5.4 Performance Optimization Strategies

Getting optimal performance from cloud-based HPC workloads requires careful attention to several factors:

19.5.4.1 Network Performance

Network performance is often the bottleneck in cloud-based HPC applications. Several strategies can help optimize network performance:

- **Placement Groups:** Ensuring that compute instances are physically close to minimize network latency.
- **Enhanced Networking:** Using SR-IOV and other hardware acceleration features.
- **Network Topology:** Designing network architectures that minimize communication overhead.
- **Bandwidth Provisioning:** Ensuring adequate network bandwidth for data-intensive applications [16].

19.5.4.2 Storage Optimization

Storage performance is equally critical for many scientific workloads. Key considerations include

- **File System Selection:** Choosing the right file system for the workload characteristics.
- **I/O Patterns:** Optimizing applications for the I/O characteristics of cloud storage.
- **Data Locality:** Ensuring that data is stored close to compute resources.
- **Caching Strategies:** Using local caching to reduce storage latency [17].

19.5.4.3 Cost Optimization

Cloud costs can quickly spiral out of control for large-scale scientific workloads. Several strategies can help manage costs:

- **Spot Instances:** Using preemptible instances for fault-tolerant workloads. Spot instances can save 30–40% in cost savings as per AWS documentation.
- **Right-Sizing:** Choosing instance types that match workload requirements that can reduce the cost by 25–30% on average.
- **Scheduling Optimization:** Running workloads during off-peak hours when costs are lower.
- **Reserved Instances:** Committing to long-term usage for predictable workloads [18].

19.5.5 Case Studies

19.5.5.1 Climate Modeling

Climate modeling represents one of the most computationally intensive areas of scientific research. Models like the Community Earth System Model (CESM) require thousands of cores and can run for weeks or months. The National Center for Atmospheric Research (NCAR) has successfully deployed CESM on AWS, achieving several benefits:

- **Elastic Scaling:** Ability to scale up for urgent climate predictions.
- **Cost Efficiency:** Paying only for the computational resources actually used.

- **Collaboration:** Easier sharing of model outputs with international research partners.
- **Experimentation:** Ability to test different model configurations without impacting production systems [19].

The AWS implementation demonstrated quantifiable improvements: simulation time reduced by 35% through optimized instance selection and parallel scaling, while costs decreased by 42% compared to traditional supercomputing allocations. Additionally, the time-to-science for exploratory runs improved from weeks to hours, enabling researchers to test 3x more model configurations within the same project timeline.

The migration wasn't without challenges. The team had to address issues with data transfer, optimize the model for cloud networking characteristics, and develop new workflows for managing cloud-based simulations. However, the results demonstrated that cloud platforms can be viable alternatives to traditional supercomputing centers for even the most demanding scientific applications.

19.5.5.2 Genomics and Bioinformatics

The genomics field has been an early adopter of cloud computing, driven by the exponential growth in sequencing data. The Broad Institute's GATK (Genome Analysis Toolkit) has been optimized for cloud deployment, running on both Google Cloud and AWS. Key benefits include:

- **Scalability:** Processing thousands of genomes in parallel.
- **Cost Efficiency:** Avoiding the need to maintain expensive on-premises infrastructure.
- **Collaboration:** Sharing datasets and analysis pipelines with international collaborators.
- **Reproducibility:** Ensuring that genomic analyses can be replicated exactly [18].

The cloud deployment has enabled new types of research that would have been impossible with traditional infrastructure. Large-scale population genetics studies, for example, can now process datasets containing millions of individuals, providing insights into human evolution and disease susceptibility.

19.5.5.3 Particle Physics

The particle physics community has unique computational requirements, processing the enormous datasets generated by experiments like the Large Hadron Collider. CERN has been exploring cloud computing as a complement to its traditional grid computing infrastructure. The experiments have shown that cloud platforms can effectively handle particle physics workloads, particularly for less time-critical analyses [20].

The challenges in particle physics are primarily around data management—experiments generate petabytes of data that need to be processed, filtered, and analyzed. Cloud platforms provide the scalability needed to handle these datasets, but the economics require careful optimization to avoid excessive data transfer costs.

19.6 Challenges and Future Outlook

19.6.1 Current Challenges

19.6.1.1 Data Transfer and Network Latency

One of the most significant challenges in cloud-based scientific computing is the "data gravity" problem. Large scientific datasets are expensive and time-consuming to transfer, creating a natural tendency for computation to migrate to where the data already exists. This can create vendor lock-in situations where researchers become dependent on a particular cloud provider simply because that's where their data resides [21].

Network latency remains a challenge for tightly coupled parallel applications. While cloud providers have made significant investments in network infrastructure, the performance of applications that require low-latency communication between nodes can still suffer compared to specialized HPC interconnects like InfiniBand.

19.6.1.2 Cost Predictability

Cloud costs can be difficult to predict for scientific workloads, particularly for researchers who are new to cloud computing. The pay-as-you-go model, while offering flexibility, can lead to unexpected bills if resources aren't managed carefully. This is particularly challenging for academic researchers who often have fixed budgets and limited cloud expertise [22].

19.6.1.3 Skills Gap

The transition to cloud-based HPC requires new skills that many researchers don't currently possess. Understanding cloud architectures, container orchestration, and cloud-native development practices requires significant investment in training and education. Many research institutions are struggling to bridge this skills gap while maintaining their research productivity.

19.6.1.4 Compliance and Security

Scientific research often involves sensitive data that must comply with various regulations and institutional policies. Ensuring that cloud deployments meet these requirements can be complex, particularly for multi-institutional collaborations that span different countries with different regulatory frameworks [23]. For sensitive genomic data in multi-institutional partnerships, specific frameworks like GDPR and HIPAA require robust technical implementations, including end-to-end encryption (AES-256), federated identity management systems, and comprehensive audit logging. Tools such as AWS Key Management Service, HashiCorp Vault for secrets management, and attribute-based access control (ABAC) systems are essential for maintaining compliance while enabling collaborative research across institutional boundaries.

19.7 Emerging Trends

19.7.1 Serverless Computing for Scientific Workloads

Serverless computing is beginning to find applications in scientific computing, particularly for event-driven processing and data analysis workflows. Functions-as-a-Service (FaaS) platforms like AWS Lambda, Azure Functions, and Google Cloud Functions enable researchers to run code without managing servers, paying only for the actual execution time [24].

While serverless platforms have limitations for traditional HPC workloads (execution time limits, memory constraints), they're well-suited for certain types of scientific applications:

- **Data Processing Pipelines:** Triggering analysis workflows when new data arrives.
- **Real-Time Analysis:** Processing streaming data from scientific instruments.
- **Microservices:** Breaking down complex applications into smaller, manageable components.
- **Cost Optimization:** Eliminating costs for idle resources.

19.7.2 Edge Computing for Scientific Applications

The proliferation of IoT devices and sensors in scientific research is creating new opportunities for edge computing. By processing data closer to where it's generated, researchers can reduce latency, minimize bandwidth usage, and enable real-time decision making [25].

Examples include

- **Environmental Monitoring:** Processing sensor data in real-time to detect environmental changes.
- **Autonomous Vehicles:** Enabling real-time decision-making for autonomous research vehicles.

- **Telescope Arrays:** Coordinating observations across multiple telescopes.
- **Laboratory Automation:** Controlling scientific instruments based on real-time data analysis.

19.7.3 Quantum Computing Integration

As quantum computing matures, cloud platforms are beginning to offer quantum computing services alongside traditional computing resources. This enables researchers to explore hybrid classical-quantum algorithms without needing access to physical quantum computers [26].

Current quantum cloud services include

- **IBM Quantum Network:** Access to IBM's quantum computers through the cloud.
- **Amazon Braket:** Quantum computing service offering access to quantum computers from multiple vendors.
- **Google Quantum AI:** Access to Google's quantum processors through Google Cloud.
- **Microsoft Azure Quantum:** Quantum development platform with access to various quantum technologies.

19.7.4 AI and ML Integration

The integration of AI and ML capabilities into cloud platforms is creating new opportunities for scientific research. Cloud providers are offering increasingly sophisticated AI services that can be applied to scientific problems without requiring deep expertise in ML [27].

Applications include:

- **Automated Data Analysis:** Using ML to identify patterns in scientific datasets.
- **Predictive Modeling:** Developing models to predict experimental outcomes.
- **Anomaly Detection:** Identifying unusual patterns in sensor data.
- **Natural Language Processing:** Analyzing scientific literature and research papers.

19.7.5 The Road Ahead: Where Scientific Computing Is Really Heading

19.7.5.1 Federated Everything (Because Nobody Wants to Put All Their Eggs in One Basket)

The future of scientific computing likely involves federated approaches that combine resources from multiple cloud providers, on-premises systems, and specialized facilities. This would enable researchers to leverage the best capabilities of each platform while avoiding vendor lock-in [28].

Key components of federated computing include

- **Unified APIs:** Common interfaces for managing resources across different platforms.
- **Data Federation:** Seamless access to data regardless of where it's stored.
- **Workload Orchestration:** Intelligent placement of workloads based on requirements and costs.
- **Identity Management:** Unified authentication and authorization across platforms.

19.7.5.2 Sustainability and Green Computing

Environmental sustainability is becoming increasingly important in scientific computing. Cloud providers are investing heavily in renewable energy and carbon-neutral operations, but there's still significant work to be done to minimize the environmental impact of large-scale computing [29].

Specific initiatives include Google's carbon-aware load balancing that automatically shifts workloads to regions powered by cleaner energy sources, AWS's Graviton2 processors delivering 20% better performance per watt, and Azure's commitment to negative carbon emissions by 2030. Researchers can actively reduce their environmental impact by selecting energy-efficient instance types like AWS's T4g or Google's Tau VMs, which offer up to 42% better price-performance while consuming significantly less energy.

Future developments may include

- **Carbon-Aware Scheduling:** Automatically scheduling workloads to minimize carbon footprint.
- **Energy-Efficient Algorithms:** Developing algorithms that minimize energy consumption.
- **Renewable Energy integration:** Directly powering computational workloads with renewable energy.
- **Carbon Accounting:** Providing detailed information about the carbon footprint of computational workloads.

19.7.5.3 Democratization of Scientific Computing

Cloud computing has the potential to democratize access to HPC resources, enabling researchers at smaller institutions or in developing countries to access computational capabilities that were previously available only to well-funded research centers [30].

This democratization could lead to

- **Broader Participation:** More researchers are able to tackle computationally intensive problems.
- **Diverse Perspectives:** Different viewpoints and approaches to scientific challenges.
- **Collaborative Research:** Easier collaboration between researchers with different resource constraints.
- **Educational Opportunities:** Students are able to access HPC for learning and research.

19.8 Conclusion

So here we are again—back to that fundamental shift I keep coming back to. We've gone from resource-constrained to essentially resource-unlimited, at least in theory. The institutional capacity bottleneck has been replaced by … well, by different bottlenecks, but ones that are much more manageable.

The technical maturation continues to surprise me. These platforms aren't just catching up to traditional supercomputing—in many ways, they're leapfrogging it. The flexibility alone changes how you approach computational problems. When you can dynamically reconfigure your entire infrastructure stack, you start thinking about problems differently.

Yeah, the challenges are real. Data transfer costs will bankrupt you if you're not careful. Network latency can kill tightly coupled applications. Managing distributed systems at this scale requires skills that most research groups don't have yet. The learning curve is steep, and the cost optimization game never ends.

But the trajectory is clear, even if the path is messy. Quantum computing integration, edge computing for real-time applications, and AI-driven workflow optimization—these aren't just buzzwords anymore. They're becoming practical tools that researchers can actually use.

19.8.1 The Economics Have Changed Everything

The CapEx to OpEx shift isn't just accounting. It's a fundamental change in how research gets planned and executed. You can be opportunistic now in ways that were impossible before. Exploratory research, where you have no idea what you'll need computationally? Not a problem. Scale up when you need to, and scale down when you don't.

This flexibility is particularly valuable for the kind of research where you're genuinely exploring uncharted territory. You're not locked into resource decisions made months in advance based on incomplete information.

The sustainability story is complex, though. Cloud providers achieve better efficiency through scale—that's well-established. But computational demands in scientific research are growing exponentially. So while individual workloads might be more efficient, aggregate environmental impact keeps climbing. We need to be honest about managing that tradeoff.

19.8.2 The Long View

I'm convinced these are still early days. The intersection points—cloud plus quantum, cloud plus edge, cloud plus AI orchestration—that's where the real breakthroughs are going to happen. The boundaries between different types of computing resources are blurring, and that's creating possibilities we're only beginning to explore.

The democratization aspect might be the most important long-term impact. When computational resources become truly accessible, innovation can emerge from anywhere. Some of the most creative work I've seen lately has come from unexpected places—small teams with big ideas who suddenly had access to infrastructure they could never have afforded before.

But success metrics need to evolve too. It's not just about performance per dollar or job throughput anymore. It's about the pace of discovery, the quality of insights, and the ability to ask questions that were computationally intractable before.

Early indicators are promising, but the real test will be how research methodologies evolve to leverage cloud-native capabilities rather than just porting traditional approaches. That's the next wave, and it's going to be fascinating to watch unfold.

The infrastructure revolution is mostly done. The methodological revolution? That's just getting started.

References

1 Hey, T., Tansley, S., and Tolle, K. (2009). *The Fourth Paradigm: Data-Intensive Scientific Discovery*. Microsoft Research. [Online]. Available: https://www.microsoft.com/en-us/research/wp-content/uploads/2009/10/Fourth_Paradigm.pdf.

2 M. Armbrust *et al.*, "A view of cloud computing," *Commun. ACM*, vol. 53, no. 4, pp. 50–58, 2010.

3 Sterling, T. L., Salmon, J., Becker, D. J., and Savarese, D. F. (1999). *How to Build a Beowulf: A Guide to the Implementation and Application of PC Clusters*. MIT Press. [Online][Book] Available: https://www.amazon.com/How-Build-Beowulf-Implementation-Application/dp/026269218X.

4 CERN, "Computing at CERN: The worldwide LHC computing grid and data processing," *CERN Computing Overview*, 2020. [Online]. Available: https://home.cern/science/computing.

5 E. Deelman *et al.*, "Pegasus, a workflow management system for science automation," *Future Gener. Comput. Syst.*, vol. 46, pp. 17–35, 2015.

6 Amazon Web Services, "AWS ParallelCluster user guide," 2021. [Online]. Available: https://docs.aws.amazon.com/parallelcluster.

7 Amazon Web Services, "Amazon FSx for lustre user guide," 2021. [Online]. Available: https://docs.aws.amazon.com/fsx/latest/LustreGuide.

8 Microsoft Azure, Azure cycleCloud documentation," 2021. [Online]. Available: https://docs.microsoft.com/en-us/azure/cyclecloud.

9 Google Cloud Platform, "High performance computing on Google cloud," 2021. [Online]. Available: https://cloud.google.com/solutions/hpc.

10 Rescale, "Rescale platform overview," 2021. [Online]. Available: https://www.rescale.com/platform.

11 Sabalcore Computing Inc. (2021). *HPC Cloud Solutions.* Orlando, FL, USA.

12 B. Burns and J. Beda, *Kubernetes: Up and Running*. O'Reilly Media, 2019.

13 P. Di Tommaso *et al.*, "Nextflow enables reproducible computational workflows," *Nat. Biotechnol.*, vol. 35, no. 4, pp. 316–319, 2017.

14 J. Köster and S. Rahmann, "Snakemake—a scalable bioinformatics workflow engine," *Bioinformatics*, vol. 28, no. 19, pp. 2520–2522, 2012.

15 Apache Airflow, "Apache airflow documentation," 2021. [Online]. Available: https://airflow.apache.org/docs.

16 Expósito, R. R. *et al.* (2013). Performance evaluation of HPC applications on low-cost cluster architectures. *Future Gener. Comput. Syst.*, 29(4), 1034–1045. https://doi.org/10.1016/j.future.2026.108374.

17 R. Thakur, W. Gropp, and E. Lusk, "Data sieving and collective I/O in ROMIO," in *Proc. 7th Symp. Front. Massively Parallel Comput.*, 1999, pp. 182–189. [Online] Available: https://web.cels.anl.gov/~thakur/papers/romio-coll.pdf.

18 G. A. Van der Auwera *et al.*, "From FastQ data to high-confidence variant calls: The genome analysis toolkit best practices pipeline," *Curr. Protoc. Bioinformatics*, vol. 43, no. 1, pp. 11–10, 2013.

19 National Center for Atmospheric Research, "CESM in the cloud," 2020. [Online]. Available: https://www.cesm.ucar.edu/models/cesm2/cloud.

20 CERN Openlab, "Cloud computing for particle physics," 2020. [Online]. Available: https://openlab.cern/projects/cloud-computing.

21 K. Keahey *et al.*, "Lessons learned from the chameleon testbed," in *Proc. 2020 USENIX Annu. Tech. Conf.*, 2020, pp. 219–233. [Online] Available: https://www.usenix.org/system/files/atc20-keahey.pdf.

22 M. A. Netto, "HPC cloud for scientific and business applications: Taxonomy, vision, and research challenges," *ACM Comput. Surv.*, vol. 51, no. 1, pp. 1–29, 2019.

23 T. Grance and P. Mell, "The NIST Definition of Cloud Computing," in *Comput. Secur. Div. Inf. Technol. Laborat.*, National Institute of Standards and Technology, 2011. [Online] Available: https://www.doria.fi/bitstream/handle/10024/93563/cloud_software.pdf.

24 G. McGrath and P. R. Brenner, "Serverless computing: design, implementation, and performance," in *Proc. 2017 IEEE 37th Int. Conf. Distribut. Comput. Syst. Workshops*, 2017, pp. 405–410. 10.1109/ICDCSW.2017.36.

25 W. Shi *et al.*, "Edge computing: Vision and challenges," *IEEE Internet Things J.*, vol. 3, no. 5, pp. 637–646, 2016.

26 J. Preskill, "Quantum computing in the NISQ era and beyond," *Quantum*, vol. 2, p. 79, 2018.

27 M. I. Jordan and T. M. Mitchell, "Machine learning: Trends, perspectives, and prospects," *Science*, vol. 349, no. 6245, pp. 255–260, 2015.

28 I. Foster *et al.*, "Federated computing for the masses: Aggregating resources for science," *Computer*, vol. 53, no. 10, pp. 56–64, 2020.

29 E. Strubell *et al.*, "Energy and policy considerations for deep learning in NLP," in *Proc. 57th Annu. Meet. Assoc. Comput. Linguist.*, 2019, pp. 3645–3650. [Online] Available: https://aclanthology.org/P19-1355/.

30 M. D. Wilkinson *et al.*, "The FAIR guiding principles for scientific data management and stewardship," *Sci. Data*, vol. 3, no. 1, pp. 1–9, 2016.

20

Ethics, Bias, and Responsible AI in Cloud Environments

Sreekanth B. Narayan[1] *and Karan Alang*[2]

[1] *Sr. IEEE Member, Okemos, MI, USA*
[2] *Independent Researcher, CA, USA*

20.1 Introduction

In this article, we emphasize the paramount value of ethics as related to the design of artificial intelligence (AI) systems and of cloud-connected systems. But as putatively AI-driven decisions become increasingly central to decisions in domains like healthcare, finance, and law enforcement, the importance of guardrails that mandate fairness, transparency, and accountability is higher than ever for the government aspect.

AI bias that originates from external, and often opaque sources, be they in benchmark datasets or embedded decisions of algorithmic design, leads to many societal challenges, as these biases can distort systems and widen existing asymmetries of privilege and class. Hence, AI-generated ethical issues become more and more important for developers, organizations, and policymakers [1, 2].

20.1.1 Cloud AI Introduces a Security Perspective

Operations/access is added but it raises the risk of loosening data privacy and ethical governance. Previously, setting up was a brain-twisting, long legal 9th vendor pricing and legal process; however, it is now released with AI, where we are at the AI governance knowledge part. Traditionally, we are comfortable with numbers in business but never uncomfortable with the data to showcase their key business portfolios, where we look and fill in the sense that we are capable of being guards of such data, which is proprietary. Our roadmaps to these challenges will need to be informed by strong-armed frameworks that emphasize responsible AI best practices. This includes the importance of doing proper ethical risk assessment, engaging diverse stakeholders, and constantly monitoring AI systems to minimize bias.

"Striking the right balance between allowing innovation and protecting against unintended harm while focusing on the development of AI is the right approach."

The responsible use of AI technology requires the cooperation of cloud providers, developers, regulators, and industry groups to establish the best practices that promote fairness and prevent biased discrimination [3–5].

The entire dialog around AI ethics is dominated by talk of the risks of biased algorithms, such as the Correctional Offender Management Profiling for Alternative Sanctions (COMPAS) system in criminal justice, and Amazon's biased hiring system. These are examples of unintended harmful consequences of AI, and they show the danger of AI mindlessly reflecting the prejudices of society and the necessity of AI having a pro-social impact and a regulatory framework.

This could be that data was loaded in without anyone ever deep diving to understand the units and work all the scenarios (especially the negative scenarios) of what's going on and the things that are weighed heavily as we start to proceed forward in the future. In addition, tools for transparency and privacy will also need an ethical AI framework to be based on users' rights and societal values, as investment amounts are getting humongous for making the Large Language Models (LLMs) work, and the humongous computing required for the data [6] too is now leading to greenhouse effects.

Overall, the failure of the "state in hand" not to embrace ethics, bias, and responsible AI in the cloud is a further compelling argument for organizations to have ethical governance at the core of all their AI implementations. The second of these is crucial to establish trust from users (and interested parties) and to play our part in developing balanced technology for the good of society on the other.

In that same vein, here is a Khan Migo instance from ChatGPT that you can learn from and copy other industry members. We must have the credentials until we can trust the practice of an ethic and learn the experience to challenge the complex world of AI, computing, and data, which shares the right to access treatment and consideration. To create an organization that will take time to turn the vision to solve such complexities too. You find drugs for COVID-19, and combining the test results, we can use it in mankind [1, 7, 8].

We have seen AI data-driven and made biased decisions, because of either incomplete or poor-quality training data, flawed algorithms, or negligence, which have negative assumptions and bad decisions that can affect individuals and communities coming from organizations that are increasingly relying on AI as their source of accurate data-driven decision-making.

Here, however, is a riposte to all that drumbeating, and if you are a member of the public, you ought to welcome what the following, shared by a Forbes Technical Council, has to say about what is what when it comes to what and where these are alarms that you, the public, need.

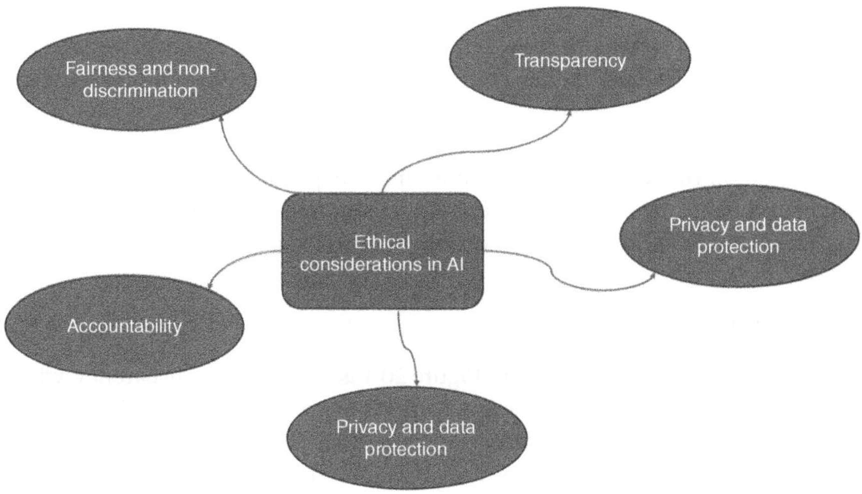

Figure 20.1 AI—Key ethical principles.

20.1.2 Ethical Considerations in AI

Attention Assembler, construct deep learning as colonizers, open-source style. AI development builders and launch builders created a unit of nine people in Eden to take the AI strata industry faster with AI out of dev cycles (The Evolution of Miles and Building for Modern Enterprises: Calculative Cycles of Development).

Ethics are up for sale, and investment is busy. AI systems are being incentivized to be the best answer to a problem in specific practical decision-making contexts—health finance, policing. Thus, observing Figure 20.1, to provide, to function, and to work such as to be as equal, transparent, and safe as possible is a major problem, which may be a strong solution, and which is not a help but a problem, and is in waiting for any other long-term view than the previous one, a very men-drug or reliance–centric treatment-oriented statistical primary dataset [1, 2].

Ethical governance for AI is not a compliance view, although it's really about how we learn about participating in this fight against the cross-cutting issues around responsibility and trust in the user, which is a big point that stakeholders made [1].

20.2 Key Ethical Principles

20.2.1 Fairness and Non-Discrimination

An AI is fair if it doesn't discriminates when deciding a specific case, on a specific person (or type of person), or on a specific group [3].

As in Figure 20.1, it is a robust philosophy of design that does not mimic or perpetuate current social inequities. The question is how we can we identify such an exposure and use the risk as an opportunity to potentially address linguistic supremacies or prejudices that are overt or covert in the training data or the algorithmic model [9].

Complete fairness is essential for building a dependable system. This ethical reliance on public trust may be a dream to achieve and not a must to achieve (like 100% fool-proofing the systems for various populations) [2].

20.2.2 Transparency

One of the promises of ethical AI in Figure 20.1 is to push for transparency, where the organizations would describe how any AI system had been designed, what data had been used, and how decisions were made [10]. For complex ones, with replays, e.g., since all players know all have asked between them, it's a matter of transparency and winning confidence and therefore can shield them from any AI scrutiny (up to end-to-end scenarios, of course, including business, e.g., anticipations). This is perceived to be the most important alignment with social values and needs in AI systems [10].

20.2.3 Accountability

An accountability lens on AI ethics places a premium on accountability, as everyone wants to know who is accountable—and how—it is essential to define and make clear the roles for responsibility along the AI implementation lifecycle. This is necessary to articulate and carry out distinct roles of responsibility in the AI implementation at or for whichever system as observed in Figure 20.1.

This principle has consequently led to the establishment of a regulator to correct for the harmful or biased nature of AI decision-making. It might thus fit a double agenda, that of possibly meeting future threats, such as those that spill over to the gender bias/retention scheme of Amazon, where whether one was female never mattered, regardless of who she was in terms of skill, and only men kept their jobs.

People like the company's former employee Emily Chao (name withheld), once a married mother of two while being a shipping clerk at one of the most popular online retail stores, Zara, must meet all payment deadlines on behalf of their employer in any situation.

For every domestic worker who fears their employer shifting their living/working territory, and themselves as well, as not being English, there was one case sent to another as a matter of course.

In fields such as healthcare, where AI has the potential to have a huge impact on patient outcomes, merely the research computation of finding any trials might land you behind bars. Accountability for and the governance principles that will be required to transition this framework from the "AS IS" of today to the "TO BE" must accompany design interventions to mitigate unintended consequences introduced in decision-making driven by AI [10].

20.2.4 Privacy and Data Protection

As we move forward under the paradigm of increasingly using and consuming customer data to train AI systems, there is a critical rush to keep all user data privacy-safe with a clear architectural setup as explained pictographically in Figure 20.1.

This even becomes a constant ethical question when big data is not managed maturely.

Meanwhile, methods like data anonymization are necessary to maintain privacy and human rights [10] by the legislation governed under privacy protection acts, including General Data Protection Regulation (GDPR) and California Consumer Privacy Act (CCPA) [3].

To maintain the quality as well as the privacy of the collected data, the organizations must take the behavior in time and adopt the data storage platforms and data transfer protocols for data collected [3].

20.2.5 Beneficence and Non-Maleficence

The concepts of beneficence and non-maleficence strongly articulate this need for AI systems to hold a place that is complementary to humanity: influencing change for good and carefully refraining from harming.

These responsibilities are critical for developers to ardently assume their role in forecasting, preventing, and remedying problems so that AI systems contribute to human well-being without triggering serious risks.

Developers must evaluate and correct so as not to induce dangerous misperceptions or any larger undesirable effects on individuals or society [7, 11].

20.3 Bias in AI

AI bias has to do with those hallucinations with systematic errors in AI decision-making that cause them to become unfair or discriminatory to some groups or individuals. That is mostly because of human biases that find their way into training data or into the algorithms themselves, leading to outcomes that are unjust for specific groups, ones based on race, gender, age, or socioeconomic status. We need to face this issue upfront and work on a way of making AI fair for all [12, 13].

Among the more widely discussed case studies of bias in AI is that of Amazon's hiring tool, aimed at making the hiring process more efficient. After Amazon trained it on a decade's worth of resumes and hiring, it found the system began penalizing resumes that included the word "women's" or that suggested the applicant was female, people familiar with the matter said. This bias most likely came from the applicant's gender distribution in the training data, where there were mostly males drawn from a mostly male-dominated tech industry. The AI system, therefore, started to downrate resumes with the word "women," leading to qualified applicants from women's colleges and with women's sports affiliations being rejected. Despite addressing bias in the model with revisions and neutrality attempts, Amazon finally abandoned the tool in 2018 due to its biases [14–16].

20.3.1 Types of AI Bias

20.3.1.1 Data Bias

Data bias is a major player in the world of AI bias, popping up at various stages of data collection and preparation. When datasets are not representative and do not harmonize well with the diverse population, they aim to serve an AI model built on such data that can churn out skewed results. Common types of data bias include selection bias, where certain demographics are left out, and labeling bias, which happens when human annotators unintentionally inject their prejudices into the data. Plus, there is always sampling bias [17, 18], which stems from flawed data collection strategies, leading to AI models that fail to accurately mirror real-world distributions, thus compromising their fairness. Thus, tackling these biases will always become a prerequisite and ensure fairness for everyone [19, 20].

20.3.1.2 Algorithmic Bias

The bias in the latter comes from errors in the construction and operation of AI algorithms. That bias can manifest itself through flawed assumptions or social bias encoded in the logic of a program, and its effect can be perpetuated as opposed to ameliorating existing inequalities. For instance, they can cause biased data in the training data to result in biased decisions in things like hiring, lending, and law enforcement. Picture AI data in which certain race groups are under-represented. This system could unfairly benefit candidates from already-privileged groups, reifying inequity and injustice. Trusted AI requires due diligence to establish that fair and unbiased AI is a necessity [21, 22].

20.3.2 Sources of Bias

Here are a few sources of AI bias, and it's important to understand these if you want to address them properly. Here are some categories:

Measurement Bias: This is the case when data are misclassified or simplified and can occur due to human errors or machine inaccuracies. This can result in incorrect AI results [22].

Reinforcement Bias: AI algorithms get repeatedly trained on the same sets of data and, as a result, are quite narrow-minded, to the point of making poor judgments. It further facilitates biased perceptions, due to which it is difficult for models to generalize well over diverse groups [19].

Implicit Bias: These are stealth bigotries that affect how information is read or studied and result in imbalance in AI despite not being evilly intended [20].

Sampling Bias: This occurs when the sampled data used to train the model is not representative of all users, penalizing the model for not being able to produce fair and unbiased insights [20]. If data gathering over-represents some groups while under-representing others, the AI automatically relies too much on these specific features, which then produce wrong predictions. To alleviate such instances or business cases, data sampling ought to be completely random or should well represent the characteristics of the population that is being proposed for or modeled [23].

Reporting Bias: This type of bias happens when the frequency with which events occur in the training set deviates from real-world distribution, which results in an incorrect understanding of the distribution of data, as observed in, e.g., sentiment analysis models [20].

20.3.3 Importance of Addressing AI Bias

Fairness in AI is important in bringing about social justice and economic success. AI-biased systems do not just violate the norms of fair play; they can also have dire consequences for a large community.

To combat AI bias, it is important to go under the hood of a variety of datasets that fully represent wider populations and to constantly audit AI outputs for bias.

In healthcare, for example, AI models that are prejudiced can result in misdiagnosis or advice for treatment that is not equal for various demographics. In education, for example, algorithms with bias could unfairly judge students based on their performance or their socioeconomic background.

It is also important to develop methods like debiasing algorithms and fairness-aware modeling, which try to mitigate the effect of biased data on the behavior that the AI models produce [21, 22].

Scrutinizing these models for biases is essential to ensure fair outcomes in AI applications, ranging from medical diagnosis to educational and loan scoring [18, 21].

20.4 Responsible AI Practices

Responsible AI describes a framework for principles that should guide the development and use of AI technology to enable AI to do good for society

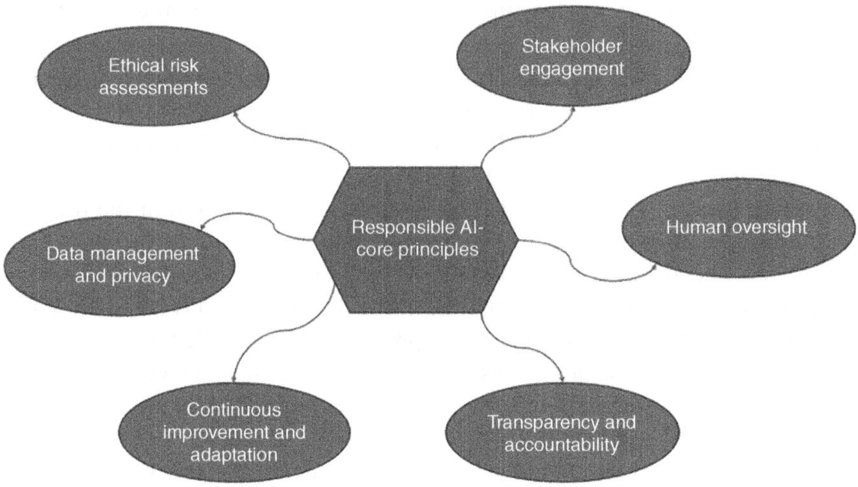

Figure 20.2 Responsible AI—Core principles.

and minimize its risks, as in Figure 20.2. These guidelines cover ethos issues, including bias, openness, respect for privacy, and conformity to regulation [2, 7]. Using responsible AI, we can at least mitigate risks and gain the trust of the users, customers, and regulators, in the end, providing a valuable solution for society [1]. It is a new spring day in the mountains, and the air is full of scent and hum. Dew hangs heavily on the pine trees, glistening in the filtered light.

20.4.1 Core Principles of Responsible AI

20.4.1.1 Ethical Risk Assessments

Companies should engage in periodic ethical risk assessments to help identify and assess any potential risks associated with AI applications prior to deployment and on an ongoing basis and upon new reviews and any other instances raised by business stakeholders with reference to Figure 20.2. This forces them to actively plan for identifying potential issues sooner rather than later and for mitigating those ethical concerns so AI systems are designed to meet customer expectations.

For instance, a company that is building an AI tool to make hiring easier might perform checks to ensure that the tool is not prejudicial against some demographics. Early detection can enable the company to tweak the algorithm to ensure that their hiring is more unbiased and symptomatic of the great dictator itself (hiring manager). This is a step toward trust and equality in hiring.

The latter can contribute to trust-building between users and the AI system and the AI system's naturalness concerning values [1, 24].

20.4.1.2 Stakeholder Engagement

Reaching out to and involving a broad range of stakeholders is key to developing inclusive AI systems grounded in a multitude of perspectives. By working together across different backgrounds, we can make sure that technology is just and serves the concerns of all the communities it reaches, as shown in Figure 20.2.

When training an AI system for healthcare, it can be more complete and fairer if doctors and patients—and those who are other ways involved in healthcare—from various groups can contribute.

Adhering to this principle ensures the AI system has been developed on a diverse and rich dataset, benefiting everyone else by becoming more accurate and fairer [1, 24].

20.4.1.3 Human Oversight

Responsible AI requires that it be guaranteed to be properly seen by a human or that humans be somewhere in the loop.

The ideal decision-maker would oversee AI outputs to see if they match comprehensive models and data sets that are fair and act as necessary, as shown in Figure 20.2.

This way, it helps to mitigate the risks and quick-fix situations related to automated systems that can become biased or produce inaccurate results [1, 25].

Take an AI system that is an active part of loan approvals, for example. Without human-in-the-loop control, the system could unintentionally privilege some demographics over others because of biased training data.

With the input of seasoned decision-makers to review the AI's suggestions, any ugly prejudices can be spotted and remedied so that the process of loan approval is fair for all who apply.

Such a proactive stance not only increases the fairness of AI systems but also fosters trust from users and stakeholders.

20.4.1.4 Continuous Improvement and Adaptation

AI fairness is an ongoing journey that requires the regular review and adjustment of AI models, as shown in Figure 20.2. While these systems advance, private and public institutions must raise their ethical level and avoid potential biases and discrepancies to meet human expectations [1, 8].

For instance, let's say your firm is creating an AI application to approve loans. At first, the system may inadvertently favor some demographics because of the biased training data. As the AI model is constantly being assessed and refined, the company can find such biases and correct them. They could be using fairness-aware algorithms and periodically auditing the system's decisions for equity. This makes it easier by preserving fairness and helps build the trust of the users, making sure that an AI-powered system is serving all the applicants fairly and with justice.

20.4.1.5 Data Management and Privacy

Introduction of data access controls and application of methods such as data masking and scrambling are important for preserving the privacy of users and safeguarding against unauthorized access to the data [2, 6].

For instance, in a medical environment, patient records may be obfuscated so that confidential information is available only to authorized users. This means that even if intercepted, the data is unreadable or secure.

We also help you further create a responsible AI framework by enabling data to be used only for its purpose and maintaining compliance with privacy and security standards, as shown in Figure 20.2.

20.4.1.6 Transparency and Accountability

Building accountability and trust requires making the decision processes of AI transparent. Ultimately, as shown in Figure 20.2, by including practical examples and explanations of how algorithms operate and the variables that influence their decision-making process, users may gain a better understanding of how such AI solutions can impact their business requirements [8, 26]. For example, consider a retail business that relies on AI to forecast consumer preferences. By describing how AI sifts through past purchases and browsing to predict what users might want to buy, the company can educate users about what technology does and does not do. Doing so not only builds trust but also ensures that AI is used responsibly and effectively.

20.5 Implementation Considerations and Good Practices

Forward-looking organizations that want to grow sustainably should infuse responsible AI into their governance to operationalize a set of best practices. These best practices involve performing ethical risk assessments to identify issues before they become problematic, involving diverse stakeholders for inclusivity, practicing good data management to optimize for data quality and privacy, deploying mechanisms for human-in-the-loop "override" in case of AI error, and continually updating and retraining AI models to adhere to ethical norms as forming a building block as presented in Figure 20.3.

Compliance with these principles and practices can enable organizations to develop AI solutions that respect fairness and accountability and create societal benefits, working toward a more equitable technology landscape [1, 7, 25].

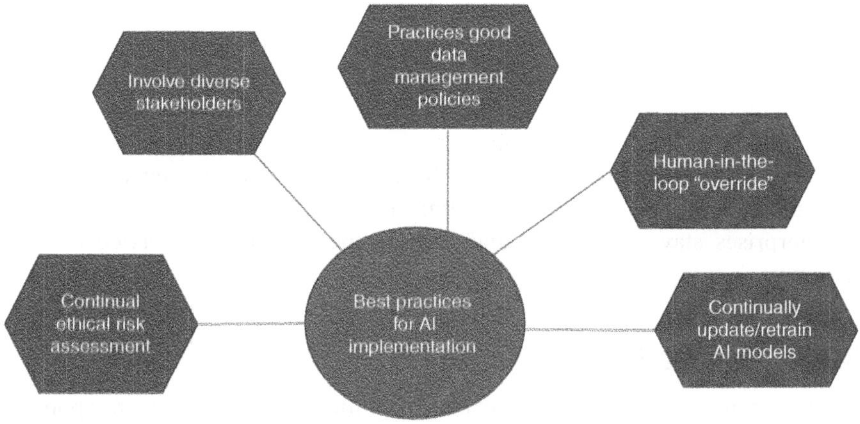

Figure 20.3 Best practices for implementation of AI.

20.6 Cloud Environments and AI

The integration of AI in cloud-based architecture is changing the game when it comes to enterprise productivity, IT usability, and data insight. Think of a retail business deploying cloud-based AI to review customer behavior and inventory. This not only adds to operational efficiency but also provides valuable decision support. With AI as a service offered through cloud computing, they provide the potential for innovation and advanced analytics across industries [4, 27].

But all these bones have their attendant risks and weaknesses. For example, a healthcare professional who employs AI to oversee patient data will need to guarantee strong data protection and compliance to prevent data breaches and preserve patient trust. By managing these risks closely, organizations can transform them into learning opportunities to develop reliable and customer error-free solutions.

In summary, AI in cloud computing has a lot of potential for growth and innovation, but the challenges that accompany such opportunities must be addressed to promote responsible and secure use. We should welcome this new, game-changing technology, not be afraid of it, and work together toward a better future.

20.6.1 Opportunities and Innovations

Cloud-based AI allows companies to harness powerful tools for instantaneous decision-making and analytics that were once exclusive to larger conglomerates

[4]. For instance, with AI-powered cloud services, a small retailer analyzing customer data and streamlining inventory can now boost its operational efficiency and fuel innovation. The scalability and affordability of cloud computing mean even smaller organizations can take advantage of AI solutions that enhance their operations and facilitate growth. This transformation has brought to the table countless opportunities for businesses to build systems that learn through a lot of data and react dynamically with the business requirements, so enterprises stay competitive and provide the best-in-class service to their customers.

20.6.2 Emerging Risks

Despite the applications, AI is facing many significant risks as it becomes popular in the clouds. While the availability and scalability-enhancing features are welcome, they carry with them the risk of introducing attack surfaces that adversaries might try to harvest [4, 5]. For instance, in a cloud-based AI service, convenience and scalability can render it vulnerable to attacks such as model stealing, in which an attacker could steal the AI model and use it inappropriately. Data poisoning, on the other hand, is another threat [5, 27], where the adversary perturbs the training data to disrupt the model's predictions. All these concerns underscore the need for strong security.

20.6.3 Ethical Considerations and Governance

The ethical AI model and program in the cloud, like SAP Joule in the SAP S/4 Cloud edition, are crucial to learn more about trust and accountability [5]. Organizations should prioritize transparency, fair play, and security when developing AI systems. For instance, an SAP Joule company can build solid data protection policies and well-documented AI decision-making processes to gain user trust.

Joint work between cloud providers, AI developers, and regulators can support the responsible deployment of these technologies, resulting in a shared set of best practices and auditing procedures that ensure protections against bias and discrimination [4, 27].

Reviewing AI models for bias, using bias detection tools, and following anti-discrimination laws are mechanisms for organizations working to keep their AI processes ethical [17, 26]. By adhering to these principles, companies will build AI that is fair and accountable and that benefits society, ultimately creating a more equitable technology industry overall, which is pictographically represented in Figure 20.4.

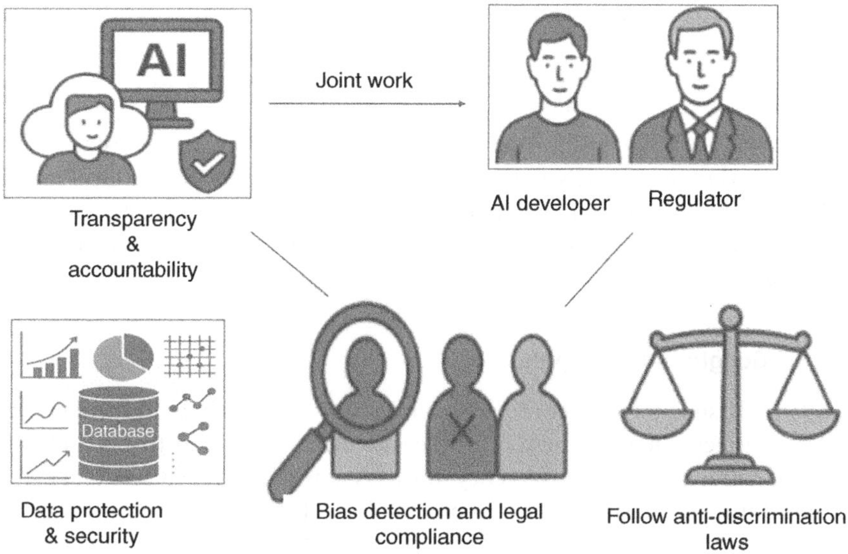

Figure 20.4 Ethical considerations and governance.

20.7 Case Studies

20.7.1 Introduction to Ethical AI Case Studies

Detailed cases in ethical AI development are extremely useful to demonstrate real-world examples of the ways in which AI can be developed and deployed in line with guiding principles [3].

These in-depth studies offer a view of the ethical issues and solutions taken by organizations with a strong ethical orientation.

A case study might, for example, demonstrate how a healthcare provider was able to use AI to improve patient outcomes with the consideration of data privacy and fairness.

Such cases are critical for developers, policymakers, and relevant parties in the AI ecosystem to learn about the ways in which ethical AI can be put into practice, as well as adopt best practices.

20.7.2 IBM's AI Ethics Board

IBM went to the next level on responsible AI by forming an AI Ethics board that oversees the ethical development of AI capabilities developed by the company.

This board is certainly important for reviewing and governing projects to make sure they meet the IBM principles of trust and openness [3].

For instance, consider a case in which IBM is building an AI that does healthcare diagnoses.

The AI Ethics Board would review the system for biases and would guarantee that it respects a patient's right to privacy.

In this way, the board encourages a culture of responsible AI usage, establishing adequate governance models and best practices to mitigate potential ethical issues.

This preventative measure will help further trust with the users and will come to demonstrate leadership in ethically deploying AI in an industry struggling with how to use it.

20.7.3 Google's AI Principles

Google has issued a clear set of AI Principles that it will follow in the development of AI technologies. These principles are centered around the idea of fairness, accountability, and transparency in AI systems to mitigate biases that could develop during the design and development phases [3].

Consider, for instance, if Google were to build an AI-based job recruitment tool. By doing this, the company's AI system can be trained in hiring processes that are fairer, not using the kind of biases that have been used in the past. This fairness ensures your organization is better equipped to have an inclusive and equitable hiring process. Moreover, by elucidating the process behind how the AI makes decisions as well as holding it accountable, Google establishes trust with its users and interest holders. This is not only raising the ethical bar for AI; it's leading by example for the industry at large.

For example, imagine a scenario where Google is developing an AI-powered tool for job recruitment. By adhering to these principles, the company ensures that the AI system evaluates candidates based on their qualifications and skills rather than any biased criteria. This commitment to fairness helps create a more inclusive and equitable hiring process. Additionally, by being transparent about how the AI makes decisions and holding the system accountable, Google builds trust with users and stakeholders. This proactive approach not only enhances the ethical standards of AI but also sets a positive example for industry.

20.7.4 The COMPAS System and Racial Bias

The COMPAS system is a notorious case of AI bias in the criminal justice system. Consider an African American defendant evaluated by the COMPAS system, which mistakenly predicts a greater recidivism probability than for a Caucasian defendant. This bias was discovered in a research exercise and showed that the system was loaded against black accused [6, 26].

In reply, the COMPAS Northpointe developers addressed these concerns by implementing a race-neutral version of the algorithm. Overall accuracy remained similar in this new version, but racial bias was substantially reduced. This case underscores that it is always necessary to assess and modify AI systems for fairness and equity. By mitigating biases and operating responsible changes, we can build AI technologies that are ethical and enable justice for everyone [6].

20.7.5 Amazon's Recruitment Algorithm

An example of AI bias is the Amazon hiring algorithm, which was scrapped after it was found to be biased against women. The algorithm had been trained to vet resumes by observing patterns in resumes submitted over the past decade, and most of the patterns were by men for the tech industry, the company says. The algorithm drew the conclusion, albeit wrongly. This is how historical biases can make their way into AI systems. This case illustrates the importance of careful design and scrutiny of the algorithms in order not to carry over existing gender gaps into the hiring process. Finally, it emphasizes the need to revisit and normalize the data for fairness and equity [26].

For example, consider the situation in which a strong female candidate gets passed over on account of her resume containing words such as "women's soccer team" or "women's college." After all, not only does this mean the organization is missing out on otherwise diverse candidates, but it also reinforces the gender biases already in place. Through thoughtful algorithm design and ongoing scrutiny of data for biases, they can build better, more equitable hiring processes.

To illustrate this, imagine a chart that demonstrates the process of recruitment, where bias can be entered along the way and how it is addressed. By taking a proactive stand, it guarantees that AI systems are built to be fair and equal, and, as a result, that we get the best and brightest to work with.

20.7.6 Healthcare AI and Racial Bias

In healthcare, one AI model, which is used to predict patient mortality rate, was found to be discriminatory toward African American patients. A study by Ober-Meyer et al. found that the system was more likely to assign high-risk scores to African American patients even when controlling for other health measures, such as chronic diseases.

These biases can result in disparate healthcare access and poor treatment outcomes for marginalized populations, highlighting the importance of fairness implemented on AI models [6, 28].

The cases will also be forced to set up a good governing model; if not, it would involve the data and bring in a lot of lawsuits that will dry up the future for the organizations that wish for a quick cut. They will create short-term benefits for the companies, and this will fade away the long-term benefits.

20.8 Future Directions

20.8.1 Enhancing Ethical Frameworks

As AI advances, the integration of robust ethical frameworks will be crucial in ensuring that AI is designed and used within the constraints of governance. Ethical aspects are becoming increasingly recognized as the key aspect in the development of AI. Through elegant risk-taking and conscious consideration for social impact, they are leading the charge toward a more just tomorrow.

Take health, for example. Ethical AI can help ensure that diagnostic tools are fueling accurate and unbiased outcomes for all patients, without them being discriminated against based on their background. In finance, it can be used to produce fair lending practices that treat no group unfairly. Ethical AI can avoid biased profiling and unfair justice in the case of law enforcement [1].

Bringing a set of comprehensive ethical AI guidelines into play is critical in reducing the risk of biases and adverse outcomes, especially in such risk-prone fields. Thus, they can gain trust and provide useful and safe AI for all [11].

20.8.2 Advancements in Bias Mitigation

Persistent use of biased AI and ML systems calls for ongoing research and innovative solutions. As generative AI techniques are becoming increasingly common, future work should focus on identifying and addressing the multiple sources of bias that such models may embed. For example, such biases may stem from historical data, algorithm design, or even interaction with a user.

It is paramount that policies that necessitate human domain opinion and review are established in decision-making processes so that fair outcomes are achieved [6].

For example, imagine a health AI system that is adopted for patient diagnosis. Without human supervision, the system could accidentally be skewed to favor specific demographics over others based on biased training data. Because human experts scrutinize recommendations from AI, they're able to address any unfair biases that have crept in, ensuring that all patients receive fair treatment.

This not only ensures fairness but also builds users' trust toward AI applications, thereby creating a fairer and more balanced technological society in the long run [29].

20.8.3 Collaborative Approaches to AI Safety

Facilitating collective advancement is key to the future of responsible AI. By investing in leading-edge, safe, and secure research and having a larger R&D spend overall, industry can pave the way with technical solutions grounded in the needs of each sector and capable of addressing potential risks and broader AI-wide impacts [30].

In these articles, the authors also propose a schema to generate sufficient open space in terms of the return on investment (ROI).

Exchange of experiences and best practices on ecosystems will be key for creating a culture of responsibility and accountability in AI areas [31].

20.8.4 Commitment to Continuous Learning

Given how fast technology enabling AI continues to evolve, it will be important to keep the door open to discovery and adjustment. Use strong and deliberate design and testing, containment, and impact strategies to prevent the abusive use of AI applications by institutions [30]. Letting managed risk transform a venture that had been born as a financial gamble into a means of bringing jobs and boosting the Gross Domestic Product (GDP) of the nation.

Such an iterative process would enable policymakers and practitioners to stay alert to the emergent problematic nature of AI systems and our concomitant obligations to respond to them in ways that dovetail with our values in efforts to promote elevating human rights principles from special instruments for decent responses into able tools for good fixes [1, 30].

20.8.5 Promoting Privacy and Security

With the shift toward a model in which more customer data is employed and consumed for training AI for research and business purposes at scale, it is a pressing requirement to keep all the user data privacy safe within a clear architectural paradigm.

This, too, becomes a crucial ethical issue when big data is not handled responsibly [10].

There is significant relevance of privacy and data anonymization as data protection under privacy acts, including GDPR and CCPA by law [3], to protect human rights and privacy, in which the associated approach to data protection will depend on and be based on.

Organizations must proactively include data storage platforms and data transfer standards for the data collected to maintain the quality and the privacy of the data needed [3].

References

1 Lumenalta, "Ethical considerations of AI," Oct. 2024. [Online]. Available: https://lumenalta.com/insights/ethical-considerations-of-ai.
2 "Navigating responsible AI: Why it matters and best practices for implementation," [Online]. Available: https://www.informatica.com/resources/articles/navigating-responsible-ai.html.
3 J. Anglen, "Ethical AI development guide," [Online]. Available: https://www.rapidinnovation.io/post/ethical-ai-development-guide.
4 "AI ethics: Navigating fairness and bias mitigation," [Online]. Available: https://www.francescatabor.com/articles/2024/4/4/ai-ethics-navigating-fairness-and-bias-mitigation.
5 Cogent Infotech, "9 ethical AI principles for organizations to follow," Jan. 2023. [Online]. Available: https://www.cogentinfo.com/resources/9-ethical-ai-principles-for-organizations-to-follow.
6 IBM, "What is AI ethics?," 2024. [Online]. Available: https://www.ibm.com/think/topics/ai-ethics.
7 J. Holdsworth, "What is a bias?," Dec. 2023. [Online]. Available: https://www.ibm.com/think/topics/ai-bias.
8 Mitra Best, "Understanding algorithmic bias and how to build trust in AI," Pwc.com. [Online]. Available: https://www.pwc.com/us/en/tech-effect/ai-analytics/algorithmic-bias-and-trust-in-ai.html.
9 H. D. Thu, "Addressing AI bias and fairness: Challenges, implications, and strategies for ethical AI," 2025. [Online]. Available: https://smartdev.com/addressing-ai-bias-and-fairness-challenges-implications-and-strategies-for-ethical-ai/.
10 "Combating bias in AI Systems: A guide for data scientists," [Online]. Available: https://www.datasciencecentral.com/combating-bias-in-ai-systems-a-guide-for-data-scientists/.
11 Law and Ethics in Tech, "Ethical artificial intelligence frameworks-fairness and equity," Jul. 2023. [Online]. Available: https://lawnethicsintech.medium.com/ethical-artificial-intelligence-frameworks-fairness-and-equity-b579c24a7a42.
12 Geeksforgeeks.org, "Fairness and bias in artificial intelligence," Apr. 2024. [Online]. Available: https://www.geeksforgeeks.org/fairness-and-bias-in-artificial-intelligence/.
13 Tigera.io, "Understanding AI safety: Principles, frameworks, and best practices," [Online]. Available: https://www.tigera.io/learn/guides/llm-security/ai-safety/.
14 "2022 volume 4 bias and ethical concerns in machine learning," [Online]. Available: https://www.isaca.org/resources/isaca-journal/issues/2022/volume-4/bias-and-ethical-concerns-in machine-learning.

15 “3 ways to minimize AI Bias–TransPerfect,” [Online]. Available: https://www.transperfect.com/dataforce/blog/3 ways to minimize AI bias.

16 Accuray.com, “Overcoming AI bias: Understanding, identifying and mitigating algorithmic bias in healthcare,” [Online]. Available: https://www.accuray.com/blog/overcoming-ai-bias-understanding identifying-and-mitigating-algorithmic-bias-in-healthcare/.

17 Trailhead.salesforce.com, “Recognize bias in artificial intelligence,” [Online]. Available: https://trailhead.salesforce.com/content/learn/modules/responsible-creation-of-artificial-intelligence/recognize-bias-in-ai.

18 Promevo, “Key strategies for ethical & efficient AI implementation,” Mar. 2025. [Online]. Available: https://promevo.com/blog/ethical-ai-implementation.

19 S. Taylor, “How to implement responsible AI, responsibly,” Sept. 2024. [Online]. Available: https://www.unisys.com/blog-post/ai/how-to-implement-responsible-ai-responsibly/.

20 T. Grenawalt, “Machine learning ethics: Understanding bias and fairness,” Oct. 2023. [Online]. Available: https://www.vationventures.com/research-article/machine-learning-ethics-understanding-bias-and-fairness.

21 E. Ferrara, “Fairness and bias in artificial intelligence: A brief survey of sources, impacts, and mitigation strategies,” Dec. 2023. [Online]. Available: https://www.mdpi.com/2413-4155/6/1/3.

22 N. T. Lee, “Algorithmic bias detection and mitigation: Best practices and policies to reduce consumer harms,” May 2019. [Online]. Available: https://www.brookings.edu/articles/algorithmic-bias-detection-and-mitigation-best-practices-and-policies-to-reduce-consumer-harms/.

23 “Tackling AI bias: Essential strategies companies should implement today,” May 2025. 10.36227/techrxiv.174611924.41516862/v1.

24 Thale, “AI regulations, cloud security, and threat mitigation: Navigating the future digital risk,” Oct. 2024. [Online]. Available: https://cloudsecurityalliance.org/blog/2024/10/02/ai-regulations-cloud-security-and-threat-mitigation-navigating-the-future-of-digital-risk.

25 A. Delaney, “Exposing the gas: Where AI and cloud introduce risk to your data protection strategy,” Apr. 2023. [Online]. Available: https://www.defendedsolutions.com/defended-solutions-blog/ai-cloud-risks-to-data-protection.

26 “Building a responsible AI: How to manage the AI ethics debate,” [Online]. Available: https://www.iso.org/artificial-intelligence/responsible-ai-ethics.

27 Sanjay, “AI in the cloud: Where ethics and governance converge,” Nov. 2023. [Online]. Available: https://ahex.co/ai-in-the-cloud-where-ethics-and-governance-converge/.

28 M. Wanyoike, “Ethical AI in the cloud,” Sept. 2024. [Online]. Available: https://medium.com/@AIandInsights/ethical-ai-in-the-cloud-68f4905e61c0.

29 Telusdigital.com, "Five strategies to mitigate bias when implementing generative AI," Mar. 2024. [Online]. Available: https://www.telusdigital.com/insights/ai-data/article/mitigating-genai-bias.

30 Aigoogle/responsibilityprinciples, "AI principles," [Online]. Available: https://ai.google/responsibility/principles/.

31 A. Ribeiro, "DHS framework offers AI security guidelines for critical infrastructure and highlights secure development and supply chain accountability," Nov. 2024. [Online]. Available: https://industrialcyber.co/ai/dhs-framework-offers-ai-security-guidelines-for-critical-infrastructure-highlights-secure-development-supply-chain-accountability/.

21

Conclusion—The Future Cloud: Ethical, Autonomous, and Planet-Aware

Pronnoy Goswami[1] *and Aditya Gupta*[2]

[1] *IEEE Senior Member, Santa Clara, CA, USA*
[2] *IEEE Senior Member, Seattle, WA, USA*

21.1 Introduction

For over two decades, cloud computing has been the primary engine of digital innovation, fundamentally altering how we build, deploy, and scale software systems. Its history is a story of relentless abstraction, a continuous effort to distance developers from the physical constraints of hardware. This journey, first chronicled in seminal papers like "A View of Cloud Computing" [1], envisioned computing delivered as a fifth utility [2], as ubiquitous and reliable as the electrical grid. We have, in large part, realized that vision. The cloud has democratized access to high-performance computing, catalyzed the growth of data-intensive artificial intelligent (AI), and become the bedrock of the global economy.

Yet, as we stand at this contemporary vantage point, the foundational principles that drove the first wave of cloud adoption—cost-efficiency, elasticity, and operational leverage—are no longer sufficient to guide its future. The cloud is not merely a technical infrastructure; it has evolved into a societal one, a distributed, semi-autonomous system that makes decisions with profound economic, environmental, and ethical consequences. The pressing questions have thus shifted. It is no longer just about "Can we scale it?" but rather:

- How do we ensure control over infrastructure that makes decisions on our behalf?
- Does it align with our human values of fairness, transparency, and accountability?

In this concluding chapter, we synthesize the critical themes explored throughout this volume to propose a research and engineering agenda for the next generation of cloud computing. We argue that the future cloud must be architected around three core imperatives: ethical governance, autonomous operation, and planet-aware sustainability. These are not independent pursuits but deeply intertwined facets of a single, overarching challenge: to build cloud systems that are not only powerful and resilient but also accountable, transparent, and responsible.

We will deconstruct this challenge by examining six interconnected domains that form the blueprint for this future:

1) **The Trajectory of Abstraction:** Analyzing the trade-offs between developer velocity and operational opacity.
2) **Multicloud Resilience and Observability:** Moving from fragmented monitoring to holistic, system-wide understanding.
3) **Governance-Aware Autonomy:** Embedding safety, fairness, and explainability into self-managing systems.
4) **Ethics as an Architectural Primitive:** Enforcing responsible behavior at the infrastructure layer.
5) **Planet-Aware Cloud Architectures:** Integrating sustainability as a first-order design principle.
6) **The New Economics of Trust and Sovereignty:** Balancing cost with compliance, security, and data integrity in a zero-trust world.

Through this exploration, we will demonstrate that the next great leap in cloud computing will not be measured in teraflops or petabytes alone, but in its capacity to earn and maintain societal trust. It requires us to move beyond thinking of the cloud as a collection of services and to begin engineering it as a global, shared utility with embedded accountability [3].

21.2 The Enduring Arc of Abstraction and Its Unseen Costs

The history of the cloud is synonymous with the history of abstraction. Each major paradigm shift, from bare-metal servers to virtual machines (VMs) [4], from VMs to containers [5], and from containers to serverless functions [6], was motivated by a desire to simplify the developer experience by concealing the complexity of the underlying infrastructure. As we discussed in "*The Evolution of Cloud Computing*," a chapter in this book, this progression has yielded tremendous gains in productivity and agility, allowing teams to focus on business logic rather than on managing operating systems, runtimes, or network fabrics.

However, this relentless pursuit of abstraction has created a fundamental tension. While it empowers developers, it simultaneously introduces new forms of opacity for platform operators, security teams, and financial analysts. When an application is disaggregated into a mesh of ephemeral, event-driven functions spanning multiple cloud providers, traditional methods of debugging, performance tuning, and cost attribution break down. The very mechanisms that make serverless platforms so powerful—managed runtimes, automatic scaling, and invisible infrastructure—also create an observability gap [7]. Troubleshooting a latency spike or a security vulnerability in such an environment becomes a forensic exercise across distributed, often inaccessible, components.

Future abstraction models must therefore be designed with an explicit goal of resolving this tension. We posit that the next evolution will not be another layer of "hiding" but rather the development of transparent abstractions. These are systems that provide the cognitive benefits of high-level interfaces while exposing rich, structured metadata about their internal operations. This requires a co-design of application frameworks and underlying platforms, centered on several key principles:

- **Structured Telemetry Propagation:** Modern distributed tracing standards like OpenTelemetry are a critical first step, enabling the propagation of context across process and network boundaries [8]. Future systems must go further, embedding application-level semantics, business transaction IDs, and policy metadata directly into the telemetry fabric.
- **Cost as an Observable Signal:** Cloud cost is currently a lagging indicator, often analyzed weeks after the fact. Transparent abstractions must surface cost data in real time, attributing it not just to high-level services but to individual functions, API calls, or even specific tenants in a multi-tenant system [9]. This transforms cost from an accounting problem into an engineering metric.
- **Explainable Runtimes:** As platforms make more autonomous decisions (e.g., placing a function in a specific availability zone and selecting a particular VM instance type), they must be capable of explaining *why* a decision was made. This requires logging not just the outcome but also the inputs, policies, and constraints that informed the decision logic [10].

Achieving this will demand a move away from siloed toolchains and toward integrated platforms where the runtime, orchestration layer, and observability framework are designed as a single, coherent system.

21.3 From Monitoring Silos to Multicloud Operational Resilience

The strategic imperative to avoid vendor lock-in, comply with data sovereignty regulations, and improve fault tolerance has driven the widespread adoption of multicloud and hybrid architectures [11]. However, this architectural choice comes at the cost of operational fragmentation. Each cloud provider offers its own bespoke suite of tools for monitoring, logging, security, and identity management. The result is a fractured operational landscape where engineering teams struggle to maintain a coherent view of application health, security posture, and compliance status.

As detailed in "*Multi-Cloud and Hybrid Cloud Strategies for Resilient Infrastructure*," the antidote to this fragmentation is not another dashboard, but a systemic approach to observability. Unlike monitoring, which tracks the health of known components (e.g., CPU utilization and disk space), observability provides the capability to ask arbitrary questions about a system's behavior without having to predefine the metrics [7]. It is a critical enabler of resilience in complex, distributed environments.

The future of multicloud resilience hinges on maturing our observability practices from passive data collection to active, intelligence-driven systems. We foresee progress in several key areas:

- **The Service Mesh as a Universal Control Plane:** Technologies like Istio and Linkerd provide a dedicated infrastructure layer for managing service-to-service communication [12]. Initially focused on traffic management and security, the service mesh is evolving into a de facto cross-cloud control plane. By instrumenting all inter-service communication, it provides a consistent source of telemetry (metrics, logs, and traces) regardless of where the services are running. Future service meshes will incorporate richer policy enforcement, enabling fine-grained control over data routing based on sovereignty rules, cost policies, and even the carbon intensity of the underlying infrastructure.
- **Open Standards as the Lingua Franca:** The success of OpenTelemetry (OTel) in standardizing telemetry generation has been pivotal [8]. Its broad adoption by cloud providers and vendors is a testament to the industry's recognition that interoperability is non-negotiable. The next frontier is to standardize the metadata and semantics *within* the telemetry signals, creating a richer, more queryable dataset for Artificial Intelligence for IT Operations (AIOps) and other autonomous systems.
- **From Anomaly Detection to Causal Analysis:** Today's AIOps platforms are adept at detecting anomalies in high-cardinality data streams. However, detecting a deviation is different from understanding its root cause and business impact. Future observability systems, powered by causal inference models and topology-aware analytics, will move beyond correlation to identify causal pathways. They will be able to answer questions like, "*Did the deployment of service X cause the checkout failure for European customers, and what is the associated revenue impact?*" [13].

Ultimately, observability is the sensory system for the autonomous cloud. It provides the ground truth necessary for self-healing, self-optimizing, and self-protecting systems to function safely and effectively.

21.4 The Challenge of Governance-Aware Autonomy

The sheer scale and dynamism of modern cloud platforms have made fully manual operation untenable. We have crossed a threshold of complexity where human operators can no longer reliably perform real-time analysis and intervention. This has given rise to a new class of autonomous systems designed to manage infrastructure through closed control loops, policy-driven automation, and machine learning-based decision engines. As explored in "*Autonomous Cloud Infrastructure and Self-Healing Systems*," technologies like the Kubernetes Operator pattern [14, 15] and practices like chaos engineering [16] are prime examples of this trend. These systems can automatically scale workloads, remediate failures, and reconfigure networks without human intervention.

However, autonomy without robust governance is a recipe for disaster. An improperly configured auto-scaler can lead to catastrophic cost overruns [9]. A biased resource scheduler can systematically starve certain workloads, violating service-level agreements (SLAs). An overly aggressive self-healing system can exacerbate an outage by repeatedly restarting a failing component. The central research challenge, therefore, is not simply to build more powerful automation but to build governance-aware autonomous systems.

But you can have autonomy without strong governance at your own peril. Misconfiguration can cause a loss of millions of dollars, representing cost [9]. A resource scheduler that is biased and systematically under-resources some workloads is in breach of SLAs. Too-aggressive self-healing may worsen an outage by repeatedly restarting a failed component. The fundamental challenge in research, thus, is not how to construct more powerful automation per se but how to construct governance-aware autonomous systems.

This requires embedding mechanisms for safety, explainability, and human oversight directly into the architecture of the automation itself. We identify three critical pillars for achieving this:

1) **Explainability and Auditability:** When an autonomous system makes a critical decision—such as terminating a set of VMs or rerouting traffic away from a region—it must be able to produce a clear, human-understandable explanation for its actions. This "explainability by design" requires the system to log the telemetry it observed, the policies it evaluated, and the decision logic it applied [10]. This creates an immutable audit trail that is essential for forensic analysis, compliance verification, and, most importantly, building operator trust.
2) **Programmable, Verifiable Guardrails:** Autonomy must operate within well-defined boundaries. These boundaries should be expressed as declarative policies that are both machine-readable and formally verifiable. For example,

a policy might state, "The auto-scaler for the payments service is not permitted to exceed a budget of $5,000 per day" or "No production data originating from the EU can be processed on infrastructure outside of designated EU regions." Technologies like Open Policy Agent (OPA) are paving the way for this kind of policy-as-code [17], but significant research is needed in formal verification techniques to prove that a system's behavior will always remain within these safety envelopes.

3) **Human-on-the-Loop Governance:** Full autonomy does not imply the absence of humans. Rather, it reframes the role of the human operator from a manual controller to a strategic supervisor. Future systems should incorporate "human-on-the-loop" models, where the autonomous system can propose a course of action for high-risk scenarios and await human approval before executing. This model combines the speed and analytical power of the machine with the contextual judgment and ethical reasoning of the human expert.

Failing to address the governance challenge will not only lead to technical failures but will fundamentally erode the trust that organizations place in the cloud. Autonomy and control must be seen as two sides of the same coin.

21.5 From Optimization to Obligation: The Rise of Ethical and Planet-Aware Architectures

For years, the design of cloud systems was driven by technical and economic optimizations: maximizing performance, minimizing latency, and reducing cost. As the cloud's influence has grown, we are recognizing that this optimization function is incomplete. The decisions made by cloud infrastructure—how to allocate resources, where to store data, which tasks to prioritize—have tangible ethical and environmental consequences. In response, we are seeing the emergence of two new, interconnected architectural drivers: ethics by design and sustainability by default.

21.5.1 Engineering Ethics into the Infrastructure Layer

As we argued in "Ethics, Bias, and Responsible AI in Cloud Environments," ethical considerations in the cloud extend far beyond the fairness of AI models. The infrastructure itself can become a source of systemic bias and inequity if not designed with intention. A resource allocation algorithm in a multi-tenant system could, for instance, consistently deprioritize smaller customers during peak load, creating a digital "poverty trap." A data retention policy might inadvertently violate user privacy by storing logs for longer than necessary.

To counter this, we must begin to treat ethics not as a compliance checklist but as an architectural principle, enforced at the lowest levels of the cloud stack. This vision of ethical infrastructure requires us to:

- **Develop Fairness-Aware Schedulers:** Orchestration systems like Kubernetes need to evolve beyond simple resource packing. Future schedulers must be able to incorporate fairness constraints, ensuring that resources are allocated equitably across different tenants, user groups, or workload priorities, especially under contention [18].
- **Embed Data Minimization by Default:** Inspired by privacy regulations like General Data Protection Regulation (GDPR) [19], cloud platforms should be architected to minimize data collection and retention. This means providing tools for automatic data anonymization, configurable time-to-live (TTL) policies on all stored data (including logs and backups), and transparent reporting on what data is being stored and for what purpose.
- **Provide Transparent Impact Assessments:** Just as developers review code for performance regressions, platform operators should have tools to assess the potential ethical impact of infrastructure changes. Before deploying a new autoscaling policy or a new data routing rule, they should be able to model its effect on different user cohorts to proactively identify and mitigate potential biases [20, 21].

21.5.2 Planet-Aware Computing: A First-Order Principle

The environmental footprint of the digital economy is immense and growing. Data centers are responsible for an estimated 1–2% of global electricity consumption, a figure that is projected to rise significantly with the proliferation of AI workloads [22]. As presented in "Sustainable Cloud Computing and Carbon-Aware Architectures," we can no longer treat sustainability as an afterthought. It must become a first-order principle of cloud architecture, on par with performance, security, and reliability.

This shift towards planet-aware cloud design requires a multi-layered strategy:

- **Infrastructure Layer: Follow the Renewables:** Data centers should be strategically located in regions with abundant and consistent renewable energy sources. Cloud providers are already making progress here, but the next step is to provide customers with the transparency and control to ensure their workloads run on carbon-free energy [23, 24].
- **Orchestration Layer: Carbon-Aware Scheduling:** Workload schedulers should be endowed with real-time data on the carbon intensity of the electrical grid. This allows them to practice "carbon-aware" scheduling, deferring non-critical batch jobs, big data analyses, or AI model training to times when

the grid is supplied by wind, solar, or other green sources [25]. This simple act of time-shifting can dramatically reduce the carbon footprint of a computation without affecting its outcome.
- **Development Layer: Green Software Engineering:** Developers must be empowered to make environmentally conscious choices. This includes providing them with APIs to specify the "greenness" requirements of a workload, libraries that optimize for energy efficiency, and observability tools that expose the energy consumption and carbon footprint of their code. Initiatives like the Green Software Foundation's Software Carbon Intensity (SCI) specification are crucial steps toward creating a standardized "carbon label" for software components [26].

By integrating both financial and environmental cost signals into our dashboards and APIs, we can empower organizations to make holistic optimization decisions that align their business goals with their Environmental, Social, and Governance (ESG) commitments.

21.6 Redefining the Economics: Financial Operations, Sovereignty, and Zero Trust

The final pillar of the future cloud involves a fundamental rethinking of its economic and security models. The traditional focus on minimizing direct financial cost is evolving into a more sophisticated, multi-dimensional optimization problem that accounts for risk, compliance, and trust. This is driven by two powerful forces: the maturation of Financial Operations (FinOps) and the non-negotiable demands of data sovereignty and zero-trust security.

21.6.1 The Evolution of FinOps: From Cost Control to Value Optimization

The FinOps movement has transformed cloud financial management from a reactive accounting exercise into a proactive, cross-functional discipline [9]. It brings together finance, engineering, and business teams to foster a culture of financial accountability. However, the first wave of FinOps focused primarily on cost visibility and optimization. The next generation of FinOps must incorporate a broader definition of "cost" and "value."

We envision a multi-dimensional FinOps framework where infrastructure decisions are balanced against:

- **Financial Cost:** The direct dollar cost of compute, storage, and network resources.

- **Environmental Cost:** The carbon footprint (e.g., CO_2 equivalent) associated with a workload, which may soon carry a direct or indirect financial price via carbon taxes or credits [27].
- **Operational Risk:** The "cost of unreliability," measured by the potential business impact of an outage for a given architectural choice.
- **Compliance Risk:** The potential financial penalties and reputational damage associated with violating data sovereignty or other regulatory mandates.

This holistic approach moves the conversation from "Which VM is cheapest?" to "What is the optimal blend of cost, performance, carbon efficiency, and risk for this specific application?"

21.6.2 Securing the Fabric: Sovereignty and Zero Trust

In our increasingly fragmented geopolitical landscape, data is subject to the laws of the jurisdiction in which it resides. Regulations like Europe's GDPR [19], California's California Consumer Privacy Act (CCPA), and India's Digital Personal Data Protection (DPDP) have made data sovereignty a critical design constraint. Simultaneously, the rise of sophisticated cyber threats has led to the broad adoption of the *Zero Trust Architecture (ZTA)* model, which operates on the principle of "never trust, always verify" [28].

These two forces, (1) sovereignty and (2) zero trust, are reshaping the very fabric of the cloud. The future cloud will not be a monolithic, borderless entity. Instead, it will be a federation of programmable trust zones, enforced by a new generation of security technologies:

- **Confidential Computing:** This emerging paradigm uses hardware-based Trusted Execution Environments (TEEs) to protect data even while it is being processed in memory [29]. This allows organizations to process sensitive data in the cloud without exposing it to the cloud provider or any other entity on the host system, providing a powerful tool for enforcing sovereignty and privacy.
- **Declarative, Verifiable Policy Engines:** Zero trust requires that every request to access a resource be authenticated and authorized. Policy engines like OPA [17] allow these authorization rules to be managed centrally as code, providing a consistent and auditable mechanism for enforcing access control across a multicloud environment.
- **Real-time Attestation Systems:** To trust a component in a distributed system, you need to be able to verify its identity and integrity at any time. Cryptographic attestation protocols allow a workload to prove that it is running the correct software on a trusted hardware platform, providing a foundational building block for establishing trust in a zero-trust world.

Together, these technologies will enable the creation of infrastructures that are both highly autonomous and verifiably compliant, ensuring that even automated actions adhere to the strictest security and jurisdictional policies.

21.7 Synthesis and a Forward-Looking Research Agenda

The domains we have explored, abstraction, resilience, autonomy, ethics, sustainability, and trust, are not isolated challenges to be solved in sequence. They are deeply intertwined threads in the complex tapestry of the future cloud. A planet-aware scheduler (sustainability) is useless without the fine-grained telemetry to inform its decisions (observability). An autonomous remediation system (autonomy) is dangerous without the verifiable guardrails to ensure its safety (governance). A multicloud strategy (resilience) is untenable without a unified security model that enforces data sovereignty (trust).

The central argument of this chapter is that progress requires a holistic, co-design approach. Engineering decisions can no longer be made in a vacuum; they must be evaluated against their operational, ethical, environmental, and economic impacts. As we conclude this volume, we propose a forward-looking research and engineering agenda to guide the community toward this vision. We believe the most pressing open questions lie at the intersections of these domains:

1) **On Verifiable and Ethical Autonomy:**
   - How can we apply formal methods to automatically verify that the behavior of an autonomous cloud management system (e.g., an autoscaler or self-healer) will never violate a given set of safety, ethical, or financial policies?
   - What theoretical frameworks are needed to measure and mitigate algorithmic bias in resource schedulers and load balancers at the infrastructure level?
2) **On The Economics of Sustainability and Resilience:**
   - What is the correct economic model for pricing the carbon externality of cloud workloads? How can we create market-based mechanisms that incentivize the development and adoption of "green" software?
   - How can we quantify the financial value of resilience (e.g., the Return on Investment [ROI] of investing in a multicloud architecture or a chaos engineering program) to better justify these investments?
3) **On Transparent Abstractions and Trust:**
   - What new language constructs and runtime features are needed to create "explainable" serverless platforms that can justify their autonomous decisions regarding function placement, scaling, and resource allocation?

- How can we build a continuous attestation fabric that can provide verifiable proof of data provenance and processing integrity as data flows through a complex, multicloud data pipeline, especially one involving confidential computing enclaves?

4) **On Human-Centric Cloud Operations:**
   - What new user interfaces and data visualizations are needed for a multi-dimensional FinOps dashboard that allows operators to intuitively understand the trade-offs between cost, performance, carbon, and risk?
   - What are the most effective models for "human-on-the-loop" governance in autonomous systems? At what points in the decision-making process is human judgment most critical?

21.8 Conclusion and Future Scope

The first era of cloud computing was defined by a relentless drive for scale and efficiency. The next era will be defined by a quest for control, responsibility, and trust. The future cloud, as we have envisioned it, is not a predetermined outcome of technological evolution. It must be built with intention. It requires a conscious and collective effort from researchers, engineers, and policymakers to embed our highest values—fairness, transparency, sustainability, and accountability—into the very architecture of our digital world.

The building blocks are here. From OpenTelemetry and confidential computing to carbon-aware scheduling and policy-as-code, we have the technical components. The great task ahead is one of synthesis and integration. We must move beyond optimizing individual components in isolation and begin architecting holistic systems that are designed from the ground up to be resilient, responsible, and aligned with the long-term interests of both people and the planet. In sum, we must elevate our ambition from delivering computing as a utility to stewarding it as a shared societal good.

Cloud computing's future lies not in isolated technical advances but in integrated, responsible architectures reflecting human and planetary values. We must deliberately design infrastructures that are transparent, fair, autonomous yet governed, and inherently sustainable. This is not merely an engineering challenge but a societal imperative.

References

1 M. Armbrust *et al.*, "A view of cloud computing," *Commun. ACM*, vol. 53, no. 4, pp. 50–58, 2010.

2 R. Buyya, C. S. Yeo, S. Venugopal, J. Broberg, and I. Brandic, "Cloud computing and emerging IT platforms: Vision, hype, and reality for delivering computing as the 5th utility," *Future Gener. Comput. Syst.*, vol. 25, no. 6, pp. 599–616, 2009.
3 OECD, "The role of cloud computing in research and innovation," 2022. [Online]. Available: https://www.oecd.org/sti/policy-papers/the-role-of-cloud-computing-in-research-and-innovation.htm.
4 P. Barham *et al.*, "Xen and the art of virtualization," in *Proc. Nineteenth ACM Symp. Oper. Syst. Principles (SOSP '03)*, New York, NY, USA: Association for Computing Machinery (ACM), 2003, pp. 164–177.
5 D. Merkel, "Docker: lightweight Linux containers for consistent development and deployment," *Linux J.*, vol. 2014, no. 239, 2014.
6 J. Schleier-Smith *et al.*, "What serverless computing is and should become: the NEXT era of cloud computing," *Commun. ACM*, vol. 64, no. 10, pp. 76–84, 2021.
7 C. Majors, "Observability: A 3-year retrospective," 2021. [Online]. Available: https://thenewstack.io/observability-a-3-year-retrospective/.
8 The OpenTelemetry Authors, "OpenTelemetry documentation," *CNCF*, 2024. [Online]. Available: https://opentelemetry.io/docs/.
9 FinOps Foundation, "State of FinOps 2023," 2023. [Online]. Available: https://data.finops.org/state-of-finops/2023.
10 A. Adadi and M. Berrada, "Peeking inside the Black-box: A survey on explainable artificial intelligence (XAI)," *IEEE Access*, vol. 6, pp. 52138–52160, 2018.
11 HashiCorp, "State of cloud strategy survey," 2023. [Online]. Available: https://www.hashicorp.com/state-of-the-cloud.
12 R. Choo *et al.*, "A survey on service mesh: architecture, security, and challenges," *Digit. Commun. Netw.*, vol. 9, no. 5, pp. 1210–1222, 2023.
13 J. Pearl, *Causality: Models, Reasoning, and Inference*, 2nd ed. Cambridge, UK: Cambridge Univ. Press, 2009.
14 "KubeCon + CloudNativeCon NA 2023 Keynotes," *CNCF*, 2023. [Online]. Available: https://www.youtube.com/playlist?list=PLj6h78yzYM2MYc0X1465RzF_7Cqf7bnqL.
15 Kubernetes Authors, "Operator pattern," 2024. [Online]. Available: https://kubernetes.io/docs/concepts/extend-kubernetes/operator/.
16 A. Al-Hawari *et al.*, "Chaos engineering: A survey on principles, techniques, and challenges," *IEEE Access*, vol. 8, pp. 157778–157802, 2020.
17 T. Sandall *et al.*, "Open policy agent," *CNCF*, 2018. [Online]. Available: https://www.openpolicyagent.org/.
18 M. Schwarzkopf, "The future of the datacenter is (still) the computer," in *Proc. 17th Workshop Hot Top. Oper. Syst. (HotOS '19)*, Association for Computing Machinery (ACM), 2019, pp. 162–169.

19 P. Voigt and A. von dem Bussche, "The EU general data protection regulation (GDPR)," in *A Practical Guide*, 1st ed. Cham: Springer International Publishing, 2017, pp. 1–383.

20 Microsoft Azure, "Microsoft responsible AI standard v2," 2022. [Online]. Available: https://www.microsoft.com/en-us/ai/responsible-ai.

21 World Economic Forum, "Ethics by design: An organizational approach to responsible use of technology," 2022. [Online]. Available: https://www.weforum.org/publications/ethics-by-design-an-organizational-approach-to-responsible-use-of-technology/.

22 N. Jones, "How to stop data centres from gobbling up the world's electricity," *Nature*, vol. 561, no. 7722, pp. 163–166, 2018.

23 Google Cloud, "Carbon-aware computing for Google Cloud," 2023. [Online]. Available: https://blog.google/outreach-initiatives/sustainability/carbon-aware-computing-location/.

24 AWS, "Sustainability pillar – AWS well-architected framework," 2023. [Online]. Available: https://docs.aws.amazon.com/wellarchitected/latest/sustainability-pillar/sustainability-pillar.html.

25 A. Wierman *et al.*, "Carbon-aware computing," *ACM SIGCOMM Comput. Commun. Rev.*, vol. 53, no. 1, pp. 1–8, 2023.

26 Green Software Foundation, "Software Carbon Intensity (SCI) specification v1.0," 2021. [Online]. Available: https://github.com/Green-Software-Foundation/sci.

27 W. D. Nordhaus, "Designing a global carbon tax," *Rev. Environ. Econ. Policy*, vol. 14, no. 1, pp. 4–22, Winter, 2020.

28 S. Rose, O. Borchert, S. Mitchell, and S. Connelly, "Zero trust architecture," NIST Special Publication 800-207, Aug. 2020. [Online]. Available: https://csrc.nist.gov/publications/detail/sp/800-207/final.

29 Confidential Computing Consortium, "Confidential computing: A technical analysis," 2023. [Online]. Available: https://confidentialcomputing.io/wp-content/uploads/sites/10/2023/03/CCC-A-Technical-Analysis-of-Confidential-Computing-v1.3_unlocked.pdf.

Glossary

Abstraction	Simplifying complex systems by hiding lower-level details.
Observability	The ability to understand a system's internal state through external outputs.
Governance-Aware Autonomy	Autonomous systems designed with embedded ethical and safety controls.

FinOps	Financial operations practice for optimizing cloud spending.
Zero Trust Architecture	A security model assuming no implicit trust, requiring continuous verification.
Confidential Computing	Protecting data during processing using secure hardware enclaves.
Planet-Aware Computing	Incorporating environmental sustainability into computing practices.

Index

a

Access control 81
Access management 250
Accountability 286, 376–377, 382
Active learning 80
Adaptive sampling techniques 60, 61
Adherence 146
Agent-based *vs.* agentless data collection 162–163
Agentic AI 46, 143–145
  orchestration 108–109
AI as a Service 4–5
AI-driven cloud services 129–148
  architecture 131
  automated provisioning and dynamic scaling 135–136
  broader impact of 132
  cloud cost optimization 141
  generative and agentic AI in 143–145
  hybrid cloud management 137
  intelligent automation principles in 134–135
  journey to 130–131
  ML capabilities of 131
  multimodal AI foundations 145–147
  performance optimization and cost management 136–137
  security and threat detection 136
  technologies empowering 133–134
AI-enhanced anomaly detection 63–64
AI for IT Operations (AIOps) platforms 5, 11, 210
  anomaly detection and root cause analysis 169–172
  with APM and DevSecOps 184
  architecture 156–161
  best practices for 179–182
  big data imperative 153
  case studies and industry implementations 175–179
  challenges and limitations 182–183
  cloud observability fundamentals 154–156
    in cloud environments 155–156
    distributed tracing and context propagation 156
    observability *vs.* monitoring 154
    pillars of observability 154–155
  data pipelines and telemetry management 161–164
    agent-based *vs.* agentless data collection 162–163
    data transport and storage considerations 163
    handling high cardinality and high velocity 164
    observability data 161–162

AI for IT Operations (AIOps) platforms (*contd.*)
    schema standardization and tagging strategies 163–164
  defining 153–154
  future directions in 183–185
  incident management workflow 172–174
  intelligent observability, AI/ML techniques for 165–168
    clustering and dimensionality reduction 167
    graph-based models for dependency mapping 167–168
    reinforcement learning 168
    supervised learning 166
    time-series forecasting 166–167
    trend analysis 166–167
    unsupervised learning 165
  manual operations to automated monitoring 152–153
  motivation and scope 151
  open-source *vs.* commercial 181
  overview 151–152
AI-powered risk assessment 272
AI workloads 113–127
  challenges in 125–126
  and cost drivers 116–117
  optimizing usage and cost 123
  quantifying business value 121
  reporting and analytics 121
  sentiment analysis workloads 122
  tagging strategy 120
  types of 114–116
Alert fatigue mitigation 169–170
Algorithmic bias 378
Amazon Braket 348–350, 367
Amazon DynamoDB 228, 231
Amazon Elastic Kubernetes Service (AWS EKS) 266
Amazon Event Bridge 230
Amazon, recruitment algorithm 387
Amazon Resource Names (ARNs) 62
Amazon Web Services (AWS) 2, 17, 26, 200, 321, 358
  AppConfig 234
  Auto Scaling 135
  CloudTrail 273
  Cognito 229
  Config 139
  Cost Explorer 137
  Customer Carbon Footprint Tool 9
  Event Bridge 220
  Event Bridge Schema Registry 227
  GuardDuty 136
  Lambda function 26, 46, 220, 228, 230–231
  Step Functions 230–231
  X-Ray 61, 62
Annotation systems 182
Anomaly detection 100, 121, 169–172
  alert fatigue mitigation 169–170
  confidence scores and explainability 171–172
  multi-modal anomaly detection 169
  probabilistic correlation and causality inference 170
  topology-aware root cause localization 171
  types of 169
Apache Airflow 362
Apache Kafka 276
Apache Log4j 195
API Gateway 229
API Security 48
Application deployment 24–25
Application-level segmentation 254
Application programming interfaces (APIs) 19–20, 37, 41, 132, 220, 320
  gateway functions 39
  versioning 48

ARPANET 15, 18
Artificial intelligence (AI) 1, 46, 113–114
  challenges and opportunities 9–10
  cloud environments and. *See* Cloud environments
  cloud's new growth engine 4–5
  and cloud use cases 6–7
  for compliance and governance automation 139
  democratization 87
  in deployment pipelines 138
  development of 75
  FinOps principles applied to 117–125
  for fraud detection 176
  and generative AI 127
  governance and regulatory frameworks 147
  and machine learning (ML) 100
  mainframes to virtualization 1–2
  methods 71
  for proactive security and compliance automation 294–295
  techniques for intelligent observability 165–168
Asynchronous communication 51
Atlassian 102
AT&T 50
Attribute-based access control (ABAC) 248, 251
Auditing needs 183
Audit management 275
Authentication 251
Autoencoders 165
Automate code generation 143
Automated governance (guardrails) 100
Automated machine learning (AutoML) 76
Automated provisioning 135–136
Automated remediation 174
Automation 33
  classification 160–161
  of cloud management 129
  compliance monitoring 65
  of customer support 145
  intelligence 129–148
  and orchestration layer 160–161
  real-time monitoring and 126
Automation-driven infrastructure management 27
AutoML 4–5, 78
Autonomic computing 210
Autonomous AI systems 147
Autonomous cloud infrastructure
  AI for IT Operations (AIOps) 210
  architectural principles for 201–203
  autonomic computing 210
  cloud-native and microservice paradigms 203–205
  cloud storage and networking fundamentals 209–210
  defining 199–200
  Function-as-a-Service architectures 206–207
  GitOps and continuous delivery 208
  Infrastructure-as-Code (IaC) 207–208
  Kubernetes 205
  monitoring, logging, and observability 208–209
  observability platforms and tools 209
  self-healing in cloud resilience 200–201
  serverless computing model 206
  traditional *vs.* cloud-native monitoring 208–209
Autonomous cloud operations 144
Autonomous governance 280
Autonomous lifecycle management 144
Autonomous systems 6

Autoregressive integrated moving average (ARIMA) models 166–167
Availability 286
Azure Activity Logs 273
Azure Functions 46, 206
Azure Quantum 350
Azure Virtual Machine Scale Sets 200

b

Backend-as-a-Service (BaaS) 220, 222
Backend for frontend (BFF) 39–40
Backward compatibility 48
Banking 306–307
Banking (US Regional Bank) 101–102
Bare-metal hypervisor 21
Batch inference 115
Batch processing 85
Batch workloads 115
Bayesian belief propagation 171
Bayesian networks model 170
Behavioral-driven development (BDD) 191
Behavior analytics 248
Benchmarking 10, 122
  results analyses 68–69
Beneficence 377
Bias 377–379
  hypocrisy 139
Bias mitigation 144
Bioinformatics 364
Black-box models 86
Blockchain technology 294
Blue-Green Deployments 47
Budgets 122
Business capability 39
Business model transformation 92
Business software alliance (BSA) 193
Business value drives decisions 96

c

Caching 85
CALMS methodology 193
Capital expenditures (CapEx) 91
  to operating expenditures (OpEx) shift 91–92, 94
Capital One 142
Carbon accounting 368
Carbon-aware architectures 319–339
  workload scheduling system 320
Carbon-aware scheduling 8, 323–324, 368
Carbon-conscious planning 320
Carbon Disclosure Project 338
Causality inference 170
Causality mapping 159
Centralized log aggregation 43
  architecture 258–259
Centralized logging 40
Centralized orchestration 226
Certification standards 311
Chaos engineering 44, 70
  for cost 99
Chaos Engineering method 139
Chaos Monkey tool 142
Chargeback models 99–100
ChargePayment Lambda function 236
ChatOps 173
Checkpointing 85
Chellappa, Ramnath 17
Chief Information Officers (CIOs) 3
China's Personal Information Protection Law (PIPL) 300, 303–304
Circle CI 47
Climate modeling 363–364
Closed-loop policy enforcement 184
Cloudability 137
Cloud Access Security Brokers (CASBs) 257
CLOUD Act 301, 303, 309, 314

Cloud architectures, event-driven 219–245
Cloud computing 1, 76, 129
  architecture and service models 3
  challenges and opportunities 9–10
  definition 16
  driving growth in 4
  evolution of 1–7, 132–137, 321–322
  growth of 11
  historical context and significance 17–18
  modern 23–25
  serverless computing. *see* Serverless computing
  service models in 15
  shifting cloud paradigm 4
  supporting AI workloads in 5
  sustainability imperative 7–9
  sustainable 319–339
  virtualization and 15
    cloud-native architectures 132–137
  virtual machines to serverless 15–27
Cloud cost optimization 91–110, 141
  AI/ML for predictive 100–101
  complexity and capital expenditures (CapEx) 91–92, 94
  cost-aware architecture and operations 99–100
  FinOps. *see* Finance+DevOps (FinOps)
  holistic cost management framework 98
  mindset for new era 92–93
  single-workload optimization 98–99
Cloud-edge continuum 147
Cloud environments
  and AI 383–388
  bias in 377–379
  ethical principles 375–377
  responsible AI 379–382
  zero trust architecture in 247–262
Cloud financial operations (CTOs) 93
Cloud Functions 26
Cloud identity 250
Cloud localization laws 299–315
Cloud-native
  applications 283–297
  computing 31–51
    applications 33
    case studies and real-world applications 49–50
    core design patterns in 39–40
    core values of 33
    data management patterns 40–42
    fundamentals of 33–35
    generation of 42
    scalability 33
    security 35
  IAM in 292
  microservices architectures (MSA) 132–137
    monolithic to 32
    principles of 32, 34
  observability systems 57, 209
  platform integration 61–62
  software 187
  tech company 102
  threat detection services 260
Cloud-Native Computing Foundation (CNCF) 288
Cloud networks 210
Cloud operations, intelligence automation in 137–143
Cloud OpEx (cloud computing) 94
Cloud security 136
Cloud security posture management (CSPM) tools 190–191
Cloud service models 3
Cloud's variable cost model 96–97
Cloud Watch Alarms 234

Cloud workload protection platforms (CWPP) 191
Clustering 165, 167
Coherence 344
"*Cold start*" latency 27, 224–225
Collaborative incident response 173
Command Query Responsibility Segregation (CQRS) 40
Committed use discounts (CUDs) 124
Common Event Format (CEF) 260
Common Gateway Interface (CGI) scripts 19
Communication patterns, of microservices 37
Communications of the Association of Computing Machinery (CACM) 221, 222
COMPAS system 386–387
Compatible Time-Sharing System (CTSS) 18
Compliance 45, 283, 365–366
  AI-enhanced 290–291
  architecting for 309–313
  automation framework 66–67
  certification management 271–272
  challenges 292–294
  CIAA model 286
  for cloud-native applications 283–297
  monitoring 272
  observability 65–67
  orchestration 275
Compliance-as-Code (CaC) 289, 312–313
Compliance automation 294–295
Compliance-driven observability 176
Compliance risk 401
Comprehensive performance evaluations 70
Computational requirement 146
Compute resources 116
Concept drift 79–80, 182
Confidence scoring 274
Confidential computing 401
Confidentiality 286
Configuration management 48–49, 234
Configuration Management Database (CMDB) systems 273
Consumer awareness 336
Consumer-driven transformation 338
Consumption-based pricing model 27
Containerization 24–25, 34, 133, 360
  concept of 41
  and Kubernetes ecosystem 35
  orchestration 25
  security 48
  technologies 204
Context propagation 60, 156
  mechanisms 63
Continuous authentication 256–257
Continuous compliance monitoring 270
Continuous delivery 208
Continuous improvement 80, 122, 381–382
Continuous integration and deployment (CI/CD) 31, 34, 38, 43, 47, 233
  pipelines 181
Continuous learning 389
Continuous monitoring 80
Continuous posture assessment 256
Contract testing 44, 48
Contrastive Language-Image Pre-training (CLIP) 145
Conventional operating system 22
Conventional threshold-based methods 65
Conway's Law 204
Core design patterns, in MSAs 39–40
Corporate social responsibility 104

Correctional Offender Management Profiling for Alternative Sanctions (COMPAS) system 374
Cost anomaly detection 141
Cost-aware
  anomaly detection 177
  architecture and operations 99–100
Cost–benefit analysis 70
Cost commitment 94
Cost-cutting techniques 259
Cost drivers 114–117
Cost efficiency 77
Cost management 86, 136–137
Cost optimization 45, 97, 141, 177–178
Cost overhead 183
Cost predictability 365
Cost visibility 94
Covariate drift 79–80
Critical Information Infrastructure (CII) 303
Critical security controls 193
Cross-cloud arbitrage 105–106
Cross-cloud security 65–67
Cross-cutting services 231–232
Cross-functional impact 126
Cross-platform coverage 256
Cross-regional/multi-cloud deployments 117
CrowdStrike 194
Cryptographic agility 295
Cultural shift 179
Custom APIs 81
Customer support systems 50
Custom ML models 273–274
Cybercriminals 247
Cybersecurity Framework (CSF 2.0) 193
Cybersecurity platforms 7
Cyber sovereignty 303–304

d

Dashboards 97
Data Access Object (DAO) 231
Database per Service 40
Data bias 378
Data center
  cooling technologies 327–328
  footprints 22
  security 260–261
  Zero Trust approach 261
Data collection 59–60
Data consistency 48
Data due diligence 279
Data encryption 81
Data governance 179–180
Data-intensive apps 3
Data labeling 78
Data lakes and warehouses 78
Data localization 299–301
Data management 40–42, 382
Data migration 38
Data preprocessing 78
Data privacy 86, 299–315
  industry case studies 306–309
  and localization 300–301
  regional regulatory landscape 301–306
    Brazil 305
    Canada 305
    China's PIPL 303–304
    European Union 301–302
    India's DPDP Act 304–305
    other notable jurisdictions and frameworks 305–306
    Russia 305
    United States 302–303
Data processing performance metrics 64
Data protection 300, 377
Data Protection Board 304

Data sovereignty 63, 299, 336
  complexity 266–267
Data standardization 335
Data summarization methods 71
Data synchronization 146
Data transfer 117
Data transport and storage 163
Data versioning 85
DBSCAN 165
Dead Letter Queue (DLQ) 240
Debugging 225, 234
  complexity 225–226
  distributed event-driven applications 239
Decentralized cloud 107–108
Decentralized computing 19
Decentralized governance 34
Declarative infrastructure management 207–208
Deep learning (DL) 76, 134
  models 86
Deep neural networks 167
Deep Q-Networks (DQNs) 168
DeFi mechanisms 107
Democratization, of scientific computing 368
Dependency mapping, graph-based models for 167–168
Deployment pipelines, AI in 138, 205
Design artifacts 144
Detection fidelity 169
Deutsche Telekom 308
Development and Operations (DevOps) 188
  automation 243
  culture 34, 38, 43, 49
  functions 135
  integration 81
  toolchains and CI/CD pipelines 181
DevSecOps 288, 309
  adoption of 192, 287
  anti-patterns 196
  APM and 184
  best practices 194–195
  cloud-native 187–197
  embedding legal rules in 312–313
  implementation 196–197
  implementation with frameworks 192–194
  maturity model 193–194
  operating model 188
  sovereignty-aware architectures and 315
  state of 188–192
Digital entertainment/tech (Spotify) 102
Digital Operational Resilience Act (DORA) 306
Digital Personal Data Protection (DPDP) Act 300, 304–305
Digital transformation 1
Dimensionality reduction 167
Directed acyclic graphs 168
Disaster recovery 22
Distributed AIOps 178
Distributed ML system 77
Distributed systems 45
Distributed tracing 156
  implementation strategy 61–63
    cloud-native platform integration 61–62
    OpenTelemetry integration framework 61
    real-time processing and analytics 62–63
  records 155
  technologies 57
  tracks 40
Distributed training 85
Docker 287
  approach 25
Domain-driven design (DDD) 38

Dot-Com Boom 19
D-Wave systems 349
Dynamic application security testing (DAST) 44
Dynamic load balancing 328–329
Dynamic scaling 135–136
Dynamic workloads 131
  scheduling 141
DynamoDB 231

e

eBPF instrumentation 60
E-commerce 50
  businesses 132
E-Commerce platform at scale 175–176
Economic rationale 2
economic scalability 17
Edge AI 5, 147, 148
Edge computing 324
  integration 70–71
  for scientific applications 366–367
Edge-optimized observability 71
Elastic stack (ELK) 271
ElectricityMap 336
Electronic health records (EHRs) 50
Embedded automated data classification 63
Emerging technologies
  AI techniques 184–185
  in security 294–295
Empowering teams 55
Encrypted telemetry management 66
End-to-end observability 55
Energy efficiency 322–323
  algorithms 368
Energy/industrial (Schneider Electric) 103
Entanglement 344
Enterprise agreements 99
Enterprise incident management 65
Enterprise risk management 275
Enterprise software architects 23
Environmental cost 401
Environmental sustainability 71, 368
Ephemeral computing 8
Error handling 236
Error mitigation research 348
Ethical AI/Ethics 139, 373–389
  accountability 376–377
  beneficence and non-maleficence 377
  development 10
  fairness and non-discrimination 375–376
  principles 375–377
  privacy and data protection 377
  transparency 376
EU AI Act 5
EU Cloud Security Scheme 311
EU's GDPR 301–302
Event Bridge 227, 233
Event-driven architecture (EDA) 32, 33
  challenges 224–226
  components in 220, 221
  evolution of 221
  and microservices architectures (MSAs) 42–43
  security 226
  serverless computing and 219–245
    architecture 229–232
    case study 235–238
    challenges and limitations 239–241
    implementation 232–235
    proposed framework 226–229
Event-driven automation 134
Event-driven choreography 226
Event-driven data sync mechanisms 63
Event-driven execution model 26
Event-driven microservices 49
Event producers 226

Event routing and bus (choreography) 227
Event-triggered functions 245
Eventual consistency 48
Executive sponsorship 179
Explainability 144
Explainable AI (XAI) techniques 171–172
Extended Berkeley Packet Filter (eBPF)-based instrumentation 57
Extended Detection and Response (XDR) systems 7

f

Fairness *vs.* non-discrimination 375–376
False positive management 274
Fast deployment 77
Fault tolerance 33
Fault-tolerant operation 69
Feature engineering 158
Federated learning 71, 86
  approach 5
Federated trust strategies 311–312
FedEx 50
FedRAMP 303, 308
Feedback loops 181
Finance 6, 306–307
Financial cost 400
Financial data 96
Financial difficulties 336
Financial operations (FinOps) 45, 400–402
  in action 101–103
  agentic AI orchestration 108–109
  for AI workloads 113–127
  collaborative nature of 114
  cross-cloud arbitrage 105–106
  cross-functional teamwork 95
  cultural mindset of 102
  decentralized cloud and new financial models 107–108
  emergence and evolution of 94–95
  FinOps Meets Sustainability (GreenOps) 104–105
  framework 119
  licensing and SaaS 125
  lifecycle 97–98
  management of 125
  multicloud 105–106
  principles 95–97
    applied to AI 117–125
  rise of 91–110
  sustainability 125
Financial risk models 274
Financial services 132, 176
FinOps Foundation 94, 95, 97, 106
FinOps Meets Sustainability (GreenOps) 104–105
FinOps open cost and usage specification (FOCUS) 98
Forecasting 101, 122
Forward-leaning developments 107
Forward-thinking organizations 94
Fragmentation problem 266
Fragmented compliance 336
Function-as-a-service (FaaS) 26, 46, 133, 226
  architectures 206–207
Function orchestration 227
Future abstraction models 395

g

Gate-model platforms 349
Gaussian mixture models (GMMs) 165
General Data Protection Regulation (GDPR) 82, 289, 301–302
Generative adversarial networks (GANs) 184
Generative AI (Gen AI) 71, 87, 113, 117, 134, 143–145

Genomics 364
"German Cloud" project 314
GET/PUT commands 20
GitHub Actions or Jenkins 44
GitLab CI 47
GitOps tools 44, 47, 208
Global democratization 346
Goldman Sachs 49
Google
  AI principles 386
  AutoML 144
  Chronicle Security Operations Suite 291
  data centers carbon-neutral 333
Google Cloud 78, 142–143, 267
Google Cloud Audit Logs 273
Google Cloud AutoML 78
Google Cloud Functions 206
Google Cloud Operations Suite 139
Google cloud platform (GCP) 2, 20, 266, 359
Google Cloud Trace 61, 62, 68
Google Compute Engine (GCE) 20
Google Quantum AI 367
Governance 45, 147
  automation, compliance and 139
  framework 265–281
  rig layer 269
  systems 280
Governance-aware autonomy 397–398
Governance, risk, and compliance (GRC) platforms 66
Government data rules 302–303
Government digital service (GDS) team 50
Granger causality tests 170
Granular policy enforcement 248
Graph-based algorithms 58
Graph-based models, for dependency mapping 167–168
Graphics processing units (GPUs) 16, 76, 114
  utilization and scarcity 126
Graph neural networks (GNNs) 168
Graph pattern matching 168
Green computing 71, 368
Green Metrics 9

h

Hardware acceleration 85
Hardware simulation 20–21
Healthcare AI 132, 387–388
Healthcare diagnostics 146
Healthcare organizations 307–308
Health Insurance Portability and Accountability Act (HIPAA) 266, 289, 301, 307
High-level architectural components 156–161
High performance computing (HPC) 355–370
  container orchestration for scientific workloads 360–361
  data challenge 357–358
  emerging trends 366–369
  Kubernetes for 361
  scientific computing 356–357
    Amazon Web Services (AWS) 358
    cloud platforms for 358–360
    Google cloud platform (GCP) 359
    Microsoft Azure 358
    Rescale 360
    Sabalcore 360
  traditional HPC *vs.* cloud HPC 357
  workflow management systems 361–365
    Apache Airflow 362
    climate modeling 363–364
    genomics and bioinformatics 364
    Nextflow 361

High performance computing (HPC) (*contd.*)
particle physics community 364–365
performance optimization strategies 362–363
Snakemake 362
High-risk automation 161
Holistic cost management framework 98
Homomorphic encryption 295
Horizontal scaling techniques 68
Hosted hypervisor 22
HTTP Application Programming Interface (APIs) 31
Human-centric design backup 139
Human-in-the-loop
vs. fully autonomous remediation 174
for remediation 177
Human oversight 381
Hybrid cloud management 137
Hybrid cloud strategies, for resilient infrastructure 55–72
Hybrid orchestration-choreography model 243
Hyperscale cloud providers 321
Hypertext Preprocessor (PHP) 19
Hypervisor—virtual machine technology 21–22

i

IBM 21
AI Ethics board 385
IBM Cloud Functions 26
IBM Qiskit 347
IBM Quantum network 347, 367
Identity access management (IAM) 35, 232, 233, 239, 242, 250, 267
zero trust governance for 252–253
Identity providers (IdPs) 252
Implementation phase analysis 67–68
Implicit bias 379
Incident management workflow 172–174
In-depth knowledge graphs 64
India's DPDP Act 304–305
Individualized content delivery 146
Industrial IoT 6
Inference workloads 115, 116
InfiniBand Networking 359
Infrastructure-as-a-Service (IaaS) 3, 17, 76, 285, 287
Infrastructure-as-Code (IaC) 31, 143–144, 190, 207–208, 232–233
Infrastructure management 48–49
Instrumentation strategy 59–60
Insurance (Nationwide Insurance) 102
Integrated risk management 275
Integrating generative AI models 87
Integration patterns 39–40
Integrity 286
Intelligence automation 129–148
in cloud ecosystems 134–135
in cloud operations 137–143
AI in deployment pipelines 138
self-healing cloud infrastructure 138
Intelligent alerting systems 65
Intelligent cloud observability, AI/ML techniques for 165–168
Intelligent data lifecycle management 71
Intelligent resource optimization 101
Intelligent scaling 243
Intelligent virtual assistants 145
Intent-driven operations 183–184
Interactive application security testing (IAST) 190
Interactive workloads 115–116
Internal cloud budgets 107–108

International Data Corporation (IDC) 113
Internet Solutions Division Strategy 18
IonQ 349
IoT edge deployment smart city Singapore 334
Isolation Forest model 176
ISO 27000 series 193
IT asset management team 95

j

Java Naming and Directory Interface (JNDI) 195
Jenkins 47
JPMorgan Chase 49
JSON Web Tokens (JWTs) 229
Juggling energy economy 335
Just-in-Time Access (JIT) 248

k

Kernel-based VM (KVM) 22
Key performance indicators (KPIs) 122, 180
KnowBe4 220
Knowledge base 159–160
Kubernetes 203–205
  autonomous cloud infrastructure 205
  clusters 290, 295
  Docker and 287
  ecosystem 35
  for HPC 361
  network policies or service meshes 290
  services 25
Kusto Query Language (KQL) 259

l

Lack of operational flexibility 22
Lambda functions 219, 227, 228, 230–231
Large language models (LLMs) 5, 6, 71, 113, 374
Leadership in Energy and Environmental Design (LEED) 320
Least privilege 248
Licensing 125
Limited customer awareness 336
Linux Foundation 94
Load balancing 85
Local Interpretable Model-Agnostics Explanations (LIME) 171
Log aggregation 259
Logging strategy 40, 234
Log4j vulnerability 195
Log4Shell (CVE-2021-44, 228) 195
Low-level virtual machine (LLVM) 353
Low-risk automation 160

m

Machine learning (ML) 46, 113–114, 134
  algorithms 63
  artificial intelligence and. *see* Artificial intelligence (AI)
  evolution of 76–77
  frameworks 78
  for fraud detection 176
  models 61, 65
  for proactive security and compliance automation 294–295
  techniques for intelligent observability 165–168
Machine Learning as a Service (MLaaS) 75–87
  challenges in 86
  cloud computing 76
  enabling scalability 82–85
  frameworks and tools in 77–85
  integration and APIs 80–81
  key drivers of 77–78

Machine Learning as a Service (MLaaS) (*contd.*)
  machine learning, evolution of 76–77
  model deployment and inference 79–80
  model development and training 78–79
  security and governance 81–82
  use cases 82
  vendors of 87
Machine learning operations (MLOps) 116
Maersk 50
Manufacturing/consumer electronics (Samsung) 102–103
Markov decision systems (MDPs) 168
Maturity model 193–194
Mean time to respond (MTTR) 139, 291
Measurement bias 378
Micro-segmentation 255
  for network control 253–254
  ultimate goal of 255
Microservices architectures (MSAs) 31–51, 132
  communication patterns 37
  core design patterns in 39–40
  data management patterns 40–42
  emerging trends 45–49
  event-driven architecture (EDA) and 42–43
  integration patterns 39–40
  migration strategies to 38
  vs. monolithic architecture 37
  monolithic to 32
  overview 36–38
  service decomposition patterns 39
  in telecommunication 50
  testing and quality assurance in 44
  Zero Trust architecture (ZTA) in 289
Microsoft 141
Microsoft Azure 358
Microsoft Azure Quantum 350, 367
Microsoft Azure Security Center 139
Microsoft Azure Sentinel 136
Microsoft Sentinel 272
Microsoft's Project Natick 333–334
Minimum viable AIOps (MVA) 180
MLOps (ML operations) 81
Model Cards 141
Model drift 182
Model storage sprawl 116
Modern cloud apps 219
Modern cloud computing 23–25
  container orchestration 25
  rise of containerization 24–25
  traditional virtual machines 23–24
Modularity 34
Monitor-analyze-plan-execute (MAPE) control loop 202–203
Monitoring 47
Monolithic architecture, microservices *vs.* 37
Monolithic/containerized apps 224
MuleSoft Anypoint platform 276
Multi-agent coordination 144
Multicloud environments
  core challenges in 266–268
  predictive risk intelligence 265–281
Multicloud FinOps 105–106
Multicloud observability foundations 56–57
  architecture framework 58–61
    components 59
    data collection and instrumentation strategy 59–60
    design principles 58–59
    service mesh integration architecture 60–61

cross-cloud security and compliance observability 65–67
distributed tracing implementation strategy 61–63
cloud-native platform integration 61–62
OpenTelemetry integration framework 61
real-time processing and analytics 62–63
emerging technological developments 70–71
implementation guidelines and best practices 67–68
multimodal data fusion and analytics 63–65
AI-enhanced anomaly detection 63–64
intelligent alerting systems 65
unified data model architecture 63
performance evaluation and verification 68–70
benchmark results analyses 68–69
cost–benefit analysis 70
scalability and resilience testing 69–70
performance optimization techniques 68
Multicloud operational resilience 395–396
Multicloud pipelines 6
Multicloud strategies, for resilient infrastructure 55–72
Multi-factor authentication (MFA) 248
Multimodal AI foundations 145–147
Multi-modal anomaly detection 169
Multimodal data fusion and analytics 63–65
AI-enhanced anomaly detection 63–64
intelligent alerting systems 65
Multivariate forecasting 167
Mutual Transport Layer Security (TLS) (mTLS) 41, 258

n

Naming conventions 120
National Institute of Science and Technology (NIST) 3, 16
Cybersecurity Framework (CSF 2.0) 193
Secure Software Development Framework (SSDF) 192–193
as virtualization 20
Nation-state actors 250
Natural language processing (NLP) 76, 130, 134, 139
Netflix 49, 142
Chaos Engineering method 139
Chaos Monkey 200
Hystrix library 202
Network control, micro-segmentation for 253–254
Networking 117
Network latency 365
Network perimeters 254
Network security policy enforcement 267
Neural network–based models 158
Neural networks 76
New financial models 107–108
Nextflow 361
Next-generation monitoring systems 153
Noise reduction 169–170
Noisy Intermediate-Scale Quantum (NISQ) 341
Nonlatency-sensitive workloads 329
Non-maleficencc 377
Novel technologies 338

o

Observability 47
 cloud-native 209
 data 161–162
 and debugging 225
 gaps 240
 patterns 40–42
 platforms and tools 209
 vs. monitoring 154
Observability-driven framework 55–72
 distributed tracing technologies 57
 multicloud observability foundations 56–57
 performance analysis for 69
 service mesh observability patterns 58
 trends and challenges 56
On-demand pricing 123
Ongoing model retraining 179
On-site renewable installations 328
Open Compute Project 338
Open Cybersecurity Schema Framework (OCSF) 258
Open Policy Agent (OPA) 288, 312
Open-source
 vs. commercial AIOps 181
 MLaaS 87
 software management 195
 technologies 19
 trace tools 62
Open Telemetry 40, 43, 56–58, 69, 232, 242
 implementation metrics 62
 instrumentation 67
 integration framework 61
 Software Development Kits (SDKs) 59
OpenTracing 40
Operating expenditures (OpEx) shift 91
 CapEx comfort to 91–92, 94
Operational complexity 24, 336
Operational risk 401
 models 273–274
Optimization, of costs 45
OrderFulfillmentNotifier Lambda 238
OrderLogger Lambda 238
"OrderPlaced" events 230, 236
"OrderProcessingStateMachine" 230
"Order Processing" system 227
Organizational readiness 179
Out-of-the-box tools 271–273
Over-provisioning 2
Oversimplified language 20

p

Particle physics community 364–365
Passwordless authentication 251
Pay-as-you-go model 76, 85
Pay-per-invocation model 235
Performance evaluation and verification 68–70
Performance metrics alignment 274
Performance optimization 136–137
 strategies 362–363
 techniques 68
Performance overheads 239
Perimeter controls 249
Personal Information Protection Law (PIPL) 300
Phased deployment strategy 67
Philips Health Suite 50
Physical qubit technologies 345
Physical to virtual infrastructure 22–23
Pillars of observability 154–155
Pipeline workloads 116
Planet-aware architectures 398–400
Platform-as-a-Service (PaaS) 3, 15, 20, 76, 285, 287
 security controls 257–258
Platform-driven automatic classification 66
Platform engineering 49

Policy and legal difficulties 336
Policy-as-Code 184
Policy management 275
Policy violations 275
Post-quantum cryptography 295
Power purchase agreements (PPAs) 8, 323, 328
Predictive autoscaling 177–178
Predictive cloud cost optimization 100–101
Predictive cost forecasting 141
Predictive models 70
Predictive risk intelligence 265–281
  Apache Kafka 276
  custom ML models and risk prediction 273–274
  data sovereignty complexity 266–267
  decisions making and taking action 274–276
    RSA Archer 275–276
    ServiceNow GRC 274
  defining 265
  identity and integration gaps 267–268
  MuleSoft Anypoint platform 276
  multicloud complexity challenge 265–266
  out-of-the-box tools for 271–273
    compliance certification management 271–272
    IBM QRadar SOAR 271
    Microsoft Sentinel 272
    Palantir Foundry 272–273
  phased implementation approach for 280
Predictive Risk Intelligence and Governance (PRIG) paradigm 265
  concept of 270
  framework architecture and components 268–269
    conceptual architecture 268
    database layer (foundation) 268
    governance rig layer 269
    intelligence engine layer 269
  implementation framework 277
  infrastructure 270–271
    elastic stack (ELK) 271
    GRC intelligence 270–271
    reality check 270
    Splunk Enterprise Security 270
  performance issues 277
  real-world case studies 277–279
Predictive threat intelligence (PTI) 290–291
Principle component analysis (PCA) 167
Privacy 146, 179–180
  data management and 382
  and data protection 377
  and security 389
Privacy-preserving analytical methods 63, 66
Privileged access management (PAM) 82
Proactive security 294–295
Probabilistic correlation 170
Project Natick 333–334
Prophet (Facebook Prophet) 166–167
Protected health information (PHI) 307
Public sector and government 308–309
Pull against push models 156

q

Quality assurance, in microservices 44–45
Quantifying business value 121
Quantum-as-a-Service (QaaS) 341
Quantum Assembly Language (QASM) 347
Quantum chemistry 348
QuantumCircuit 347

Quantum computing 338, 341–353
- advantage domains 352
- challenges and future 351–353
- classical and quantum performance 351
- frameworks and cloud platforms 345–346
- fundamental 342
- integration 147
- key strengths 350–351
- operations and execution 342–343
- theory 343–344

Quantum development kit (QDK) 350
Quantum RAM (qRAM) 344
Quantum-safe encryption 295
Qubit Virtualization 345

r

Racial bias 387–388
Rate optimization 123
Real-time analytics 100
Real-time monitoring 126
Real-time processing and analytics 62–63
Regulatory compliance 183
- models 273–274

Regulatory frameworks 147
Reinforcement bias 379
Reinforcement learning (RL) 71, 134, 168
Remote job entry (RJE) 18
Renewable energy 335
- commitments 7–8
- integration 323, 333

Reporting bias 379
Rescale 360
Research gaps 223
Reserve Bank of India 300
Reserve Inventory Lambda 237
Resilience testing 69–70
Resilient infrastructure, multicloud and hybrid cloud strategies for 55–72
Resource optimization tools 85
Resource overhead 23–24
Resource utilization 21
Responsible AI 139–141, 379–382
Rigetti computing 349
Risk-based alerting 271
Risk-based authentication 251
Risk management 275
Risk prediction 273–274
RL-based optimization 144
Robotic process automation (RPA) 134
Role-based access control (RBAC) 248, 251
Root cause analysis 57, 169–172
RSA Archer 275–276
RSA Security 277–278
Runbook integration 159–160, 173
Runtime application self-protection (RASP) 190

s

Sabalcore 360
SafeCode 193
Saga pattern 40, 43, 48
SageMaker 79
Sampling bias 379
Samsung 102–103
Scalability 33
- cost optimization 85
- and cost overhead 183
- data pipelines 85
- enabling 82–85
- inference 79, 85
- infrastructure 82
- model training 82–85
- testing 69–70

Scalable AI 75–87

Schema standardization strategies 163–164
Schmidt, Eric 17
Schneider Electric 103
Schrems II ruling 301–302, 314
Scientific computing 356–357
  benefits for 360
  democratization of 368
Scientific research 355–370
Scientific workloads
  container orchestration for 360–361
  serverless computing for 366
SDLC 189–190
Search Engine Strategies (SES) Conference 17
Seasonal decomposition 165
Secrets management 48
Sectoral Rules 304–305
Sector cooperation 338
Secure SDLC 189, 192
Secure Software Development Framework (SSDF) 192–193
Security 81–82, 86, 144, 179–180, 365–366
  AI-enhanced 290–291
  automation 272
  challenges 292–294
  for cloud-native applications 283–297
  complexity 277
  compliance frameworks 289–290
  current security frameworks and processes 287–289
  emerging technologies in 294–295
  enhancements 242
  monitoring 146
  observability metrics 66
  and privacy 139
  privacy and 389
  and threat detection 136
  threats 131
Security Information and Event Management (SIEMs) 7, 259–260, 268
Security Orchestration, Automation, and Response (SOAR) systems 259–260
Segmenting functions 49
Segregation of duties 251
Self-healing
  cloud infrastructure 138, 140
  in cloud resilience 200–201
  systems 135, 184
Semantic Versioning (SemVer) 48
Sentiment analysis workloads 122
Serverless architectures 75–82, 330–332
  sustainable cloud computing 325
Serverless computing 8, 20, 133, 219–245
  architecture 229–232
  benefits and limitations of 27
  case study 235–238
  challenges and limitations 239–241
  cold start latency 224–225
  concept of 26
  debugging complexity 225–226
  evolution of 220
  foundational principles of 26
  implementation 232–235
  key platform 26
  model 206
  multicloud and federated serverless 242
  observability and debugging 225
  proposed framework 226–229
  security 226
  state management 225
Server-side innovations 19
Service catalogs 49
Service decomposition patterns (SDP-s) 39
Service discovery 41

Service-level agreements (SLAs) 130, 173
Service-level objectives (SLOs) 173, 200, 201
Service mesh 40
  integration 258
  integration architecture 60–61
  performance characteristics 60
  technology 46, 58
Service models, in cloud computing 15
ServiceNow 275
ServiceNow GRC 274
Service-to-service
  communications 40
  conversations 41
Session monitoring 256–257
Shadow IT discovery 257
SHapley Additive explanations (SHAP) 171
"Shared responsibility" model 293
Shifting cloud paradigm 4
Shift-left security practices 187–197
Showback models 99–100
Simulation 20
Single sign-on (SSO) 252
Single-workload optimization 98–99
Site reliability engineering (SRE) 34
Small and medium-sized enterprises (SMEs) 75
Smart cloud automation 129
Smart grid-enabled power management 329
Smart grids technologies 328–329
Smart sampling strategies 61
Snakemake 362
Social and adoption difficulties 336–337
Software 102
Software-as-a-Service (SaaS) 3, 15, 19, 102, 220, 285, 287
  licensing and 125
  predictive autoscaling and cost optimization 177–178
  vs. self-hosted solutions 122
  Zero Trust strategies 257
Software composition analysis (SCA) 190
Software-defined networking (SDN) 210
Software Development Kits (SDKs) 59
Software simulation 20–21
Solid-state drives (SSD) 327
Sophisticated orchestration tools 355
Sovereignty 299–315, 400–402
  cloud services and regionalization 310–311
  Compliance-as-Code (CaC) 312–313
  multicloud and federated trust strategies 311–312
  public-sector demand for 309
  requirements 306–309
    finance and banking 306–307
    healthcare organizations 307–308
    public sector and government 308–309
  technical approaches to 309–313
Splunk Enterprise Security 270
Spotify 50, 102
Stakeholder engagement 381
Standardizing green cloud metrics 10
StatefulSets 205
State management 225
State privacy laws 302–303
Static application security testing (SAST) 44, 190
Step Functions 227–228, 230–231
Storage optimization techniques 68
Stream-based systems 62
Stream processing 85
Strong mitigating techniques 257
Structured telemetry propagation 395
Subdomain 39

Supervised learning 166
Sustainability 1, 368
  by design 9
  in FinOps 125
Sustainable cloud computing 319–339
  core frameworks for 325–332
    cooling systems and energy-efficient hardware 325–328
    integrated renewable energy 328–329
  difficulties and future vision 334–337
    financial difficulties 336
    policy and legal difficulties 336
    social and adoption difficulties 336–337
    technical difficulties 335–336
  foundation 321–322
  principles of 322–325
    carbon-aware scheduling 323–324, 329–330
    edge computing 324, 330
    energy efficiency 322–323
    renewable energy integration 323
    serverless architecture 325
  prospect 337–338
  use cases and industry relevance 332–334
"Sustainable FinOps" 105
Swift progression 124
Synthetic data generation 144
Synthetic minority over-sampling technique (SMOTE) 166

t

Tactics, strategies, and procedures (TTPs) 291
Tagging strategies 163–164, 261
Tech companies 15
Technical difficulties 335–336
Technology business management (TBM) 98
Telecommunication 50
Telecom network 178
Telemetry collection 155–156
Tenable Cloud Security 278
Tensor processing units (TPUs) 78
Terraform 38
Test automation 44
Testing complexity 241
Text-to-image generation models 87
Threat actors 250
Threat detection 136
Threat intelligence integration 272
Throttling 233
Ticket generation 172–173
Time-based sharing systems 18
Time-series forecasting 166–167
Time sharing 21
  concept of 18
Token-based billing 126
Tool selection framework 68
Topology-aware root cause localization 171
Total cost of ownership (TCO) 120
Trace-based anomaly detection 159
Trace compression techniques 62
Tracing tracks 40–42
Traditional CapEx (on-premises IT) 94
Traditional computing environment 21
Traditional cost reviews 100
Traditional HPC *vs.* cloud HPC 357
Traditional SDLC 189
Traditional virtual machines 23–24
Traditional *vs.* cloud-native monitoring 208–209
Training frontier models 5
Training workloads 116
Transaction management 48
Transparency 9, 139, 376, 382
Trend analysis 166–167

Troubleshooting 225
Trustworthy AI 139–141
12-factor app methodology 204

u
Unified data model architecture 63
Unified endpoint management (UEM) 255–256
Unit economics 122
UNIX operating system 18
Unpredictable costs 86, 126
Unsupervised learning 165

v
Validation 234
Variable cost model 96–97
Vendor and platform fees 117
Vendor lock-in 86, 117, 239
Vendor-specific tools 265
Virtualization 15
  advantage of 21
  to cloud-native architectures 132–137
  concept of 20–21
  early 20–21
  foundation of 18
  hardware/software 21
  hypervisor—virtual machine technology 21–22
  prominent verticals 21
  technologies 321
  virtual machines and 20–23
Virtual machines (VM) 15–27
  hypervisor—virtual machine technology 21–22
  physical to virtual infrastructure 22–23
  and virtualization 20–23
Virtual memory 19
Virtual private clouds (VPCs) 210
Vodafone 50

w
Walmart 50
WattTime 336
Workflow automation 275
Workflow management systems 361–365
  Apache Airflow 362
  climate modeling 363–364
  genomics and bioinformatics 364
  Nextflow 361
  particle physics community 364–365
  performance optimization strategies 362–363
  Snakemake 362
Workload optimization techniques 123, 124
World Wide Web 19
Write-once-read-many (WORM) 183

y
Yet another Markup Language (YAML) 240

z
Zero Trust architecture (ZTA) 247–262, 288–289, 400–402
  "assume breach" philosophy of 258
  behavioral biometrics for 290
  centralized log aggregation architecture 258–259
  in cloud computing 249–250
    perimeter controls 249
    threat actors 250
  cloud identity and access management 250
  cloud-native threat detection services 260
  concepts 247
  continuous authentication and session monitoring 256–257
  data-centric security 260–261

data encryption 261
governance for IAM 252–253
least privilege 248
least privilege access 251
micro-segmentation for network control 253–254
in microservices architecture 289
PaaS security controls 257–258
security information and event management (SIEM) 259–260
Security Orchestration, Automation, and Response (SOAR) systems 259–260
Software-as-a-Service (SaaS) 257
strong authentication 251
traditional network model 247
unified endpoint management (UEM) 255–256
verify explicitly 248
visibility, logging, and threat detection 258
zero trust network access (ZTNA) 254–255
Zero trust network access (ZTNA) 254–255
Zero-Trust observability implementation 65–66
Zero Trust security
architectures 58
model 43, 47

Printed and bound by CPI Group (UK) Ltd, Croydon, CR0 4YY
17/09/2026
14964235-0006